Fostering Sustainable Businesses in Emerging Economies

Fostering Sustainable Businesses in Emerging Economies: The Impact of Technology

EDITED BY

QUAZI TAFSIRUL ISLAM

North South University, Bangladesh

RICHA GOEL

Symbiosis Centre for Management Studies, Noida
Symbiosis International Deemed University, Pune, India

AND

TILOTTAMA SINGH

Uttaranchal Institute of Management
Uttaranchal University
Dehradun, Uttarakhand, India

United Kingdom – North America – Japan – India – Malaysia – China

Emerald Publishing Limited
Emerald Publishing, Floor 5, Northspring, 21-23 Wellington Street, Leeds LS1 4DL

First edition 2024

Editorial matter and selection © 2024 Quazi Tafsirul Islam, Richa Goel and Tilottama Singh.
Individual chapters © 2024 The authors.
Published under exclusive licence by Emerald Publishing Limited.

Reprints and permissions service
Contact: www.copyright.com

British Library Cataloguing in Publication Data
A catalogue record for this book is available from the British Library

ISBN: 978-1-80455-641-2 (Print)
ISBN: 978-1-80455-640-5 (Online)
ISBN: 978-1-80455-642-9 (Epub)

Printed and bound by CPI Group (UK) Ltd, Croydon, CR0 4YY

INVESTOR IN PEOPLE

To my daughter, Quazi Myra Islam Ayaat, who is my source of inspiration and resilience and inspires me to build a more sustainable world for her future and future generations.

—Quazi Tafsirul Islam

Table of Contents

List of Contributors

M.U. Adehi	Nasarawa State University, Nigeria
Vasim Ahmad	Uttaranchal University, India
Jashim Uddin Ahmed	North South University, Bangladesh
Khawaja Sazzad Ali	North South University, Bangladesh
Md. Yasir Arafat	Islamic Univerfsity of Technology, Malaysia
Sukanta Kumar Baral	Indira Gandhi National Tribal University (A Central University), India
Bilkisu Maijamaa	Nasarawa State University, Nigeria
Pratim Chatterjee	Amity University Kolkata, India
Anupkumar Dhore	Dr. Ambedkar Institute of Management Studies & Research, India
Anisur R. Faroque	University of Vaasa, Finland
Michela Floris	Univerisity of Cagliari, Italy
Richa Goel	Symbiosis Centre for Management Studies, Noida Symbiosis International Deemed University, Pune, India
Lalit Goyal	Graduate School of Business, Tula's Institute Dehradun, India
Vijay Prakash Gupta	IBM-GLA University, Mathura, India
Quazi Tafsirul Islam	North South University, Bangladesh
Jakia Sultana Jane	Islamic Univerfsity of Technology, Malaysia
Vijay D. Joshi	Dr. Ambedkar Institute of Management Studies & Research, India
Rita Karmakar	Amity University Kolkata, India
Zarjina Tarana Khalil	North South University, Bangladesh
Amir Hafizullah Khan	Shri Ramdeobaba College of Engineering and Management, India

Jugander Kumar	Milwaukee Electric Tool Corporation, USA
Babagana Modu	Yobe State University, Nigeria
Farzana Nahid	North South University, Bangladesh
Sudhansu Sekhar Nanda	Kirloskar Institute of Management, India
Samira Rahman	Putra Business School, Malaysia
Mashiur Rehman	Bank Asia, Bangladesh
Bhabajyoti Saikia	Assam Down Town University, India
Sudipa Sarker	Edinburgh Napier University, UK
Afnan Sayed	North South University, Bangladesh
Mohd Asif Shah	Kebri Dehar University, Ethiopia
Ajay Sidana	Amity International Business School, India
Pooja Singh	Sharda University, India
Tilottama Singh	Uttaranchal Institute of Management Uttaranchal University Dehradun, Uttarakhand, India
Tushar Soubhari	NSS College Manjeri, Kerala, India
Mehadi Hassan Tanvir	Islamic Univerfsity of Technology, Malaysia
Mohammad Shamsu Uddin	Islamic Univerfsity of Technology, Malaysia
Muhammad Idris Umar	Nasarawa State University, Nigeria
Surabhi Yadav	Independent CSR Consultant, India

Foreword

In an era of rapid technological advancements and shifting economic landscapes, the role of sustainable businesses in emerging economies has never been more significant. As we grapple with the challenges of climate change, social inequality, and economic development, it is essential to explore the transformative potential of technology to build sustainable businesses that not only contribute to economic growth but also address pressing societal and environmental issues. "Fostering Sustainable Businesses in Emerging Economies: The Impact of Technology" provides a timely and insightful analysis of this critical subject, offering readers a comprehensive understanding of the interplay between technology, sustainability, and entrepreneurship in emerging economies.

The editor's extensive research and expertise in the field of sustainable business shine through in the carefully structured chapters, each of which delves into various aspects of technology's role in fostering sustainable businesses in emerging economies. Drawing on a wealth of case studies, this book presents innovative solutions, best practices, and success stories that demonstrate the power of technology in driving positive change and creating value for both businesses and society at large.

One of the key strengths of this book is its practical approach. The editors not only present a compelling case for the importance of sustainable businesses in emerging economies but also provide actionable guidance and strategies for entrepreneurs, policymakers, and investors to harness the potential of technology in their pursuit of sustainable business growth. By doing so, this book serves as both an inspiring read and a valuable resource for those seeking to make a meaningful impact in the world.

In my own experience, I have witnessed firsthand the transformative power of technology in shaping the trajectory of sustainable businesses. As a reader, I found the editor's and author's insights and analysis to be both informative and thought-provoking, sparking new ideas and challenging conventional wisdom. This book is a testament to the editor's dedication and passion for the subject matter, and I have no doubt that it will inspire and empower readers to think differently about the role of technology in fostering sustainable businesses in emerging economies.

As our world continues to evolve and face new challenges, the importance of fostering sustainable businesses in emerging economies cannot be overstated. "Fostering Sustainable Businesses in Emerging Economies: The Impact of Technology" serves as a vital guide for anyone interested in understanding and contributing to this crucial endeavor. By showing how technology can be harnessed for positive change, this book not only inspires hope for a brighter future but also equips readers with the knowledge and tools needed to play their part in building a more sustainable and equitable world.

Preface

In the rapidly evolving global landscape, emerging economies have become the focal point for sustainable development and growth. As businesses and governments alike strive to create a more resilient and sustainable future, the role of technology in fostering sustainable businesses in these economies cannot be overstated. This book, "Fostering Sustainable Businesses in Emerging Economies: The Impact of Technology," aims to explore the intersection of sustainability, technology, and business innovation in the context of emerging markets.

The recent "eco-awakening" among consumers worldwide has driven a growing demand for sustainable products and services. This book acknowledges the need for businesses to adapt their models and practices to meet these expectations while balancing economic growth and social responsibility. It also recognizes the role that governments play in creating the right environment for sustainable businesses to thrive, as seen in the study of emerging economies' performance over 50 years.

Drawing from various fields and international perspectives, this book delves into the concept of corporate social responsibility (CSR) as a tool to promote sustainable development in developing and emerging markets. It examines how technology can be harnessed to enhance CSR initiatives, thereby contributing to a greener and more inclusive economy.

One of the critical aspects covered in this book is the role of technology in driving sustainable behavior and enabling businesses to adapt their operations accordingly. We will discuss various technological innovations that have the potential to shape sustainable business practices, from renewable energy sources to advancements in supply chain management and digital communication.

Furthermore, the book highlights examples of entrepreneurs and businesses that have thrived in challenging and restrictive conditions, showcasing the resilience and adaptability of enterprises in emerging economies. These case studies provide valuable insights into the strategies and best practices that can be adopted by businesses seeking to create a sustainable competitive advantage.

"Fostering Sustainable Businesses in Emerging Economies: The Impact of Technology" serves as a comprehensive guide for business leaders, policymakers, and academics interested in understanding the complex interplay between sustainability, technology, and economic growth in emerging markets. Through this book, we hope to inspire readers to contribute to building a more sustainable and inclusive global economy.

Acknowledgement

Our heartfelt appreciation goes to our families, who have been our pillars of strength during the challenging times of compiling and editing this book. Their unconditional love, patience, and understanding have been instrumental in empowering us to focus on our passion and achieve our goals.

We extend our sincerest thanks to all the contributors, reviewers, and editors who have been an integral part of this project. Their invaluable expertise, dedication, and hard work have significantly enriched the content of "Fostering Sustainable Businesses in Emerging Economies: The Impact of Technology." We are truly grateful for their commitment to this publication, as their collective wisdom has elevated the quality and coherence of the chapters.

Many of the contributors graciously took on the additional role of reviewers, and, for that, we are especially thankful. Their constructive feedback, attention to detail, and critical analysis have allowed us to refine our ideas, delve deeper into specific concepts, and bolster the arguments presented in this book. Their efforts have undoubtedly contributed to the overall excellence of this publication.

Lastly, we express our gratitude to all the mentors, colleagues, and friends who have supported us throughout our careers, providing invaluable insights and encouragement in our exploration of sustainable businesses and the transformative power of technology.

With profound appreciation, we dedicate "Fostering Sustainable Businesses in Emerging Economies: The Impact of Technology" to everyone who has played a part in its creation. May this book inspire and empower readers to contribute to the growth of sustainable businesses and harness the potential of technology for the betterment of our world.

Quazi Tafsirul Islam, Richa Goel and Tilottama Singh

Chapter 1

Technology-Driven Social Innovation in the Emerging Market

Bilkisu Maijamaa, M.U. Adehi, Babagana Modu
and Muhammad Idris Umar

Abstract

This book chapter focuses on firstly social innovation and tools used to address the social needs and foster social innovation initiatives. Looking at the world economic forum and how it supports the social innovations, currency swings, low paying jobs growing rapidly, rapid change and growth as a result of high volatility and high returns, respectively. Secondly looking at the emerging market brought about by the social innovations and how they interconnect. Leading innovation emerging market has three main industries semiconductors, fin-tech, and electric cars. It also looks at the significance of technology in the development of business emerging markets, the role of technology in the emerging market and activities over the decades. Small firms in emerging areas face three major challenges which technology might help overcome. The challenges are trust, sustainability, and network. The role of technology replacing analog chip used for power supply, sensors, wideband signal make up the large semiconductors in the United States replaced with digital chip such as logical operations, data storage, computer information management all this have given birth to artificial intelligence, autonomous machines, self-driving cars, supply-chain management, cloud computing, and software-as-a-service (SaaS) applications are all made possible by digital chips. These are also used for e-commerce, mobile pay-ment, fine-tech, 5G telecom, health-care advancement, remote learning, online entertainment, and cloud computing. Technical advancements that has sparked a revolution that would be especially advantageous for emerging market and small-cap enterprises are the causes of these benefits of how it has affected countries such as Europe, the United States, China, and India to mention a few.

Fostering Sustainable Businesses in Emerging Economies, 1–21
doi:10.1108/978-1-80455-640-520231001

Keywords: Emerging market; challenges; innovative technology; social innovation; rapid change; computer information management

Introduction

Both academics and policymakers have noted a remarkable growth of social innovation (SI) over the past few decades (Adams & Hess, 2010). Innovative actions that are driven by a social need are referred to as social innovations (SI), according to Mulgan (2006).

According to Howaldt and Schewarz (2010), innovation is "social" in the sense that it may not always be "excellent," but it is socially desirable and meets a social need that the market does not consider to be important (Mulgan, Tucker, Ali, & Sanders, 2007). The definition of SI given by Auerswald (2009, p. 52) is "a innovative solution to a social problem that is more effective, efficient, sustainable, or just than existing solutions and for which the value gained accrues predominantly to society as a whole rather than private individual."

SI, thus, is tied to all social and societal demands and issues where any kind of innovation can bring about an advancement based on novelty and advancement. Identifying new concepts or social structures is how some scholars define SI as a means of addressing needs or solving issues. This explanation prompts a change to a demand-pull paradigm where solutions are embraced by a large number of people who actively contribute to their growth with a clear focus on social interactions.

While there are very few empirical investigations, a significant discussion concerning the definition of social innovation (SI) is emerging in the literature. Information technology (IT) tools and applications now account for a significant portion of new solutions. According to Bulut, Eren and Seckin Halac (2013), the social context in which SI emerged was investigated, as well as the causal links between technological innovation and SI. They also clarify SI's "relativity" and the way that it is oblique to various geographical and socioeconomic activity (which suggests it is important to understand how SI initiatives develop and grow based on cross-industry flows of opportunities and cross-scale processes).

This evidence is noteworthy since there is little information about which digital tools are really used to meet social requirements in the literature that examines the crucial role that IT and digital tools play in altering how people interact, enabling technology's impact on social innovation.

Digital tools and IT play a key role in changing how people interact because interactions among people are complex, especially when there are many players involved. These tools and technologies help to make information explicit, enable participants to stay in touch, and help to solve social and societal problems more quickly and effectively, highlighting its capacity to support the collective aspect of decision-making and knowledge flows.

Many people can now actively engage in the production and implementation of new ideas as a result of the introduction of an incredibly broad range of digitalized tools (Hutter, Hautz, Füller, Mueller, & Matzler, 2011). Digitalization of social issues, especially related to the importance of social connectivity, according to Vaccaro and Madsen (2009) Technologies based on the internet can help businesses improve interactions between customers and corporate operations in respect to moral dilemmas and social issues.

The technologies of the Fourth Industrial Revolution (4IR) provide us a wide range of opportunities for social and human services, allowing us to address our most difficult environmental and social issues while also reaching more people, particularly the disadvantaged and hard-to-reach.

Utilizing 4IR capabilities, social innovators are addressing some of the biggest issues facing the planet. More than 622 million people's lives have been better thanks to the social entrepreneur community at The Schwab Foundation, which has also given out $6.7 billion in loans or the value of goods and services to help people improve their standard of living.

Here are some examples of how social innovators are using disruptive technology to better address the world's pressing issues, from changing mental healthcare to giving a billion people digital identities.

How Does the World Economic Forum Support Social Innovation?

Social innovators are tackling some of the most pressing and pervasive problems in the world, such as illiteracy, access to clean water and sanitation, the education of girls, prison reform, financial inclusion, and disaster assistance.

Over 400 of the world's top social innovators working in over 190 nations are supported by the Schwab Foundation for Social Entrepreneurship. A total of 722 million lives have been directly enhanced thanks to the efforts of this group of eminent social innovators since its founding in 1998. Outstanding social innovators are invited to be nominated by our international network of experts, partner organizations, and World Economic Forum members.

Giving each individual a legal identity, more than just opening a bank account is involved with a legal identity. Your right to vote and access to healthcare may be at stake. However, the World Bank estimates that slightly fewer than 1 billion individuals worldwide lack identity documentation. It's a problem that Joseph Thompson has managed to solve. Due to his new venture, people without official documentation can now build a personal legal identity using a digital app made by AID:Tech.

The user's digital identity is protected from tampering by Thompson's software using block chain, and it is only available to the individual whose ID it stores. It fits well with the way many individuals in emerging nations use smart phones to manage their accounts as a digital solution. In addition to working on projects for financial inclusion in Uganda, Nigeria, and Southeast Asia, AID:Tech recently approved a project that will assist 2 million individuals. It is now focusing on providing financial services to the nearly 40 million Europeans who are unable to access them. Preparing delectable scientific goodies to benefit the environment.

The existing meat-based food system is doomed to fail as the world's population approaches 10 billion, posing urgent problems with regard to climate change, food poverty, and public health, according to David Yeung, CEO and Founder of Green Monday. One of Asia's top manufacturers of plant-based foods is called Green Monday. By encouraging people to adopt a plant-based diet at least once a week, Green Monday is establishing new social norms and providing realistic alternatives to diets based on meat.

The decrease of animal protein should be a primary objective as we rethink and re-engineer the entire food supply chain, according to Yeung. Alternative protein technology is an innovation that benefits the environment, human health, and animal welfare all at once. To increase its reach, OmniPork has formed partnerships with regional eateries as well as fast-food chains like Taco Bell and White Castle. Long before sustainability became a common consideration for investors, social considerations have been a key driver of firm performance in emerging markets.

Rising inequality, lower average household incomes, and more official meddling in domestic affairs are all characteristics of emerging market nations. Due to the combination of these forces, businesses that make socially incorrect decisions typically pay a hefty price from both their customers and regulators. Companies that seize the chance to improve people's lives, communities, or countries, on the other hand, can provide a lot of value.

To Assist, Put This Idea Into Practise; Let's Look at Three Groups of Business Examples

First, Take Into Account the Company's Relationship With Its Employees

It goes without saying that businesses with happier workers are more likely to perform well, but we believe this is especially true in developing economies where the difference between the best and median employment experiences is likely to be substantially higher. For all of our investee firms who declare it, we track staff attrition as a significant statistic, and we engage with those that do not want to encourage them to reveal the data.

Our investment case for Tata Consultancy Services (TCS) is based on the company's current attrition rate of 7%, which is between one-third and one-half lower than that of its competitors and fosters a positive feedback loop between employee happiness, client satisfaction, and growth (Table 1).

How does it keep its employees happy? How does it keep its staff content?

(1) *By providing them a great deal of discretionary power.*
    By examining the organizational structure, this is best understood. Even though the corporation generates $25 billion in revenue and has 500,000 workers, it is divided into roughly 50 distinct business divisions, each with its own P&L and "mini CEO." As a result, decision-making can go more quickly and empowers lower levels of management.

(2) *By making management decisions with the welfare of the workforce in mind.*
    The Covid-19 incident significantly disrupted the Indian IT sector, but TCS not only returned workers home without suffering any financial losses, but

Table 1. TCS Employee Figures.

Global, Diverse Workforce	
Employees	488,649
Nationalities	154
Women	36%
Talent Development	
Learning hours logged	43 million
Trained in agile	457K
Employees trained in new technologies	457K
Talent Retention	
Attrition on IT services	72%

Source: TCS annual reports.

also built a new working model called Secure Borderless Workspaces TM, which has since become the norm for remote working. Following that, it personally coordinated vaccinations for all employees and their families and provided personnel with a 24-hour medical helpline.

(3) *By providing them with substantial training opportunities.*
TCS established its own internal learning platforms to promote employee involvement through gamification and by connecting skills acquired to employee career trajectories, and its employees completed over 43 million training hours in the most recent fiscal year.

How did this improved treatment of employees affect the success of the business?

A better customer experience and greater profit growth have been fueled over time by TCS's decreased attrition rate. The aforementioned graphs contrast its personnel turnover and profit growth with those of its closest rival.

Second, think at how a company interacts with the communities that surround it. In recent years, it has been especially profitable to ask "How can we improve the lives of people around us?", in growing nations. In order to help the massive domestic unbanked population gain access to financial services, Safaricom, the top telecom provider in Kenya, launched its mobile money service M-Pesa in 2007. One of the earliest large-scale financial inclusion programs ever created, it has brought about far-reaching advantages.

These are what?

(4) *Increasing production and employment.*
Safaricom believes that despite having only 6,230 permanent, contract, and temporary employees, it directly and indirectly supports more than 1 million employments in the local economy.

(5) *Making payment distribution possible.*
Because the nation has a digital payments layer, the Kenyan government was able to provide payments to its citizens during the Covid crisis in an effective and secure manner. To encourage the local community to use electronic money rather than cash and lower the danger of disease transmission, Safaricom has banned payment costs for peer-to-peer money transactions with a value of less than KES 1,000.

(6) *Assisting the neighborhoods.*
Safaricom's operations are profitable enough to generate excess funds that the corporation can put back into charitable endeavors. For instance, the business launched the Keeping Girls in School project in 2021, through which it provided 800,000 girls with a 3-month supply of sanitary napkins, underwear, and education on menstrual hygiene.

In 2016, Safaricom aligned their business strategy with the UN Sustainable Development Goals, becoming one of the first companies to do so. In addition to helping the community, Safaricom has also been a world-beating investment, with profits increasing by 5 times and share price increasing by 10 times in the last 10 years. This indicates that societal impact, profitable expansion, and return to shareholders don't necessarily have to be trade-offs.

The true value assessment calculates the Safaricom sustained over 1,92,747 direct and indirect jobs during the year and, if the wider effects on the economy are included, this number increases to over 1,013,728 jobs (Table 2).

Because to the nation's nts layer, Kenya's government was able to provide payments to its citizens during the Covid issue in an effective and secure manner. Safaricom has also stopped using Paym.

Last but not least, think about how a business interacts with its clients and ultimately its regulators. A failure to uphold social commitments to customers has repeatedly been observed to come back to haunt businesses, especially in emerging markets where the state is frequently more interventionist than in other places. Let's use the past 10 years in China as an illustration.

Table 2. True Value Assessment.

Percentage True Value: Impact on Society		
Impact on society	9 times profit generated	0.6%
Economic value added	358.6bn direct and indirect through operations and taxes	6%
Social value of M-PESA	234.1bn	9.7%
Environmental externalities	406.2m	1.5%

Source: extracts from Safaricom annual report, March 31, 2011 to March 31, 2021.

Due to consumer fear of domestic brands, foreign firms continue to hold a majority of the market. This is a result of the 2008 newborn milk scandal, which revealed that baby formula contained melamine. After Baidu's search engine pushed potentially harmful medical treatments in 2016, the company faced long-lasting regulatory and reputational issues that cost it its former monopoly as a reliable information source.

Of course, customer trust may be restored with the appropriate approach. Yum China was eventually able to win back customers' hearts after a food quality controversy in 2015 thanks to a shift in management and business strategy; today, we consider it to be best-in-class in terms of sustainability.

What Steps did Yum China Take to Improve Its Brand Image?

It has consistently prioritized doing the right thing over maximizing immediate profits.

I. *Giving salaries and conditions first priority.*
The business has made sure that pay and working conditions are far above minimal legal requirements or industry standards. This goes beyond and beyond simple financial aid; as the Covid pandemic began, for instance, it offered health insurance to restaurant owners and their families. Even more simply put, delivery drivers employed by KFC receive meals at significantly reduced prices, in contrast to their colleagues who work for delivery platforms.

II. *Investing in guidelines for food safety.*
Yum China has made enormous financial investments to guarantee that food safety regulations are upheld. Most recently, this meant making a large investment in an upstream poultry farmer who is a crucial supplier to the business. Yum China has tried to take a more balanced, long-term approach, which might not be pleasing to short-sighted investors who prefer their companies to be "asset light." It can generate good profits and free cash flow even with this investment, and it has secured the resources to continue doing so far into the future.

III. *Assisting the neighborhoods.*
The business has leveraged its on-site physical infrastructure, which includes upwards of 10,000 stores and 400,000 employees, as a basis from which to support the neighborhoods, for instance by establishing educational initiatives like reading clubs.

This kind of engagement improves brand quality and government relations while also boosting employee morale.

The businesses above are merely being used as examples. Their inclusion shouldn't be taken as a buy/sell recommendation. In conclusion, societal issues and rising markets are emphasized. The prospects for individuals who can solve problems are extensive, and the gap between the greatest and worst performers is wide. This is why any strategy for investing in emerging markets must incorporate social considerations into decision-making.

Looking at developing nations.

Developing Nations

Emerging markets are those of developing nations that are quickly urbanizing and growing their economies. Nations in emerging markets are putting money into expanding their capacity for production. They are leaving behind economies that have historically been based on agriculture and the export of basic resources. The goal of leaders in developing nations is to improve the standard of living for their citizens. They are embracing a free market or mixed economy and industrializing quickly. Brazilian, Chinese, Indian, and Russian markets are a few examples of emerging ones.

Workings of Emerging Markets

A growing market has these five characteristics:

(1) Low earnings.
(2) Rapid expansion.
(3) Extreme volatility.
(4) Changes in currency.
(5) Potentially lucrative.

All sizes of emerging markets exhibit these qualities.

Low-Paying Jobs Quick Growth

The first trait that distinguishes developing markets is that their per capita income is lower than the global average. The first crucial condition is low income because it encourages the second crucial criterion, rapid expansion. Emerging market leaders are ready to make the quick transition to an industrialized economy in order to support their citizens and hold onto power.

The World Bank no longer categorizes nations as "developing," but rather according to their yearly per capita income, with low-income and lower-middle-income nations having an income of $4,095 or less. A per capita income of $12,696.2 is found in high-income economies. Major advanced economies like the United States, Germany, and the United Kingdom experienced an economic growth of 5.4% in 2021. Asia's emerging and developing nations, including China, saw their economies expand by more than 8%.

High Volatility Is Caused by Rapid Change

The third characteristic of emerging economies is significant volatility, which is a result of rapid societal change. Natural disasters, outside price shocks, and unstable internal policies are three potential causes of that. Agriculture-based traditional economies are particularly susceptible to catastrophes like the Haitian earthquake, the Thailand tsunami, or the Sudanese drought. But as it did in Thailand, these catastrophes can pave the way for more commercial expansion.

Emerging markets are particularly vulnerable to abrupt changes in the value of currencies, such those affecting the dollar. They are also susceptible to fluctuations in the price of commodities like food and oil. That is as a result of their lack of ability to sway these movements. For instance, energy and food prices skyrocketed in 2008 as a result of American subsidies for maize ethanol production. Food riots were sparked by this in numerous emerging market nations.

Many parts of the population suffer when leaders of emerging economies make the reforms required for industrialization, such as farmers who lose their land. This might eventually cause social discontent, uprisings, and regime changes. If industries are nationalized or the government defaults on its debt, investors risk losing everything.

High Returns Can Result From Growth

This expansion calls for a substantial investment budget. However, compared to industrialized markets, these nations' financial markets are less developed.

Currency Swings Are the Fourth Characteristic

Foreign direct investment in emerging markets has not been very consistent. Getting information on companies listed on respective stock markets is frequently challenging. Selling debt, such as corporate bonds, on the secondary market could not be simple. These factors together increase the risk. This implies that investors who are prepared to conduct in-depth study will receive a higher payout.

Rapid expansion can also result in the fifth attribute, which is a higher-than-average return for investors, if it is successful. This is so because many of these nations prioritize an export-focused approach. They generate lower-cost consumer products and commodities for export to industrialized countries since they don't have the domestic demand. The businesses that support this expansion will make money. Investors benefit from rising stock prices as a result of this interplay. It also entails a greater yield on bonds, which are more expensive due to the increased risk associated with emerging market businesses.

This characteristic attracts investors to emerging markets. Emerging markets are not always wise investments. They must have a booming labor market, less debt, and an honest administration. China and India are the two primary emerging market powerhouses. More than 35% of the world's population and labor force reside in these two nations. Their predicted total gross domestic output in 2021 was $17.3 trillion, which was higher than either the European Union's $15.2 trillion or the United States' ($21 trillion) estimates.

Investing Individuals: What it means take advantage of emerging economies' rapid growth rates and potential in a variety of ways. Selecting an emerging market fund is the best option. Many funds either attempt to outperform the

MSCI Index or follow it. It helps you save time. You are not required to research international businesses and economic strategies. By spreading out your investments across a number of emerging markets rather than just one, it also lowers risk.

Emerging Markets Aren't All Equal

Emerging markets are not always profitable investment opportunities. Some nations have benefited from higher commodity prices after the 2008 financial crisis to expand their economies. They did not make infrastructure investments. Instead, they used the extra money to fund government employment and subsidies. As a result, their economies expanded swiftly, the population made significant purchases of imported commodities, and inflation quickly became an issue. Brazil, Hungary, Malaysia, Russia, South Africa, Turkey, and Vietnam were among these nations.

There wasn't much local money for banks to lend to support the expansion of local enterprises because their citizens didn't save much. By keeping interest rates low, the governments attracted foreign direct investment. This contributed to higher inflation, but it was worthwhile. The nations' economies expanded significantly in return. Commodity prices decreased in 2013. These governments were forced to reduce subsidies or expand their debt to foreign countries because they were dependent on the high price of a particular product. Foreign investments fell as the debt-to-GDP ratio rose. Currency dealers started offsetting their positions in 2014 as well. As currency prices dropped, a panic set in, causing a massive sell-off of both currencies and investments.

Other nations, on the other hand, spent their money on building infrastructure and funding workforce education. This type of investment was made by China, Colombia, Czech Republic, Indonesia, Korea, Peru, Poland, Sri Lanka, and Taiwan. Additionally, there was a lot of local currency available to finance new firms because the citizens of these nations preserved a lot of their money. These nations were prepared in 2014 when the crisis struck.

Emerging market economies are those that are undergoing the industrialization process. They present enormous growth potential, but this is tempered by extreme volatility. Emerging markets present significant opportunities for foreign investment, but they may also expose investors to significant risk. Investing in an emerging market fund, which diversifies your investment over a number of emerging markets rather than just one, is one way to lower risk.

Leading in Innovation Are Emerging Markets

Three main industries, semiconductors, fintech, and electric cars, are dominated by developing market nations, and innovation is fueling this expansion. In the world of developing markets, we are discovering businesses that provide special investment prospects.

Growth is being fueled by innovation in developing market nations. We believe that the industrialized world is no longer the sole source of invention. As a result of leadership roles in STEM (science, technology, engineering, and mathematics) education, innovation in technology applications, and a growing number of tech-savvy people, we think many of the top businesses of the next 20 years may come from emerging markets. According to us, the dominance in the three key sectors of electric vehicles (EVs), fintech, and semiconductors is generating some interesting investment opportunities.

Connected Devices and Semiconductors

The World Intellectual Property Organization said in 2019 that more than two thirds of all patent, trademark, and industrial design applications in 2018 originated in Asia. Since that time, Asia has maintained its status as the region with the highest volume of patent filings. In addition, since 2003, China has generated more STEM PhDs than any other country.

According to a report released in August 2021 by CSET, a policy research organization at Georgetown University, China, was producing 50% more STEM Ph.D. students than the United States by the year 2020. In addition, a February 2021 article in the Harvard Business Review said that China now generates 30% of all research publications on artificial intelligence (AI).

The big and important talent pool in Asia is quantified by the mix of STEM PhDs and AI research. Additionally boosting the digital economy in many of these nations are population expansion and a younger generation that is more tech-savvy.

According to an article in the May–June 2021 issue of Harvard Business Review, a money transfer app from a major China-based technology company, for instance, recorded more than a billion transactions every day in 2018. We think that Asia's emergence as a global leader in the field is largely due to this mix of talent and technologically advanced thought.

The Internet of Things (IoT), which consists of digital technologies or devices integrated in all types of consumer and industrial items, is growing as a result of scientific research leadership in AI. These include home appliances, smart watches, and more industrial uses in industries like precise manufacturing and agriculture.

The use of the Internet of Things is most prevalent in China. (%, Number of IoT connected devices).

Semiconductors have become a more essential part of our daily lives as more and more objects are redesigned and reinterpreted as "smart" tools. Many of the top businesses in this industry worldwide have a disproportionately large presence in Asia.

The worldwide semiconductor market is now dominated by two South Korean and Taiwanese businesses. These two companies employ over 135,000 people and invest more than $65 billion in capital projects every year to increase their technological advantages. The number of IoT-connected devices is expected to triple from their present amount to 43 billion by 2023 as more enterprises adopt the technology.

Brazil and India Accept Digital Wallets

Many businesses in emerging markets have moved quickly from credit cards to mobile payments. From Brazil to India, mobile payments are being accepted as the norm. According to a research by Blackhawk Network, as of April 2021, 93% of internet users in India and 43% of those in the United States used digital wallets.

Another Key Factor in This Market Is Internet Connectivity

Additionally, the expansion of online banking and alternative financing platforms is increasing the number of people in developing nations, especially Latin America, who have access to banks. These nations' citizens and small-business owners have historically had restricted access to financial services. Businesses can receive banking services outside of the traditional financial infrastructures with the use of accessible technology, particularly in fintech. In the long run, this can improve livelihoods and increase consumer spending, promoting economic growth.

In China, Electric Vehicles Are Making a Splash

China outsells both the United States and Europe in terms of global EV sales. According to data from EV-volumes.com, EV sales in China in 2020 accounted for 8% of all vehicle sales, compared to 4%–5% globally. By 2030, according to the same data, Chinese penetration will increase to more than 30%. Additionally, Chinese EV businesses profit from government assistance, which includes local consumer subsidies. Since January 2020, the number of absolute monthly units sold has increased most as a result of this.

In our opinion, Chinese EV producers are especially well-situated to profit from this market trend. Comparing China to Europe and the United States, electric vehicle models are among the best-selling ones. The battery is a crucial part of EVs, and at the moment, all of them are created and manufactured by Korean, Japanese, or Chinese firms. According to a piece written by the Institute of Electrical and Electronics Engineers in August 2021, three businesses presently control over 70% of the market (IEEE). As of July 2021, according to Putnam, some of the most popular car models in China are electric vehicles.

We have long held the opinion that developing nations are best suited to lead the globe in technological advancement. A potent incubator for innovation in the emerging markets is created by the potent mix of leadership in STEM academic resources, a strong pipeline of innovative new and affordable technological solutions, and a responsive and expanding tech-savvy population.

Learn more about the Putnam Emerging Markets Equity Fund for additional details. We have long held the opinion that developing nations are best suited to lead the globe in technological advancement. A potent incubator for innovation in the emerging markets is created by the potent mix of leadership in STEM academic resources, a strong pipeline of innovative new and affordable technological solutions, and a responsive and expanding tech-savvy population.

The Critical Significance of Technology in the Development of Business in Emerging Markets

For established enterprises in industrialized nations, the endeavor is challenging enough. Working with Digital Boost to develop a platform that offers digital consultancy to charities and small companies in the United Kingdom affected by COVID-19 throughout the summer, we have seen that even developed economies need digital support for their small- and medium-sized businesses due to the large skills gap that even established businesses struggle with.

Emerging Markets Considerably Exacerbate the Issue

Analyzing the major problems that small- and medium-sized firms (SMEs) in emerging countries deal with in the new COVID-19 age as part of the work with The MASH Foundation Trust. Small firms in emerging areas face three major challenges and think technology might help them overcome them.

I. *Trust*: In a completely virtual environment, how can we foster trust? The abrupt digitalization of payments has created a significant trust barrier between SMEs, recipients, local communities, and the government in developing economies where cash is king. Traditionally done in person, bookkeeping, transaction processing, and payments now all have to be done online. This paradigm has compelled the use of digital technology, and in nations like Kenya, programs like M-PESA mobile payments have played a crucial role. I think the payments sector can accelerate digitalization in the future while fostering trust and transparency to support emerging economies.

II. *Sustainability*: It's an important feature of SMEs that I observed while working in Kenya with local residents. Business models frequently depend too heavily on a particular geographic setting, cater to a relatively narrow social group, or depend on a strong and stable value chain. With COVID-19, that playbook has been abandoned. Particularly when finance sources are not necessarily steady, developing a self-sustaining firm is challenging in emerging nations. To drive multi-year stability in revenue and reduce macroeconomic shocks, it is essential to increase digital capacity in terms of online e-commerce in order to diversify company models.

III. *Networks*: In developing economies, establishing a successful firm can depend as much on who you know as it does on your knowledge. As important as the concept it is the ability to sell it. In my opinion, bringing together communities virtually (with digitalization basically mandated as a result of COVID-19) creates a more level playing field with limitless opportunity to forge alliances, tap into global networks, and apply lessons across various sectors to spur economic impact.

How Can We Assist Companies in Emerging Areas to Fully Utilize Their Digital Potential?

For London Business School, the nexus of consulting and technology is a crucial growth sector. "Digital for Impact" is a brand-new initiative that the Experiential Learning team, in association with professors Rajesh Chandy and Costas Markides, has started. Students will be able to apply what they learn in the classroom to the workplace, bridging the digital divide in developing nations. Students will work in groups to serve as (virtual) digital consultants in emerging markets, bringing their ideas and viewpoints to bear on firms to help them utilize technology and effect long-term change.

Growing Role of Technology in Emerging Markets

We believe that technology is now the dominant force, replacing commodity production as the main economic driver in emerging nations. One of the best instances of technological advancement worldwide is semiconductor manufacture. Analog chips, which are frequently utilized for power supply, sensors, and wideband signals, make up a large portion of the semiconductors made in the United States (e.g., speech, music, and video). Logic operations, data storage, computer processing, and information management are examples of applications for digital chips.

Digital chips are generally regarded as being far more technologically sophisticated than analog chips. They are primarily manufactured in emerging nations, with Taiwan leading the pack. Artificial intelligence, autonomous machines, self-driving cars, supply-chain management, cloud computing, and software-as-a-service (SaaS) applications are all made possible by digital chips. They are also required for e-commerce, mobile payments, fintech, 5G telecom, health-care advancements (such as telemedicine and drug discovery), remote learning, online entertainment, and cloud computing.

Health care is one industry that hasn't ranked highly in the Index. But given the rising demand for healthcare services in developing countries and the use of technology to increase access to healthcare for these people, we anticipate a significant change in this over the next 10 years.

For instance, China's Ping An Healthcare & Technology operates the web platform "Ping An Good Doctor" as a provider of mobile and online medical services. Health management, wellness services, hospital appointments, remote consultations, and the referral of healthcare resources are all done through the platform. Ping An's mission is to leverage cutting-edge technologies, such as artificial intelligence, to more efficiently allocate primary care and hospital resources.

Another such is Wuxi Biologics, a Chinese company that works internationally. The business creates biological and antibody drugs and offers added-value services to other pharmaceutical companies. Wuxi is involved in the production of the Covid-19 vaccine as part of an increasing pipeline of operations.

Activity Over the Decades

After talking about the sectors that have influenced emerging markets over the past 20 years, let's compare the market capitalization-adjusted performance of developing market stocks to that of U.S. stocks.

The MSCI Emerging Markets Large Cap Index, MSCI Emerging Markets Small Cap Index, Russell 1000® Index of US Large Caps, and Russell 2000® Index of US Small Caps are all included in Fig. 2. The figures displayed are cumulative total returns that have not been annualized and have all been calculated in US dollars.

The 20 years that ended on December 31, 2020, show that emerging-market stocks outperformed American stocks over a longer length of time. What we also observe is that over the past 20 years, small caps have outperformed large caps both in emerging economies and in the United States. This makes sense to us since, although typically having greater risk profiles, emerging-market and small-cap companies typically have more possibility for growth.

Let's now examine a shorter time frame, the 10 years that ended on December 31, 2020. The story during this time is considerably different. Both small caps and large caps underperformed, with emerging-market equities underperforming U.S. stocks by a significant margin. Further back, in the 10 years that ended on December 31, 2010, emerging-market equities and small caps outperformed large caps. Additionally, as will be discussed below, we think that investors may once again favor these places.

Expectations for the Long Term and Cyclical Improvements

After outlining the expanding significance of technology and the overall performance of stocks over the past 20 years, we have some ideas about what may be in store going forward. We think small caps and equities from emerging markets will offer better potential to produce lucrative returns over very lengthy stretches of time. The key reason is that a valuation that appears to be higher may be less of a barrier to long-term investing success in certain industries because there is typically more possibility for growth there.

We think that accurate evaluations of business models, management teams, and competitive environments – particularly in emerging-market and small-cap companies – are more important for successful investment outcomes than accurate evaluations of valuations. For our part, we focus the majority of our research efforts on business models, management teams, and competitive landscapes, among other essential elements. Take Latin American e-commerce and financial pioneer MercadoLibre as an illustration. The company's market value was roughly US$2 billion in 2010. Since then, MercadoLibre's market value has soared to around US$78 billion. Another illustration is the growth of India's HDFC Bank, which went from having roughly $15 billion in 2010 to having about 106 billion now.

We are aware, however, that market prices are also influenced by cyclical forces. For instance, the past 10 years have not tracked with what we would anticipate over the longer term. In other words, we think emerging-market equities and small caps will perform better cyclically than American stocks and large caps. Prices that are comparably reasonable, the aforementioned headroom for expansion, and technical advancements that could spark a revolution that would be especially advantageous for emerging-market and small-cap enterprises are the causes of these benefits.

The US dollar's value in relation to other currencies is another cyclical factor. In general, during the decade that ended on December 31, 2020, emerging-market currencies declined in value against the dollar, which negatively impacted the governments, businesses, and equities of emerging-market nations. These obstacles might disappear if the direction of currency exchange rates shifts generally in the upcoming 10 years, increasing investor interest in emerging markets. As a side note, because China, Taiwan, and Korea have typically been able to keep their currencies within normal ranges compared to the dollar, we think exchange rates are less crucial when investing in these nations.

An Economical New Period

We believe it's crucial to remember that "getting back on track" may not mean "going back to normal" because "normal" may have changed as global economies start to recover in 2021. In other words, a company that appeared to be well-positioned a year ago may now be obsolete due to a new economic paradigm that may have been sparked by the coronavirus pandemic and facilitated by technology that has irreversibly changed how people live and work.

We believe that our bottom-up research methodology meant we were well-prepared for this unexpected new paradigm that has benefitted IT and healthcare companies based on the recent performance of the Wasatch strategies and funds, which you can view at wasatchglobal.com. The persistence of this paradigm will also have an impact on our future investment choices because it may open up previously unimagined opportunities as well as accelerate those that we have anticipated.

Opportunities for Investment in Central China

Some mainland Chinese businesses are currently viewed as security risks by the United States. As a result, the United States has prohibited the export of key crucial technologies, including semiconductors, to China. Additionally, China is the world's largest importer of semiconductors, making it susceptible to this restriction. We believe China may begin taking significant steps to disconnect its semiconductor industry from the rest of the world as a result.

We must take into account the situation in Taiwan in order to comprehend this problem more fully. The island's economy grew at the quickest rate in 4 years during the third quarter, according to a recent report from Taiwan's statistics department. Exports were a major factor in this rise, with Taiwan Semiconductor Manufacturing (TSMC), the largest company in the nation, contributing significantly to this growth. As China's Huawei Technologies stocked up on semiconductors before to the US-imposed sales restriction taking effect in September, TSMC's revenues increased in 2020.

The belief that the current state of affairs represents a low point in US–China relations seems to be reflected in the financial markets. Even if relations don't significantly improve during Joe Biden's presidency, the argument goes, they're not likely to get substantially worse. We think this chapter is plausible. At the very least, we believe the Trump administration would approach China with more nuance and give priority to the needs of American friends like Taiwan. We believe China's long-term plan is to substantially invest in developing a Chinese-centric infrastructure for semiconductor design and manufacture, in part because of Taiwan's strong economic relationships in the United States and Europe.

However, start-to-finish semiconductor fabrication is a challenging process that takes a lot of time and effort to master. Countries like Taiwan can find themselves caught in the crossfire between China's drive to increase its economic clout and the United States' determination to rein it in. Despite this, dangers associated with emerging markets have always included trade disputes and other forms of geopolitics. Despite these dangers, we believe there could be profitable investment opportunities tied to China's building out its own semiconductor infrastructure. These prospects may extend beyond design and fabrication, as the manufacture of semiconductors necessitates a wide range of equipment, tools, and other resources.

Aside from semiconductor manufacturing, which is still in its infancy, China already boasts a wide array of investable businesses across a spectrum of market capitalizations. Additionally, a lot of these businesses meet domestic Chinese demand, which is a market niche we find very alluring. For additional information on the new Wasatch Greater China Strategy and Fund, please visit wasatchglobal.com.

Chances in Other Broader Markets

Investors valued emerging markets most highly for their energy reserves, mineral deposits, and other natural resources when they were originally identified as a distinct asset class. Many emerging-market economies were driven by the extraction of these resources, which heavily relied on the export of commodities to the developed world for growth and hard cash. Emerging markets were able to

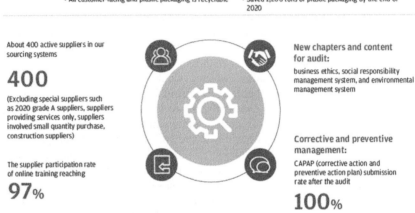

Fig. 1.   Sustainability Highlights. *Source:* extracts from Yum China annual report: http://www.yumchina.com.

evolve well beyond their initial responsibilities as producers of commodities because of this mutually beneficial connection.

Comments like "tech is 'eating' the world" no longer only apply to rich countries since technology now makes up a growing portion of emerging-market economy. This change is also reflected in the MSCI Emerging Markets Index, as shown in Fig. 1 above. For instance, TSMC's stock has benefited greatly from the company's technological edge over Intel Corp. in the semiconductor business. However, TSMC and Taiwan as a whole are susceptible to Chinese meddling – at least in the short run.

Korea may benefit the most from increased semiconductor production, outside of Taiwan, in order to meet global demand. While Korean firms have behind TSMC, much like Intel in the United States, they may have the best chances to catch up. Again, in addition to design and fabrication, the manufacture of semiconductors necessitates the involvement of numerous other regional business sectors in the supply chain.

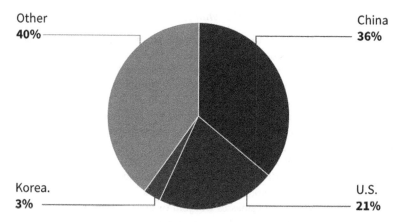

Fig. 2.   Use of the Internet of Things in China. *Source:* Statista, as of August 2021.

Therefore, semiconductors might help a new generation of "Asian Tigers" emerge. India is a technical innovation powerhouse, despite the fact that it isn't yet a leader in semiconductors. India, for instance, has a wealth of human capital that may be used by technology. Shivank Patel, a fifth-grade student at the age of nine, was highlighted in a recent Bloomberg Businessweek piece. Shivank has been learning how to write software code for a year and has already produced a number of apps.

Patel's most recent project, which he aims to release in the Google Play Store, is made to assist parents and medical professionals in keeping track of prematurely delivered children. India has seen a rise in the popularity of online coding programs for primary school students as worried parents try to give their children the skills they need to get a career that pays well.

Visit wasatchglobal.com to access our white paper titled India's Virtuous Circle of Amazing Progress for a thorough examination of India. The three megatrends that the study discusses are formalization, financialization, and digitization, all of which are made possible by technology.

Outlook for Wasatch

It is obvious that the tensions between the United States and mainland China will not be eased anytime soon. Although these tensions may be unsettling, we think they may hasten the creation of technologically sophisticated supply chains, some of which will serve China's domestic requirements while others will serve various channels. The coronavirus pandemic, which led to severe shortages of safety equipment and pharmaceutical ingredients, also brought attention to the need for nations and businesses to diversify their supply chains and exercise greater control over production.

Low Price Can No Longer Be the Main Factor

Apple, for instance, intends to increase iPhone manufacture there. Additionally, Samsung will begin producing TVs in India, where it currently has its largest factory for the production of smart phones. According to us, improved and new supply chains will present lucrative investment opportunities. Consider the cover title of the TIME Magazine edition from December 14: "2020: The Worst Year Ever" if you have any remaining doubts about the ability of businesses and their stocks to perform successfully in the face of geopolitical tensions between the United States and China.

The majority of Wasatch strategies and funds, which concentrate on high-quality businesses with robust cash flows, experienced double-digit percentage gains in 2020. Additionally, many global broad stock indexes performed nicely. We anticipate that hundreds of businesses will join or enlarge their participation in the highly developed supply chains that pass through emerging economies in the coming years. And because there are so many businesses, particularly in China, some will prosper wildly while others will suffer. As a result, we believe active stock selection will be crucial.

In this regard, we keep expanding the capabilities of our team of researchers on new markets. Neal Dihora, CFA, who joins Wasatch as a Portfolio Manager from the esteemed Nicholas Company, is the newest member of our team. Neal is a Gujarati speaker and was born in Bhavnagar, India.

Wasatch's expertise in evaluating cutting-edge, technologically focused businesses ought to be well equipped for negotiating the rapidly evolving landscape of new markets. Additionally, while some of our strategies and funds concentrate on small caps, our "select" strategies and funds enable us to make investments in mid- and large-cap firms that we think have a strong potential for future growth.

To sum up, we aim to own many of the tech-related businesses that have long provided industrialized nations with significant efficiency and modern conveniences – including during the coronavirus pandemic – in emerging regions. We may also benefit from an even larger tailwind if it turns out that the investment cycle and the currency cycle have moved in favor of several emerging markets.

We believe that it is hard to foresee precisely how the dynamics we have described here will play out. But by being prepared through ongoing research into individual companies' prospects and by keeping a close eye on emerging markets, we think we'll be better able to seize opportunities when they present themselves. This is crucial because a small number of individual equities frequently exceed a related benchmark index. And we're especially thrilled that commodity production may no longer be the dominant driver in emerging countries, as technology – an area in which we believe ourselves to have great expertise – may have done so.

Bibliography

Adams, D., & Hess, M. (2010). Social innovation and why it has policy significance. *The Economic and Labour Relations Review, 21*(2), 139–155.

Bulut, C., Eren, H., & Seckin Halac, D. (2013). Social innovation and psychometric analysis: World conference on psychology and sociology 2012. *Procedia - Social and Behavioral Science, 82,* 122–130.

Corporate Finance Institute. *Emerging markets.* Retrieved from https://corporate financeinstitute.com/resources/knowledge/economics/emerging-markets/. Accessed on August 5, 2021.

Howaldt, J., & Schewarz, M. (2010). *Social innovation: Concepts, research fields and international trends.* MA/ZLW.

Hutter, K., Hautz, J., Füller, J., Mueller, J., & Matzler, K. (2011). Communitition: The tension between competition and collaboration in community-based design contests. *Creativity and Innovation Management, 20*(1), 3–21.

International Monetary Fund. *World Economic Outlook Database.* Retrieved from https://www.imf.org/external/pubs/ft/weo/2020/01/weodata/index.aspx. Accessed on August 5, 2021.

International Monetary Fund. *Report for Selected Countries and Subjects.* Retrieved from https://www.imf.org/external/pubs/ft/weo/2020/01/weodata/weorept.aspx?pr. x=58&pr.y=11&sy=2007&ey=2014&ssm=1&scsm=1&ssd=1&sort=country& ds=.&br=1&c=924%2C233%2C293%2C964%2C935%2C524%2C528%2C536% 2C542&s=NGDP_RPCH%2CPCPIEPCH&grp=0&a=. Accessed on August 5, 2021.

Moon, S., Armstrong, J., Hutler, B., Uphur, R., Katz, R., Atuire, C., & Wolff, J. (2022). Governing the access to Covid-19 tools accelerator; towards greater participation, transparency, and accountability. *The Lancent, 399*(10323), 487–494.

Mulgan, G. (2006). *Collaboration and collective impact; how can founders, NGOs and governments achieve more together?* London: NESTA.

Mulgan, G., Tucker, S., Ali, R., & Sanders, B. (2007). Social innovation: What it is, why it matters and how it can be accelerated.

National Center for Biotechnology Information. Food vs. fuel: Diversion of crops could cause more hunger. *Environmental Health Perspectives.* Retrieved from https://www.ncbi.nlm.nih.gov/pmc/articles/PMC2430252/. Accessed on August 5, 2021.

The World Bank. *World Bank country and lending groups.* Retrieved from https:// datahelpdesk.worldbank.org/knowledgebase/articles/906519. Accessed on August 5, 2021.

The World Bank. *Population, Total.* Retrieved from https://data.worldbank.org/ indicator/SP.POP.TOTL. Accessed on August 5, 2021.

The World Bank. *Labor Force, Total.* Retrieved from https://data.worldbank.org/ indicator/SL.TLF.TOTL.IN?view=chart. Accessed on August 5, 2021.

The World Bank. *GDP (current US$) – European Union.* Retrieved from https://data. worldbank.org/indicator/NY.GDP.MKTP.CD?end=2018&locations=EU&start= 2018&view=bar. Accessed on August 5, 2021.

The World Bank. *GDP (current US$).* Retrieved from https://data.worldbank.org/ indicator/NY.GDP.MKTP.CD. Accessed on August 5, 2021.

U.S. Securities and Exchange Commission. *T. Rowe Price: Institutional emerging markets equity fund.* Retrieved from https://www.sec.gov/Archives/edgar/data/ 852254/000031321213000035/iiefpta-march39.htm. Accessed on August 4, 2021.

Vaccaro, A., & Madsen, P. (2009). Corporate dynamic transparency: The new ICT-driven ethics? *Ethics and Information Technology, 11*(2), 113–122.

Chapter 2

Digitization and Integration of Sustainable Development Goals (SDGs) in Emerging Economies

Quazi Tafsirul Islam, Jashim Uddin Ahmed and Afnan Sayed

Abstract

Digitization is the process of transforming analog systems into digital ones, and it has become a crucial factor in the sustainable development of emerging economies. Although implementing digitization may be challenging due to limited budgets, missing strategies, pushback from employees, and the existing organizational structure, it can bring multifaceted benefits to the economy, such as improved employment and income, enhanced access to knowledge and education, and reduced costs for companies and countries. Moreover, digitization can significantly impact economic growth, as it can create new job opportunities, foster innovation, and improve infrastructure, among other benefits. The United Nations Sustainable Development Goals (SDGs) provide a global agenda for creating a more sustainable, equitable, and prosperous future by 2030, and digital technologies have become increasingly important in addressing the challenges of achieving these goals, particularly for emerging economies. However, achieving these ambitious goals presents significant challenges, particularly for emerging economies. Hence, this literature review aims to discuss the potential impact of digital technologies on the implementation of the SDGs in emerging economies, supported by scholarly research and opinions. In conclusion, digital technologies have significant potential to contribute to the achievement of the SDGs by promoting economic growth and innovation while also promoting sustainability, creating a more prosperous and equitable world for all.

Keywords: Digitization; SDGs; emerging economy; development; sustainability; technology

Fostering Sustainable Businesses in Emerging Economies, 23–38
Copyright © 2024 Quazi Tafsirul Islam, Jashim Uddin Ahmed and Afnan Sayed
Published under exclusive licence by Emerald Publishing Limited
doi:10.1108/978-1-80455-640-520231002

Introduction

Digitization refers to transforming analog systems into digital ones, which is an impactful factor in the sustainable development of emerging economies (Gobble, 2018). Due to the lack of means of providing services digitally, emerging economies often waste their valuable resources on bottlenecks, making the entire process bizarre, enigmatic, and time-consuming for the end consumers. From keeping records manually to not providing services on time, citizens in emerging economies often go through a rollercoaster ride. However, as more countries understand the importance of digitization, they are taking and integrating more sustainable development approaches into their economy. Digitization can have multifaceted benefits in the economy, such as the improved condition of life through more and better employment and income, enhanced access to knowledge and education, and most importantly, how it reduces cost in a company and hence a country. Emerging economies such as Bangladesh, Kenya have taken initiatives to include their citizens financially under their digital roof. The more people use these transaction methods, the more likely the country will achieve sustainable development. Healthcare in such economies also substantially improved as patients can now consult their doctors with the help of their phones sitting at home. This improved the quality of life and increased efficiency and productivity. Children can now grasp new knowledge through the internet's interactive use and collaboration with other digital platforms. Agriculture businesses also reaped the benefits of digitization as many nations whose primary source of gross domestic product (GDP) is based on agriculture benefit the most. From raising funds to generate harvest through digital platforms to farmers having the means of communicating with the field and vegetation experts from miles away is one of the best examples of integration of digitization for achieving Sustainable Development Goals (SDGs).

Nevertheless, digitization can rope in several challenges, among which limited budget, missing digitization strategy, pushback from employees, the structure of the existing organization, and absence of expertise to deal with digitization, to name a few (Sabbagh, Friedrich, El-Darwiche, Singh, & Koster, 2013). Whenever a company goes through digitization, facing any of these challenges is possible. Bringing in a new strategy to carry out a business requires money. However, companies may need more funds to implement the strategy. Even when the company knows that digitization can be cost-effective and generate higher revenue totaling higher profit, they may need more money to do so.

Moreover, because digitization improved efficiency and proved cost-effective, only some companies have solid strategies to implement. The importance of research and how to successfully transform into a new form of strategy is substantial. Lack of strategy or poor strategy can be costly for the company, which they may not recover from (Sabbagh et al., 2013). Additionally, employees at an organization's heart may find it challenging to adopt the new business strategy. The company has to give the employees on-the-job training and incentivize them to adopt the new strategy.

Nevertheless, a company's primary concern should be to look into the organization's existing structure. Digitization transforms the manual system into digital form through state-of-the-art technology; however, if a company's existing structure does not support such technology or if it becomes more costly to change the existing structure to digitize, digitization can be a barrier to be implemented. Even if a company digitizes itself, the importance of experts is significant. Experts are needed to train the employees in the organization and solve any company's dilemma (Sabbagh et al., 2013). The recruitment of such skilled labor can be expensive and time-consuming.

The government of a country can face the same challenges. Before implementing such a strategy, the government must find out if the citizens are ready to transition. Emerging economies may fail to implement such a strategy right away due to the citizens' lack of human capital to navigate this journey, along with the country's poor infrastructure. Digital literacy can be a big question here. A country where people need access to digital platforms may find it daunting to deal with such digitization. Digital literacy consists of knowledge or human capital to navigate digital gadgets in everyday life (Firmansyah & Susetyo, 2022). If the country's citizens have sufficient knowledge of how to use different kinds of digital products, the government can easily make the transition. However, in emerging economies, this may be different. This is mainly because of the digital divide within a country and compared with countries around the globe. The digital divide refers to the endowments of digital products among the citizens of a country (Ragnedda, 2019). People from the lower income group may need a smartphone or internet connectivity to gain knowledge about digital products and information worldwide.

On the contrary, people from higher income groups can handle such difficulty. This discrimination in income groups leads to the divide where different people have different degrees of accessibility. Hence, digitization in emerging economies may take time to bring productivity and efficiency.

Literature Review

The United Nations SDGs encompass a global agenda for creating a more sustainable, equitable, and prosperous future by 2030. However, achieving these ambitious goals presents significant challenges, particularly for emerging economies. Digital technologies have become increasingly important in addressing these challenges, as they offer a range of solutions to help bridge the gaps in sustainable development. This literature review aims to discuss the potential impact of digital technologies on the implementation of the SDGs in emerging economies, supported by scholarly research and opinions.

Digitization is the process of converting analog systems into digital ones, and it significantly impacts the long-term development of developing economies (Gobble, 2018). Emerging economies frequently waste their valuable resources on bottlenecks, making the entire process strange, cryptic, and time-consuming for the end users since they need more capabilities to provide services digitally.

People in emerging economies frequently experience a variety of ups and downs, from manually maintaining records to needing help to deliver services on time. Nonetheless, more nations are adopting and incorporating more sustainable development practices into their economies as they realize the value of digitization. The economy can gain from digitization in various ways, including increased access to knowledge and education, better employment opportunities and income, and – most importantly – cost savings for businesses and, by extension, entire nations.

Sabbagh et al. (2013) added that the importance of digitization in enhancing GDP per capita and decreasing unemployment is unparalleled. The author claimed that a 10% increase in digitization in an emerging economy raises the GDP per capita by 0.75% and decreases unemployment by 1.02%. Economies need more adequate ICT ecosystems to ensure their chance of growth. The author measured the index for digitization using variables such as ubiquity, affordability, reliability, speed, usability, and skill.

The most common case of digitization today is digital financial inclusion through mobile financial services. A similar case is India's Aadhaar Pay which allows the citizens of India to transact money to any part of the country with just their fingerprint (Singh & Malik, 2019). Another revolutionary mobile app that made the transaction process smoother and safer is Paytm. The creation of mobile banking services is another illustration of digitization in Bangladesh. Since 2010, bKash, the market leader, has an equity of over $320 million (Alo, 2022), followed by Nagad, which holds 35% of the market share.

Digital Technologies and Economic Growth

Digital technologies are recognized as vital drivers of economic growth, particularly in emerging economies (ITU, 2018). The rapid expansion of the internet and mobile technologies has led to increased connectivity, enabling businesses to tap into new markets and creating opportunities for innovation and entrepreneurship (UNCTAD, 2017). Digital technologies have become increasingly important in driving economic growth and achieving sustainable development. Furthermore, digital technologies have the potential to accelerate progress toward several SDGs, including;

Goal 8: Decent work and economic growth: Digital technologies can create new job opportunities and promote economic growth. A study by the International Labor Organization (ILO) found that digitalization can create more than 60 million new jobs by 2030 (ILO, 2019). Another study by the World Bank found that expanding broadband connectivity could increase economic growth by 1.38 percentage points in low- and middle-income countries (World Bank, 2016).

Goal 9: Industry, innovation, and infrastructure: Digital technologies can foster innovation and improve infrastructure. A study by the European Union found that digitalization can increase productivity by up to 30%, with the potential to add €2.2 trillion to the European economy by 2025 (European Commission, 2016). Digital technologies can also improve infrastructure by making it more efficient and connected, as seen in the development of smart cities (Bibri & Krogstie, 2017).

Goal 12: Responsible consumption and production: Digital technologies can help businesses improve their sustainability practices. A study by Accenture found that digital technologies can enable a circular economy, where waste is minimized and resources are kept in use for longer periods of time (Accenture, 2014). E-commerce and digital marketplaces can also facilitate more sustainable consumption patterns by reducing the need for physical goods and enabling the sharing economy.

Goal 13: Climate action: Digital technologies can help mitigate climate change by enabling more efficient and sustainable energy systems. A study by the International Energy Agency found that digitalization could reduce global carbon emissions by 20% by 2030 (International Energy Agency, 2017). Another study found that the use of digital technologies could help reduce energy consumption in buildings by up to 30%.

Goal 17: Partnerships for the goals: Digital technologies can facilitate global partnerships and collaboration. They enable people to connect and collaborate across borders and can facilitate the sharing of knowledge and best practices. Digital technologies can also enable greater transparency and accountability, which are essential for achieving the SDGs.

Overall, digital technologies and economic growth have significant potential to contribute to the achievement of the SDGs. By promoting economic growth and innovation while also promoting sustainability, digital technologies can help create a more prosperous and equitable world for all.

Digital Technologies and Education

Digital technologies have the potential to revolutionize education and contribute to the achievement of SDG 4, which focuses on ensuring inclusive and equitable quality education for all (Bulman & Fairlie, 2016). In emerging economies, where access to education is often limited, digital tools can facilitate learning and bridge the educational gap, particularly in rural areas. Digital technologies are transforming the landscape of education around the world, particularly in emerging economies. In the context of SDGs, digital technologies can play a critical role in addressing global education challenges, such as improving access to quality education, reducing disparities, and enhancing lifelong learning opportunities.

SDG 4 specifically aims to ensure inclusive and equitable quality education and promote lifelong learning opportunities for all. Digital technologies can help achieve this goal by providing access to online learning resources, virtual classrooms, and remote education. With the help of digital technologies, students from remote and underprivileged areas can access quality education that was previously out of their reach.

Digital technologies can also assist in the monitoring and evaluation of education programs to ensure that they are meeting the SDG targets. By using data analytics, education stakeholders can track progress toward achieving the SDGs and identify areas where more resources are needed.

Furthermore, digital technologies can be used to create innovative teaching and learning approaches that can enhance students' learning outcomes. Technologies such as virtual reality, artificial intelligence, and gamification can provide immersive and engaging learning experiences that stimulate students' interest and facilitate knowledge acquisition.

However, there are challenges associated with integrating digital technologies into education, particularly in emerging economies. For example, lack of infrastructure, limited internet connectivity, and inadequate teacher training can hinder the effective implementation of digital technologies in education.

Therefore, it is essential to ensure that digital technologies are used in a way that aligns with the principles of sustainable development. This means that digital technologies should be accessible, affordable, and environmentally friendly. Additionally, teacher training programs should be developed to enable educators to effectively use digital technologies in their teaching practices. However, careful planning and implementation are necessary to ensure that digital technologies are used to create sustainable and equitable education systems.

Digital Technologies and Health

The SDGs provide a framework for global development and call for action on issues such as poverty, inequality, and climate change. Two of the SDGs, SDG 3 and SDG 9, are particularly relevant to the intersection of digital technologies and health. The integration of digital technologies into healthcare systems can contribute to the achievement of SDG 3, which aims to ensure healthy lives and promote well-being for all at all ages (Mechael et al., 2010). Digital health solutions, such as telemedicine, electronic health records, and mobile health applications, can improve access to healthcare services, enhance the quality of care, and reduce costs in emerging economies (Labrique, Vasudevan, Kochi, Fabricant, & Mehl, 2013).

SDG 3, "Good Health and Well-being," aims to ensure universal access to quality health care and to address the underlying determinants of health, such as poverty, lack of education, and inadequate sanitation. Digital technologies have the potential to help achieve this goal in a number of ways.

One-way digital technologies can contribute to SDG 3 is by increasing access to health care services. Telemedicine, for example, allows health care providers to remotely diagnose and treat patients using digital communication technologies. This can be especially beneficial for people in remote or underserved areas who may not have access to traditional health care facilities.

Another way digital technology can contribute to SDG 3 is by enabling better tracking and management of health data. Electronic health records (EHRs), for example, can help health care providers track patients' medical histories, which can improve diagnosis and treatment. Additionally, health data can be analyzed to identify trends and patterns, which can inform public health policies and interventions.

SDG 9, "Industry, Innovation and Infrastructure," aims to promote sustainable industrialization and technological innovation, as well as to improve access to infrastructure and technology. Digital technologies are crucial to achieving this goal, as they can drive innovation and increase access to infrastructure and technology.

One-way digital technologies can contribute to SDG 9 is by facilitating the development of new technologies and products that can improve health outcomes. For example, wearable devices and health apps can help individuals monitor their health and prevent or manage chronic conditions. Similarly, artificial intelligence (AI) and machine learning (ML) can be used to analyze health data and develop personalized treatment plans.

Another way digital technology can contribute to SDG 9 is by improving access to health care infrastructure. For example, mobile health clinics equipped with digital technologies can provide basic health care services to underserved populations. Additionally, digital technologies can be used to improve the efficiency and effectiveness of health care facilities, such as hospitals and clinics.

Overall, the intersection of digital technologies and health has the potential to contribute significantly to the achievement of SDGs 3 and 9. However, it is important to ensure that these technologies are accessible and affordable for all, and that they are developed and used in an ethical and responsible manner.

Digital Technologies and Gender Equality

Digital technologies can play a crucial role in advancing gender equality (SDG 5) by empowering women and girls through increased access to information, services, and opportunities (World Bank, 2016). One crucial aspect of this goal is the role of digital technologies in advancing gender equality. Digital technologies have the potential to empower women and girls by providing access to information and knowledge, expanding economic opportunities, and enhancing their social and political participation. For example, digital technologies can provide women with access to online education and training, allowing them to acquire new skills and knowledge that can enhance their economic opportunities. Digital platforms can also enable women to connect with potential employers, customers, and business partners, thereby expanding their economic opportunities. Moreover, digital technologies can help women and girls participate more fully in the social and political life of their communities. Online platforms can provide spaces for women to share their experiences, voice their opinions, and participate in decision-making processes. Social media can also help women to form networks and communities that provide support and resources for achieving their goals. However, the gender digital divide remains a significant challenge in achieving SDG 5. Women and girls continue to have lower levels of access to digital technologies, and they are less likely to have the skills and knowledge necessary to use them effectively. This digital divide is especially pronounced in developing countries, where women are more likely to have limited access to digital technologies and digital literacy.

To achieve gender equality in the context of SDG 5, it is essential to address the digital divide and ensure that women and girls have access to digital technologies and the skills and knowledge to use them effectively. This can be achieved through policies and programs that promote digital literacy and digital inclusion for women and girls. It is also important to address the underlying social and cultural factors that limit women's access to digital technologies and their participation in the digital economy and society.

In conclusion, digital technologies have the potential to play a significant role in achieving gender equality in the context of SDG 5. However, to realize this potential, we must address the digital divide and ensure that women and girls have equal access to digital technologies and the skills and knowledge to use them effectively. By doing so, we can create a more inclusive and equitable digital economy and society that empowers women and girls to achieve their full potential.

Examples From Emerging Economies

Digital Financial Services

Digital financial services have been transforming the economies of many emerging markets in recent years. Here are some examples of how digital financial services are being used in emerging economies:

bKash & Nagad in Bangladesh: bKash and Nagad have been instrumental in promoting financial inclusion in Bangladesh, making essential financial services accessible to the country's unbanked population. As leading mobile financial service providers, they have simplified money transfers, bill payments, and savings account management through their user-friendly platforms. By partnering with local retail stores and mobile phone shops, these services have expanded their reach, particularly in rural areas. Furthermore, their involvement in disbursing government social safety net allowances ensures transparency and security in the process. Overall, bKash and Nagad have significantly contributed to poverty reduction and economic growth in Bangladesh.

Mobile Money in Kenya: M-Pesa is a mobile phone-based money transfer service that was launched in Kenya in 2007. Since then, it has become a critical financial tool for millions of Kenyans who do not have access to traditional banking services. M-Pesa allows users to deposit, withdraw, and transfer money using their mobile phones, and it has helped to spur economic growth by enabling small businesses to transact more easily.

Digital Banking in India: India has seen a significant rise in digital banking in recent years, with many people using their smartphones to access financial services. Apps like Paytm, PhonePe, and Google Pay allow users to transfer money, pay bills, and even invest in stocks and mutual funds. The government's Digital India initiative has helped to drive this growth by promoting the use of digital technologies in various sectors of the economy.

Blockchain in South Africa: The South African Reserve Bank has been exploring the use of blockchain technology to improve the efficiency and security of its payment system. The bank has launched a pilot project that uses blockchain to settle interbank transactions, and it is also exploring the use of blockchain for cross-border payments (Ahmed, Gazi, Iqbal, Islam, & Talukder, 2020).

Online Lending in China: China's peer-to-peer (P2P) lending market has grown rapidly in recent years, with platforms like Lufax and Yirendai offering loans to small businesses and individuals. These platforms use technology to assess credit risk and match borrowers with lenders, and they have helped to fill a gap in the traditional banking system, which often overlooks small borrowers.

Digital Remittances in the Philippines: The Philippines is one of the largest recipients of remittances in the world, and digital remittance services have become increasingly popular in recent years. Apps like GCash and PayMaya allow Filipinos to receive money from abroad directly into their mobile wallets, making it faster and more convenient than traditional remittance methods.

These are just a few examples of how digital financial services are being used in emerging economies to drive economic growth and financial inclusion. As technology continues to evolve, we can expect to see even more innovative solutions emerge in the years to come.

Digital Technologies and Education

Digital technologies have transformed the way we learn, and emerging economies have not been left behind in adopting these technologies. Here are some examples of digital technologies being used in literacy and education in emerging economies:

One Laptop per Child (OLPC): OLPC is a nonprofit organization that provides low-cost, rugged, and power-efficient laptops to children in emerging economies. The laptops are preloaded with educational software that helps children learn basic reading, writing, and numeracy skills.

eLearning platforms: Various eLearning platforms like Udemy, Coursera, and edX have made it possible for learners in emerging economies to access high-quality education from anywhere in the world. These platforms offer courses on various subjects ranging from coding, business, language, and arts.

Virtual classrooms: Virtual classrooms have become increasingly popular in emerging economies, especially during the COVID-19 pandemic. Platforms like Zoom, Microsoft Teams, and Google Meet have made it possible for learners to attend classes from the comfort of their homes.

Mobile learning: Mobile learning has gained popularity in emerging economies because of its affordability and accessibility. Many organizations have developed mobile apps that offer educational content, such as Duolingo, which offers language learning courses.

Interactive whiteboards: Interactive whiteboards are becoming increasingly popular in emerging economies. They allow teachers to use digital content, such as videos and images, to make their lessons more engaging.

Digital libraries: Digital libraries like World Digital Library and Project Gutenberg have made it possible for learners in emerging economies to access a vast collection of books and other educational resources at no cost.

These are just a few examples of digital technologies being used in literacy and education in emerging economies. With the increasing adoption of digital technologies, learners in these economies have the opportunity to access high-quality education, regardless of their location or economic status.

Digital Healthcare Services

Here are some examples of digital healthcare services that are being used in emerging economies:

Helium Health (Nigeria): Helium Health is a Nigerian startup that offers a product suite that digitalizes data, formalizes monetization, and enables telemedicine for healthcare systems in West Africa (Ahmed, Islam, Ahmed, & Amin, 2022).

We Care Solar: An innovative solar energy firm based in South African region providing energy solution for healthcare sector in remote Africa (Ahmed et al., 2022).

Practo (India): Practo is a digital healthcare platform in India that connects patients with doctors and allows them to book appointments, order medicines, and store their medical records securely. It has a presence in over 50 cities in India and also offers telemedicine services.

Halodoc (Indonesia): Halodoc is a digital healthcare platform in Indonesia that offers teleconsultations, medicine delivery, and lab services. It also has a feature that allows users to chat with a doctor and ask for medical advice.

Ping An Good Doctor (China): Ping An Good Doctor is a digital healthcare platform in China that provides online consultations, medical prescriptions, and appointments with doctors. It also offers AI-assisted diagnosis and health management services.

Zocdoc (Brazil): Zocdoc is a digital healthcare platform in Brazil that connects patients with doctors and allows them to book appointments online. It also offers a feature that helps users find doctors who accept their insurance.

Doctor on Demand (Mexico): Doctor on Demand is a digital healthcare platform in Mexico that provides online consultations with doctors and mental health professionals. It also offers services such as prescriptions, lab tests, and referrals to specialists.

Swasth (India): Swasth is a digital healthcare platform that is creating a national digital health stack in India, with a vision to improve healthcare access and affordability. It aims to create a seamless and integrated platform that connects all stakeholders in the healthcare ecosystem, including patients, healthcare providers, and insurers.

eDoctor (Vietnam): eDoctor is a digital healthcare platform in Vietnam that provides online consultations with doctors, prescriptions, and medicine delivery. It also offers a health diary feature that allows users to track their health records and schedule reminders for appointments and medication.

SeeDoctor (Nigeria): SeeDoctor is a digital healthcare platform in Nigeria that offers online consultations with doctors, medical advice, and prescriptions. It also has a feature that allows users to book appointments with doctors for in-person consultations.

Teladoc Health (Brazil): Teladoc Health is a digital healthcare platform in Brazil that provides telemedicine services, including online consultations with doctors, mental health professionals, and specialists. It also offers services such as medical opinions, second opinions, and remote patient monitoring.

Mfine (India): Mfine is a digital healthcare platform in India that connects patients with doctors and specialists through telemedicine. It also offers medicine delivery, lab tests, and health packages.

Digital Technologies to Promote Gender Equality

Here are a few examples of how digital technologies are being used to promote gender equality in different emerging countries:

India: Using digital technologies to promote gender equality in an emerging country is the "She Leads Digital" program in India. This program is designed to provide training and support to women entrepreneurs in the country, particularly those who are operating small- and medium-sized businesses. The program is delivered through a digital platform, which includes online training modules, webinars, and mentoring sessions. Participants can access the platform from anywhere, which is especially important in a country as vast as India, where many women entrepreneurs may live in remote areas with limited access to resources. Through the She Leads Digital program, women entrepreneurs can learn about a range of topics, including business planning, financial management, and marketing. They can also connect with other women entrepreneurs and mentors for advice and support. The program is designed to help women entrepreneurs overcome the many challenges they may face in starting and growing a business, such as limited access to capital, lack of business networks, and cultural barriers. Overall, the She Leads Digital program is a great example of how digital technologies can be used to promote gender equality in emerging countries. By providing women entrepreneurs with the training and support they need to succeed, the program is helping to break down barriers and empower women to take their place as leaders in the business world.

Uganda: The Women of Uganda Network (WOUGNET) has developed a mobile app called "Her Visions App" to help rural women in the country access information and resources related to gender equality, reproductive health, and other key issues. The app provides access to online courses, community forums, and other resources, and also allows users to report instances of gender-based violence.

Kenya: The AkiraChix organization provides training and mentorship to girls and young women in the country who are interested in pursuing careers in technology. Through its training programs and community outreach initiatives,

AkiraChix is helping to address the gender gap in the tech industry and promote greater gender equality in the country.

Pakistan: The "Girls' Voice" project is a digital platform that allows girls in the country to share their stories and experiences of gender-based violence, discrimination, and other issues. The platform provides a safe and anonymous space for girls to speak out and connect with others who have had similar experiences, and also provides access to resources and support services.

Mexico: The "Women's Digital Center" is a program run by the Mexican government that provides training and support to women entrepreneurs and workers in the technology sector. The program includes training in coding, web development, and other key skills, as well as mentorship and networking opportunities to help women build their careers in the industry.

These are just a few examples of how digital technologies are being used to promote gender equality in emerging countries around the world. As technology continues to evolve and become more widely accessible, there is tremendous potential for these initiatives to make a real difference in the lives of women and girls.

Challenges and Future Opportunities

Despite the potential benefits of digital technologies for the SDGs, several challenges and limitations exist. One major concern is the digital divide, which refers to the gap between those who have access to digital technologies and those who do not (Hilbert, 2016). In emerging economies, issues such as inadequate infrastructure, limited access to affordable devices and services, and insufficient digital literacy can exacerbate this divide.

Implementation of digitization and integrating sustainable development goals in emerging economies can be challenging for any government. Financial literacy, digital literacy, lack of expertise, and poor infrastructure are a few of its many challenges. However, the benefits outweigh the challenges. The quality of lives of the people of a country enhance through sustained development of education and healthcare, organizations get efficient and generate more profit, human capital develops, reducing unemployment and more skilled labor is produced, and a more significant number of people is included under the financial sector. Therefore, the importance of integration of digitization for sustainable development goals in emerging economies is significant.

In conclusion, the literature highlights the potential of digital technologies in advancing the United Nations SDGs in emerging economies. Digital technologies can contribute to economic growth, education, health, and gender equality, among other areas, which are crucial for sustainable development. However, the digital divide, inadequate infrastructure, limited access to affordable devices and services, and insufficient digital literacy present challenges that must be addressed to fully harness the benefits of digitalization in emerging economies. Governments have a pivotal role to play in bridging these gaps and ensuring that the potential of digital technologies is effectively harnessed for achieving the SDGs.

Firstly, governments must invest in the development of robust digital infrastructure to ensure widespread access to digital technologies, particularly in underserved and remote areas. This includes upgrading and expanding broadband networks, as well as enhancing the availability and affordability of digital devices and services. Investment in digital infrastructure can be achieved through public–private partnerships, which can help mobilize resources and expertise from both sectors to address the challenges of digitalization.

Secondly, governments should prioritize digital literacy and skills development to ensure that their populations can effectively utilize digital technologies. This can be achieved through the incorporation of digital literacy programs into formal education systems and the promotion of vocational training and lifelong learning opportunities. By equipping citizens with the necessary digital skills, governments can help bridge the digital divide and create a more inclusive digital economy.

Moreover, governments can play a key role in fostering innovation and entrepreneurship in the digital sector. This can be done through the establishment of supportive regulatory frameworks, the provision of financial incentives for startups and SMEs, and the promotion of research and development in the digital technology sector. By fostering a conducive environment for digital innovation, governments can help drive the development and adoption of new digital solutions that can contribute to the achievement of the SDGs.

Additionally, governments should collaborate with various stakeholders, including the private sector, civil society, and international organizations, to develop and implement comprehensive and integrated digital strategies for the SDGs. Such strategies should be tailored to the unique needs and priorities of each country and should address cross-cutting issues such as data privacy, security, and the ethical use of digital technologies.

Finally, governments should take targeted measures to address the digital gender divide, which is particularly pronounced in many emerging economies. This can include promoting equal access to digital technologies and services for women and girls, as well as supporting initiatives that empower women through digital skills development and entrepreneurship. By addressing the digital gender divide, governments can help ensure that women and girls are not left behind in the digital transformation and can actively contribute to the achievement of the SDGs.

Conclusion

In summary, the role of governments in attaining the SDGs through the use of technology in emerging economies is crucial. By investing in digital infrastructure, promoting digital literacy, fostering innovation, collaborating with stakeholders, and addressing the digital gender divide, governments can help unlock the full potential of digital technologies for sustainable development. By leveraging these technologies effectively and inclusively, emerging economies can accelerate progress toward the SDGs and build a more sustainable, equitable, and prosperous future for all.

References

Accenture. (2014). *Circular advantage: Innovative business models and technologies to create value in a world without limits to growth.* Retrieved from https://www. accenture.com/_acnmedia/Accenture/Conversion-Assets/DotCom/Documents/ Global/PDF/Dualpub_15/Accenture-Circular-Advantage-POV.pdf

Ahmed, J. U., Gazi, M. A., Iqbal, R., Islam, Q. T., & Talukder, N. (2020). Value co-creation through social innovation in healthcare: A case of we care solar. *World Journal of Entrepreneurship, Management and Sustainable Development, 16*(4), 341–357. doi:10.1108/WJEMSD-03-2020-0024

Ahmed, J. U., Islam, Q. T., Ahmed, A., & Amin, S. B. (2022). Extending resource value-based circular economy business model in emerging economies: Lessons from India. *Business Perspectives and Research.* doi:10.1177/22785337211070363

Alo, J. N. (2022, March 27). *How the mobile phone and bKash revolutionized financial transaction.* The Business Standard. Retrieved from https://www.tbsnews.net/ economy/how-mobile-phone-and-bkash-revolutionised-financial-transaction-392218. Accessed on March 4, 2023.

Bibri, S. E., & Krogstie, J. (2017). Smart sustainable cities of the future: An extensive interdisciplinary literature review. *Sustainable Cities and Society, 31*, 183–212. doi: 10.1016/j.scs.2017.02.017

Bulman, G., & Fairlie, R. W. (2016). Technology and education: Computers, software, and the internet. In *Handbook of the Economics of Education* (Vol. 5, pp. 239–280). Elsevier. doi:10.1016/B978-0-444-63459-7.00005-1

European Commission. (2016). *Digital Economy and Society Index 2016.* Retrieved from https://ec.europa.eu/digital-single-market/en/scoreboard/2016

Firmansyah, D., & Susetyo, D. P. (2022). Financial behavior in the digital economy era: Financial literacy and digital literacy. *Jurnal Ekonomi Dan Bisnis Digital, 1*(4), 367–390. doi:10.55927/ministal.v1i4.2368

Gobble, M. A. M. (2018). Digitalization, digitization, and Innovation. *Research-Technology Management, 61*(4), 56–59. doi:10.1080/08956308.2018.1471280

Hilbert, M. (2016). The bad news is that the digital access divide is here to stay: Domestically installed bandwidths among 172 countries for 1986–2014. *Telecommunications Policy, 40*(6), 567–581.

International Energy Agency. (2017). *Digitalization & energy.* Retrieved from https:// www.iea.org/reports/digitalization-energy

International Labour Organization. (2019). *Work for a brighter future: Global commission on the future of work.* Retrieved from https://www.ilo.org/global/topics

ITU. (2018). *Measuring the information society report 2018.* Retrieved from https:// www.itu.int/en/ITU-D/Statistics/Pages/publications/misr2018.aspx

Labrique, A. B., Vasudevan, L., Kochi, E., Fabricant, R., & Mehl, G. (2013). mHealth innovations as health system strengthening tools: 12 common applications and a visual framework. *Global Health Science and Practice, 1*(2), 160–171.

Mechael, P., Batavia, H., Kaonga, N., Searle, S., Kwan, A., Goldberger, A., ... Ossman, J. (2010). *Barriers and gaps affecting mHealth in low and middle-income countries: Policy white paper.* Columbia University. Earth Institute. Center for Global Health and Economic Development (CGHED): with mHealth Alliance.

Ragnedda, M. (2019). Conceptualising the digital divide. *Mapping Digital Divide in Africa*, 27–44. doi:10.2307/j.ctvh4zj72.6

Sabbagh, K., Friedrich, R., El-Darwiche, B., Singh, M., & Koster, A. (2013). Digitization for economic growth and job creation: Regional and industry perspectives. *World Economic Forum – The Global Information Technology Report*, 35–42.

Singh, R., & Malik, G. (2019). Impact of digitalization on Indian rural banking customer: With reference to payment systems. *Emerging Economy Studies, 5*(1), 31–41. doi:10.1177/2394901519825912

UNCTAD. (2017). *Information Economy Report 2017: Digitalization, trade and development.* United Nations Conference on Trade and Development. Retrieved from https://unctad.org/system/files/official-document/ier2017_en.pdf

World Bank. (2016). *World Development Report 2016: Digital Dividends.* Washington, DC: World Bank.

Further Readings

Amankwah-Amoah, J., Khan, Z., Wood, G., & Knight, G. (2021). Covid-19 and digitalization: The great acceleration. *Journal of Business Research, 136*, 602–611. doi:10.1016/j.jbusres.2021.08.011

Aziz, A., Islam, M. M., & Zakaria, M. (2021). *Covid-19 exposes digital divide, social stigma and information crisis in Bangladesh.* doi:10.31235/osf.io/j3hux

Bangladesh Bank. (2022). Retrieved from https://www.bb.org.bd/en/index.php/financialactivity/mfsdata. Accessed on March 4, 2023.

Behera, J. K. (2021). Digital transformation and its impact: An analytical study. In *Digitization of economy and society* (pp. 27–49). Apple Academic Press. doi:10.1201/9781003187479-3

Centre For Public Impact (CPI). (2022). *Mobile currency in Kenya: The M-Pesa.* Retrieved from https://www.centreforpublicimpact.org/case-study/m-currency-in-kenya. Accessed on March 4, 2023.

Chona, J. S. (2021). Entrepreneurship with a design for social justice mindset: A case for hello tractor. In *2021 IEEE International Symposium on Technology and Society (ISTAS).* IEEE. doi:10.1109/istas52410.2021.9629132

Dhaka Tribune. (2021, June 30). *Bangladesh health watch launches Covid-19 research repository.* Retrieved from https://archive.dhakatribune.com/bangladesh/2021/06/30/bangladesh-health-watch-launches-covid-19-research-repository. Accessed on March 4, 2023.

Future Startup. (2022, May 30). *Agritech startup ifarmer raises $2.1 million in new funding, eyes expansion.* Retrieved from https://futurestartup.com/2022/05/30/agritech-startup-ifarmer-raises-2-1-million-in-new-funding-eyes-expansion/. Accessed on March 4, 2023.

GSMA (2015). *Bridging the gender gap: Mobile access and usage in low and middle-income countries.* Retrieved from https://www.gsma.com/mobilefordevelopment/wp-content/uploads/2016/02/GSM0001_03232015_GSMAReport_NEWGRAYS-Web.pdf

Hilbert, M. (2011). Digital gender divide or technologically empowered women in developing countries? A typical case of lies, damned lies, and statistics. *Women's Studies International Forum, 34*(6), 479–489.

Himel, M. T., Ashraf, S., Bappy, T. A., Abir, M. T., Morshed, M. K., & Hossain, M. N. (2021). Users' attitude and intention to use mobile financial services in Bangladesh: An empirical study. *South Asian Journal of Marketing, 2*(1), 72–96. doi:10.1108/sajm-02-2021-0015

Kagan, J. (2022, December 7). *What is M-pesa? definition, how service works, and example.* Investopedia. Retrieved from https://www.investopedia.com/terms/m/mpesa.asp. Accessed on March 4, 2023.

Kemp, S. (2021, November 4). *Digital in Saudi Arabia: All the statistics you need in 2021 – DataReportal – Global digital insights.* DataReportal. Retrieved from https://datareportal.com/reports/digital-2021-saudi-arabia. Accessed on March 4, 2023.

Molla, M. A.-M. (2021, November 7). *Silent heroes of 'surokkha'.* The Daily Star. Retrieved from https://www.thedailystar.net/news/bangladesh/news/silent-heroes-surokkha-2224306?amp. Accessed on March 4, 2023.

OECD iLibrary. (2022). *Going Digital in Brazil.* Retrieved from https://www.oecd-ilibrary.org/economics/oecd-reviews-of-digital-transformation-going-digital-in-brazil_e9bf7f8a-en. Accessed on March 4, 2023.

The Business Post. (n.d.). *Bkash dominates while Nagad grows fast.* Retrieved from https://businesspostbd.com/front/bkash-dominates-while-nagad-grows-fast-2022-06-09. Accessed on March 4, 2023.

Yesmin, S., Paul, T. A., & Mohshin Uddin, M. (2018). Bkash: Revolutionizing mobile financial services in Bangladesh? *Business and Management Practices in South Asia,* 125–148. doi:10.1007/978-981-13-1399-8_6

Chapter 3

A Dimensional Mapping and Comparative Study of CSRs and SDGs in Emerging Economies

Pooja Singh and Surabhi Yadav

Abstract

Sustainable Development Goals (SDGs) are forming a blueprint for attaining the prosperity and peace for the entire world as it is an accomplishing goal of the UN agenda of 2030. SDGs focus on ending poverty and creating new life in a better way. These goals give a clear vision to achieve the optimum growth in a sustainable manner. Corporates are now mandated by law in India to contribute a certain percentage of profits to the cause of social development, ultimately helping the nation develop. The main aim of business is to earn money, and all the related decisions affect the board of directors, associated stakeholders, customers, etc.; all these practices also affect the internal employees in an ethical way. In order to prevent the companies to do any unethical practices, government has mandated some laws; all the corporates need to spend and utilize their corporate social responsibility (CSR) contribution in a particular time frame. All the prescribed activities need to be accomplished in a particular time frame. Along with profit maximization, the business is shifting their attention toward the conservation of natural resources. In this study, the researcher has provided a linkage between CSR and SDGs. Through this research, the objective is to attain the mapping between schedule seven of companies act 2013, section 135 and 17 goals of SDGs.

Keywords: CSR; SDG; companies act 2013; emerging economies; schedule seven; COVID-19

Fostering Sustainable Businesses in Emerging Economies, 39–52
Copyright © 2024 Pooja Singh and Surabhi Yadav
Published under exclusive licence by Emerald Publishing Limited
doi:10.1108/978-1-80455-640-520231003

Introduction

Sustainable Development Goals (SDGs)

SDGs came into force in September 2015, replacing Millennium Development Goals (MDGs) with 193 countries to reduce and eliminate poverty, protect the Earth, and ensure prosperity as a part of the agenda of sustainable development. SDGs focus on ending poverty and creating new life in a better way. These goals give a clear vision to achieve the optimum growth in a sustainable manner (Fukuda-Parr & McNeill, 2019).

The Millennium Development Goals were set up in 2015 focusing on only eight significant areas for the nation. The major goal for formation of MDG is to make the nation prosper and competitive on all grounds. The MDG focused on development of underdeveloped countries at the cost of funding by the developed nations. Critics further argued over the limited scope of MDG as it has the difficulty in measuring the targets and uneven progress among other countries, and hence SDGs came into existence (Satapathy & Paltasingh, 2022). All the shareholders require collaborative effort to make the sustainable goals achievable. All the businesses have roles to play for delivering the SDGs and contributing the services and products, building opportunities and requirement of jobs through innovation and technology (WHO report, 2018).

SDGs are 17 goals set up by the United Nations to attain a sustainable future for people across the planet Earth. SDGs are the keystones impacting on the environment, society, and economy at large. SDGs are basically forming a blueprint for attaining the prosperity and peace for the entire world as it is an accomplishing goal of UN agenda of 2030 (Witte & Dilyard, 2017). The SDGs have 17 parameters that encompass almost 169 targets that are to be achieved with the multi-stakeholder commitments. On that basis, they provide a universal outline for the society, government, businesses, and organizations to work in the most permissible manner toward the development of the entire community (Nonet, Gössling, Van Tulder, & Bryson, 2022).

One of the most important objectives of SDGs is good health and well-being which includes National Health Mission including NRHM and support to National Health system. Since 2015, the collective efforts of the countries are indulging toward advancements and development. The Sustainable Development Goals Report of 2020 reveals that the child health has improved, people have access to the water and electricity, and a number of women are participating in the Ministries. Nevertheless, many goals have shown no or minimal advancement (Murray, 2015). The unbearable pain of COVID-19 has also impacted the goals of SDGs, as it includes the health care-related issues all over the nation (Singh, Dharwal, Alam, & Sharma, 2021).

Role of SDGs in Emerging Economies

- *Circular economy* – Circular economy is the phenomenon which promotes reusing, recycling, refurbishing, sharing, leasing, and repairing the existing goods with its optimum usage. This process actually reduces the wastage of the products. The tendency to use the goods again and again creates further value. In order to achieve SDGs, the concept and practice of circular economy is considered a very important initiative (Karuppiah, Sankaranarayanan, Ali, Jabbour, & Bhalaji, 2021).

- *Gross Domestic Product (GDP)* – In emerging economies, the United States has set up the association of sustainable development with the Gross Domestic Product (GDP). GDP has been identified to measure economic health and progress while SDGs measure the healthy development of the nation (Adrangi & Kerr, 2022).
- *BRICS* – Renewable energy and energy security also plays a critical role in attaining the SDGs in emerging economies. BRICS stands for Brazil, Russia, India, China, and South Africa, constitutes 36% of primary energy of the world. One of the important goals of SDGs is renewable energy, securing energy and resources (Jana, 2022).

Role of Technologies in Emerging Market

Green Intellectual Capital (GIC) plays a vital role of competitive market in the long run time period. With the increasing development and competitor, a company can be quickly wiped off from the industry. Technological advancement is pushing the companies toward inclusive growth and attaining sustainability. In order to compete with the industry, there is a need of technological awareness and its proper implication in propagating the business. The technological awareness is associated with the sustainability and business performance. "The creativity, knowhow, technology and financial resources from all of society is necessary to achieve the SDGs in every context" (Ullah et al., 2021).

Corporate Social Responsibility

Corporates are now mandated by law in India to contribute a certain percentage of profits to the cause of social development, ultimately helping the nation develop. The main aim of business is to earn money, and all the related decisions affect the board of directors, associated stakeholders, customers, etc.; all these practices also affect the internal employees in an ethical way (Singh, Dharwal, Alam, Sharma, & Kumari, 2020). In order to prevent the companies to do any unethical practices, government has mandated some laws; all the corporates need to spend and utilize their CSR contribution in a particular time frame. All the prescribed activities need to be accomplished in a particular time frame. Along with profit maximization, the business is shifting their attention toward the conservation of natural resources. Customer-friendly policies and balancing the resources and population is the foremost and interesting appeal nowadays (Latapí Agudelo, Jóhannsdóttir, & Davídsdóttir, 2019). The logic behind social responsibility is to fill the gaps in society through responsible and conscious actions and to gain an optimum utilization of resources. Hence, businesses are encouraged to socially utilize their CSR fund through a CSR framework prescribed by the government. The whole phenomenon of returning to the society without the implication and indulgence of any personal benefit is known as CSR (Carroll & Shabana, 2010).

CSR is a well-known practice all over the globe in which companies are working for the development of the society by contributing 2–2.5% of their average net profit for the development of the nation. The work is done by keeping in mind the society welfare along with the company's goodwill. CSR is a global aspect, but it has a significant history from India. "Dharma" focuses on the producer who gives a stimulated amount of percentage out of their goods into the philanthropic activity. In the Mauryan dynasty, Kautilya believed that the practice of giving charity to the underprivileged has a significant impact on the goodwill of the dynasty as well as on the person who is donating their personal belongings for the betterment of others (Walton, 1982). The basic phenomenon of CSR is to contribute to the Maslow's theory of food, clothing, and shelter. In the early 1800s, the rich and wealthy businessmen used to visit the temple and donate some money for the poor (Aspect1, Philanthropy). During the 1900s, Mahatma Gandhi promoted the concept of Trusteeship among the business community. As per him every business, every individual is a trustee of society and thus one must keep only as much with him as is required to fulfill one's necessities and rest should be given back to the society, especially for the betterment of the weaker section of society. The weaker section included marginalized poor, underprivileged, disabled, backward communities and tribes, and rural development (Aspect 2, Trusteeship). After the introduction of Public Sector Units in India in the early 1950s, the government has made sure the proper implication of charity through a channelized manner along with the customer satisfaction and business growth which inculcated the social responsibility so deeply in our country (Aspect 3, Social Accountability and Transparency). In the 1900s, sustainability came into existence and social responsibility has now become a sustainable practice which leads to globalization and privatization in India for the first time (Aspect 4, Sustainable Business Strategy) (Bajic & Yurtoglu, 2018).

All the CSR laws are now governing through a proper body known as the Ministry of Corporate Affairs (MCA), and the act is known as the Companies Act 2013 act.

Objectives

- To study the SDGs in a comprehensive manner.
- To study the linkage between SDGs and CSR in emerging economies.

Leveraging CSR for the SDGs – Sustainable development and social responsibility have their own significant impact on society. CSR and SDGs both were regulated in the year 2014–2015 and have tremendous potential to optimize a growth model of the nation. CSR sets a broad parameter for the functioning and attaining the sustainable future and SDG gives a defined goal to attain and measure the results of activities. All the companies are now strategically trying to prepare and regulate the risks as well as competitive gains through expanding the performance and market opportunities. Companies are offering the roadmap to align the CSR, citizenship, international development, and national agendas of sustainability. Companies are actively participating in the valuation in the strategy formation especially for the corporate citizenship. There is a cooperative need for business drivers to attain the social and environment goals along with the practices of enhancing the competition. On the level of industry, companies are focusing on the corporate citizenship, which is going to be linked to the appropriate business models (Warhurst, 2001).

Another important factor to measure the progress and outcome of both the business and its related environment is CSR. Now, companies will be able to quantify the social and environment of CSR activities that are related to business benefits. Since last 5 years, more potential is needed from all the related stake-holders to gain effective SDGs. There is a clear understanding that the private sector is using its expertize to focus on retaining the development goals. However, many companies are falling short apart in quantifying the business. There is a wide gap between schedule seven of the Companies Act 2013 and SDGs (Mitra & Chatterjee, 2020).

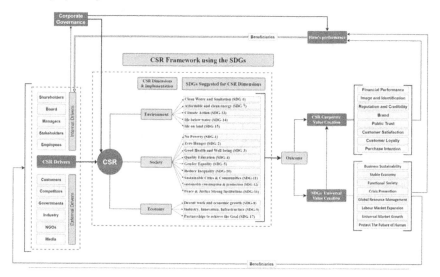

Mapping SDGs With Section 135 Schedule Seven

CSR activities	SDGs
Central Government has set up Swach Bharat Kosh to encourage sanitation, eradication of poverty and hunger and safe drinking water available.	• No poverty • Zero Hunger • Good health and Well-being • Clean Water and Sanitation
Encouraging the women, children, differently abled and elderly people for education such as special education, vocational skills and other enhancement projects.	• Eradicating poverty • No Hunger • Quality in Education • Decent work and economic growth
Empowering women through setting up homes and hostels for those who are homeless and orphans, Providing day care centers, and other facilities for working females, retired and senior citizens. Encouraging gender equality for those who are facing inequalities (socially and economically backward groups).	• Reducing Poverty • Balancing Gender Equality • Reduced Inequalities

Figure Representing the Aspects and Drivers of Corporate Social Responsibility (CSR) (Dhanesh, 2015).

Ensuring and balancing the ecological equilibrium, preserving the soil, air and other natural resources along with environmental sustainability.	<ul><li>Encouraging Clean Water and Sanitation facilities</li><li>Inexpensive and Clean Energy</li><li>Development of 3 Is' (Industry, Innovation and Infrastructure)</li><li>Sustainable communities and cities</li><li>Climatic Action</li><li>Water management (including below water life).</li><li>Life on earth</li></ul>
Preserving the national heritage, cultural-art includes re-establishment of buildings and sites of antique importance and promoting and developing traditional handicrafts.	<ul><li>Industry, Innovation, and Infrastructure</li><li>Sustainable cities and societies</li></ul>
Providing different measures for the benefit of war widows and their dependents Armed forces veterans.	<ul><li>Encouraging Good health and well being</li><li>Quality of education (special and vocational both)</li><li>Standard work with Economic growth</li></ul>
Encouraging the training of rural sports, nationality-recognized sports, Paralympic sports and Olympic Sports	<ul><li>Standard work with Economic growth</li></ul>
Encouraging and supporting the scheduled castes and under privileged people through contributing in PM's national relief fund or any other Central government fund.	<ul><li>Eradicating poverty</li><li>No Hunger</li><li>Quality in Education</li><li>Decent work and economic growth Balancing the 3Is (Industry, Innovation and Infrastructure).</li><li>Life on earth.</li></ul>
Involvement to Central Government or State Government or any agency or Public Sector Undertaking of Central Government or State Government funded incubators.	<ul><li>Balancing the 3Is (Industry, Innovation and Infrastructure). Climatic Action</li><li>Responsibility towards Consumption and Production</li></ul>

(Continued).

Rural Development projects, Slum Area Development	<ul><li>Eradicating poverty</li><li>No Hunger</li><li>Good health and well being</li><li>Quality in education</li><li>Balancing the 3Is (Industry, Innovation and Infrastructure).</li></ul>
Managing Disaster, including relief, rehabilitation and reconstruction activities	<ul><li>Eradicating poverty</li><li>No Hunger</li><li>Good health and well being</li><li>Quality in education</li><li>Balancing the 3Is (Industry, Innovation and Infrastructure).</li></ul>

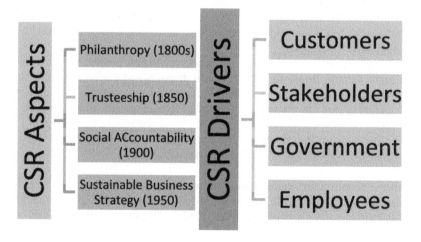

(Continued).

Advancing Sustainable Development with Reference to Technology

Nowadays businesses are catering toward the complex opportunities of the market. The entire market gets disrupted in a very short span of time and with the involvement of various factors, such as technological advancement and insufficient natural resources. New markets are emerging with the growth of natural resources. The business is characterized by the unparalleled, fast tracking, and complex opportunities and risks. Business leaders and stakeholders are growing their understanding toward the natural disasters, economic disproportions and this can eventually disturb the long-term prosperity. In order to overcome this challenge, the businesses are taking strategic efforts (OECD report, Policy responses to the economic crisis 2022).

The Sustainable agenda of Sustainable Development 2030 set up 17 goals that needed to be accomplished by the world giant leader in UN summit, and then it came into force. All the countries came together to achieve the targets in the upcoming 15 years of time such as eradication of poverty, reducing inequalities, and climatic change. SDGs not only define the sustainable world and 17 goals that need to be achieved in 2030, but it also provides new market areas and technologies where we can grow along with the society development. The best way to achieve the big targets is to divide the work into small pieces, same goes with the global goals as global goals also need to be divided into small local businesses to assure the results (Poddar & Narula, 2020).

- Reducing poverty rates by almost 50% and assuring no children, male, or female will suffer by the poverty and hunger by the end of 2030.
- Implementation of social protection system and substantial coverage for the poor and vulnerable people of the society.
- Ensuring all the equal rights for males and females to access the basic service related with the ownership of land, natural resources, financial services, technology, and inheritance.
- Building the infrastructure for the underprivileged people suffering from drought, famine, flood, and other natural disasters and environmental shocks.
- Ensuring mobilizing of resources through various sources, including the cooperation and development of countries to eradicate all the aspects of poverty.
- Creating a sound framework of regional, national, and international levels to support the poor and gender related issues, etc.

All the countries are working and putting their efforts for attaining the SDGs successfully by the end of 2030. The SDGs have 17 goals with 169 indicators and 241 indicators to measure the progress of the agenda (SDG Progress Report, 2022).

Progress Monitoring

As per the leading environment global authority, United Nations Environmental Program (UNEP) covers the entire topic related to management of resources, water protection, global ecosystem, and sustainable management with the optimum utilization of resources. All the organizations are cooperating well on the scaling method of investment to attain the sustainable goals. In order to increase the investment promotion, there is a need of sustainable investment especially in reaching the climatic goals. Turkey is now implementing the SDGs through a simple strategy of Foreign Direct Investment (FDI) (UN Environment SDG report, 2022).

The most preferred SDG is SDG 4 which is about quality education. Nearly 28% of entire CSR fund of the nation is spent for the achievement of this goal. This is followed by SDG 3 and SDG 1 which talks about good health and no poverty, respectively. The least preferred SDGs are peace and justice (SDG 16), sustainable production and consumption (SDG 12), and SDG 14, which talks about life below water. Aspirational districts have been the center of spend where maximum number of projects were carried out for quality education (SDG 4) and clean water and sanitation (SDG 6) (De Haan, Dales, & McQuilken, 2020).

Some of the parameters for monitoring of SDGs are:

- Reducing poverty rates by almost 50% and assuring no children, male, or female will suffer by the poverty and hunger by the end of 2030.
- Implementation of social protection system and substantial coverage for the poor and vulnerable people of the society.
- Ensuring all the equal rights for males and females to access the basic service related with the ownership of land, natural resources, financial services, technology, and inheritance.
- Building the infrastructure for the underprivileged people suffering from drought, famine, flood, and other natural disasters and environmental shocks.
- Ensuring mobilizing of resources through various sources, including the cooperation and development of countries to eradicate all the aspects of poverty.
- Creating a sound framework of regional, national, and international levels to support the poor and gender-related issues, etc.

The rate of poverty has declined from 36% to 10% from 1998 to 2015, respectively. COVID-19 has had a bad effect on the entire nation, which ultimately increased the fallout rate. The 10% of the entire population of the world is still deprived of the basic needs of food, clothing, and shelter. Job security is still a big issue which is giving a feeling of insecurity for the persons who have job. According to the latest estimates, 10% of our Earth's population is living on approximately 150 rupees per day wages. As a result of pandemic, the entire region of South Asia and Africa are facing the extreme verge of poverty and most of the population of the respective area is living below the poverty line. The ratio of the working poor has decreased from 14.3% to 7.1% in the year 2019. The projection technique has suggested that 6% of the entire population would still be living under the poverty rate by the end of 2030. Out of five children, one child is living below the poverty line. Promising a healthy life and well-being at all the age bars is a very critical issue (UN Report, 2021).

To achieve sustainable development, we must first ensure healthy lifestyles and work to improve the welfare of people of all ages. There is now a global health crisis that is unlike any other that has ever occurred: COVID-19 is wreaking havoc on the lives of billions of people, generating economic instability, and spreading anguish throughout the globe. On the other hand, more effort has to be taken in order to completely eliminate the number of diseases and address the number of other continuing and emerging health problems. It is possible to make significant headway in the effort to save the lives of millions of people if the focus is placed on enhancing sanitation and hygiene, obtaining more efficient funding for health systems, and increasing access to medical professionals (Wang & Huang, 2021).

The urgent need of being prepared has been brought to light by the global hazards posed by health catastrophes such as COVID-19. The United Nations Development Program emphasized the significant gaps that exist between countries' capacities to respond to and recover from the COVID-19 scenario. The pandemic presents a pivotal opportunity to invest in essential public services for the twenty-first century and to make adequate plans for responding to public health emergencies (OECD report: response to Coronavirus COVID 19, 2022).

Results and Implications

On detailed mapping and analysis of the 17 SDG goals and 12 activities mentioned in the schedule seven, the researcher could establish a strong corelation between SDGs and schedule seven of the Section 135 of Companies Act, 2013, the CSR Act in India. CSR can act as a catalyst to achieve the SDGs in India. To explain, the researcher would present the work in the following tabular form:

(1) The first goal of SDG is "no poverty," this goal aims at bringing an end to the poverty in the various forms that it exists everywhere. This can be again achieved through the three activities mentioned under the schedule seven. Three of the thematic areas – number I, X, and XI out of 12 in schedule seven are focused toward achieving these goals. Where the first activity talks about eradication of poverty, malnutrition, and hunger; the thematic area X talks about development of the rural projects thereby leading to reduction in poverty; and thematic area 11 deals with development of the slum area, which focuses on the development of the poor and malnourished people living in these areas.

(2) The second SDG "zero hunger" aims at achieving the food security and improvement in nutrition and leading to promotion of sustainable agriculture; this can further be achieved by providing food and nutrition to each and everyone, which is again the focus of first activity of schedule seven. Furthermore, the achievement of sustainable agriculture can also be achieved by taking up the activities as mentioned under the fourth item of schedule seven which talks about environmental sustainability, agroforestry maintenance of natural resources, quality of soil, air, water, etc.

(3) The third SDG goal focuses on the good health and well-being; the aim of this goal is to ensure well-being for all humans. Healthcare and well-being is the first activity that is mentioned in schedule VII, which talks about various preventive health-care measures that can be adopted by the corporate and government policies, ensuring environmental sustainability.

(4) The fourth SDG is to provide "quality education," which focuses on inclusivity and equality in providing quality education and providing lifetime of learning opportunities for everyone. This SDG goal can be mapped with the second activity of schedule seven which is talking about promoting education and it includes vocational training, skills development activities,

education for all age females (girls and women) to lead enhancement in their livelihood.

(5) The fifth SDG is "gender equality". This particular goal aims to achieve equality and inclusiveness of women and girls and empower them. This SDG can be directly mapped with the third activity on schedule seven which also talks about the similar activities like empowerment of women, promoting gender equality, and adopting various measures for reducing inequalities in achieving inclusiveness.

(6) The sixth SDG goal is about clean water and sanitation. The purpose of this goal is to confirm the availability of clean drinking water for drinking and availability of water for sanitation for all. On mapping with the schedule seven, this goal can be directly achieved by following the activities as mentioned in the first activity which is talking about the projects which can make drinking water available for all and inclusion of Bharat Kosh, which is a center set up by the government to promote sanitation.

(7) The seventh SDG goal is the achievement of affordable and clean energy. Though this goal cannot be directly mapped to any of the activities as mentioned in schedule seven but the researcher strongly recommend that the fourth activity which is talking about conservation of natural resources and ensuring environmental sustainability, all the activities which will actually lead to usage of clean energy somewhere. Similarly the activities nine and 10, which mention about contribution to the incubators and research development in various fields of science, technology, and medicine, are finally into developing a system which helps us in promoting SDGs.

(8) The SDG number eight is decent work and economic growth. This talks about the sustainable and inclusive economic growth for each and everyone in the society. It aims at providing decent work for all; this cannot be mapped directly but if we focus on the activities mentioned under activity two and three of schedule seven – which are talking about promotion of education, environment, employment enhancing vocational training skills, livelihood enhancement projects, and various measures for reducing inequalities faced by people of economically weaker section (EWS) groups – similarly under the activity seven, the contribution to any of the funds for the welfare of the backward classes minorities and welfare of women and disease would lead to achievement of this SDG goal, which is talking about the inclusivity.

(9) The ninth SDG is about industry innovation and infrastructure. Here the focus is more on building a resilient infrastructure and promoting sustainable industry and promote innovation; this can however be directly linked to the ninth activity of schedule seven which is focusing on building up the incubators & research centers and focuses on the development in the area of technology and engineering, science of medicine. This activity further mention various institutions – the public funded universities where the CSR fund can go for the promotion and development of projects, which are sustainable – which can lead to achieving the SDG goals.

(10) The SDG goal number 10 is talking about reducing inequalities and here the focus is reduction of inequality among communities of member countries. However, CSR in India focuses on the development of its own communities and tribes, which include the disabled, communities from economically weaker sections, women, SCs and STs, etc. This SDG can be easily mapped to the eight thematic areas as mentioned in the schedule seven which deals with PM Cares fund and PMNRF: the objective of both these funds is the social economic development of weak and poor and thus providing equal opportunity of growth and future to marginalized woman, tribes, and communities.

(11) The 11th SDG goal focuses on sustainable cities and communities. Most of the countries lack or do not have well-defined urban policies or, even if they have, they are hardly implemented. This SDG focuses on better living standards and conditions for each and everyone in the city. The 11th thematic area as mentioned in the schedule seven encompasses all the activities and policies for slum area development. The Indian government is further extensively working under PM Awas Yojna and PM Awas rental Yojna to provide better dwellings to every individual, touching the last milestone by taking care of migrant labor as well. Besides the first thematic area as mentioned in schedule seven focuses on sanitation activities and Swachh Bharat Kosh is mentioned under it. This enables the corporate to support the sanitation system of not only slums but also encourages corporates to invest in sanitation system across as part of the urban development plan. Clean and hygienic toilets are one of the first steps in providing dignity of living to any human being.

(12) The 12th SDG "sustainable consumption and production" can be easily mapped to the fourth theme of schedule seven, whereby it also brings the attentions of corporates on sustainability of environment, balancing and protecting ecological system and flora and fauna, and conservation of natural resources and maintaining air, water, and soil.

(13) The 13th SDG goal is on "climate action," the aim of this goal is to combat the impact of climate change. This goal can again be mapped to thematic area four, where the focus is on environment and ecological balance. Further the area specified in schedule seven, point 9 lays emphasis on disaster management which includes relief, rehabilitation, and reconstruction activities majorly caused by natural calamities.

(14) Life below water (iv) assuring environmental sustainability, ecological equilibrium, flora and fauna preservation, animal welfare, agroforestry, resource conservation, and soil, air, and water quality maintenance (It includes contribution to the Clean Ganga Fund for rejuvenation of river Ganga, set up by the Central Government).

(15) Life on land.

(16) Peace, justice, and strong institutions and partnerships for the goals.

Global Implications

This research shows a direct linkage between CSR in India and SDG as set by the United Nations. The awareness regarding environment, social, and governance issues have increased many folds ever since the law on CSR came in India, i.e., 2014. Moreover the MCA reports by government of India shows that Indian incorporations have spent more than Rs. 24,800 crore for areas mentioned under CSR. This spend is strategically planned and as per law based on actual need assessment of ground and community. Globally, if corporates adopt similar framework like Indian CSR, then it would become easier for corporates to develop a framework for sustainable development. Each country has its own ranking on various SDG indexes. Such frameworks like schedule seven can be developed by each country based on their ranking and need. These frameworks can be a guiding map for corporates globally to achieve the SDGs by 2030 as targeted by the United Nations (Jain & Willer).

References

Adrangi, B., & Kerr, L. (2022). Sustainable development indicators and their relationship to GDP: Evidence from emerging economies. *Sustainability, 14*(2), 658.

Bajic, S., & Yurtoglu, B. (2018). Which aspects of CSR predict firm market value? *Journal of Capital Markets Studies, 2*(1), 50–69.

Carroll, A. B., & Shabana, K. M. (2010). The business case for corporate social responsibility: A review of concepts, research and practice. *International Journal of Management Reviews, 12*(1), 85–105.

De Haan, J., Dales, K., & McQuilken, J. (2020). *Mapping artisanal and small-scale mining to the Sustainable Development Goals*. Newark, DE: University of Delaware (Minerals, Materials and Society program in partnership with PACT). Retrieved from http://www.pactworld.org. https://sites.udel.edu/ceoe-mms/. Accessed on January 10, 2021.

Dhanesh, G. S. (2015). Why corporate social responsibility? An analysis of drivers of CSR in India. *Management Communication Quarterly, 29*(1), 114–129.

Fukuda-Parr, S., & McNeill, D. (2019). Knowledge and politics in setting and measuring the SDG S: Introduction to special issue. *Global Policy, 10*, 5–15.

Jana, S. K. (2022). Sustainable energy development in emerging economies: A study on BRICS. In *Environmental sustainability, growth trajectory and gender: Contemporary issues of developing economies* (pp. 23–35). Bingley: Emerald Publishing Limited.

Karuppiah, K., Sankaranarayanan, B., Ali, S. M., Jabbour, C. J. C., & Bhalaji, R. K. A. (2021). Inhibitors to circular economy practices in the leather industry using an integrated approach: Implications for sustainable development goals in emerging economies. *Sustainable Production and Consumption, 27*, 1554–1568.

Latapí Agudelo, M. A., Jóhannsdóttir, L., & Davídsdóttir, B. (2019). A literature review of the history and evolution of corporate social responsibility. *International Journal of Corporate Social Responsibility, 4*(1), 1–23.

Mitra, N., & Chatterjee, B. (2020). India's Contribution to the Sustainable Development Goals (SDGs) with respect to the CSR mandate in the Companies Act,

2013. In *The Future of the UN Sustainable Development Goals* (pp. 383–396). Cham: Springer.

Murray, C. J. (2015). Choosing indicators for the health-related SDG targets. *The Lancet, 386*(10001), 1314–1317.

Nonet, G., Gössling, T., Van Tulder, R., & Bryson, J. M. (2022). Multi-stakeholder engagement for the sustainable development goals: Introduction to the special issue. *Journal of Business Ethics*, 1–13.

OECD report. Policy responses to the economic crisis: Investing in innovation for long-term growth. Retrieved from https://www.oecd.org/sti/42983414.pdf. Accessed on April 14, 2022.

OECD Policy Responses to Coronavirus (COVID-19). *The territorial impact of COVID-19: Managing the crisis across levels of government.* Retrieved from https://www.oecd.org/coronavirus/policy-responses/the-territorial-impact-of-covid-19-managing-the-crisis-across-levels-of-government-d3e314e1/. Accessed on January 10, 2022.

Poddar, A., & Narula, S. A. (2020). A study of corporate social responsibility (CSR) and sustainable development goal (SDG) practices of the states in India. In *Mandated corporate social responsibility* (pp. 85–94). Cham: Springer.

Satapathy, J., & Paltasingh, T. (2022). CSR practices and Sustainable Development Goals: Exploring the connections in Indian context. *Business and Society Review, 127*(3), 617–637.

SDG report. (2022). *UN SDG Report.* Retrieved from https://unstats.un.org/sdgs/report/2022/. Accessed on July 7, 2022.

Singh, P., Dharwal, M., Alam, J., & Sharma, A. (2021). Corporate social responsibility in the time of COVID-19. *Turkish Journal of Physiotherapy and Rehabilitation*, 5476–5479.

Singh, M. P., Dharwal, M., Alam, J., Sharma, A., & Kumari, D. (2020). Environmental CSR – Evidences of top manufacturing units in India. *PalArch's Journal of Archaeology of Egypt/Egyptology, 17*(6), 7679–7693.

Ullah, H., Wang, Z., Bashir, S., Khan, A. R., Riaz, M., & Syed, N. (2021). Nexus between IT capability and green intellectual capital on sustainable businesses: evidence from emerging economies. *Environmental Science and Pollution Research, 28*(22), 27825–27843.

UN environment report. Retrieved from https://www.unep.org/about-un-environment. Accessed on July 20, 2022.

United Nation report on peace, dignity and equality on a healthy planet. Retrieved from https://www.un.org/en/global-issues/ending-poverty. Accessed on July 15, 2022.

Walton, C. C. (1982). Corporate social responsibility: The debate revisited. *Journal of Economics and Business, 34*(2), 173–187.

Wang, Q., & Huang, R. (2021). The impact of COVID-19 pandemic on sustainable development goals – A survey. *Environmental Research, 202*, 111637.

Warhurst, A. (2001). Corporate citizenship and corporate social investment: Drivers of tri-sector partnerships. *The Journal of Corporate Citizenship, 1*, 57–73.

WHO report. Retrieved from https://www.who.int/news-room/fact-sheets/detail/millennium-development-goals-(mdgs). Accessed on January 16, 2022.

Witte, C., & Dilyard, J. (2017). Guest editors' introduction to the special issue: The contribution of multinational enterprises to the Sustainable Development Goals. *Transnational Corporations, 24*(3), 1–8.

Chapter 4

Understanding the Level of Digitization in Emerging Economies: Implications for Sustainable Development Goals

Farzana Nahid and Sudipa Sarker

Abstract

Micro, small, and medium enterprises (MSMEs) can play a significant role in achieving sustainable development goals (SDGs) as they have the ability to reduce unemployment. Digitalization helps MSMEs in a number of ways, including lowering transaction costs, quickening access to information, and bettering communication with extended supply chain members. This chapter aims to understand the level of digitalization in MSMEs in an emerging economy such as Bangladesh. MSMEs in Bangladesh account for 25% of the gross domestic product and employ 87% of civilians. This chapter builds on qualitative data from 60 MSMEs from various manufacturing and service sectors such as textile, retail, food delivery, IT companies, etc. The interviews were semi-structured and followed an interview protocol. The length of interviews varied between 40 and 50 minutes. Content analysis was used to analyze the data. Findings suggest that counterintuitively the level of digitization in MSMEs is not low in Bangladesh. Many micro and small enterprises use MS Excel to help them manage customer and product data. Medium Enterprises use Enterprise Resource Planning (ERP) software for planning enterprise-wide resources. Some medium enterprises also use powerful data analytics software such as Oracle, Power BI, Google Analytics, Python, and SPSS. Results also reveal barriers to digitization in MSMEs, which include a lack of employee awareness, training, and motivation of top management. This chapter maps the digitalization levels in MSMEs in Bangladesh and provides implications for SGDs. The chapter also presents policy recommendations for improving the digitalization level in emerging economies.

Fostering Sustainable Businesses in Emerging Economies, 53–69
Copyright © 2024 Farzana Nahid and Sudipa Sarker
Published under exclusive licence by Emerald Publishing Limited
doi:10.1108/978-1-80455-640-520231004

Keywords: MSMEs; digitization; sustainable development goals (SDGs); emerging economy; innovation barrier; digital literacy

Introduction

Today's business competency and sustainability are highly dependent on technological capabilities. Digital technologies are transforming all types of business aspects, and thus new challenges are coming. Neugebauer (2019) argues that digital transformation requires the application of digital capabilities to products, processes, and assets with the goal to enhance efficiency, and customer value as well as managing risk, and tapping gap into new business opportunities. Similarly, Bertini (2016) claims that digital transformation affects not just lives, but also individual experiences. This is how digitalization significantly correlates with the sustainable development components, not only through economic development through higher competitiveness, innovativeness, and entrepreneurial activities, but also through social aspect (Jovanović, Dlačić, & Okanović, 2018; Levi Jakšić, Rakićević, & Jovanović, 2018b) Therefore, sustainable development is a priority now where digitalization highly affects. According to Brundtland Commission (1987, p. 41), sustainable development (SD) refers to the development that meets the requirements of the present without compromising future generations' ability to fulfill their own needs. SD suggests that the well-being of humanity can only be accomplished through social equity, environmental protection, and economic growth.

However, cultural differences do have a significant impact on digitalization status. More hierarchy, risk-taking capacity, individualism, and flexibility can lead to higher digitalization. Because of today's complexity of society, culture can be considered as another dimension to achieve sustainable development (Commonwealth Secretariat, 2007; Hawkes, 2001), culture determines the meaning of development done and how people act, react and accept with that changes/development (Organization Culture 21, 2014). Consequently, this development or change could be a crucial factor while adoption of digital transformation. Benner (2017) analyzed the cultural acceptance impact of digitalization, "Facebook" in particular on the Gross Domestic Product (GDP) in West and East Germany. The study measured the data from Google Trends and the results showed that GDP is increased by a positive cultural acceptance of digitalization. Again, Srite and Karahanna (2006) compared cultural value and technology acceptance in their study where the results again confirmed that behavioral intention to use technology is influenced by cultural values. Moreover, Layton (2007) argues that cultural context helps to define and explore the marketing environment as culture interacts with other factors like technological level, economic development, and the physical environment in the environment to ensure a society's sustainable development. Therefore, it can be said that culture, society, and the macro-marketing approach are interconnected.

Although emerging economies are becoming more engaged with global markets as they growing, however, the status of technology adoption, and digitization of operations and processes by SMEs which varies from culture to culture are still insignificant (Meyer & Peng, 2016). Technology can guide new business creation, sustain competitive advantage, and survive in the post-COVID-19 pandemic and the interconnected global economy. Therefore, achieving sustainable development in emerging economies is quite expected where technology can take a major contribution. Achieving sustainability in businesses means knowing the business's impact and purpose for which they need right type of data and technologies. That is how emerging economies should consider digitalization to achieve sustainability.

Data analytics plays a crucial role in digitization. Organizations can be more holistic, transparent, proactive, and accountable by having analytics and business intelligence capabilities while making business decisions. Data analytics/analytical tools can help businesses to accomplish their goals. Companies have widely embraced the use of analytics, especially big data analytics to streamline operations and to improve processes in the developed economy (Basuony, Mohamed, Elragal, & Hussainey, 2020; Sun & Huo, 2021). But what is the scenario of analytics use in the companies of developing economies? This chapter, therefore, not only analyzes the digitalization scenario in the MSMEs in emerging economies, Bangladesh in particular, but also aims to explore the status of using analytical tools in the MSMEs in Bangladesh.

Research Objectives

Digitalization can be done in process and in operation. Here this chapter will examine the effects of digitalization in the operations of firms. The chapter will also explore the effects of technology in decision making, customer handling, and communication. Keeping the significance of the digital transformation process and its vitality in achieving sustainable development goals in an emerging economy, this chapter proposes three research questions: How does digital transformation impacts sustainable development in an emerging economy such as Bangladesh? To what extent analytics is being used in MSMEs in Bangladesh and its impact in firms' operation. What are the barriers that are still hindering the digitalization process among firms?

Literature Review

Digitalization is a new game changer and has changed the ways of thinking and shaping up things. Now, a physical store, an e-Store, physical payments and e-Payments, and virtual reality can coexist. Katz, Koutroumpis, and Callorda (2013, p. 6) defined digitalization as the social transformation triggered by the massive adoption of digital technologies to generate processes, share, and transact information. A digital firm can transform business enterprises by streamlining unnecessary activities in the value-creating entities or in the logistics pipelines (BarNir, Gallaugher, & Auger, 2002).

There are significant payoffs from e-business initiatives; for example, if all the value creating entities are digitally connected, firms can quickly optimize both operational performance and financial cost-effectiveness (Barua, Konana, Whinston, & Yin, 2001). In a digital firm, all the significant business relationships with customers, suppliers and employees are digitally enabled and mediated (Laudon & Laudon, 2012, p. 11), and businesses can attain better customer relationships, engender information resource exchanges, increase employee performance, and augment operational efficiencies (BarNir et al., 2002). Organizations can experience economic stability in the short run and sustainable development in the long run through digitization of business operations because digitization can bring in cost efficiency and numerous growth opportunities by adopting newer and innovative technologies and processes (Bhutani & Paliwal, 2015).

Kshetri (2007) addresses the issue as to why developing countries are not in a position to digitalize themselves as he found that economic factors, sociopolitical factors, and cognitive factors all hinder the adoption of competitive models like e-commerce at the consumer and business levels in Nepal. In fact a country's transition to a digitally intensive society requires technology adoption, use and affordability of technologies, quality and capacity of network (Katz et al., 2013, p. 6). Keil et al. (2001) said it right that the transformation of business needs to be connected with the supply push and the demand-pull through ICT. According to Zhu, Kraemer, and Xu (2002), technological, organizational and environmental can be interconnected for better adoption of e-business which will lead to the creation of e-business value. Besides, in order to digitalize an organization, adopting an enterprise system, leveraging customers, supply chain, human resources and financial accounting are also needed (Davenport, 1998; Mathrani, Mathrani, & Viehland, 2013). Therefore, digitalization is not merely the adoption of technology, but the readiness of users backed by enormous levels of support from employees, management, customers, suppliers, and all other involved stakeholders.

Firms today are required to adapt swiftly and boldly to survive and thrive in today's turbulent and competitive global environment. Firms seek opportunities to recognize the constraints to advance their business processes that can impact their ability to respond to customer demands. Agility is characterized by firms that are identifying and developing new advantages continuously to orchestrate their business processes and so through organizational agility, firms can respond to environmental business changes in a proper and timely manner (Bi, Davidson, Kam, & Smyrnios, 2013; Chakravarty, Grewal, & Sambamurthy, 2013; Tallon & Pinsonneault, 2011) and thus can develop capabilities to explore new opportunities to enhance firm performance (Chakravarty et al., 2013).

This study supports considers the resource-based theory which argues that a firm can achieve competitive advantage by the right use of its resources, which in turn can generate superior long-term performance (Barney, 1991; Mata, Fuerst, & Barney, 1995; Ray, Muhanna, & Barney, 2005). This is how the resource-based theory establishes a clear link between resources and sustained advantage (Wade & Hulland, 2004). A firm to establish a solid IT base needs to work on several types of capabilities like e.g., agility (Sambamurthy, Bharadwaj, & Grover, 2003), knowledge management (Tanriverdi, 2005), and innovation-supportive organizational culture (Benitez-Amado, Llorens-Montes, & Perez-Arostegui, 2010) as intermediate variables in order to have superior performance. IT capability is defined as the ability to mobilize, deploy, and use IT-based resources to improve the firm's business processes (Santhanam & Hartono, 2003).

Analytics to Achieve Digitalization Among MSMEs in Emerging Economies

Digitalization and transaction automation investments facilitated organizations to grow substantially to develop abilities to capture the behavioral data of customers. Organizations more or less deal with data on a regular basis where data analytics or analytical tools are extremely helpful. Data analytics unlock the potential of the wide variety of data organizations generate today and can deliver valuable insights from the data to enable smarter decisions and drives/improves performance (Mukhopadhyay, 2022). With the help of data analytics, an organization can personalize marketing pitches to individual customers to identify and mitigate business risks.

Although companies of developed economies heavily use analytics in their regular business operations and decision making, however unfortunately, wide and deep analytics adoption is yet limited in developing economies (Kalema & Mokgadi, 2017; Orhan & Guajardo, 2022). The common challenges the firms face there are scarcity/unavailability of quality data and lack of investments in setting up data analytics infrastructure. This is even more challenging for small and medium-sized companies in emerging markets as they struggle to afford expensive purchases because of their tight budget. However substantial reduction in data storage costs and analytics tool and technologies has also made the development and implementation of analytics solutions more affordable. Therefore, the use of analytics in an emerging market is in novice stage and has been benefitting firms there. Thanks to the COVID-19 pandemic, which in fact forced these developing economies in a way to invest in data analytics for greater adoption. The use of data analytics among small businesses has been steadily increasing over the past few years. According to SCORE Association, in 2020, only 45% of small businesses were actually using analytics, while 51% of respondents considered data analytics important. Allied Market Research predicts that the big data and business analytics market will grow by 13.5% from 2021 to 2030, reaching an estimated $684.12 billion. According to Dresner's Business Intelligence Market Study (2021), business intelligence investments will be increased by as much as 50% across tech firms, manufacturing, retail, as well as finance by the end of 2022.

Bangladesh Scenario

Digitalization is playing a leading role in the production, operation, and distribution of businesses in a global and shared economy. Entrepreneurs can be facilitated by digitalization's actual benefits which generate accurate estimates of business benefits (Brynjolfsson & Collis, 2019). According to Sakata (2018), the digital revolution will help immediate application of technological solutions to move quicker and perform deep analysis of an era abundant in data.

Bangladesh is one of the mostly densely populated countries of the world with a population of 166,303,494 (The World Bank, 2022b). Bangladesh has a literacy rate of 74.66% (The Daily Star, 2022). The growth rate of gross domestic product in 2021 was 6.9% (The World Bank, 2022a). According to Katz et al. (2013) Bangladesh placed in the constrained cluster in the index of digitalization among 184 countries. Government of Bangladesh has put significant effort to foster digitalization of Bangladesh (Rahman, 2015). Research on current position in digitalization of Bangladesh is fairly limited (Uddin, Sohel, Mohammad, & Rahman, 2014).

According to Huawei Global Connectivity Index 2019, Bangladesh topped the chart of "Top Movers" for its significant digital economy growth. Bangladesh is a labor-intensive country but skill of labor is still low. Bangladesh entered 4G era through initiating "Digital Bangladesh" in 2018. According to Sung (2018), in an agriculture-based country like Bangladesh, the fourth industrial revolution can be helpful for the farmers to determine weather conditions by using mobile phones. Bangladesh has slowly introduced home delivery, mobile clinics, and telemedicine services. According to Ali (2020), BASIS which is the association in Bangladesh of Software and Information Services is working to disseminate information, communication expertise, and for access to information.

Bangladesh is gradually introducing telemedicine centers, satellite clinics in rural areas, and online home delivery services of goods. According to the 2022 data from the Bangladesh Telecommunication Regulatory Commission (BTRC) website, the total internet users stood at 113.73 million by 2021 while achieving the goal of Digital Bangladesh. According to Huawei Global Connectivity Index 2019, Bangladesh was on the list of "Top Movers" for its significant digital economy growth. However, Bangladesh still requires synchronization of advanced technological changes at all stages in the pyramid.

Unfortunately, full digitization of the education system is yet to be achieved in Bangladesh. Just 16% people in Bangladesh undertake vocational and technological education. Many training and skill development centers are government run but lack necessary equipment to provide state of the art training to the uneducated adults. The banking sector in Bangladesh has been already digitalized and uses online banking and SMS banking. However, the cost of e-banking is much higher for lower and middle-income segments of society. Top 8 digital wallets of Bangladesh called DESHIZ have gone cashless in Bangladesh. They are bKash, iPay, Rocket, NexusPay, Upay, GPAY, Easy.com.bd, and Dmoney. In fact, the first digital cattle market named Digital Haat was introduced in Dhaka city in 2020.

According to Hassan (2020), digitalization in financial services in Bangladesh is increasing, its implementation is still behind other sectors. Hassan (2020) reported that to reduce inequality the state-owned company Nagad is providing mobile financial services. During the COVID-19 pandemic, reaping and harvesting crop with agricultural tools saved the farmers in Bangladesh because of a short fall of agricultural laborers. Also, educational institutions used technology and could continue classes by Zoom and Google Meet.

Methodology

This study follows a qualitative approach where 60 micro, small, and medium company personnel were interviewed while using a convenience sampling method. A semi-structured interview questionnaire was used to interview 80 mid and top management people from 60 companies where each interview took about 40–50 minutes. Interviews were taken in person, over phone and through email. Among 60 companies, 10 are micro, 30 are small, 20 are medium sized companies. Among 60, 37 companies are manufacturing and 23 are service based enterprises. Among manufacturing companics, we have restaurant, FMCG, book publishing house, printing press, retail shop, furniture shop, hardware shop, cement companies, and pharmaceuticals. In service-based companies we have ed-tech, fin tech, marketing agency, agro tech, online grocery, food delivery app, ride sharing app, software company, entertainment, insurance, bank, and interior design firms.

Findings

From the interviews, three different perspectives can be pointed out here as triggering factors to have digitization. Firstly, the type of company. Service-based companies, especially IT-related companies or online based businesses, tend to use analytics more often due to their daily handling with data compared to those that run businesses manually. Secondly, age of the company. Comparatively, new companies are opting for digitalization and analytics compared to old companies as they have few people yet young professionals with more technical/analytical skills. Thirdly, country-based skill and infrastructural lacking. Unavailability of enough digitally skilled people, high cost of automation or analytical tools, lack of capital and poor infrastructural facilities are hindering the companies' acceptance and learning of digitization, adoption of analytics in particular.

Advantages Mentioned for Using Analytics

Some quotes are mentioned from the interviews where interviewees did mention about and the advantages they get from analytics. Some interviewees did mention that many businesses struggle to optimize their inventory levels where data analytics are helpful in determining ideal product supply based on holidays and seasonality. In fact, gathering and analyzing data about the supply chain can detect production related delays or even can predict any possible future problems. In case of a company's overestimation of product demand, data analytics is useful to determine the optimal price for a clearance sale to reduce inventory, as mentioned by the interviewees. Fig. 1 and 2 shows the replies in Yes/No when the very basic question was asked to the companies (manufacturing and service-based) about if they use analytics in day-to-day business operations or not.

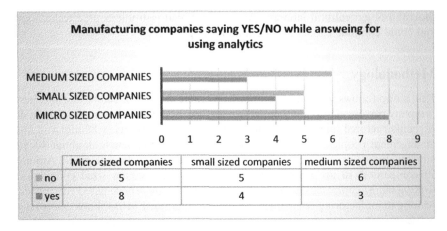

Fig. 1.   Manufacturing Companies Saying Yes/No While Answering
for Using Analytics. *Source:* Authors (2023).

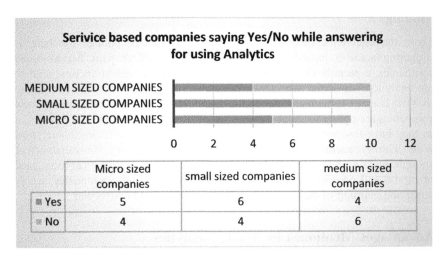

Fig. 2.   Service-Based Companies Saying Yes/No While Answering
for Using Analytics. *Source:* Authors (2023).

Moreover, as per the interviews, analyzing data doesn't only increase business efficiency, but also helps identify new business opportunities, such as untapped customer segments. The owner of a software manufacturing company said, "Computer models based on data analytics help our company see shifts in what customers buy and give us a clear picture of what products should be highlighted or updated." Data analytics can also be utilized as a human resources tool. Applications of AI and machine learning are transforming the hiring process in many organizations, while applications of data analytics in people management are informing decisions on promotions, performance evaluations, employee engagement, and professional development. A pharmaceutical company CEO opined that "we use analytics to train and promote our employees. Also, data analytics can visualize and diagnose the causes of historical events and can propose better future acts."

Furthermore, the CEO of a retail tech company opined that "Our company works with large amounts of data. For accuracy and fast response, the analytical tools provide us with much-needed quantitative insights. We use MS Excel and Power BI for operations, admin management, Human Resource management, customer handling, and competitor analysis. They help us use a few people and thus save our money and time." A manager of a software company stated that "Our company is currently using several analytical tools to collect data and to find several statistics. These tools are helping us to structure, for data cleaning, manipulating, managing, analyzing, tracking, and visualizing the data for solving real-life business problems our clients bring in." Another online food delivery company owner opined that "We are using Python, Django, docker, woo-commerce, IBM SPSS, Tableau, Power BI, Google Analytics, and these tools are helping us to structure, analyze, track, and visualize the data for everyday operations. They not only help us to decide what went wrong but also help us predict ways to improve our service." An Ad agency owner said "For our business, we use Google Spreadsheets or Excel. With the help of Excel, we create tasks for employees, record their job responsibilities and track monthly performance. Also, for internal communication, we use Slack which makes our life comfortable. For YouTube management, keywording, and engagement we use Tube Buddy." A medium-sized textile factory manager opined that "We have created our own proprietary software 'Prosperity ERP' system. The integrated system fits in with our company's requirement and as we do not have to manually connect databases, this software helps us do the required visualization."

Limited Use of Analytics

We also got some companies both manufacturing and service based who use only Excel in daily business operations. An HR manager of a marketing agency shared his view. He said "The role of MS Excel in our company is mostly for the organization of the data rather than data analysis. We don't need any sort of complex data analytics as we don't deal with large amounts of data." Another Ed-tech company manager said "We just use MS Excel for daily operational data management and other necessary work. We are aware of a few software, but we don't need them. Our work is simple, and Excel can easily solve it. But as we grow, we might need other software in the future, we are open to it." An owner of a wholesale packaging company said "We are not aware of other efficient software or analytical tools other than Excel. For excel is saving us." A mobile and electronic shop owner opined similarly as he also said they are not aware of other tools. Excel seems friendlier and more common so they use it. They did some market research and keep the data somewhat in excel and Microsoft word and later they analyze it. A Radio channel owner said "We use only Microsoft Excel because of its easier usability. We are aware of other analytical tools but not willing to take the hassle of using them, while excel is enough to keep track of the outcome of a marketing campaign, inventory, and so on. We think the charts and graphs provided by the Excel are enough for us to evaluate everything." A furniture shop owner said "I am aware of analytical software like IBM SPSS, Microsoft Power BI, SAS, etc. as I studied engineering. But my business is comparatively small, and MS excel fulfills most of my purpose. Therefore, trying out another software might be overwhelming for me. Also, any employee can operate Excel." A medium-sized book publishing house owner opined that "Our company mainly uses Excel and can efficiently manage customers, product data, and make reports."

Barriers Mentioned

When COVID-19 emerged out of nowhere, it was the biggest challenge to face in digitalization for many companies. Some learned by force to survive whereas some businesses had to shut down as they felt lost and didn't know what to do. On the other hand, the companies which knew about technology adopted it more and could survive the toughest days. It was in fact challenging for so many established companies. They could have run a bit smoother if they could forecast a better plan for such a situation. Many companies just had to wait for things to be normal as they didn't know they could run operations virtually using technology. Fig. 3 shows the barriers mentioned by the interviewees from MSMEs they think for not using analytics or for their limited use of analytics.

While expressing some barriers for which companies are reluctant to use analytics we found frustration regarding the lack of skilled employees, trained employees, lack of awareness, reluctance to learn, lack of sufficient capital, and running operations manually are some notable ones. From the interviews, some companies both medium and small were found who don't use any digitization or analytical tools. They still operate business manually. Employees from a garment company, two printing press, and three fast food restaurants reveal the similar scenario. Although these companies are on average over 25 years old, surprisingly they don't use any analytics or tools. They are not even aware of these tools' benefits. They said they don't need any tool for maintaining anything of their businesses and they are not interested because they are fine doing everything manually. A manager from the garment factory said "We have enough employees to work. We don't want to spend money to train employees to use any tools, it's trouble. We also fear that our employees will leave if they are told to use the new analytical tools. We are not even sure how these tools will bring us any profit or more revenue."

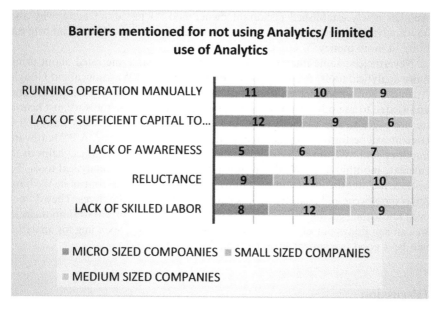

Fig. 3. Barriers Mentioned by the Interviewees From MSMEs for Not Using Analytics or Limited Use of Analytics.

As small companies, some do struggle to provide in-depth training for analytical tool knowledge and usage while baring the cost and insufficient capital. A trading house owner said, "There is an absence of strategic alignment. We find analytical tools very difficult to use. Learning to use them is time-consuming and needs money. This is a luxury for small companies like ours." Again, some of the interviewees expressed their frustration about sweating while finding skilled employees who can operate software. A medium sized fast food restaurant company said "We wanted to have an app to deliver food, but we lack skilled employees. There is no one who can train them." Another garment factory owner said "A notable problem is our aged employees who are happy to work manually although it takes more time to manage customers, they are scared to learn technology." An insurance company owner said "The major pressing concern with any analytical system is the risk of information leak. We handle sensitive information, and an error in the process if get exposed can harm our company's reputation. Also, the tool installation is expensive."

A small media and ad agency company owner said "Our firm produces films/ TVCs/OVCs as required by the advertising agencies or companies. Using analytics could help us to keep track of how their content is performing on social media, competitors act, and to better plan the future. However, small production houses are oversaturated in the industry, they don't make much profit and so don't see the value of keeping an analyst even spending 25k per month."

Another newly established restaurant owner said, "I just don't know why and how analytics can help me in making my business operation easy and can help me bring in more money."

Nevertheless, some interviews were quite positive and interested about using more analytical tools. A content marketing agency said "We know about Google Analytics and sometimes we use it casually. But we don't have the expertise and knowledge to use other kinds of tools. As the benefits of the tools we just heard, we are eager to use analytics to predict current trends and forecast how well a content will perform if they can find someone with the expertise." A PC hardware importer said "We are collecting data through Microsoft Excel. Excel helps us to calculate monthly sales. We do not use any other software or analytical tools. To operate our website, we are using a third party to manage and control it. We have fewer employees and from those, it is hard to find skilled employees. They do not even know the benefits of these tools. I now think it is important to train them so we can run things ourselves and can save time and money. Spending for analytics will be a good investment for long term."

Discussion

Digital transformation has become a norm nowadays (Ufua et al., 2021). This study tries to comprehend the variables that are related to the usage of analytics among MSMEs. There is a need to create a digital economy driven by technology to gain the sustainable development of individuals, firms, and nations (Karakara & Osabuohien, 2020). Digitalization can help countries like Bangladesh to achieve many sustainable development goals (SDG). For instance, digitalizing the education sector can help Bangladesh attain SDG 4, which is quality education (Unterhalter, 2019). There are many barriers to digitalization in emerging economies such as Bangladesh. One of the key ones is the lack of financial resources for small and medium enterprises. Furthermore, for SMEs it is difficult to have workforce that would like to adopt digitalization fully. Digitalization level in Bangladesh is still low compared to neighboring countries such as India, Sri Lanka, and Pakistan (Katz et al., 2013).

Bangladesh should work on improving its innovation scenarios through continuous process. In the country, investment policies, foreign direct investment, and outsourcing are becoming more convenient. Proper activities and directions can be aligned for seed money, angel investors, start-up ventures, crowdfunding, and investments for starting digital ventures. Also, establishing entrepreneurial promotion-based data center with international standards can expand access to economic activities. Electronic fund transfer and electronic data interchange together can be helpful.

Unfortunately, ICT preparedness in Bangladesh for a digital economy is relatively low compared to countries such as India and China. Therefore, it is high time for Bangladesh to work with proper guidance to motivate digital labor force so that workers with digital literacy prove their innovativeness. In addition, there is a need to develop and approach which is human-centric and technologically advanced. Internet connectivity in rural areas requires to be upgraded to minimize the gap between rural and urban areas. This can help Bangladesh to reduce poverty (SDG 1) as SDG 1 has strong co-relation with digitalization (Perez-Martinez, Hernandez-Gil, San Miguel, Ruiz, & Arredondo, 2022).

Digitalization can also help Bangladesh to achieve SDG 9 which is about creating resilient infrastructure, fostering sustainable industrialization, and promoting innovation (Ufua et al., 2021). However, there is a need to develop effective policies to promote digitalization specially to foster technological innovation. Bangladesh government can improve the structure of the incentives as well as train the people so that SMEs can have necessary skill set to implement digitalization (Onyango & Ondiek, 2021).

Moreover, local youth should be encouraged through funding support for their entrepreneurial work with digitization. To attain sustainable competencies, Bangladeshi firms should focus more on providing digital skill training. Also, widespread adoption of telemedicine and healthcare using mobile phones can improve promote the good health and well-being (SDG3) (Perez-Martinez et al., 2022). Nevertheless, the government should utilize data-driven innovation as consumer well-being can be achieved by creating a digital economy in Bangladesh (Brynjolfsson & Collis, 2019).

Conclusion

At present, digitalization is a crucial issue for organizations all over the world. It is elemental for organizations in emerging economies because digitalization can bring in ample opportunities to become efficient and effective. Thereby, for Bangladesh, it is instrumental to invest in education, training as well as digitalization of all services. It is great that Bangladesh is digitalizing almost all the sectors (Hossain, Syeed, Fatema, & Uddin, 2022). The interviews reveal that technology adoption, digitalizing operation, and analytics usage are in early stage of development among Bangladeshi MSMEs. Bangladesh suffers from having a large share of population who are digitally illiterate (Bhowmik et al., 2023). Educational institutes should focus more on teaching technology and analytics, so more graduates are available with the right digital awareness and knowledge. Foreign investment in digitalization of Bangladesh, especially in providing MSMEs to adopt digital solutions, can be encouraged by the Government of Bangladesh.

Bangladesh should concentrate on modernization of the education system and advancement of skills to tackle today's challenges. There needs to be adoption of digital economy to unlock the potential of a globalized market. To reduce disparity between rich and poor, the digital economy is a must. To help people adopt a digital economy, Bangladesh needs to popularize digitalization through innovative technologies, research, and development. The digital economy can create new jobs through social and human development. Each education institution can think of having data and learning centers. Digitalization can ensure talent management and enhancement by taking consideration of learner's age.

Digital preparedness must entail require ICT skills for spheres of the population. Digitalization should not replace low skilled labors, rather it must educate and enhance the skill level for all.

Limitations

For this study subjectivity in sample selection might have been a limitation and, therefore, generalization of the findings may be questioned in some respects. Random sampling in place of convenience sampling might have brought about more representative results for further generalization. In any case, this is quite a limited number of respondents to use for predicting the results for an entire country. Causal inferences to data that have been collected and measured without error might further limit the generalizability of this research. Further study can be done on large firms to see the overall status of digitization, and the result can be compared with that of MSMEs.

References

Ali, M. M. (2020). Digitization of the emerging economy: An exploratory and explanatory case study. *Journal of Governance and Regulation, 9*(4), 25–35.

Barney, J. (1991). Firm resources and sustained competitive advantage. *Journal of Management, 17*, 99–120.

BarNir, A., Gallaugher, J. M., & Auger, P. (2002). Business process digitization, strategy, and the impact of firm age and size: The case of the magazine publishing industry. *Journal of Business Venturing, 18*, 789–814.

Barua, A., Konana, P., Whinston, A. B., & Yin, F. (2001). Driving e-business excellence. *MIT Sloan Management Review*, 36–44.

Basuony, M. A., Mohamed, E. K., Elragal, A., & Hussainey, K. (2020). Big data analytics of corporate internet disclosures. *Accounting Research Journal, 35*(1), 4–20.

Benitez-Amado, J., Llorens-Montes, F. J., & Perez-Arostegui, M. N. (2010). Information technology-enabled intrapreneurship culture and firm performance. *Industrial Management & Data Systems, 110*, 550–566.

Benner, E. (2017). Cultural acceptance of digitalization and growth of an economy: A comparison of East and West Germany. *Economics Student Theses and Capstone Projects*, 53.

Bertini, P. (2016). Focus on technology hinders true digital transformation. Retrieved from http://www.brandknewmag.com/focus-on-technology-hinderstrue-digital-transformation/

Bhowmik, M., Ashraf, F., Fatema, T., Habib, F., Kabir, M. L., Islam, I., & Islam, M. N. (2023). Evaluating usability of mobile financial applications used in Bangladesh. In *Springer series in design and innovation* (Vol. 27, Issue November). Springer Nature Switzerland. doi:10.1007/978-3-031-20364-0_15

Bhutani, S., & Paliwal, Y. (2015). Digitalization: A step towards sustainable development. *OIDA International Journal of Sustainable Development, 8*(12), 11–24.

Bi, R., Davidson, R., Kam, B., & Smyrnios, K. (2013). Developing organizational agility through IT and supply chain capability. *Journal of Global Information Management (JGIM)*, *21*, 38–55.

Brundtland Commission. (1987). *Our common future: Report of the World Commission on Environment and Development*. United Nations.

Brynjolfsson, E., & Collis, A. (2019, November–December). *How should we measure the digital economy?* Boston, MA: Harvard Business Review. Retrieved from https://hbr.org/2019/11/how-should-we-measure-the-digital-economy

Chakravarty, A., Grewal, R., & Sambamurthy, V. (2013). Information technology competencies, organizational agility, and firm performance: Enabling and facilitating roles. *Information Systems Research*, *24*, 976–997.

Commonwealth Secretariat. (2007). Culture as the fourth pillar of sustainable development. In *Small states: Economic review and basic statistics* (Vol. 11, pp. 28–40). London: Commonwealth Secretariat. doi:10.14217/smalst-2007-3-en

Culture 21. (2014). Culture: Fourth pillar of sustainable development. Retrieved from www.agenda21culture.net/sites/default/files/files/documents/en/zz_culture4pillarsd_eng.pdf

Davenport, T. H. (1998). Putting the enterprise into the enterprise system. *Harvard Business Review*, *76*(4), 121–131.

Hassan, R. (2020). The economy of digitality: Limitless virtual space and network time. In *The condition of digitality: A post-modern Marxism for the practice of digital life* (pp. 97–128). doi:10.16997/book44

Hawkes, J. (2001). *The Fourth Pillar of Sustainability: Culture's essential role in public planning*. Melbourne, Australia: Cultural Development Network.

Hossain, S. (2020, January 18). Fintech: Revisiting financial inclusion. The Financial Express. Retrieved from https://thefinancialexpress.com.bd/views/fintech-revisiting-financial-inclusion-1579359721

Hossain, M. S., Syeed, M. M. M., Fatema, K., & Uddin, M. F. (2022). The perception of health professionals in Bangladesh toward the digitalization of the health sector. *International Journal of Environmental Research and Public Health*, *19*(20). doi:10.3390/ijerph192013695

Jovanović, M., Dlačić, J., & Okanović, M. (2018). Digitalization and society's sustainable development–Measures and implications. *Zbornik radova Ekonomskog fakulteta u Rijeci: časopis za ekonomsku teoriju i praksu*, *36*(2), 905–928.

Kalema, B. M., & Mokgadi, M. (2017). Developing countries' organizations' readiness for Big Data analytics. *Problems and Perspectives in Management*, *15*(1 (cont.)), 260–270.

Karakara, A. A. W., & Osabuohien, E. (2020). ICT adoption, competition and innovation of informal firms in West Africa: A comparative study of Ghana and Nigeria. *Journal of Enterprising Communities*, *14*(3), 397–414. doi:10.1108/JEC-03-2020-0022

Katz, R. L., Koutroumpis, P., & Callorda, F. (2013). The Latin American path towards digitization. *Info*, *15*(3), 6–24.

Keil, T., Eloranta, E., Holmstrom, J., Jarvenpaa, E., Takala, M., Autio, E., & Hawk, D. (2001). Information and communication technology-driven business transformation – A call for research. *Computers in Industry*, *44*, 263–282.

Kshetri, N. (2007). Barriers to e-commerce and competitive business models in developing countries: A case study. *Electronic Commerce Research and Applications, 6*, 443–452.

Laudon, K. C., & Laudon, J. P. (2012). *Management information systems* (12th ed.). Upper Saddle River, NJ: Pearson Education, Inc.

Layton, R. A. (2007). Marketing systems – A core macromarketing concept. *Journal of Macromarketing, 27*(3), 227–242. doi:10.1177/0276146707302836

Levi Jakšić, M., Rakićević, J., & Jovanović, M. (2018b). Sustainable technology and business innovation framework – A comprehensive approach. *Amfiteatru Economic, 20*(48), 418–436. doi:10.24818/ea/2018/48/418

Mata, F. J., Fuerst, W. L., & Barney, J. B. (1995). Information technology and sustained competitive advantage: A resource-based analysis. *MIS Quarterly, 19*, 487–505.

Mathrani, S., Mathrani, A., & Viehland, D. (2013). Using enterprise systems to realize digital business strategies. *Journal of Enterprise Information Management, 26*(4), 363–386.

Meyer, K. E., & Peng, M. W. (2016). Theoretical foundations of emerging economy business research. *Journal of International Business Studies, 47*(1), 3–22.

Mukhopadhyay, B. K. (2022, 17 August). Decision making: Using the tool of business analytics. The Financial Express. Retrieved from https://thefinancialexpress.com.bd/views/views/decision-making-using-the-tool-of-business-analytics-1507986642

Neugebauer, R. (Ed.). (2019). *Digital transformation*. Springer Berlin Heidelberg.

Onyango, G., & Ondiek, J. O. (2021). Digitalization and integration of Sustainable Development Goals (SGDs) in public organizations in Kenya. *Public Organization Review, 21*(3), 511–526. doi:10.1007/s11115-020-00504-2

Orhan, C. C., & Guajardo, M. (2022). Analytics in developing countries: Methods, applications, and the impact on the UN Sustainable Development Goals. *International Transactions in Operational Research, 29*(4), 2041–2081.

Perez-Martinez, J., Hernandez-Gil, F., San Miguel, G., Ruiz, D., & Arredondo, M. T. (2022). Analysing associations between digitalization and the accomplishment of the Sustainable Development Goals. *SSRN Electronic Journal, 857*(May 2022), 159700. doi:10.2139/ssrn.4122952

Rahman, L. (2015). Digital Bangladesh: Dreams and reality. The Daily Star, Part 1. Retrieved from https://www.thedailystar.net/supplements/24th-anniversary-the-daily-star-part-1/digital-bangladesh-dreams-and-reality-73118

Ray, G., Muhanna, W. A., & Barney, J. B. (2005). Information technology and the performance of the customer service process: A resource-based analysis. *MIS Quarterly, 29*, 625–652.

Sakata, T. (2018, April 24). *The good, the bad and the ugly of artificial intelligence and machine learning*. Retrieved from https://medium.com/applied-innovation-exchange/the-good-the-bad-and-the-ugly-of-artificial-intelligence-and-machine-learning-3f7e663c317a

Sambamurthy, V., Bharadwaj, A., & Grover, V. (2003). Shaping agility through digital options: Reconceptualizing the role of information technology in contemporary firms. *MIS Quarterly, 27*, 237–263.

Santhanam, R., & Hartono, E. (2003). Issues in linking information technology capability to firm performance. *MIS Quarterly*, 125–153.

Srite, M., & Karahanna, E. (2006). The role of espoused national cultural values in technology acceptance. *MIS Quarterly, 30*(3), 679–704. doi:10.2307/25148745

Sung, J. (2018). *The Fourth Industrial Revolution and precision agriculture.* doi:10. 5772/intechopen.71582

Sun, Z., & Huo, Y. (2021). The spectrum of big data analytics. *Journal of Computer Information Systems, 61*(2), 154–162.

Tallon, P. P., & Pinsonneault, A. (2011). Competing perspectives on the link between strategic information technology alignment and organizational agility: Insights from a mediation model. *MIS Quarterly, 35*, 463–484.

Tanriverdi, H. (2005). Information technology relatedness, knowledge management capability, and performance of multi-business firms. *MIS Quarterly, 29*, 311–334.

The Daily Star. (2022, November 11). *Bangladesh's literacy rate now 74.66%.* The Daily Star. Retrieved from https://www.thedailystar.net/tags/population-census-2022#:~:text=Bangladesh's%20literacy%20rate%20now%2074.66,Population%20 and%20Housing%20Census%202022%E2%80%9D

The World Bank. (2022a). *GDP growth (annual %) – Bangladesh.* The World Bank. Retrieved from https://data.worldbank.org/indicator/NY.GDP.MKTP.KD.ZG? locations=BD

The World Bank. (2022b). *Population, total – Bangladesh.* The World Bank. Retrieved from https://data.worldbank.org/indicator/SP.POP.TOTL?locations=BD

Uddin, M. A., Sohel, S. M., Mohammad, A., & Rahman, A. (2014). The state of the digitization of business enterprises in Bangladesh: A stakeholders' perspective. *SIU Journal of Management, 4*(1), 89–103.

Ufua, D. E., Emielu, E. T., Olujobi, O. J., Lakhani, F., Borishade, T. T., Ibidunni, A. S., & Osabuohien, E. S. (2021). Digital transformation: A conceptual framing for attaining Sustainable Development Goals 4 and 9 in Nigeria. *Journal of Management and Organization, 27*(5), 836–849. doi:10.1017/jmo.2021.45

Unterhalter, E. (2019). The many meanings of quality education: Politics of targets and indicators in SDG4. *Global Policy, 10*(January), 39–51. doi:10.1111/1758-5899.12591

Wade, M., & Hulland, J. (2004). Review: The resource-based view and information systems research: Review, extension, and suggestions for future research. *MIS Quarterly, 28*, 107–142.

Zhu, K., Kraemer, K. L., & Xu, S. (2002). A cross-country study of electronic business adoption using the technology-organization environment framework. In *Twenty-Third International Conferences on Information Systems.* Center for Research on Information Technology and Organizations, UC Irvine. Retrieved from https://studycrumb.com/alphabetizer

Chapter 5

Green Technology Practices and Local Well-Being: Inspiring Insights From a Brazilian Case Study

Michela Floris

Abstract

The current era is characterized by hyperturbulence, population growth, attention to food security, the need to identify sustainable strategies to reduce pollution and poverty, and the disparity between developed and undeveloped economies. These circumstances force a global paradigm shift based on sustainable practices and processes that put people and the environment at the core of each activity, contributing to sustainable, social, and economic development and promoting well-being in the community.

In this spirit, a strong impulse can derive from the practices of Green Technology, considered here as that set of processes aimed at eco-sustainability that acquire undisputed relevance, especially for emerging economies.

This chapter focuses on the role that Green technology practices exert in generating local well-being in the world's fifth-largest country: Brazil. Dynamic growth and effective social policies lifted millions of people out of poverty in the 2000s, even if socio-economic development varies widely across the country. Brazil is a leading global agricultural, minerals, and oil producer. The natural environment represents the primary source of Brazil's development that deserves to be protected and push firms and citizens to find new sustainable solutions based on green policies. Drawing inspiration from a Brazilian case study, this chapter proposes a set of building blocks that foster sustainable business practices in emerging countries.

The chapter is organized as follows: the first part introduces the concept of green technology practices; the second highlights the opportunities of green technologies; the third focuses on a single case study.

Fostering Sustainable Businesses in Emerging Economies, 71–86
Copyright © 2024 Michela Floris
Published under exclusive licence by Emerald Publishing Limited
doi:10.1108/978-1-80455-640-520231005

Keywords: Green technology; local well-being; case study; Embrapa; agriculture; sustainability

Introduction

Population growth, industrial development, and growing food needs have significantly impacted the environment (Salvador et al., 2019), contributing to the attention enhancement toward environmental sustainability (Alam & Murad, 2020; Naimoğlu, 2022) and sustainable development. As Brundtland's (1987) report states, sustainable development is the development that allows present generations to meet their own needs without compromising future generations to satisfy theirs.

Recently, the 2030 Agenda for Sustainable Development (UN, 2015) enriched the meaning of sustainable development, proposing an action program for people, the planet, and prosperity. It incorporates 17 Sustainable Development Goals, SDGs – into an extensive action program for 169 "targets" or milestones. The SDGs consist of common goals for all countries and individuals and refer to a set of essential development issues: the fight against poverty, the eradication of hunger, and the fight against climate change, to name a few.

This renewed attention toward sustainable development, considered broadly, generates new conditions for countries, people, firms, and organizations and pulls to identify new strategies to achieve personal and collective objectives by following sustainable paths. In such a scenario, adopting sustainable technologies seems essential to promoting sustainability practices within different contexts (Hu, Wang, Huang, & Zhang, 2019). These practices focus on reducing environmental impact and improving quality in many other sectors, such as health, energy saving, and countries' wealth (Zhu & Ye, 2018). In this sense, Green Technology represents the right way to spread sustainable practices (Wang, Nie, Peng, & Li, 2017). Fujii and Managi (2019), adopting the definition of the Organization for Economic Co-Operation and Development (OECD), underline that the term "Green Technology" includes technologies that promote mechanisms to reduce pollution, produce alternative energy, save energy, and manage waste. These technologies balance environmental protection and economic development and create a sustainable society (Sun, Lu, Wang, Ma, & He, 2008).

Notwithstanding the importance of green technology has increased worldwide (Fujii & Managi, 2019), there is a scarcity of studies focused on how sustainable technologies are developed in the BRICS (Brazil, Russia, India, China, and South Africa) countries (Fujii & Managi, 2019; Miranda, Moletta, Pedroso, Pilatti, & Picinin, 2021). As these developing economies operate in several economic contexts that generate a high worldwide environmental impact (Aswathy & Saravanan, 2019), understanding how these countries can follow sustainable principles by adopting green technologies practices is particularly relevant (Aldakhil, Nassani, Awan, Abro, & Zaman, 2018; Awan, Arnold, & Gölgeci, 2021).

This chapter aims to contribute to filling this gap by problematizing the topic (Alvesson & Sandberg, 2011), reviewing the main literature on green technology to introduce the concept, and analyzing a successful Brazilian case study that appears to be inspiring in terms of behavior, strategies, and contribution for local well-being.

Literature Background

Defining "Green Technology"

Green Technology represents a suitable way of achieving sustainable development (Ulucak, 2020), encouraging green economic growth (Sohag, Taşkın, & Malik, 2019), and reducing pollution (Yin, Zhang, & Li, 2020). Several studies argue that the improvement of technical efficiency is relevant (Gu, Zhao, Yan, Wang, & Li, 2019; Kwon, Cho, & Sohn, 2017), especially concerning renewable energy (Gu et al., 2019; Lin & Zhu, 2019) that generates clean energy and reduces environmental impact (Alam & Murad, 2020). In other words, green technologies are essential to driving countries toward sustainable development (Ulucak, 2020). In this perspective, green technology is "environmentally friendly by definition" (Miranda et al., 2021, p. 2), taking care of energy efficiency, safety, recycling, and other relevant aspects (Awan et al., 2021).

Over time, the concept of green technology has been made more explicit, starting from the contribution of Braun and Wield (1994), who have generically used this term to define technologies, products, and processes that aim to reduce environmental impact. More recently, other scholars have defined green technologies as those innovations that ensure customer value by reducing environmental impact (Bartlett & Trifilova, 2010); as the production process respectful of the environment and resources (Kemp & Pearson, 2007); as a lever to achieve an equilibrate development considering economic and environmental needs (Corsi, de Souza, Pagani, & Kovaleski, 2021). Other scholars have differentiated between green technological innovation and green managerial innovation (Qi, Shen, Zeng, & Jorge, 2010; Rennings, 2000), dividing those innovations that are based on environmental scientific knowledge and technology from those that refer to the adoption of new managerial practices or organizational structures to cut environmental impacts (Li, Rollins, & Yan, 2018).

In sum, in the light of this brief and not exhausting literature review, it is evident that the concept is broad and includes innovations, technologies, processes, and products that can be considered environmentally friendly and, contemporarily, it embodies new managerial and organizational perspectives able to reduce environmental impact and to spread sustainable behavior within and outside the firm.

Green Technology Practices in Brazil

A recent literature review (Miranda et al., 2021) focusing on green technology practices in BRICS states that Brazil primarily focuses on adopting production processes, products, and raw materials that reduce the environmental, social, and economic impact (Glänzel & Zhou, 2011). The goal is to preserve the natural resources and energy stand out (Ferreira et al., 2018; Pereira, Ferreira, de Santana Ribeiro, Carvalho, & de Barros Pereira, 2019).

The attention toward internal environmental practices and the search for alternative sources of water and energy push identifying and conceiving new ways to link practices to strategies, promoting process, product, and market innovation, and implementing operations based on green policies (green purchases, green distribution, green supply chain, and others), and because of the adoption of green technologies, Brazil has reduced the consumption of energy and materials.

Diana, Jabbour, de Sousa Jabbour, and Kannan (2017) underline that manufacturing plays a pivotal role in promoting sustainable operations, while others spotlight agriculture as the driver to spread humanistic sustainable development (dos Reis, do Nascimento, Felizardo, & da Silva Santos, 2015).

Furthermore, other scholars (Walker, Seuring, Sarkis, & Klassesn, 2014) argue that green technologies are essential for the sustainable management of operations because "the improvement of environmental conditions results from the adoption of environmental technologies and innovations and the analysis of ecological resources and modernization, which claim the possibility of the combination of environmental legislation, industrial solutions, and innovation and improvement of firms' environmental performance" (Miranda et al., 2021, p. 7).

Green technologies in Brazil encompass particular products, processes, and raw materials (Ferreira et al., 2018); sustainable agriculture (Castro-Vargas, Baumann, Ferreira, & Parada-Alfonso, 2019); sustainable practices for water retention (Loise de Morais Calado, Esterhuizen-Londt, Cristina Silva de Assis, & Pflugmacher, 2019); waste management (Madeira & Macedo, 2015); reduction of greenhouse gas emissions (Forster, Vaughan, Gough, Lorenzoni, & Chilvers, 2020); green buildings (Kasai & Jabbour, 2014); and sustainable policies (Gramkow & Anger-Kraavi, 2018, 2019).

The literature on the topic is relatively novel, and studies are still scarce (Fujii & Managi, 2019; Miranda et al., 2021). This chapter aims to contribute to this gap by focusing on a Brazilian case study to uncover how and why green technologies are adopted and can promote local well-being.

Method

Research Design and Data Collection

This study is based on a single case study (Yin, 1994, 2013), consistently with recent studies on green technologies (Chan, Darko, Olanipekun, & Ameyaw, 2018; Si, Marjanovic-Halburd, Nasiri, & Bell, 2016; Wicki & Hansen, 2019; Xia, Zhang, Yu, & Tu, 2019). The case analyzed refers to a contemporary phenomenon based on real-life contexts; the boundaries between the phenomenon and its context are not identifiable; the case is unique and revelatory (Yin, 2008). Moreover, it is in line with Patton's suggestions (1990), which underlines that the "logic and power of purposeful sampling lies in selecting information-rich cases for study in depth. Information-rich cases are those from which one can learn a great deal about issues of central importance to the purpose of the research." The study was conducted in July and August 2022. Primary data consisted of 15 documents for understanding the context of Brazil (demographic, technological, and socio-economic features), more than 50 official documents of the case study (available online), and several official websites and social media. Secondary sources comprised archival data from business publications and other documents related to Brazil's green technologies practices and policies. Because of the exploratory nature of this study, additional documents were retrieved and analyzed until theoretical saturation was reached (Glaser & Strauss, 1979; Sebele-Mpofu, 2020; Suddaby, 2006; Walsh & Bartunek, 2011).

Research Context

Brazil is, by extension and population, the most important country in South America and borders most of the continent's other nations. Given the territory's wing, it is impossible to define Brazil precisely; there are huge tropical forests (Amazonia above all), hilly and mountainous areas, and vast coastal plains; the population composition is also very varied. Brazil is a federation comprised of 26 states and one federal district, and the urbanization rate is 85%, which is relatively high. Many cities exceed a million inhabitants, starting from one of the most populated cities in the world as well as the first in South America, São Paulo (12,214,000 inhabitants, 22,495,000 urban agglomerates), which exceeds 10 million people considering the urban area also, Rio de Janeiro (6,748,000 inhabitants, 12,486,000 urban agglomerates). In this ranking also the capital Brasilia (2,951,000 inhabitants, 3,429,000 urban agglomerates), Salvador (2,886,000 inhabitants, 3,430,000 urban agglomerates), Fortaleza (2,687,000 inhabitants, 3,621,000 agglomerates urban), Belo Horizonte (2,522,000 inhabitants, 5,271,000 urban agglomerates), and Manaus (2,208,000 inhabitants, 2,308,000 urban agglomerates).

Brazil possesses a large stock of natural resources and a relatively diverse economy. The country is the world's largest coffee, sugarcane, and oranges producer and one of the world's largest soy producers. With forests covering half the country, and the largest rainforest in the world, Brazil is the world's fourth-largest exporter of timber. In addition, Brazil is among the most prominent livestock producers for commercial purposes and attracts investment from multinationals in the food and biofuel industry. However, even though agriculture accounts for 40.1% of exports, it contributes relatively little to GDP (5.9%) and employs only 9% of the population. Agriculture grew significantly in 2021, mainly driven by increased soybean production and rising agricultural commodity prices. Moreover, Brazil is a significant industrial power and has significantly benefited from its mineral wealth. The country is the world's second-largest exporter of iron and one of the world's leading producers of aluminum and coal. As an oil producer, Brazil aims to become energy independent shortly, with reserves that could make it one of the top five oil producers in the world. In addition, the country is increasingly establishing itself in the textile, aeronautical, pharmaceutical, automotive, steel, and chemical industries. Many world's leading car manufacturers have set up manufacturing plants in Brazil. The service sector accounts for 62.9% of the Brazilian GDP and employs 70.9% of the active workforce. In recent years, the country has started the production of services with high-added value, especially in the aeronautics and telecommunications sectors. Tourism has also grown, making it an important segment of the tertiary sector. The service sector was the hardest hit by the Covid-19 pandemic but significantly recovered in 2021 as vaccination rates and people's mobility increased. The recovery in the industry was mainly driven by household services, information and communication, and transport, as well as a slight rebound in the tourism sector.

Brazil is part of the group of countries known as BRIC (Brazil, Russia, India, and China). This group consists of emerging countries, which may become, in the next 50 years, the main strength of the global economy (Vieira & Veríssimo, 2009). Demands for economic growth challenges countries classified as emerging economies in terms of climate change, lack of affordable and sustainable energy, low capital, environmental degradation, lack of availability and investment in technology, lack of sufficient food supplies in remote areas, food security, high rate of unemployment, high population growth, lack of transport and communication (mainly in rural areas), lack of infrastructure in education, and poverty (Anand, Fennell, & Comim, 2020; Anghinoni et al., 2021; Lustig, Pabon, Sanz, & Younger, 2020; Troyano & Martín, 2017). Furthermore, Sambuichi et al. (2019) highlight that Brazil shows hunger and food insecurity, although it represents one of the largest agricultural areas of the world and one of the largest global food producers. Moreover, the agricultural industry impacts the environment dramatically, worsening environmental conditions and not contributing to the promotion of sustainable development (Rajão et al., 2020). In this regard, green technologies can help sustain Brazilian agriculture toward sustainability.

The Case Study

The case study analyzed is the Brazilian Agricultural Research Corporation (Embrapa).

Embrapa is a "case of successful institutional innovation whose main characteristics are: a public corporation model of organization; scale of operation at the national level; spatial decentralization; specialized research units; enhanced training and remuneration of human resources; and a vision of an agriculture based on science and technology" (Martha, Contini, & Alves, 2012, p. 211).

Embrapa is an innovative firm that promotes knowledge and technology for Brazilian agriculture. It was established in 1973 to spread technology for agriculture and farming to ensure food security and a leading position in the international food, fiber, and energy market. Embrapa, on its official internet site, declares its mission, which is creating research development and innovation solutions to ensure the sustainability of agriculture for the benefit of Brazilian society. At the same time, its vision is to be a protagonist in the generation and use of knowledge for the sustainable development of Brazilian agriculture.

Embrapa bases its strategy and vision on five pillars: excellence in agricultural research, production efficiency and quality, social aspects, network, and environmental sustainability. Its central values can be summarized as follows:

- reliability and integrity, concerning spreading ethics and integrity in all activities;
- respect toward people and opinion viewpoints;
- connectivity by interacting with stakeholders to generate knowledge and applied technology;
- innovation, to identify and conceive innovative and creative solutions apt to increase the value of products and services;
- excellence, to enhance the quality of products, services, and processes;
- sustainability that encompasses all business aspects to achieve Sustainable Development Goals.

Since the 2010s, Embrapa has focused on sustainability, or, better, on sustainable agricultural technology for the tropics. Brazil was on the frontline of agricultural science and technology and now has unique expertise in sustainability in tropical agriculture. Zero tillage and crop-forestry-livestock integration illustrate farming practices and systems that combine efficiency with economic and environmental sustainability. A range of other green technologies (biological carbon sequestration, renewable energy, geo-referencing technologies, and machinery for accurately assessing fertilizer and pesticide needs) are highlighted in document of Embrapa's "low carbon agriculture" (Cabral, 2021).

Embrapa is organized in several research units distributed throughout the national territory and is specialized in products, resources, and themes, with well-structured power distribution and task attribution (Alves, 2010).

Embrapa possesses an extensive portfolio of projects – based on green technologies and focused on promoting sustainability and local well-being – that follows a top-down strategy. Following this perspective, the projects are focused on specific themes which are strategic for the organization and meaningful for the territory (Crespi, da Costa, Preusler, & Porto, 2019).

Embrapa is an institution with the ambition of persisting for a long time into the future, serving Brazilian and world societies. In this sense, it invests heavily in human capital to accomplish immediate and future needs (Alves, 2008, 2010). In fact, the most relevant key to achieving Embrapa's success is human resource policies. The policy intends to develop human capital, stimulate creativity, and ensure an organizational environment to motivate workers. Specifically, Embrapa assures decent work regarding workers' careers, good salaries, retirement plans, health plans, activities to accumulate knowledge and experience, training programs, entrepreneurial orientation, and transparent communication. In this sense, Embrapa takes care of human resources because it considers them the firm's most relevant force in facing current and future challenges. The challenges are primarily related to production efficiency to ensure: an increase in productivity; scientific excellence, as a result of solid attention toward R&D; sustainable production to ensure the rational use of natural resources and the interest in preserving the environment; inclusion in production, that is the intention of informing policies to solve social and economic inequalities, to reduce rural poverty in Brazil. In other words, Embrapa stimulates the acquisition of scientific knowledge and technological skills to have high-professional workers, creating a vigorous and creative climate that allows the development of new environmental-friendly technologies to achieve sustainability broadly.

Embrapa's contribution is fundamental to Brazil's economy, society, and environment due to the strong development of the agriculture industry. More in detail, Embrapa has introduced technologies to introduce new varieties, cultural practices, zoning, tillage, biological fixation of nitrogen, livestock development for meat and milk, vegetables, fruit, irrigation, and knowledge.

Discussion

The proposed case study appears particularly relevant because, from the documents analyzed, the role of extraordinary importance that Embrapa plays in Brazil emerges. Embrapa is not only a successful firm, but it is an organization that embodies a development model that, by basing its business on the primary local resource and, consequently, by investing in the main economic activity of the territorial context, contributes to the development of the whole of Brazil. By investing in human resources, Embrapa bases its success on an unstoppable process of research and development of new green technologies and new sustainable practices to modernize its agricultural sector. Embrapa conceives and develops green technologies that aim to reduce the environmental impact, tending to implement and diversify production, improve production practices and procedures and converge at the same time toward reducing local problems linked to food security and hunger and toward the positioning of the agricultural output in international markets. In this sense, Embrapa also promotes local well-being and stimulates the population's awareness of the importance of their local resources, which, in compliance with the philosophy of sustainable development, must be valued and used in the present but also preserved for their future use. This vision has also generated a sense of pride in the citizens, who perceive the quality of the work carried out by Embrapa, its relevance, as well as the evident ability to create relationships with various public and private stakeholders to amplify the positive effects of the firm's behavior and strategies.

From the documents and data analyzed, which made it possible to study the case in depth, it is possible to extrapolate some building blocks. These elements can represent the foundations and pillars of a successful business model that contributes to the definition of business strategies that have continuous attention to sustainability, considered according to the most recent contributions from the UN Agenda 2030.

The building blocks are summarized in Fig. 1.

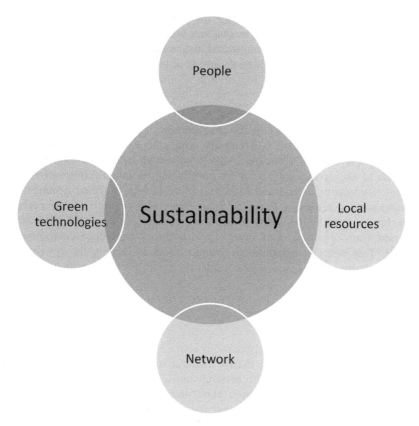

Fig. 1.   The Interpretive Model. *Source:* Author's elaboration.

People, local resources, networks, and green technologies appear to be the four pillars of achieving sustainability and local well-being.

People

The case of Embrapa underlines that human resources represent the firm's main strength in terms of continuous research, strong commitment, hard work and efforts, and searching for new ways to enhance and develop Brazilian agriculture. At the same time, Embrapa shows attention to citizens' legitimization. This situation means that Embrapa acts by trying to achieve its objectives, keeping its roots very firm with the local populations, strengthening the bond of trust, and obtaining solid legitimacy. This makes Embrapa's activity even more vital as it is recognized as a company that collaborates to achieve the common good and, therefore, to be supported and appreciated. In this scenario, the communication adopted by Embrapa is also particularly relevant and based on information transparency. Furthermore, following the development of policies aimed at reducing poverty and the gap in inequalities and promoting inclusion, Embrapa embodies the principles of Humanistic Management, placing the whole person at the center of its work and creating a context of better working and operational.

Local Resources

The case of Embrapa shows how the enhancement of local resources can increase the nation's wealth. Brazil is a country with extensive lands, and Embrapa, respecting the country's vocation, has contributed to the development and progress of the agricultural sector by introducing meaningful innovations that increase the quantities produced without causing damage to the environment and without wasting resources. Embrapa is an exceptional example of entrepreneurship characterized by the ability to use local resources, improve the processes of use and transformation, and invest in innovations to reduce environmental impact. This behavior generates a virtuous circle as keeping the environment unchanged also benefits those who consider the environment the primary resource to be valued.

Network

A strong network internally and externally characterizes Embrapa. Internally, it is organized as a network of more than 47 research units spread across all regions of Brazil (Lopes et al., 2012). The research units include: (a) specialized centers devoted to research and innovation about important crop species in Brazilian agriculture; (b) strategic organizational units responsible for developing knowledge, processes, and innovations in biotechnology, genetic resources, advanced instrumentation, information technology (IT), agroenergy, soils, agrobiology, and tropical agroindustry; (c) eco-regional units that undertake adaptations of technologies, information, and production systems to enable the sustainable use of natural resources. In addition, there are also service units dedicated to production and marketing, plant quarantine and land management, and areas dedicated to international technical cooperation and corporate management units (Figueiredo, 2016).

Externally, Embrapa bases its activities on worldwide collaborative innovation networks and a strong network of qualified professionals. At the same time, Embrapa takes care of the creation of solid and robust relations with local individuals, policymakers, and other organizations, to create a shared Brazilian development.

Green Technologies

As underlined by Cabral (2021), Embrapa is well-known for incorporating the Cerrado – a tropical savannah characterized by incredible biodiversity of fauna and flora – into Brazil's modern agriculture. This has been done through essential discoveries on improving infertile soils and developing soybean seeds adapted to the tropics, giving origins to the Green Revolution. Following this perspective, Embrapa has developed and promoted an indefinite series of green technologies to introduce in the agricultural industry.

Embrapa's success focuses on selected technological breakthroughs, highly trained and motivated scientists, and a sense of mission toward Brazilian society. At the same time, several other aspects appear to be the input and output of green technologies conceived and adopted. The first relates to Embrapa's concerns about the environmental and social impacts of the spread of large-scale farming. The second refers to an exciting action Embrapa promoted, which is the foundation of a national seed bank to preserve biodiversity. The third refers to the fact that several researchers in Embrapa collaborate with local expertise and ethnoscience to enrich and broaden their studies and offer their scientific results to the communities.

In sum, Embrapa bases its activities on green technologies to improve the agriculture industry by pursuing environmental sustainability and conservation of agricultural biodiversity, preserving climate change, achieving social fairness, and involving farmers and local communities with specific knowledge and practices in further studies and research.

Sustainability

Since 1997, Embrapa has published its Social Report annually, which includes the impact of each proposed activity. All Embrapa Research Units apply an integrated system of environmental indicators to assess the environmental impact and confirm the close interaction between research and development teams and manufacturers that adopt the promoted technologies (Rodrigues, de Almeida Buschinelli, & Dias Avila, 2010). The assessment results suggest that Embrapa occupies a place in the first line of promoting sustainability.

The mentioned pillars – people, local resources, networks, and green technologies – appear to be the drivers of achieving sustainability. Specifically, the interplay among these pillars enhances the embodiment of sustainable principles in the whole of Embrapa's activities and strategies. Thus, Embrapa, building on local resources, networks, and green technologies, contributes to improving the management and sustainable use of Brazilian biomes and their natural resources; increasing the resistance of native ecosystems and production systems, and improving the adaptability of Brazilian agriculture to climate change and water scarcity, supporting public policy design and improvement.

Moreover, focusing on people, Embrapa generally promotes peaceful and inclusive societies for sustainable development in Brazil and other developing countries. It also provides access to information and, through its actions, supports effective, accountable, and inclusive institutions at all levels for peace and global justice.

Specifically, Lopes et al. (2021) underline that in several documents, Embrapa declares its commitment to sustainable development by comprising all 17 UN

Sustainable Development Goals (SDGs). This alignment with SDGs represents an undoubted opportunity for Embrapa and its partners to be recognized and appreciated worldwide and achieve economic, social, environmental, and cultural benefits through agricultural research and innovation.

Conclusion

This chapter aimed to analyze the role of green technologies in sustainability promotion and development, paying attention to the experience of Embrapa. This Brazilian company designs and develops agricultural field innovations to consolidate and implement Brazilian agricultural production.

The successful case of Embrapa shows the great opportunities that the adoption of green technologies in the agricultural sector can offer in terms of the achievement of SDGs in the emerging economies.

From the case study, it emerged that the continuous tension toward sustainability and the achievement of all the SDGs of the UN 2030 Agenda is the result of the interaction between four pillars which are synergistically related and feed each other. These pillars are people, local resources, networks, and green technology. The latter, in particular, benefits from the previous ones and represents the result of their continuous and constant interaction and, together with them, contributes to sustainable development in an ample sense. The case described, therefore, appears to be a best practice that other developing areas could draw inspiration to promote socio-economic development within them in line with the philosophy and the most recent aims of sustainable development. In other words, Embrapa represents an exceptional explanatory case of how and why aligning one's objectives with the more general ones can allow acquiring a competitive advantage and appreciation in the market that is difficult to imitate by competitors. In this sense, operating in compliance with sustainability, developing technologies to reduce the environmental impact, creating a network with local and international actors, taking advantage of local relationships to enhance the territory's resources, and creating conditions for reducing poverty can represent a development model to pursue economic, social, and environmental goals jointly.

References

Alam, M. M., & Murad, M. W. (2020). The impacts of economic growth, trade openness, and technological progress on renewable energy use in organization for economic cooperation and development countries. *Renewable Energy, 145,* 382–390.

Aldakhil, A. M., Nassani, A. A., Awan, U., Abro, M. M. Q., & Zaman, K. (2018). Determinants of green logistics in BRICS countries: An integrated supply chain model for green business. *Journal of Cleaner Production, 195,* 861–868.

Alves, E. (2008). Vernon Ruttan e a Embrapa. *Revista de Política Agrícola, 17*(4), 95–96.

Alves, E. (2010). Embrapa: A successful case of institutional innovation. In *Brazilian agriculture development and changes. Brasília: Embrapa,* 143–160.

Alvesson, M., & Sandberg, J. (2011). Generating research questions through problematization. *Academy of Management Review, 36*(2), 247–271.

Anand, P. B., Fennell, S., & Comim, F. (2020). *Handbook of brics and emerging economies.* Oxford: Oxford University Press.

Anghinoni, G., Anghinoni, F. B. G., Tormena, C. A., Braccini, A. L., de Carvalho Mendes, I., Zancanaro, L., & Lal, R. (2021). Conservation agriculture strengthen sustainability of Brazilian grain production and food security. *Land Use Policy, 108,* 105591.

Aswathy, S., & Saravanan, G. (2019). Green technology literature from India as reflected in Web of Science from 2000 to 2015. *Library Philosophy and Practice,* 1–13.

Awan, U., Arnold, M. G., & Gölgeci, I. (2021). Enhancing green product and process innovation: Towards an integrative framework of knowledge acquisition and environmental investment. *Business Strategy and the Environment, 30*(2), 1283–1295.

Bartlett, D., & Trifilova, A. (2010). Green technology and eco-innovation: Seven case-studies from a Russian manufacturing context. *Journal of Manufacturing Technology Management, 21*(8), 910–929.

Braun, E., & Wield, D. (1994). Regulation as a means for the social control of technology. *Technology Analysis & Strategic Management, 6*(3), 259–272.

Cabral, L. (2021). Embrapa and the construction of scientific heritage in Brazilian agriculture: Sowing memory. *Development Policy Review, 39*(5), 789–810.

Castro-Vargas, H. I., Baumann, W., Ferreira, S. R., & Parada-Alfonso, F. (2019). Valorization of papaya (Carica papaya L.) agroindustrial waste through the recovery of phenolic antioxidants by supercritical fluid extraction. *Journal of Food Science and Technology, 56*(6), 3055–3066.

Chan, A. P. C., Darko, A., Olanipekun, A. O., & Ameyaw, E. E. (2018). Critical barriers to green building technologies adoption in developing countries: The case of Ghana. *Journal of Cleaner Production, 172,* 1067–1079.

Corsi, A., de Souza, F. F., Pagani, R. N., & Kovaleski, J. L. (2021). Technology transfer oriented to sustainable development: Proposal of a theoretical model based on barriers and opportunities. *Scientometrics, 126*(6), 5081–5112.

Crespi, T. B., da Costa, P. R., Preusler, T. S., & Porto, G. S. (2019). The alignment of organizational structure and R&D management in internationalized public company: The Embrapa case. *Innovation & Management Review, 16*(2), 193–216.

Diana, G. C., Jabbour, C. J. C., de Sousa Jabbour, A. B. L., & Kannan, D. (2017). Putting environmental technologies into the mainstream: Adoption of environmental technologies by medium-sized manufacturing firms in Brazil. *Journal of Cleaner Production, 142,* 4011–4018.

dos Reis, A. A., do Nascimento, W. L. N., Felizardo, A. O., & da Silva Santos, A. R. (2015). Agricultura Familiar e Economia Solidária: a experiência da Associação MUTIRÃO, na região do Baixo Tocantins, Amazônia Paraense. *Revista Tecnologia e Sociedade, 11*(22), 120–142.

Ferreira, A., Kunh, S. S., Fagnani, K. C., De Souza, T. A., Tonezer, C., Dos Santos, G. R., & Coimbra-Araújo, C. H. (2018). Economic overview of the use and production of photovoltaic solar energy in brazil. *Renewable and Sustainable Energy Reviews, 81,* 181–191.

Figueiredo, P. N. (2016). New challenges for public research organisations in agricultural innovation in developing economies: Evidence from Embrapa in Brazil's soybean industry. *The Quarterly Review of Economics and Finance, 62*, 21–32.

Forster, J., Vaughan, N. E., Gough, C., Lorenzoni, I., & Chilvers, J. (2020). Mapping feasibilities of greenhouse gas removal: Key issues, gaps and opening up assessments. *Global Environmental Change, 63*, 102073.

Fujii, H., & Managi, S. (2019). Decomposition analysis of sustainable green technology inventions in China. *Technological Forecasting and Social Change, 139*, 10–16.

Glänzel, W., & Zhou, P. (2011). Publication activity, citation impact and bi-directional links between publications and patents in biotechnology. *Scientometrics, 86*(2), 505–525.

Glaser, B. G., & Strauss, A. L. (1979). *The discovery of grounded theory* (10 ed.). Hawthorne, NY: Aldine Publishing.

Gramkow, C., & Anger-Kraavi, A. (2018). Could fiscal policies induce green innovation in developing countries? The case of Brazilian manufacturing sectors. *Climate Policy, 18*(2), 246–257.

Gramkow, C., & Anger-Kraavi, A. (2019). Developing green: A case for the Brazilian manufacturing industry. *Sustainability, 11*(23), 6783.

Gu, W., Zhao, X., Yan, X., Wang, C., & Li, Q. (2019). Energy technological progress, energy consumption, and CO2 emissions: Empirical evidence from China. *Journal of Cleaner Production, 236*, 117666.

Hu, J., Wang, Z., Huang, Q., & Zhang, X. (2019). Environmental regulation intensity, foreign direct investment, and green technology spillover—An empirical study. *Sustainability, 11*(10), 2718.

Kasai, N., & Jabbour, C. J. C. (2014). Barriers to green buildings at two Brazilian Engineering Schools. *International Journal of Sustainable Built Environment, 3*(1), 87–95.

Kemp, R., & Pearson, P. (2007). Final report MEI project about measuring eco-innovation. *UM Merit, Maastricht, 10*(2), 1–120.

Kwon, D. S., Cho, J. H., & Sohn, S. Y. (2017). Comparison of technology efficiency for CO2 emissions reduction among European countries based on DEA with decomposed factors. *Journal of Cleaner Production, 151*, 109–120.

Lin, B., & Zhu, J. (2019). Determinants of renewable energy technological innovation in China under CO2 emissions constraint. *Journal of Environmental Management, 247*, 662–671.

Li, K., Rollins, J., & Yan, E. (2018). Web of Science use in published research and review papers 1997–2017: A selective, dynamic, cross-domain, content-based analysis. *Scientometrics, 115*(1), 1–20.

Loise de Morais Calado, S., Esterhuizen-Londt, M., Cristina Silva de Assis, H., & Pflugmacher, S. (2019). Phytoremediation: Green technology for the removal of mixed contaminants of a water supply reservoir. *International Journal of Phytoremediation, 21*(4), 372–379.

Lopes, D. B., de Oliveira, Y. M. M., Sampaio, M. J. A. M., FOGACA, F. d. S., de MELLO, L., de FREITAS, M., ... MOZZER, G. (2021). *Challenges and opportunities for Embrapa*. Retrieved from http://www.alice.cnptia.embrapa.br/alice/handle/doc/1131468

Lopes, M. A., Faleiro, F. G., Ferreira, M. E., Lopes, D. B., Vivian, R., & Boiteux, L. S. (2012). Embrapa's contribution to the development of new plant varieties and their impact on Brazilian agriculture. *Crop Breeding and Applied Biotechnology*, *12*(S2).

Lustig, N., Pabon, V. M., Sanz, F., & Younger, S. D. (2020). *The impact of COVID-19 lockdowns and expanded social assistance on inequality, poverty and mobility in Argentina, Brazil, Colombia and Mexico* (Vol. 558). Washington, DC: Center for Global Development.

Madeira, J. V., Jr, & Macedo, G. A. (2015). Simultaneous extraction and biotransformation process to obtain high bioactivity phenolic compounds from Brazilian citrus residues. *Biotechnology Progress*, *31*(5), 1273–1279.

Martha, G., Jr, Contini, E., & Alves, E. (2012). Embrapa: Its origins and changes. In *The regional impact of national policies: The case of Brazil* (pp. 204–222). Cheltenham: Edward Elgar Publishing.

Miranda, I. T. P., Moletta, J., Pedroso, B., Pilatti, L. A., & Picinin, C. T. (2021). A review on green technology practices at BRICS countries: Brazil, Russia, India, China, and South Africa. *Sage Open*, *11*(2). doi:10.1177/21582440211013780

Naimoğlu, M. (2022). The impact of economic growth, trade openness and technological progress on renewable energy use in Turkey: Fourier EG cointegration approach. *Ege Akademik Bakis*, *22*(3), 309–321.

Patton, M. Q. (1990). *Qualitative evaluation and research methods*. Newbury Park, CA: Sage.

Pereira, E. J. d. A. L., Ferreira, P. J. S., de Santana Ribeiro, L. C., Carvalho, T. S., & de Barros Pereira, H. B. (2019). Policy in Brazil (2016–2019) threaten conservation of the Amazon rainforest. *Environmental Science & Policy*, *100*, 8–12.

Qi, G., Shen, L. Y., Zeng, S., & Jorge, O. J. (2010). The drivers for contractors' green innovation: An industry perspective. *Journal of Cleaner Production*, *18*(14), 1358–1365.

Rajão, R., Soares-Filho, B., Nunes, F., Börner, J., Machado, L., Assis, D., ... Rausch, L. (2020). The rotten apples of Brazil's agribusiness. *Science*, *369*(6501), 246–248.

Rennings, K. (2000). Redefining innovation—Eco-innovation research and the contribution from ecological economics. *Ecological Economics*, *32*(2), 319–332.

Rodrigues, G. S., de Almeida Buschinelli, C. C., & Dias Avila, A. F. (2010). An environmental impact assessment system for agricultural research and development ii: institutional learning experience at Embrapa. *Journal of Technology Management and Innovation*, *5*(4), 38–56.

Salvador, R., Barros, M. V., Rosário, J. G. D. P. D., Piekarski, C. M., da Luz, L. M., & de Francisco, A. C. (2019). Life cycle assessment of electricity from biogas: A systematic literature review. *Environmental Progress & Sustainable Energy*, *38*(4), 13133.

Sambuichi, R. H. R., Kaminsk, R., Perin, G., de Moura, I. F., Januário, E. S., Mendonça, D. B., & de Almeida, A. F. C. (2019). *Programa de Aquisição de Alimentos e segurança alimentar: modelo lógico, resultados e desafios de uma política pública voltada ao fortalecimento da agricultura familiar.* (p. 59)

Sebele-Mpofu, F. Y. (2020). Saturation controversy in qualitative research: Complexities and underlying assumptions. A literature review. *Cogent Social Sciences*, *6*(1), 1838706.

Si, J., Marjanovic-Halburd, L., Nasiri, F., & Bell, S. (2016). Assessment of building-integrated green technologies: A review and case study on applications of Multi-Criteria Decision Making (MCDM) method. *Sustainable Cities and Society*, *27*, 106–115.

Sohag, K., Taşkın, F. D., & Malik, M. N. (2019). Green economic growth, cleaner energy and militarization: Evidence from Turkey. *Resources Policy*, *63*, 101407.

Suddaby, R. O. Y. (2006). From the editors: What grounded theory is not. *Academy of Management Journal*, *49*(4), 633–642. Retrieved from http://aomarticles.metapress.com/content/CRA0TWNT83U3T4GJ

Sun, Y., Lu, Y., Wang, T., Ma, H., & He, G. (2008). Pattern of patent-based environmental technology innovation in China. *Technological Forecasting and Social Change*, *75*(7), 1032–1042.

Troyano, M. C., & Martín, R. D. (2017). Poverty reduction in Brazil and Mexico. Growth, inequality and public policies. *Revista de Economia Mundial*, *45*, 23–42.

Ulucak, R. (2020). How do environmental technologies affect green growth? Evidence from BRICS economies. *Science of the Total Environment*, *712*, 136504.

UN. (2015). *Transforming our world: The 2030 agenda for sustainable development*. New York, NY: United Nations, Department of Economic and Social Affairs.

Vieira, F. V., & Veríssimo, M. P. (2009). Crescimento econômico em economias emergentes selecionadas: Brasil, Rússia, Índia, China (BRIC) e África do Sul. *Economia e Sociedade*, *18*, 513–546.

Walker, H., Seuring, S., Sarkis, J., & Klassesn, R. (2014). Sustainable operations management: Recent trends and future directions. *International Journal of Operations & Production Management*, *34*(5).

Walsh, I. J., & Bartunek, J. M. (2011). Cheating the fates: Organizational foundings in the wake of demise. *Academy of Management Journal*, *54*(5), 1017–1044.

Wang, C., Nie, P.-y., Peng, D.-h., & Li, Z.-h. (2017). Green insurance subsidy for promoting clean production innovation. *Journal of Cleaner Production*, *148*, 111–117.

WCED, U. (1987). *Our common future—The Brundtland report*. Report of the World Commission on Environment and Development.

Wicki, S., & Hansen, E. G. (2019). Green technology innovation: Anatomy of exploration processes from a learning perspective. *Business Strategy and the Environment*, *28*(6), 970–988.

Xia, D., Zhang, M., Yu, Q., & Tu, Y. (2019). Developing a framework to identify barriers of Green technology adoption for enterprises. *Resources, Conservation and Recycling*, *143*, 99–110.

Yin, R. K. (1994). *Case study research* (3 ed.). Thousand Oaks, CA: Sage.

Yin, R. K. (2008). *Case study research* (4 ed.). Thousand Oaks, CA: Sage.

Yin, R. K. (2013). Validity and generalization in future case study evaluations. *Evaluation*, *19*(3), 321–332.

Yin, S., Zhang, N., & Li, B. (2020). Enhancing the competitiveness of multi-agent cooperation for green manufacturing in China: An empirical study of the measure of green technology innovation capabilities and their influencing factors. *Sustainable Production and Consumption*, *23*, 63–76.

Zhu, S., & Ye, A. (2018). Does the impact of China's outward foreign direct investment on reverse green technology process differ across countries? *Sustainability*, *10*(11), 3841.

Chapter 6

Contributions of ML in Industry 5.0 to Sustainable Development

Mohammad Shamsu Uddin, Mehadi Hassan Tanvir, Md. Yasir Arafat and Jakia Sultana Jane

Abstract

Industry 5.0 is referred to the subsequent industrialization. The ultimate goal of this transformation is to enable manufacturing solutions through collaboration with man and machine which are more user-friendly and increase work quality in comparison to Industry 4.0. This will be accomplished through the consumption of the creative potential of human specialists in the creation of an industry with more efficient, clever, and precise machines. It is predicted that several exciting breakthroughs and apps will help Industry 5.0 in its plan to gain more productivity and supply personalized goods in an open system. On the other hand, Industry 5.0 has had a greater global and international renown from the very beginning of its existence. Machine learning (ML) technology, the Internet of Things (IoT), and big data will create a collaboration with people, robots, and other intelligent devices. Industry 5.0 continues to serve as an attractive driver for our society's workforce skills and young talent in search of purposeful professional lives. There are some challenges as well, such as working with advanced robots requires people to develop skills. People need to gain proper knowledge about collaboration with smart machines and the robot manufacturers industry. However, this ultimate overhaul is necessary for the industry to certify its reason as a solution provider for our society. These things will unquestionably ensure the long-term sustained development (SD) of any nation's economy.

Keywords: Industry 5.0; Industry 4.0; machine learning (ML); sustainable development goals (SDG); Internet of Things (IoT); blockchain

Fostering Sustainable Businesses in Emerging Economies, 87–107
Copyright © 2024 Mohammad Shamsu Uddin, Mehadi Hassan Tanvir, Md. Yasir Arafat and Jakia Sultana Jane
Published under exclusive licence by Emerald Publishing Limited
doi:10.1108/978-1-80455-640-520231007

Introduction

In any event, the origins of the idea of Industry 5.0 may be traced back to Germany, where it first emerged. At the trade fair that was held in Hannover in 2017 under the name CeBIT, Japan showed its claim vision for the end of the age of mechanical robotization, mechanical technology, and sharp fabrication. At that point in time, we referred to it as Society 5.0. It is said that the Japanese vision gave rise to the notion of Industry 5.0 as an improvement of the first concept with a greater proportion of humans, carrying trade value alongside robots. Industry 5.0 has a proper framework for achieving sustainable development (Maddikunta et al., 2022). It has the potential to go past Industry 4.0's for-profit-centric efficiency and development sustainability objectives such as individuals, socio-environmental supportability, and flexibility. The automation and digitization of processes are the primary priorities of Industry 4.0.

On the other hand, people and robots will collaborate in the same workplace in the 5.0 version of the industry (Are We Ready for MICE 5.0? An Investigation of Technology Use in the MICE Industry Using Social Media Big Data - ScienceDirect, n.d.). In addition to this, it should also emphasize the customer experience, hyper-customization, responsive supply chains, and on-site manpower (Identifying Industry 5.0 Contributions to Sustainable Development: A Strategy Roadmap for Delivering Sustainability Values - ScienceDirect, n.d.). Machines will be intelligent enough to carry out complex actions all by themselves, while also working together with people to help the task go by more quickly and effectively. It is not unusual for an unproductive trend to be promoted and encapsulated under the concept of "revolution" in logical conversation and in the mainstream media. The current application of the IoT and CPS to production lines, management of supply chain operations, and manufacturing have been dubbed "Industry 4.0" or "the 4th technological transformation." At this time, we are beginning to get closer to the Fifth Industrial Revolution. And despite the fact that Industry 4.0 and its revolutionary decentralization and interconnectedness are still operating at full speed, it is general knowledge that it will be inexorably superseded by Industry 5.0, the full integration of the social aspect of commercial activity and sophisticated systems (Paschek, Luminosu, & Ocakci, 2022). The combination of people and machines will blend the potential exactness of full mechanization with the basic and cognitive aptitudes of trade pioneers. Besides industry 5.0 will contribute to the following fields:

- It will create more job facilities.
- It will provide mass customization opportunities.
- More focus will be on customer satisfaction.
- It is the arrangement of a greener solution that centers on ensuring a normal environment.
- It will use predictive analysis to make more accurate decisions.
- The use of real-time data by machines will be ensured by automated production systems, which will also involve the participation of trained individuals.

As companies started to understand Industry 4.0, the Fifth Mechanical Transformation appeared on the scene. Industry 5.0 is taking control as a way to recognize that the industry must realize social objectives beyond employment and development, becoming a powerful provider of development, and so on. It is also adopting regulation as a way of recognizing that the industry must realize social objectives beyond work and progress. Industry 4.0 focuses not so much on the fundamental values of social rationality and supportability and on advances in internet technology and intelligence to expand generational skills and quality (Silvestri, Forcina, Introna, Santolamazza, & Cesarotti, 2020). This perception or suspicion is the foundation of the presentation of Industry 5.0 (Zonta et al., 2020). Therefore, the concept of Industry 5.0 provides a unique focus and emphasizes the need for exploration and development to strengthen business in its prolonged utility for humans while staying within the limits of the planet.

In point of fact, there have been a few conversations virtually on the topic of the "Age of Augmentation," which refers to a situation in which people and machines interact to the benefit of both parties before this official introduction of Industry 5.0 (Fino, Martín-Gutiérrez, Fernández, & Davara, 2013). Also, Bednar and Welch illustrated what they called "Smart Working" principles. The incorporation of contemporary technologies plays a vital role in Industry 5.0. In this chapter, we have discussed various emerging technologies, such as machine learning (ML), edge computing (EC), digital twins (DTs), collaborative robotics (CR), the Internet of Things (IoT), big data analytics, blockchain, and potential future 6G systems and beyond. In addition to something like this, we talk about the ways in which these technologies contribute to Industry 5.0.

The chapter focuses on the potential applications of these technologies in the future, for example, predictive maintenance, hyper customization, and cyber-physical cognitive systems (CPSs). We developed this chapter to show the contribution of ML in Industry 5.0 for sustained development (SD). We briefly present Industry 5.0, ML, and SD and the relation between all of these terms. The distinctions between Industry 4.0 and Industry 5.0 are not significant at all. The factors responsible for this difference are discussed in this chapter as well. We endeavored to investigate the role that ML plays in Industry 5.0 as well as its effects on the sector. After then, we spoke about the difficulties that would be presented by Industry 5.0, including how it will affect human existence and the aims of sustainable development. In the end, we attempted to offer a few introductions and analyzed the overall impact that Industry 5.0 has had on the new industry.

The Different Factors Between Industry 4.0 and 5.0

Industry 4.0 aims to increase mass production via the use of developing technology. Some of the technologies have been incorporated into the industrial sector as part of the Industry 4.0 standard (Fig. 1), which has resulted in an upheaval in that field. For example, artificial intelligence (AI), the IoT, cloud computing, CPSs, and cognitive computing. In parallel to this, it is planned to create the

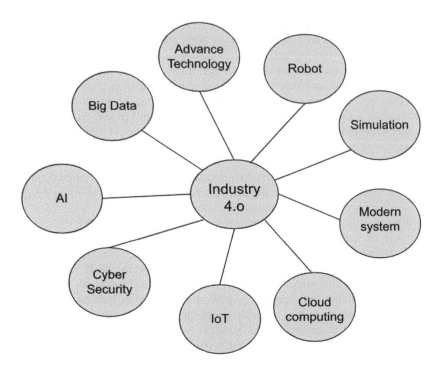

Fig. 1.   Contributions of Industry 4.0. *Source:* Author's original work.

industry more "intelligent" by integrating machines and other equipment that are capable of exercising control over one another during the product's entire life cycle (Zhong, Xu, Klotz, & Newman, 2017). The initial goal of the Fourth Industrial Revolution was to raise overall productivity and performance levels by distributing intelligence across devices and software programs utilizing ML. As a result of the rise in problems that industries face in the internet age, like market uncertainty and shorter product lifespans cycles as a result of rapidly shifting electronic needs, necessary changes of buyers, and the urgent need to manufacture wiser and more new products, manufacturers are under expanding pressure to produce products that are both intelligent and more creative (Khin & Kee, 2022).

   Accordingly, it is assumed that machines may be made more autonomous, communicate more effectively with one another, and keep tabs on their performance. Manufacturing companies and overall economic growth benefit greatly from 4.0 (Critical Components of Industry 5.0 Towards a Successful Adoption in the Field of Manufacturing, n.d.). Flexibility in production, mass customization, intelligent goods, higher quality, and higher productivity were some of the most often claimed advantages of Industry 4.0.

   In addition, the idea behind Industry 4.0 is also that electronics, advanced technologies, and intelligent machines can interact with their surroundings and make choices with little to no human intervention if they are capable of conversing with each other. But nowadays it has changed a lot. The incorporation of CPSs and the IoT into the manufacturing process as well as the connection of technology, people, and other systems are what set Industry 4.0 apart from its predecessor, Industry 3.0 (Critical Components of Industry 5.0 Towards a Successful Adoption in the Field of Manufacturing, n.d.). Technical developments such as adaptive robots, data analytics, artificial intelligence, cloud systems, 3D printing, and distributed systems are necessary for the transition to 4.0 (Aslam, Aimin, Li, & Ur Rehman, 2020).

On the other hand, to implement Industry 5.0, the important driving factors are efficiency and productivity. Manufacturing firms are considering adopting 5.0 because of the operational benefits as well as the market opportunities (Souza, Ferenhof, & Forcellini, 2022). According to the literature, businesses must concentrate on the person rather than the hurdles that increase 4.0 rollout because possibilities outnumber restrictions and hurdles may be overcome by people. Strong incentives for 4.0 adoption were also discovered in the literature, and they included strategic, logistical, economic, and cultural potential, as well as chances for new business models.

As such, numerous research studies have also found that state subsidy may favorably affect the choice to adopt 4.0 for enterprises that have the additional resources needed to execute 4.0 (Adel, 2022b). Nonetheless, organizations must be careful of the impediments to 4.0 uptake before making the right choice to begin on the 4.0 path. Studies have shown that moves toward 4.0 may be considerably hampered by problems related to profitability and future growth. We also identify three essential activities as the part that defines Industry 4.0 integration: education for employees, conducting research before beginning any Industry 4.0 program, and making frequent use of existing corporate data. Leaders may boost their likelihood of a successful deployment and subsequent company development by familiarizing themselves with any of these elements.

Industry 5.0, in contrast, combines the analytical and mental capacities of people with the rapidity and accuracy of modern technologies (Fig. 2). Another major advancement made possible by Industry 5.0 is global personalization, which allows consumers more leeway in selecting items that are tailored as per their preferences. With the help of Industry 5.0, people may focus on more intellectually demanding activities while robots do routine ones.

In addition, Industry 5.0 is primarily concerned with product variety, with workers-friendly machines. Users may acquire goods tailored to suit unique needs due to Industry 5.0. Such scientific age allows the sector to adhere to a standard production method. This promotes design flexibility allowing things to be further personalized through improving production rates. It also helps automation. The contemporary manufacturing industry's objective is to become more competent and efficient. With new technical breakthroughs, it reduces human contact in production. It tries to make zero contact, and it will play a crucial role in meeting customers' tailored needs. This revolution's various characteristics increase client happiness. Diverse ITs are utilized in Industry 5.0 to increase robot productivity, which in turn allows for less time and money in the operation.

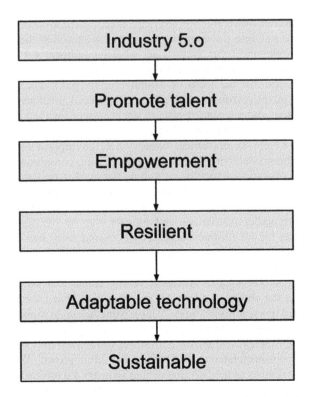

Fig. 2.   Contributions of Industry 5.0. *Source:* Author's original work.

On the other hand, mass customization gives way to vast customizing in this era, with a focus on meeting the needs of specific customers (Narvaez Rojas, Alomia Peñafiel, Loaiza Buitrago, & Tavera Romero, 2021). According to existing literature, the most notable change between Industry 4.0 and Industry 5.0 is indeed the increasing social contact that allows individuals more freedom of expression via the creation of unique merchandise and services. Because individuals are more involved in the imagination in Industry 5.0, users may receive more personalized goods and services. The precise ways in which Industry 5.0 will disrupt current industries are still unclear, but one thing is certain: it will eliminate the boundaries that separate the physical and digital worlds (Akundi et al., 2022).

In addition to this, the research indicates that for IoT and Industry 5.0 to function effectively, a breakthrough technology management structure is necessary. They also stressed that the IoT and Industry 5.0 need a framework for innovation management that is capable of striking a balance between the interests of businesses and customers, and also between the amount of availability and the degree of security. On the other hand, the emphasis of Industry 5.0 is placed more on the combination of human brain capacity and creativity with an eye toward longevity and dexterity. The IoT boom is what is driving the development of Industry 5.0, and it is anticipated that these two ideas will converge in the not-too-distant future.

These days, the frameworks of many sectors and marketplaces have been revolutionized, and as a result, new items (both commodities and services) that were never even conceived of in the past have come into existence. Due to this surge of the industrial revolution, the flexibility of goods is now possible, which means that a manufacturer may accommodate a client's specific personal preferences for goods at a price that is negligible or nonexistent to the consumer. In this way, Industry 5.0 offers clients more personalized merchandise and services than ever before. This is something that is only achievable with the greater participation of people in the creation of products and services, and it is a key element of Industry 5.0. An examination of the relevant literature reveals that a growing number of businesses are putting greater emphasis on the role of humans in their production processes in order to improve product customization and operational efficiencies. Businesses that adhere to 5.0 principles, on the other hand, should be mindful that transition does not occur immediately. The standardization of decision-making across job site workers is a major leap, but it has to be accompanied by supervisors who will evaluate and collaborate in the changing process.

Modern Technologies

The following step with the progression of the IR 4.0 required for the industry to be advanced fortified. Industry 4.0 rebellious, such as the web, digitization, blockchain, added substance fabricating, fake insights, swarm integration, robots, advancements in vitality, biotechnology, and virtual and upgraded reality are likely to alter (Xu, Lu, Vogel-Heuser, & Wang, 2021). The objective of this is often to examine and comprehend the past investigation on mechanical transformation. In expansion, this idea makes a conceptual system for Industry 5.0; at long last, the activity and implementation of an integrated Industry 5.0 demonstrate within the manufacturing industry.

Machine Learning (ML)

- ML is a subfield of AI that applies data to educate in a manner that is intended to be analogous to how humans learn, with the end objective of creating more complex outcomes. There is a long tradition of ML at IBM. When checkers expert Robert Nealey challenged an IBM 7094 computer to a game in 1962, the machine defeated him. This achievement seems small in light of current capabilities, but it was a major breakthrough in the development of AI.
- Recent decades have seen a meteoric rise in storage and processing power, allowing ML to be used in cutting-edge technologies.
- ML is becoming more important in the area of big data, which is growing at a fast pace. In information extraction, statistical approaches are used to train

systems for classification, prediction, and discovery. Then, these discoveries inform decisions inside apps and enterprises, which in turn affects crucial growth indicators. As big data continues to grow in importance, so too will the need for skilled data scientists. They'll need to help prioritize business issues and identify the information needs associated with those queries.

Edge Computing

- Using multiple data science architectures called "edge computing," data from end users is handled at the channel's side, as near to its point of entry as feasible.
- Cloud technology redistributes certain processing and storage resources away from centralized data centers and toward the objects or people who generate the data itself. Instead of sending raw data to a centralized data center, processing and analysis may take place closer to the point of origin, whether it is a storefront, a factory floor, a utility network, or a city's streetlights. Results from computations performed at the periphery, such as real-time trading data, hardware support predictions, or other notable replies, are often sent back to the main data center for human review and further processing.
- ERP systems may be made more responsive by locating them physically near the data frame via the use of sensor nodes and border computing, which is the main goal of edge computing. There are many advantages to doing business close to the origin of data, such as quicker insights, quicker response times, and more available bandwidth.
- The original goal of combining cloud computing with AI was to accelerate innovation through automation and increased insight from collected data. However, the ability of networks and infrastructure to handle the massive volume and variety of data produced by interconnected devices has been overwhelmed.
- Bandwidth and latency issues arise when all these data are transmitted from disparate devices to a single location in a data center or the cloud (Botton & Lee-Makiyama, 2018). By processing and analyzing data near its point of creation, edge computing is more efficient. Compared to sending data to a cloud or data center, this method drastically decreases latency. Faster and more thorough data analysis is made possible by edge computing, and mobile edge computing on 5G networks, opening the door to greater insights, quicker response times, and enhanced customer experiences.

Digital Twins

It is an identical digital copy of an existing physical object. A wind turbine, for example, may be outfitted with a battery of sensors to monitor its vitals and provide insight into its operation. Various operational data, such as energy production, temperature, and ambient variables, are gathered by such devices. These data are transferred and then utilized to update the backup version.

Dependent on the scale at which a product is being viewed, different digital twins exist. The primary distinction between these identical twins is their field of use. Multiple digital twins may coexist in the same system or procedure. Digital twins can be broken down into their smallest component, known as a "twin," which is the smallest example of a fully functional twin. An analogous concept, parts twins refer to similar but less crucial parts.

- *Paradoxical asset pairs*
  An asset is the sum of two or more parts that work together successfully. With the help of asset twins, you can analyze how those parts work together, statistical information which could be translated into advanced analytics.
- *Identical systems or units*
  System or unit twins provide a further level of detail, revealing the interdependencies between individual components of a larger whole. Understanding how your assets work together is made easier with the help of system twins, which can also suggest ways to improve performance.
- *Twin processing*
  The macro level of magnification offered by process twins elucidates the interdependencies of the various components that comprise a factory as a whole. How well do these systems work together, and how do delays in one system affect the others? Through the use of process twins, we can better understand the optimal timing schemes that shape efficiency.

Collaboration Robot

The term "collaborative robot" can be shortened to "cobot," which refers to an upgraded robotic arm that has been combined with cognitive capabilities that make it possible for the robot to engage directly with humans and work amicably alongside them. Cobots or the Fourth IR Performer play a significant role in smart manufacturing as both a byproduct of this movement and a significant player in its ecosystem (Vysocky & Novak, 2016). Cobots possess the following characteristics:

- They are able to connect with other cobots and computer systems, which results in an automated procedure that is more simplified.
- They include capabilities such as built-in vision and image processing, which enable them to recognize items and read barcodes.
- They are equipped with sensors that immediately stop any movement in order to prevent colliding accidentally with either humans or other machines.
- Manufacturers of collaborative robots, such as Techman Robot, are able to accommodate shifting requirements. The end effectors of our cobot are highly adaptable, which enables users to use it for a wide variety of tasks.

Collaboration, in its most basic sense, means "the action of working with someone to produce or create something," which is precisely what collaborative robots are meant to do. Common understanding holds that a collaborative robot is one that can operate in close proximity to humans without the need for fences. Okay, so now it's cooperative, but it's still not a team player.

There are many varieties of collaborative robots, but only one requires no additional safeguards to operate. Characterized by a focus on mechanical power, this type as it limits force, it can safely operate alongside humans in the workplace without any additional protections. Strange forces are being felt by the robot as it moves. Indeed, it is preset to shut down if it detects too much force being applied. One of the reasons why these robots are more spherical is so that they can dissipate force in the event of an impact on a broad surface. These robots' most distinctive feature is their capacity to sense and respond to forces at their joints. This equips them with the ability to sense any unnatural forces applied to them while they are at work. They can be made to slow down or even switch directions in these scenarios, reducing the severity of the initial collision. In the event of a collision with a human, they will be able to react quickly enough to absorb and dissipate some of the impact's energy.

IoT

To put it simply, the "IoT" is the concept of linking almost any device that has an on/off toggle to the web as well as other such gadgets (Singh & Singh, 2015). IoT refers to the global network of computers, mobile phones, and other electronic gadgets that can collect, process, and disseminate data concerning their use and environmental circumstances. Fitness tracking gadgets that analyze your pulse rate and steps over time and then prescribe a workout routine based on available evidence; smart heaters that can calculate how long to prepare food; ego autos that utilize complicated sensors to spot obstructions in their route. In fact, there are now "connected footballs" that can record data about how far and fast a ball is thrown, then be accessed later via an app for use in practice (Aslam et al., 2020). For example, if we own a car factory, for instance, we might be interested in sales data regarding the most popular aftermarket additions, such as leather upholstery or aluminum wheels. With the help of IoT technology, we will be able to: Install sensors to find out where in a showroom people spend the most time and which items get the most attention; determine which parts are selling the best by digging into the available sales data; keep popular items in stock by automatically adjusting for fluctuations in demand based on sales data. With the help of real-time data from my linked gadgets, we might efficiently and economically decide which components to restock with.

Big Data Analysis

Data might be in a number of formats (structured, semi-structured, or unstructured), have sizes (terabytes to zettabytes), and come from a variety of origins and all amenable to the sophisticated reporting tools that comprise big data analytics (Özdemir & Hekim, 2018). Creativity, commercial insight, pattern discovery, pattern discovery, statistical modeling, and data assessment are all steps inside the methodology. Raw information is what we refer to as data. In order to locate valuable information, draw conclusions, and provide support for decision-making, it has become necessary to check, clean, convert, and model data (Akundi et al., 2022). Analysis of large amounts of data is referred to by its acronym. Strategic planning, analyzing, and forecasting future events, as well as gathering corporate knowledge, may all benefit from its use. Due to their scalability, low cost, and ability to handle and retain the enormous volumes of data getting made right, open-source technologies like Apache Hadoop, Apache Spark, and the whole Hdfs ecosystem may be employed as a component of the big data approach. The big data tsunami has brought about fundamental shifts in the operation of several sectors. The demand to apply more complex analytics to it has evolved in tandem with the rise of big data. Now specialists may make judgments that are both more accurate and lucrative.

Blockchain

Durability, endurance, data storage, network congestion, integrity, atomicity, and visibility are just some of the difficulties that existing security solutions haven't been able to address since they've tended to concentrate on just a few areas (Understanding Blockchain Technology for Future Supply Chains: A Systematic Literature Review and Research Agenda | Emerald Insight, n.d.). One possible solution to the issues discussed above is to use blockchain-based (Fig. 3). Bitcoin is a distributed, immutable ledger that allows for the recording of transactions and the tracking of assets in a business network. Capital investments include things like homes, cars, cash, and property (intellectual property, patents, copyrights, branding) (Bodkhe et al., 2020). To keep track of and transact almost any asset with little cost and in a completely secure manner, blockchain technology is needed.

Data is the engine that drives the economy. If information can be received promptly and precisely, that's even better (Rupa, Midhunchakkaravarthy, Hasan, Alhumyani, & Saeed, 2021). It is particularly suited for supplying such information as it delivers an immediate, shareable, and entirely transparent list of selected on an immutable viewable only by subscribers of a trusted network. A blockchain ledger may be used to record transactions for everything from purchasing to manufacturing. Having consistent, up-to-date information available to all parties increases confidence, paves the way for more efficient processes, and may even create completely fresh industries.

6G Technology

It seems premature to start using the term "6G" when 5G networks are still being deployed and many parts of the world are still using 4G and even 3G networks. Technology advances relentlessly, and standards develop slowly, so we've always been headed in the direction of a 6G world. The fact that people are already discussing 6G networks before 5G infrastructure is even fully developed is a testament to how rapidly this industry evolves. After jumping from 1G to 5G in such a short amount of time, the next logical step in wireless connectivity speed is undoubtedly 6G. Every decade or so, a new mobile network standard emerges as the dominant one. In other words, most telecom companies will begin trial runs and we will start seeing teases of 6G-capable phones around 2030. It's possible that you'll hear about 6G before you even get your hands on a 5G phone because it's common for work to begin as long as a decade prior to any real implementation of a new network techno.

Uses of the Technology

Predictive Maintenance

Proactive maintenance is a type of assistance that particularly monitors a stock's well-being, state, and action in real-time. It is aimed at lowering prices, shocking problems, and allowing the company to schedule maintenance within their revenue vitality (Adel, 2022b). The most difficult difficulties in this area are the ability to predict the need for resource upkeep at a certain upcoming minute. It is feasible, which improves equipment failures, costs, management, and output quality. Although predictive maintenance strategies and their structure are important, Industry 5.0 is primarily concerned with tackling information ML and AI technologies to alter manufacturing routines.

Hyper Customization

When it comes to providing each customer with more relevant information on the products they purchase and the advantages they get, it makes use of both artificially intelligent insights (AI) and actual information. Industries are presently moving from a time of mass generation to a time of mass customization, where the essential center is to form a super-empowered customer. There are numerous ways to require this to begin with a step, but companies like Platform E, focused on the generation of digital twins and within the consultancy for this other way of generation, are as of now prepared to roll. Fabricating at scale comes about in productivity and higher efficiency. However, there are those customers who value the prized belonging and would appreciate their one-of-a-kind signature as a frame of self-expression. They'll offer personalized things utilizing different levels of program and 3D digital item creation capacities. They'll be able to give more customization options and create the items effectively and without any human mediation on the off chance that they've got a way to effectively deliver in little batches. Brands are expanding the benefits of 3D resources to offer an assortment of item combinations at point-of-sale, where clients are welcome to customize items to enjoy some time recently any physical thing is created. This methodology brings not as it were client engagement and fulfillment but moreover an increment in edges and transformations. Embed cash enrolls clamor.

Hyper customization can help an industry by:

- Reducing Cost.
- Workflow automation.

- Maximizing revenue.
- Dynamic pricing.
- Elevating customer experience.

It zeroes in on minute distinctions that may be used to target clients on a micro scale, while division creates groups of customers that share common likes, loathes, and activities. Companies have always employed customer segmentation as a component of their marketing strategies to increase the likelihood that customers will get messages and offers that are of value to them. Rather than using this strategy because it improved customer happiness, businesses should do it because it increases brand loyalty, consumer spending intent, and overall marketing efficiency. Based on the objective, hyper-personalization may be achieved in a variety of methods, including the use of algorithms, the integration of online and offline streams, the prediction of customer desires, the production of customized goods, and the supply of estimations. Fig. 4 shows an example of hyper-personalized marketing.

Cyber-Physical Cognitive Systems

Industry 5.0 aims to bring about a computer shift in the industrial sector via a distributed system of data repositories, workers, procedures, management structures, and power plants. Cyber-physical cognitive parts may generate, use, and exploit relevant data to render true, coordinated judgments (Edge Computing: A Survey - ScienceDirect, n.d.). Smart Manufacturing Systems (SMS) is the end outcome of this "cyber-physical transition." Cognitive capabilities refer to the ability of the human brain or Artificial Intelligence (AI) to perform mental tasks (such as awareness, observation, logic, and evaluation) necessary to complete a specific goal within specific circumstances. Certain cognitive tasks are taxing, distressing, and ultimately harmful to humans because tiring, risky, and difficult physical tasks can phase shift. Because these sorts of physical duties are ideal for automation, it stands to reason that certain rather difficult cognitive tasks should be automated as well (Leng et al., 2022).

Contribution of ML

The most important components of Industry 5.0 will be the usage of AI and ML for such cellular devices to ease manufacturing. All parts and foundation elements of a digital network, such as the hardware, protocol, and programing model, that we are now associated with from our understanding of mobile systems up to 5G, will require one or more AI/ML approaches. The fifth iteration of the factory output model, known as Industry 5.0, puts a premium on collaboration between people and automated systems. The tools that make this model feasible enabled the development of this concept. Intelligent machines are intended to cooperate with people, and this cooperative effort is what enables the machines to achieve their full potential. Automation has been an important contributor to the expansion of industry ever since the beginning of the First Industrial Revolution

(European Commission. Directorate General for Research and Innovation, 2020). Many different kinds and forms of automation have been implemented in various industries, such as assembly lines and robotic arms. The dream of a manufacturing process in which everything is handled by a machine has not yet been realized, but ML holds the promise of making that a reality in the not-too-distant future, probably in a short time. Utilizing intelligent machines to carry out individual tasks without any or minimal intervention from human workers is the definition of industrial automation. Because of this, the amount of time required to finish a task is cut down, along with the risks associated with human error and the amount of manual labor required, which results in a significant reduction in the cost of production while simultaneously increasing production itself (Mele & Magazzino, 2020). Its modification results in a large increase in income, which has a strong influence on the development of a firm as well as the extension of the market in general. The second decade of the twentieth century saw significant advancements in mechanization, which led to the production of products that were not expected or anticipated.

However, after reaching a high point in its development, mechanical automation came to a halt. Even though some advancements were being made, nothing of significant value appeared to be on the horizon. This was at the dawn of the Internet Age, which coincided with the beginning of a boom in the computer industry. Nobody could have predicted the magnitude of the influence that computing would soon have on the expansion of the industrial sector. ML allows for the production of industrial goods to be sped up, improved in reliability, and accomplished at a lower cost. This is accomplished by feeding massive amounts of historical and statistical data into the system, which is then compiled, analyzed, and utilized to develop knowledge about the enhancement of the production process. It is not a simple "plug and play" system but rather a detailed and laborious procedure that requires time but ultimately proves to be well worth the investment of that time. Businesses are able to maintain their position as aggressive players in the industry as a result of the enhanced speed of entry and decreased costs. This helps the firms to keep offering what consumers want, as well as even extra. Automation may also be used to research and comprehend consumer behavior in order to better understand customer needs and preferences and modify production appropriately. Toward that purpose, the unforeseen issues of employing ML in managing resources, resource transfers, information minimization, and network modeling are discussed.

Challenges and Impact on Human Life

The Challenges of Industry 5.0

Industry 5.0 is the latest phase of inventions made for sophisticated and effective machinery. Both human laborers and ubiquitous robots are contributing to an increase in the industrial sector's overall productivity. The executive teams are assigned to differentiate the production line by using technologies (Liu et al., 2020). Next, they are to monitor the critical performance identification and make certain that the procedures run smoothly. The production of robots, both consumer and commercial, will be an important focus for business in the years to come. Modern technology like AI and advanced analytics has led to an acceleration in the world of production and an improvement in the effectiveness of company operations. Industry 5.0 not only has advantages in the realm of manufacturing, but it also has advantages in the realm of sustainability, since its primary objective is the development of a stable solution that is powered by green sources. Yet, it is far simpler to ignore the possible difficulties that may arise with Industry 5.0. Because it is thought to be a new kind of manufacturing paradigm in which the emphasis is placed on the interaction between people and technology.

There are a few challenges in this sector (Fig. 3). In order to gain capabilities like dealing with autonomous technologies, laborers must first learn about intelligent devices and collaborate with the robot producer. Human employees have difficulties in gaining technical abilities. Challenging operations require a significant amount of technical expertise to handle new roles and automate machine coding and languages. But it will take more time to adopt new technologies. To modify the firm, they need customized software, collaborative robotics, real-time information, AI, IoT, etc.

Putting money into cutting-edge technology is essential. Users should expect to pay a fair penny for a UR Cobot. Expenditures on retraining existing human labor forces to do novel tasks are rising. Upgrading manufacturing lines to Industry 5.0 standards proved challenging for such firms. Implementing Industry 5.0 is costly since it necessitates intelligent machinery and extremely qualified workers to boost work quality. One of the key challenges is security for Industry 5.0 since confidence in communities is vital. Its scaling employed in the business for verification is the capacity to connect with different platforms and devices, to fight with real quantum software packages to install devices. AI is risky to businesses in Industry 5.0, thus they must be protected by trustworthy cybersecurity. Because Industry 5.0 initiatives are focused on IoT, strict safety requirements are crucial for preventing vulnerabilities. Humans collaborating with intelligent technology and machines is what Industry 5.0 implies. Robotic systems will accelerate human labor by utilizing splitting techniques such as big data analytics. However, without prior expertise, it might be challenging to handle the cooperation of AI and the cerebral cortex simultaneously.

Impact on Human Life

Robots will take on new meaning with the arrival of Industry 5.0. Robots will go from just being programed devices that really can carry out mundane duties to being the perfect human partner in certain settings. The next industrialization will usher in the next series of robots, popularly referred to it as cobots, that will either be programed to execute their jobs precisely or will be able to learn them very rapidly, bringing a more human element to robotic manufacturing (Demir, Döven, & Sezen, 2019). Due to the awareness of human presence, these autonomous robots will manage the prevention and risk standards. Apparently, supreme automation executive will be a whole new job title in the industrial sector, thanks to Industry 5.0 (Yin et al., 2020). One who can interpret the

Fig. 3.   Challenges of Industry 5.0. *Source:* Author's original work.

behavior of robots and how they could communicate with individuals is called a chief robot officer (CRO). The CRO will have the final say over which equipment and robots stay and which go on the production line in order to maximize productivity. In contrast, issues arising from the automation of operations formerly performed by humans will be addressed. People are no more required to undertake any activity that may be digitized, even the tedious, filthy, and boring work in the manufacturing system.

Industry 5.0 and Sustainable Development Goals (SDG)

Industry 5.0 acknowledges the ability of the economy to accomplish aims that extend beyond workforce development, to become a self-sustaining factor of growth. This may be done by ensuring that manufacturing takes into consideration our planet's restrictions and prioritizes well-being (Identifying Industry 5.0 Contributions to Sustainable Development: A Strategy Roadmap for Delivering Sustainability Values - ScienceDirect, n.d.). It gives a high level of importance to the well-being of workers and makes use of innovative technologies in order to generate wealth that goes above job creation and expansion while still taking into account the limitations of the earth. Employees are given more autonomy, and the ever-evolving expertise and education needs of the business are met; as a result, the company's viability is increased, and top talent is attracted.

As a result, the foundation of Industry 5.0 is indeed not science but rather concepts like sentient, industrial ecology, and the public good. This course correction is rooted in the belief that technology can be customized to inspire qualities, and that product advancement can be constructed on ethical goals, instead of the manner (Paschek, Mocan, & Draghici, n.d., p. 0). Specifically, this adjustment is based on the idea that morals can be encouraged through the use of new tech. To provide a brief overview, the notion of Industry 5.0 refers to an initiative that aims to transform the manufacturing sector into a more ecological, living thing, digitalized twins and modeling, and robust (Fig. 4).

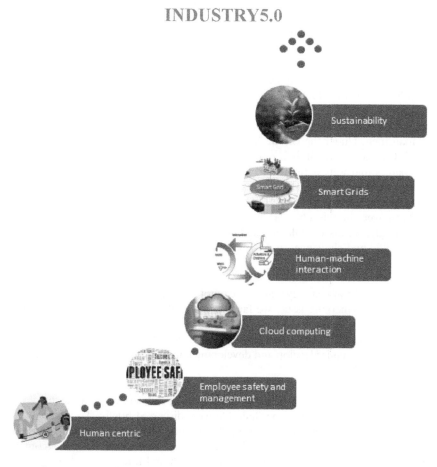

Fig. 4.   Sustainable Development Goal. *Source:* Author's original work.

Conclusion

In the chapter, we have discussed various factors of Industry 5.0 and the importance of modern technologies in incorporating Industry 5.0. The limitations of Industry 4.0 and the benefits of Industry 5.0 are discussed in detail. Learning approximately the Industry 5.0 concepts and the history of this term can in fact be to some degree befuddling, particularly since it tends to cover Industry 4.0, not fair in terms of advances and arrangements but moreover from the transient viewpoint. Industry 5.0 had more worldwide notoriety from the exceptionally starting (Nahavandi, 2019). The roots of this concept, in any case, can moreover be followed back to Germany. It was at the CeBIT 2017 exchange in Hannover where Japan displayed its claim vision for the long run of mechanical mechanization, mechanical technology, and keen fabricating. At a certain period, we referred to it as Society 5.0 (Adel, 2022a). It is said that the Japanese vision gave rise to the notion of Industry 5.0 as a development of the earlier notion with increased participation of humans, carrying trade value alongside machines. Industry 5.0 is an improvement of the original proposal. Later encounter of worldwide COVID-19 widespread and financial turbulence related to it is another eminent calculation that played a huge part in the rising ubiquity of Industry 5.0 as a modern innovation drift (Supply Chain and Logistics Operations Management Under the Era of Advanced Technology: Business & Management Book Chapter | IGI Global, n.d.). A huge supply of modern information from companies that were actualizing Industry 4.0 arrangements and practices – prior to and amid the COVID-19 crisis – shed light on numerous inadequacies of this concept and uncovered zones that clearly required change.

Moreover, in this chapter, we try to develop an outline of Industry 5.0; accordingly, we discuss related technologies, their contributions, their impact on human life, and challenges as well. However, this chapter has a few limitations, like:

- We didn't do any surveys. So, we cannot provide any empirical outcomes.
- As it is an emerging issue, we faced some challenges in the case of data and theory.
- We have seen that the implementation of modern technology is the biggest challenge for underdevelop and developing countries. As yet they cannot adopt Industry 4.0.

Finally, in this chapter, the positive elements of Industry 5.0 and the impact of technological advancements on daily life were discussed briefly. To adapt to the human-collaborative company setting of the future, our current understanding of machines will have to evolve. In addition, if Industry 5.0 is capable of overcoming its constraints, it will guarantee sustained growth and lead to even better future innovations. We firmly believe that this chapter will work as the foundation of the future study on Industry 5.0. It has practical significance to understand and for the adoption of Industry 5.0 in developed, and developing countries and provide a path way for the underdeveloped country toward sustainability.

References

Adel, A. (2022a). A conceptual framework to improve cyber forensic administration in Industry 5.0: Qualitative study approach. *Forensic Sciences, 2*(1). Article 1. doi: 10.3390/forensicsci2010009

Adel, A. (2022b). Future of industry 5.0 in society: Human-centric solutions, challenges and prospective research areas. *Journal of Cloud Computing, 11*(1), 40. doi: 10.1186/s13677-022-00314-5

Akundi, A., Euresti, D., Luna, S., Ankobiah, W., Lopes, A., & Edinbarough, I. (2022). State of Industry 5.0—Analysis and identification of current research trends. *Applied System Innovation, 5*(1). Article 1. doi:10.3390/asi5010027

Are we ready for MICE 5.0? An investigation of technology use in the MICE industry using social media big data—ScienceDirect. (n.d.). Retrieved from https://www.sciencedirect.com/science/article/abs/pii/S2211973622000563. Accessed on September 21, 2022.

Aslam, F., Aimin, W., Li, M., & Ur Rehman, K. (2020). Innovation in the era of IoT and Industry 5.0: Absolute innovation management (AIM) framework. *Information, 11*(2). Article 2. doi:10.3390/info11020124

Bodkhe, U., Tanwar, S., Parekh, K., Khanpara, P., Tyagi, S., Kumar, N., & Alazab, M. (2020). Blockchain for industry 4.0: A comprehensive review. *IEEE Access, 8*, 79764–79800. doi:10.1109/ACCESS.2020.2988579

Botton, N., & Lee-Makiyama, H. (2018). *5G and national security after Australia's telecom sector security review (Research Report No. 8/2018).* ECIPE Policy Brief. Retrieved from https://www.econstor.eu/handle/10419/202509

Critical components of Industry 5.0 towards a successful adoption in the field of manufacturing. (n.d.). doi:10.1142/S2424862220500141

Demir, K. A., Döven, G., & Sezen, B. (2019). Industry 5.0 and human-robot co-working. *Procedia Computer Science, 158*, 688–695. doi:10.1016/j.procs.2019.09.104

Edge computing: A survey—ScienceDirect. (n.d.). Retrieved from https://www.sciencedirect.com/science/article/abs/pii/S0167739X18319903. Accessed on September 22, 2022.

European Commission. Directorate General for Research and Innovation. (2020). *Enabling technologies for Industry 5.0: Results of a workshop with Europe's technology leaders.* Publications Office. Retrieved from https://data.europa.eu/doi/10.2777/082634

Fino, E. R., Martín-Gutiérrez, J., Fernández, M. D. M., & Davara, E. A. (2013). Interactive tourist guide: Connecting web 2.0, augmented reality and QR codes. *Procedia Computer Science, 25*, 338–344. doi:10.1016/j.procs.2013.11.040

Identifying industry 5.0 contributions to sustainable development: A strategy roadmap for delivering sustainability values—ScienceDirect. (n.d.). Retrieved from https://www.sciencedirect.com/science/article/pii/S2352550922002093. Accessed on September 21, 2022.

Khin, S., & Kee, D. M. H. (2022). Factors influencing Industry 4.0 adoption. *Journal of Manufacturing Technology Management, 33*(3), 448–467. doi:10.1108/JMTM-03-2021-0111

Leng, J., Sha, W., Wang, B., Zheng, P., Zhuang, C., Liu, Q., ... Wang, L. (2022). Industry 5.0: Prospect and retrospect. *Journal of Manufacturing Systems, 65*, 279–295. doi:10.1016/j.jmsy.2022.09.017

Liu, Y., Yuan, X., Xiong, Z., Kang, J., Wang, X., & Niyato, D. (2020). Federated learning for 6G communications: Challenges, methods, and future directions. *China Communications, 17*(9), 105–118. doi:10.23919/JCC.2020.09.009

Maddikunta, P. K. R., Pham, Q.-V., Prabadevi, B., Deepa, N., Dev, K., Gadekallu, T. R., ... Liyanage, M. (2022). Industry 5.0: A survey on enabling technologies and potential applications. *Journal of Industrial Information Integration, 26*, 100257. doi:10.1016/j.jii.2021.100257

Mele, M., & Magazzino, C. (2020). A Machine Learning analysis of the relationship among iron and steel industries, air pollution, and economic growth in China. *Journal of Cleaner Production, 277*, 123293. doi:10.1016/j.jclepro.2020.123293

Nahavandi, S. (2019). Industry 5.0—A human-centric solution. *Sustainability, 11*(16). Article 16. doi:10.3390/su11164371

Narvaez Rojas, C., Alomia Peñafiel, G. A., Loaiza Buitrago, D. F., & Tavera Romero, C. A. (2021). Society 5.0: A Japanese concept for a superintelligent society. *Sustainability, 13*(12). Article 12. doi:10.3390/su13126567

Özdemir, V., & Hekim, N. (2018). Birth of industry 5.0: Making sense of big data with artificial intelligence, "the internet of things" and next-generation technology policy. *OMICS: A Journal of Integrative Biology, 22*(1), 65–76. doi:10.1089/omi.2017.0194

Paschek, D., Luminosu, C.-T., & Ocakci, E. (2022). Industry 5.0 challenges and perspectives for manufacturing systems in the Society 5.0. In A. Draghici & L. Ivascu (Eds.), *Sustainability and innovation in manufacturing enterprises: Indicators, models and assessment for Industry 5.0* (pp. 17–63). Springer. doi:10.1007/978-981-16-7365-8_2

Paschek, D., Mocan, A., & Draghici, A. (n.d.). Industry 5.0 – The expected impact of next industrial revolution. In Thriving on future education, industry, business and society; Proceedings of the MakeLearn and TIIM International Conference 2019 (Vol. 8). ToKnowPress.

Rupa, C., Midhunchakkaravarthy, D., Hasan, M., Alhumyani, H., & Saeed, R. (2021). Industry 5.0: Ethereum blockchain technology based DApp smart contract. *Mathematical Biosciences and Engineering, 18*, 7010–7027. doi:10.3934/mbe.2021349

Silvestri, L., Forcina, A., Introna, V., Santolamazza, A., & Cesarotti, V. (2020). Maintenance transformation through Industry 4.0 technologies: A systematic literature review. *Computers in Industry, 123*, 103335. doi:10.1016/j.compind.2020.103335

Singh, S., & Singh, N. (2015). Internet of Things (IoT): Security challenges, business opportunities & reference architecture for E-commerce. In 2015 International conference on green computing and internet of things (ICGCIoT) (pp. 1577–1581). doi:10.1109/ICGCIoT.2015.7380718

Souza, R., Ferenhof, H., & Forcellini, F. (2022). Industry 4.0 and Industry 5.0 from the lean perspective. *International Journal of Management, Knowledge and Learning, 11*. doi:10.53615/2232-5697.11.145-155

Supply chain and logistics operations management under the era of advanced technology: Business & management book chapter | IGI Global. (n.d.). Retrieved from https://www.igi-global.com/chapter/supply-chain-and-logistics-operations-management-under-the-era-of-advanced-technology/297646. Accessed on September 16, 2022.

Understanding blockchain technology for future supply chains: A systematic literature review and research agenda | Emerald Insight. (n.d.). Retrieved from https://www.emerald.com/insight/content/doi/10.1108/SCM-03-2018-0148/full/html?casa_token=js7E9bsLtF8AAAAA:jmfBKb5cuXmRnPVe8wksrJdw4pFh2qRWgQllhZ lWYxCntnOT1uyGqtSufqlLTsYUEQwEXIoyvzCxkqloJG0P9tV5BuWD7KgWj q-j81PzhSt-kEp5eqfU. Accessed on September 16, 2022.

Vysocky, A., & Novak, P. (2016). Human—Robot collaboration in industry. *MM Science Journal, 2016*, 903–906. doi:10.17973/MMSJ.2016_06_201611

Xu, X., Lu, Y., Vogel-Heuser, B., & Wang, L. (2021). Industry 4.0 and Industry 5.0—Inception, conception and perception. *Journal of Manufacturing Systems, 61*, 530–535. doi:10.1016/j.jmsy.2021.10.006

Yin, Z., Zhu, L., Li, S., Hu, T., Chu, R., Mo, F., ... Li, B. (2020). A comprehensive review on cultivation and harvesting of microalgae for biodiesel production: Environmental pollution control and future directions. *Bioresource Technology, 301*, 122804. doi:10.1016/j.biortech.2020.122804

Zhong, R. Y., Xu, X., Klotz, E., & Newman, S. T. (2017). Intelligent manufacturing in the context of Industry 4.0: A review. *Engineering, 3*(5), 616–630. doi:10.1016/J.ENG.2017.05.015

Zonta, T., da Costa, C. A., da Rosa Righi, R., de Lima, M. J., da Trindade, E. S., & Li, G. P. (2020). Predictive maintenance in the Industry 4.0: A systematic literature review. *Computers & Industrial Engineering, 150*, 106889. doi:10.1016/j.cie.2020.106889

Chapter 7

Industry 5.0 – Its Role Toward Human Society: Obstacles, Opportunities, and Providing Human-Centered Solutions

Bhabajyoti Saikia

Abstract

The fifth industrial revolution, known as Industry 5.0, envisions an industry that is innovative, resilient, socio-centric, and competitive while minimizing negative environmental and social impacts, respecting people, the planet, and prosperity. Industry 5.0 is replacing earlier advancements and it is successful because it reaches the pinnacle of perfection. Additionally, machine work saves human workers time and effort. It is built on the concept of fusing digitalization elements from the fourth industrial revolution with Sustainable Development Goals through human-centric solutions, bio-inspired technologies, and secure data transfer. Industry 5.0 mentions about the various opportunities, constraints, and potential directions for future research. Industry 5.0 places less emphasis on technology and focus on human collaboration for progress, it supposed to have a shift in existing paradigm. Industry 5.0 is necessary in contemporary business with the paid technology advancements in order to get competitive advantages as well as economic growth for the manufacturing and it has three drivers: "green transition", "digital transition", and "competitive transition". The goal of green transition is to prevent climate change and environmental degradation. This necessitates changes to current economic growth strategies. The goal of digital transition is to support the circular economy by modernizing digital strategies in terms of digital skills, data, technologies, and infrastructure. Competitive transition aims to convert marketing policies, regulations, standards to increase people's prosperity and business value. It focuses on business and marketing rules that are fair, competitive, innovative, and adaptable.

Fostering Sustainable Businesses in Emerging Economies, 109–126

Copyright © 2024 Bhabajyoti Saikia

Published under exclusive licence by Emerald Publishing Limited

doi:10.1108/978-1-80455-640-520231008

Keywords: Human society; industry; solutions; sustainable development; technology advancements; transitions

Introduction

The first industrial revolution (Industry 1.0), which took place in the eighteenth century, brought about a significant change by allowing machines to make goods using methods and techniques that had been invented. By the end of the eighteenth century, it had spread to the United States after beginning in England in 1760. Industry 1.0 had an impact on sectors including mining, textile, agriculture, glass, and others as it signaled a transition from a handcraft economy to one dominated by machinery.

Between 1871 and 1914, the industrial sector saw a subsequent transition known as Industry 2.0, which facilitated the quick exchange of people and creative ideas. This revolution is a time of economic expansion and as company productivity rises, machines take the place of factory workers but as a result, unemployment rates got increased.

The digital revolution also known as Industry 3.0 began in the 1970s of the twentieth century as a result of the automation of memory-programmable controls and computers. This phase's focal point is mass production and the use of integrated circuit chips with digital logic; related technologies include computers, digital cellular phones, and the internet. In the world of business, technology has alternately played both role of the villain and the hero. Companies have had to contend with the prospect of either embracing a digital revolution or resignedly watch while rivals become stronger, faster, more efficient, and more prosperous, which has started for more than 10 years.

However, this embrace of digital technology, notably Industry 4.0 has had substantial good effects while occasionally replacing humans in the workflow process. As a silo unto itself, technology frequently accomplishes goals while putting people at bay and relegating them to less active and more analytical positions. The ability of businesses to align priorities to fully utilize new capabilities is being rapidly outpaced by the power of technology, necessitating the need for vision and advice to help put things into perspective. Making processes more human-centric is one of Industry 5.0's fundamental principles. The desire to allay labor union and political objections to automation stems in part from the belief that Industry 4.0 could lead to a crisis of technical unemployment.

Practically speaking, highly automated processes can produce an output that is extremely consistent and repeatable, but this does not solve the requirement to offer progressively individualized or customized items (as client expectations grow more complex). The European Union has placed a strong emphasis on sustainability and has made it a key component of policy. The European Union has pledged its full support to achieving all 17 of the Sustainable Development Goals of the United Nations, including increasing the use of renewable energy, reducing environmental impact, and advancing social objectives like the empowerment of women, especially in developing nations.

Sustainability as the foundation is the key goal of the Industry 5.0, whose vision is to counteract the usual increases in energy use and carbon emissions that come with increased industrial production. Increased energy efficiency, the use of clean energy sources, a focus on lowering pollutants and their negative effects on the environment, and the use of novel materials can all result in improvements. The idea of the "circular economy" in which materials and garbage are recycled to reduce any adverse effects on the environment is prominent, although this will require a great deal of future study and innovation. Given the dedication of the European Union and other parties interested in a more sustainable future, it is simple to understand why Industry 5.0 is viewed correctly as an evolution, merging key components of Industry 4.0 into a bigger vision that benefits a wider range of stakeholders.

Instead of concentrating solely on shareholder value, the mission is more expansive and is driven by the concepts of regenerative purpose and the transformation of industrial production. The human-centric worldview combines people and machines working actively together. As investors place a greater emphasis on environmental, social, and governance (ESG) aspects when making investment decisions, sustainability is becoming a larger concern for firms.

Herein lays the role of Industry 5.0. In order to advance the cause of human–machine symbiosis and ensure that the economic, environmental, and societal effects of digital transformation are held in the same respect as technological advancements, it was designed to build on the foundation created by Industry 4.0. Data is the fuel that drives an innovative industry. The enormous developments in connectivity, storage, and data analytics including cloud and edge-based systems are the cornerstones of every sort of global organizational endeavor not just business.

Traditional goods and business practices are changing as a result of technological developments. Technology is being converted to digital format thanks to the digital revolution. The loss of human touch has been observed in the industry as a result of digitalization and automation of setup. However, the goal of Industry 5.0 is to restore human intelligence to the forefront. It aspires to use human creativity, innovation, and judgment to mitigate the disadvantages of technology-driven industries. It has been observed that the industry driven by human technology collaboration outperforms the industry driven by either commodity. With Industry 5.0, it is time to think of employees as assets rather than liabilities. Industry 5.0 wishes to promote techniques that reduce the dangers to nature. The revolutions that preceded the fifth revolution never aimed to create a sustainable environment. Industries could be designed to generate as little waste as possible. Circular manufacturing and the use of renewable energy are other viable options. Smart materials and bio-inspired technologies must be promoted in tandem with this. The term "Industry 4.0" refers to the fusion of physical assets with cutting-edge technologies like AI, IoT, robots, 3D printing, cloud computing, etc. Organizations that have implemented Industry 4.0 are adaptable and ready to make decisions based on data. The upcoming technology of the previous generation known as "Industry 5.0" is made for effective and intelligent machines. Industry 4.0 technologies like the IoT, automation and digitization, cyber-physical systems (CPS), blockchain, additive manufacturing, artificial intelligence (AI), robotics, drones, virtual reality (VR), and augmented reality (AR) can support the Industry 5.0 vision by offering human-centric solutions and encouraging the strength of the human machine integrated system. Industry 5.0 is supported by for instance, intelligent materials with features for recycling and intelligent factories with energy-efficient automation techniques. The objectives of the fourth generation smart industry are being met and practices in that sector are being strengthened, as part of the socioeconomic development stage that is currently underway. The potential for ongoing growth of wealth and sustainable production and consumption are being scientifically examined and specified, while at the same time exposing flaws and limitations in the progress thus far. This perspective is taken to analyze and more precisely formulate how smart Industry 4.0 will affect the economy and society globally. The new Industry 5.0 development model outlines notable advancements in the automation, robotization, and digitization of hypothetical operations that promote economic growth with clear reserves and societal dangers.

Industry 5.0, as we know it now, incorporates this "human" touch and a number of subjects that are trendy right now. Resilience (both in business and in cyberspace), sustainability and the environment, purpose and values/ethics/diversity, circular economy, the role of people in a future of work with increased human–machine collaboration, human-centric solutions, and some technical issues are among these topics.

According to definitions of Industry 5.0, it is an innovative production model with a focus on interaction between humans and machines. It is concerned with maximizing collaboration among increased power and efficiency machinery as well as the innovative potential of humans. Existing projects on which Industry 5.0 is based involve the optimization of AI which results in customized products. This industry is being adapted to international standards. Industry 5.0 provides benefits to the industry as well as to the workers and society. There is also an increase in business competitiveness which helps attract the best talent. Adoption of this industry supports technologies that make proper use of natural resources. The return of the human element to systems and processes that have been automated to an extremely high level of efficiency through the use of information technology is possibly the most significant innovation of Industry 5.0. By enabling collaborative production, the human element in manufacturing in a sense, restores the soul of the industry. The capacity to use collaborative robots advances and empowers human workers' creativity and flexibility (*or cobots*). True "mass personalization" and more nimble production will be possible thanks to the collaboration of intelligent machines and astute humans. The shift to electric vehicles from fossil fuel-powered vehicles is quickening. At the same time, the use of wind and solar electricity is expanding because of the dropping cost curves and scalability in the production of batteries. The development of autonomous technology is expected to open up new economic opportunities for enhancing security and lowering pollution and transportation. The vision of revised Industry 5.0 will require new economic priorities to value, innovative business model structure and design and industry performance supply chains, current goals for digital transformation and innovative approaches to policymaking that better align the interests with business and industry also new ways to drive innovation and research capabilities, while better aligning the interests of businesses with broader society, government, and environment. Industry 5.0 can be correctly viewed as a development, combining key components of Industry 4.0 into a broader, all-encompassing vision that benefits a wider range of stakeholders which can be seen from the figure below (see Fig. 1).

When the world came to a halt as a result of the pandemic, society witnessed its negative impact. As certain businesses closed, there was a lot of strain on the common man's pockets, which led to the belief that there was a need for a sustainable society that could thrive through the difficult times. The goal of Industry 5.0 is to completely eliminate the 9–5 work culture. The idea is to use technology to reduce tedious and repetitive tasks performed by people so that they can work for the betterment of society. People should be given the opportunity to use their creativity and innovation to start a side business that will contribute to the growth and prosperity of society. As technologies help to connect and make setups more accessible, they are frequently vulnerable to various threats. The goal is to create setups that can withstand the system's drastic effects and if necessary adapt to sudden changes. As Industry 5.0 is considered to be value-driven, there are still some gaps that must be filled. Because their role is to create and innovate the unique product for customized personalized experience, the required manpower must be highly skilled in terms of technological advances. The creation of intelligent materials which would enable us to decrease the usage of nonbiodegradable materials that have a negative impact on the environment which does not receive enough research and development. The use of conventional energy sources has its own drawbacks and has been shown to have harmful consequences on the environment. Therefore, unconventional renewable energy sources must be used.

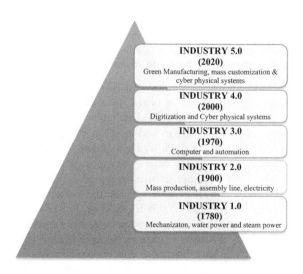

Fig. 1.   Industry Revolution From Industry 1.0 to Industry 5.0.

However, the necessary infrastructure and technology are not up to par, thus it is unable to enable the effective and efficient use of these energies on a broad scale.

Industry 5.0 – Justification and Advancement

Industry 5.0 creates a collaborative and automated working environment, changing the way businesses conduct their operations. Organizations now manage resources and capability differently, particularly in regard to people, culture and procedure while developing new business models. Prior research on creating innovation based on customer experience and organizational agility has mostly focused on the concept, relationships between factors and implications. Industry 4.0 focuses on adopting digital technologies including the IoT, big data, AI, blockchain, and cloud computing which mostly discusses digitalization. These technologies enable flexible and agile organizations to concentrate on the customer experience. Companies need to start considering the transition into Industry 5.0 when they are having trouble managing the new technologies and agility in Industry 4.0. Industry 4.0 and Industry 5.0 both continue to place a strong emphasis on technology but in order for these organizations to remain viable; they will need to develop organizational agility so that technology can be used to meet client demands.

Industry 5.0 Emphasizes Technology That is Human-Centered

The Industry 5.0 revolution indicates that humans and machines are collaborating to increase the effectiveness of industrial output. The manufacturing sector is becoming more productive, thanks to human labor and universal robotics. Each of the manufacturing company's executive teams must establish the production line which adhere to the KPIs and check that all of the procedures are carried out without a hitch.

Manufacturing of Industrial Robots and Robots is the Future of Industry 5.0

The development of cognitive computing and AI technologies is accelerating the pace of manufacturing and boosting organizational effectiveness. Industry 5.0 enables intelligent human community and collaboration, as well as intelligent technology to replace manual labor and routine chores while incorporating human creativity to improve the quality of goods and services and improve the consumer experience. Quality customer service, organizational agility, and customer experience work together to strike a balance between social progress and economic advancement. The challenge for the corporation to thrive and continue their operation in Society 5.0 is brought on by the shift in the societal paradigm. Thus, when the relationship between customer experience and business model can be made more effective, it becomes a source of competitive advantage. Industry 5.0 introduces a new paradigm for how businesses should operate. Through the interconnection of growing, interoperable information and communication technologies, the use of the IoT facilitates the collaboration shift from individual collaboration to society collaboration.

In addition to the advantages for the manufacturing sector, Industry 5.0 also has advantages for sustainability because it strives to create a sustainable system powered by renewable energy. The employees must properly engage with the machines and operators in order for businesses to implement Industry 5.0. It consists of expertise in areas like robotics and AI. Making judgments based on complex circumstances is the foundation of the corporate organization's function. Because production does not have to stop while employees receive training, firms must teach their employees via virtual education to cut costs. It offers safe training so that the employees won't be exposed to unnecessary problems throughout the training sessions. Interactive knowledge environments improve communication and staff motivation. Jobs that involve communicating with robotic and AI systems are available.

Robots that work in teams are being developed for natural human interaction. Technology in Industry 5.0 requires the expansion of digital twins. Better comprehension and testing will be possible with the use of visual models of the products, processes, and creation. The software necessary to propel the industrial company's change in Industry 5.0 is the Nexus Integra platform. It is a comprehensive solution for the extensive management of industrial assets that enables businesses to accelerate their digital transformation. In the past, people changed their habits to accommodate machinery. However, Industry 5.0 differs from all earlier solutions since humans are now at the focus of manufacturing processes. The release of any restrictions brought on by the nature of the internet and digital technology has been impacted by interconnection and interoperability, which has accelerated the growth of the smart society. Since the knowledge society is being recognized and incorporated into the online society enabled by technology, Industry 5.0 also has a positive impact by resolving social difficulties and fostering abundance for society. The long-term goal to support sustainable development shall be taken into consideration while measuring the transformation program's progress. The sustainable development factor in Society 5.0, which is the prospective performance originating from the technology and the ecosystem associated to society development, as well as current performance must be taken into account when measuring transformational performance.

Clarifications and Modernization

The phrase "Industry 5.0" describes workers who use robots and intelligent machines. By utilizing cutting-edge technology like big data analytics, robots will assist people in working more quickly. Industry 5.0 is referred to as the revolution in which man and machine are figuring out how to collaborate for increased manufacturing production efficiency and productivity. With the help of several industry technologists, philosophies, and others, Industry 5.0 is required to concentrate on the human elements and technologies in the manufacturing systems. Industry 5.0 is seen as the frontier of the intelligent factory, where it interacts with both humans and robots. Social networks are utilized for inter-human and interelectronic component communication. Human-centric, sustainable, and resilient ideas were introduced to the industrial revolution in Industry 5.0. By removing humans from monotonous jobs, it will transform production processes around the world. The supply chains for manufacturing as well as the production workflow will be significantly disrupted by intelligent robots. Customers' experiences have changed in Industry 5.0 from personalization of customization to mass customization based on societal growth and the development of technological platforms to increase the scale of product customization while providing freedom to the consumer. Using technology to gather accurate information and provide feedback to the business is crucial for decision-making. As a result, the use of big data to support the evolution of the customer journey in Society 5.0 has a huge impact on generating economic and social value which points out of experiences could supply different firm capability with technology capability. Since humans are the center of invention in Industry 5.0, collaboration between technology and people is emphasized. As a result, Industry 5.0's organizational agility was centered on people as the source of agility. The adaptability of the company to change its strategic direction to fit with its core business in order to create value could be characterized as organizational agility.

Key Features of Industry 5.0

Due to its maximum level of perfection, Industry 5.0 is replacing earlier advancements, and it is a successful process because machine work saves human workers' time and effort. A few features inspire corporate organizations to deploy Industry 5.0 despite the difficulties. For instance, in the medical field, experts are pursuing the development of a synthetic pancreas. This project is still in its early stages. Patients who have been diagnosed with Type-1 diabetes have been given a monitoring device that measures their blood sugar levels. The ability to release insulin into the body is provided by a separate device that is coupled to this one. In terms of offering a dependable and practical control system for the patient, this is one of the innovative technologies that has been developed and customized for patients. Industry 5.0 is bringing this personalization to the next level by enabling doctors to give their patients an application to download on their smart phones, allowing for their lifestyle and daily routine to be tracked and a personalized treatment plan to be created for them. Given that the technologies being used are based on AI systems, this could drastically alter the lives of people with Type 1 diabetes. These AI systems have the capacity to comprehend and learn the many bodily reactions and respond appropriately. The fundamental goal of Industry 5.0 was to reintroduce the human touch into development and production. This partnership between humans and robots will make difficult activities much easier to complete and introduce a high level of control. Long-lasting and very valuable careers will result from this relationship. This partnership ensures that the flow, quality, and data collecting are consistent. The Internet of Everything can be seen of as an extension or growth of the IoT because it stresses both machine-to-machine and machine-to-person communication in addition to machine-to-machine communication. It also emphasizes interpersonal communication, which is enabled by technology. Cisco was the company that first popularized the idea of the "Internet of Everything" which brings together people, process, data, and things to make networked connections more relevant and valuable than ever before-turning information into actions that create new capabilities, richer experiences, and unprecedented economic opportunity for businesses, individuals, and countries.

As it needs effective monitoring and maintaining of failures in smart equipment, predictive maintenance is essential for smart sensors, IoT, and customized software. The equipment will undoubtedly malfunction, but a maintenance schedule will prevent it.

Sustainability

Industry 5.0 promises to use resources that are tailored to the current needs of the manufacturing industry. Human–machine collaboration results in flexible business models. Waste and overproduction must be reduced in order to be eliminated. Local production, in conjunction with new efforts, ensures economic sustainability (Fraga Lamas, Lopes, & Fernández Caramés, 2021; Majumdar, Garg, & Jain, 2021). Corporate technologies are changing the trend with Industry 5.0. It leads to the emergence of sustainable policies, such as waste minimization and management, which can increase the effectiveness of businesses. Industry 5.0 is designed to be applicable by focusing on creative research and putting knowledge at the forefront of the evolution. It is distinguished by a determination that goes beyond simply producing goods for profit. Sustainability, human-centricity, and resilience are the fundamental principles of Industry 5.0.

Human Efficiency and Productivity

In terms of human efficiency and productivity, Industry 5.0 with the help of the most advanced technologies, it is helping people return to the production center. People focus on creativity and efficient business solutions while collaborative robots perform repetitive and dangerous tasks. The skills lead to an increase in business productivity, as people are more motivated to do the work and see the results. A human-centered methodology prioritizes human needs over manufacturing processes. Producers must recognize what technology can do for people and focus on how technology can adapt to the needs of workers rather than the other way around. It is critical that technology address issues of autonomy and privacy.

Control of the Environment

Smart, networked sensors and specialized software offer a real-time, predictive picture of the weather, temperature, energy use, and other factors. Loss prevention and increased output are beneficial for commercial organizations. Iterative processes for asset recovery, recycling, and repurposing must be improved for the manufacturing process to remain sustainable. Reduced environmental influence is required. Utilizing cutting-edge technologies, such as AI, sustainable producers can increase personalization while reducing waste and maximizing source productivity.

Efficiency of the Production Line Forecast

Industrial automation, machine learning (ML), and smart and networked equipment are predicting the production efficiency based on current activities. It improves operational effectiveness since processes are modified in accordance with the criteria to prevent losses. To strengthen and protect their industrial production against disruptions and disasters like COVID-19, manufacturers must increase production resilience.

Creativity

Technology advancements are not enabling a level of personalization that can satisfy client desires. Industry 5.0, which may take advantage of the potential of the technology, includes personnel. It looks for ways to offer fresh concepts that might result in product development with customization in mind.

Innovations and Modernization

The fourth industrial revolution was primarily concerned with the development of interconnected systems capable of complete automation. In a nutshell, the core value of Industry 4.0 was to use technology to boost production and profits. The fifth revolution, on the other hand, focuses on the same things, but the principles or pillars are flipped on their heads to focus more on achieving sustainability, resilience, and putting humans at the center with the help of technologies. The industries should be value-driven, with profits as a by-product. Industry 5.0 does not seek to be the next chronological revolution, but rather to coexist with Industry 4.0.

Industry 5.0 is developing across a variety of industries, including healthcare, manufacturing, textile, education, and food. As for example, a woolen pavilion with a robot hand created by a partnership of the companies discusses the items. The product in question is the KR 500 FORTEC robot. It can carry out a variety of carpentry activities, including moving the parts, putting adhesive down, and allowing the robots to work together. The majority of sectors are transitioning to the smart social factory by embracing Industry 5.0. A Repsol project on intelligent management was chosen to help in understanding the ideas of Industry 5.0. To increase its security and productivity, the company uses robotic process automation and blockchain technologies. The automated guided vehicle is Repsol's first cobot to perform logistics tasks like garbage deposition, raw material transportation from a warehouse, and lab visualization. Repsol is carried out on the Block Lab project, where the company is sending private information via the blockchain. The project manages 10,000 samples appropriately each year and is intended to streamline the safety issue samples.

Some of the Creative Applications Under Industry 5.0

Smart Hospital

The goal of Industry 5.0 is to build a real-time, intelligent hospital. In the field of healthcare, technology can offer remote monitoring systems. It is essential to improving the quality of life for doctors. During the COVID-19 pandemic, clinicians can concentrate on infected patients and give effective data for better treatment by using this smart healthcare technology. The COVID-19 outbreak aids both students and medical students in obtaining the necessary medical training. Medical imaging, natural language processing, and genetic data are all used in ML applications. It is concentrated on disease diagnosis, detection, and disease prediction.

Industry 5.0 enables proper production of the tailored smart implant in accordance with changing customer requirements. The measurement of numerous issues, such as glucose levels, is heading toward AI technologies in the medical field. By making implants in accordance with the patent match, which are the initial necessities for orthopedics, it aids in the implementation of mass personalization. Even the typical process for creating patient implants has changed, and it is now capable of modernizing a number of instruments and medical devices. The employment of technology is a revolution because they enable accurate surgical execution. Medical students benefit from better teaching, learning, research, and expansion processes. In orthopedics, Industry 5.0 necessitates high-quality, long-lasting implants that are personalized. It aids in the resolution of various issues such as overproduction, improper tool selection, and a lack of transparency.

Manufacturing Sector

Industry 5.0 is a new production model that emphasizes interaction between humans and machines. Industry 5.0 is concerned with leveraging collaboration between increasing precision machinery and human ingenuity. Manufacturing processes that repurpose and recycle resources are being developed to make it more sustainable. Reduced environmental impacts in the manufacturing industry are also required. To maximize resource efficiency and waste, additive manufacturing is required to increase personalization. Industry 5.0 is transforming manufacturing systems around the world by removing repetitive tasks from human workers where intelligent robots and systems are penetrating supply chains and manufacturing shop floors to unprecedented levels.

Designers are allowed to locate manufacturing plants near raw materials and in areas with low manufacturing costs. Cloud manufacturing will handle machine control in the plant as well as manufacturing lifecycle operations. The service-oriented model assists manufacturing in integrating production capabilities with services in order to provide appropriate solutions to clients. Adding service factors to the manufacturing process aims to improve production efficiency, value-added, and market share for the manufacturing business. The cloud-based platform manages manufacturing services and is used in a cost-effective manner. Cloud manufacturing is a networked system with distributed production resources (Deepa et al., 2022).

Supply Chain Management

The importance of collaboration among smarter machines such as cobots and humans is highlighted in supply chain management. Industry 5.0 aims to meet customers' hyper-personalization and hyper-customization needs, which necessitate a combination of human originality and machine competence. Robots are needed for supply chain management in standardized procedures at high production volumes, and this is a challenge where the robots require proper guidance.

Products can be personalized and customized without a human touch. However, it also makes sure that the supply chain's end-to-end operations run smoothly, including choosing the raw materials after understanding the needs of each customer's unique personalization and customization. Industry 5.0 aims to combine the human touch with automated and intelligent digital ecosystems. In a process like this, the human factors are leveraged to help customize end-user experiences and create efficient operations (Longo, Padovano, & Umbrella, 2022).

Hyper-personalization is made possible by empowering human intellect with cognitive computing and intelligent automation. Technologies like ML, robotic automation, and others are assisting staff members in developing their business acumen and speeding up the delivery of high value to clients. The ERP system controls the supply chain for the company organization, including raw material delivery, transactions, and transportation. The technology to support the digital supply chain is being created and implemented by the next generation of supply chain solutions. It entails introducing personalization into the supply chain, raising customer happiness, and managing corporate productivity and profit margins. The risks associated with the supply chain and waste are reduced and that there has been an improvement in supply chain integration for strategic partnerships, allowing supply chains to spend more time on experimentation and less time on fighting forces on project executions.

Technologies of Industry 5.0

Cloud computing, blockchain, big data analytics, IoT, and 6G networks are examples of enabling technologies for Industry 5.0.

Cloud Computing

Cloud computing refers to the delivery of computing services such as databases, software, intelligence analytics, networks, and so on. This technology provides efficient innovation as well as large-scale economics. This technology makes use of the internet to store and manage data on remote servers, which are then accessed via the internet. It provides on-demand computing services such as applications, storage, and processing power. The industrial cloud is a virtual environment that serves as a platform for industry applications. Cloud providers are developing applications such as IoT monitoring tools for mobile and web use. The cloud also allows for the use of APIs to automate data normalization from various data production sources. Devices that handle edge computing are supplied with constrained computing resources to manage business analysis.

A scalable infrastructure is offered by cloud computing to accommodate data edge devices. The edge of IoT platforms are supported by cloud infrastructure. The platforms are being utilized to control the edge devices, including diverse and autonomous shop floor robots. The industry often accesses the data from the local servers in order to manage crucial data. The amount of data delivered to the centralized server can be decreased thanks to Industry 5.0. Through the use of more workforce and preventive data, cloud computing enables the detection of machine faults.

Collaborative Robots

The goal of Industry 5.0 is to restore the human touch to development and production. It provides human operators with robot benefits such as technical precision and heavy lifting capabilities. Humans have a high ability to perform critical tasks, allowing for the implementation of a high degree of control and the ability to individualize the production phases. One of the major implications of collaborative robotics and Industry 5.0 is the need for human inputs to extend existing iterations. Collaborative robots, as well as Industry 5.0, represent a new era in robotics and manufacturing. Industry 5.0 and cobots are the beating heart that can combine human creativity and craftsmanship with the efficiency and consistency of robots. People-centric products and specialist skills are becoming more widely available. The goal of Industry 4.0 is to ensure consistency in quality and data collection. Industry 5.0, in contrary, focuses on using highly qualified workers along with robots to produce customized goods for consumers, such as smart devices and cars. With Industry 5.0, robot collaboration has begun. While experienced humans are given the cognitive skills of the craftsperson, collaborative robots are capable of heavy lifting and ensuring uniformity. Robots are transforming the way that humans and machines interact in the framework of production, which is to be expected (Pathak, Kothari, Vinoba, Habibi, & Tyagi, 2022).

People working with robots and smart machines are referred to as "Industry 5.0." Robots are assisting humans in their work by utilizing advanced technologies such as the IoT. It gave industry 4.0 a human touch for automation and business efficiency. It is defined as a network of physical objects and things that have sensors, software, and other technologies embedded in them. It is a method of connecting and exchanging data with devices and systems via the internet. IoT is a new paradigm that will change the traditional way of living in the high-tech lifestyle. Through IoT, research is being conducted to improve advanced technologies.

Even IoT is regarded as a means of providing effective solutions to data and information security issues. As a hot topic among IoT developers, there is the development of secure interaction among social networks, as well as privacy issues. Because it includes smart homes, the smart city is regarded as an important area for IoT. It includes IoT-enabled home appliances, heating systems, security systems, and other systems that communicate with one another to provide better comfort and save energy.

The issues in IoT are authentication and access control; these are required to have promising solutions to have strong security. To reduce the loss of sensitive data, a solution to verify communication parties is required. It includes an authentication scheme and verifies various security threats, such as man-in-the-middle attacks, against the key security controls. The proposed authentication and access control approaches aid in providing authenticity and confidentiality while reducing end-to-end latency in IoT-based communication networks. It is a flexible approach for data-centric applications on cloud platforms.

Big Data Analytics

Industry 5.0 is a cutting-edge technology that enables the use of 3D symmetry in the design of innovation ecosystems. Big data analytics is a complex procedure for examining big data to uncover data such as hidden patterns, market trends, and others. It employs a sophisticated analytic method with a wide range of data sets, including structured and semi-structured data. It has massive data sets that must be stored and processed using traditional tools. It is used as real-time data to improve the business industry's competitive advantages, with a focus on providing possible recommendations on predictive discovery. Big data analytics is used to detect discrepancies while the organization employs a list of the underlying causes of the problems. The majority of businesses rely on big data analytics to make strategic decisions. The company gathers information about customer preferences by utilizing various factors such as population, location accessibility, and others. Customer experiences are improved by monitoring customer experiences and addressing problem solutions in order to build strong customer relationships. When detailed information on the manufacturing cycle is not gathered, even big data poses a challenge for Industry 5.0.

Big data has gained a lot of attention in academia and industry as it moves from Industry 4.0 to Industry 5.0. Big data is a diverse and large collection of information gathered from various sources. Big data technology is used in AI, ML, data fusion, data mining, and a variety of other data analysis techniques. Many industries use big data analytics in Industry 5.0 to optimize product prices, increase productivity, and reduce overall costs because it allows them to easily understand consumer behavior. Big Data Analytics, with its available resources, aids in the creation of mass customization processes. Continuous process improvement is a critical challenge because it necessitates detailed knowledge of the manufacturing cycle.

Blockchain

It is a decentralized and distributed technology in which the digital ledger contains records called blocks that are used to record transaction data. It is a shared ledger that can help with transaction recording and asset tracking in a business network. The information drives the business. As a result, blockchain technology delivers data by storing shared and complete information in an immutable ledger that network members can access. Customers benefit from blockchain technology by tracking orders, payments, production, and so on. To avoid duplication of efforts and records in the database system, network participants keep distributed ledger records of transactions. A smart contract is recorded on blockchain and is intended to be carried out automatically to speed up transactions. It is described as company policies, such as those governing paid travel insurance. In order to strengthen the verification of earlier blocks, the transactions are to be blocked in irreversible chains. This is how a blockchain transaction is completed. For the firm to verify the transactions that are recorded, data accuracy is necessary. Time wastage is reduced with the distributed ledger since network participants share.

Introduction of 6G and Beyond

It's a sixth-generation standard for creating wireless communication tools that can support cellular data networks. It is expected that 6G organizations would exhibit much more heterogeneity than their forebears. They will likely support applications that go beyond the existing portable use scenarios, such as VR and AR, omnipresent instant correspondences, and unavoidable IoT knowledge. With local authorization, range sharing, framework sharing, and intelligent automated administration supported by flexible edge processing, AI, short-parcel communication and blockchain advancements, flexible organization administrators will typically embrace adaptable decentralized plans of action for 6G. 6G networks are anticipated to give ultra-high reliability for Industry 5.0 by meeting the norms of the intelligent information society. To assure network connectivity, AI techniques are applied to obtain mobility prediction solutions (Fraga Lamas et al., 2021; Majumdar et al., 2021). High data rates for numerous applications were a problem for Industry 5.0. Energy management is a concern for Industry 5.0 as more and larger smart devices are connected. Through the use of energy consumption and energy harvesting techniques, energy management can be optimized.

Industry 5.0 and Its Challenges

It is simpler to disregard the possible difficulties with Industry 5.0. The issues that must be resolved for Industry 5.0 developments to be successful for the business are now being recognized. People must acquire competency skills in order to work with sophisticated robots, and they must learn how to collaborate with robot and smart machine manufacturers. In addition to the soft skills needed, human workers often face difficulties learning technical skills. In the new jobs, managing translation and programing industrial robots are challenging duties demanding a high level of technical expertise (Angelopoulos et al., 2022).

The use of cutting-edge technology demands greater time and effort from human workers. Industry has to adopt collaborative robotics, AI, customized software-connected manufacturing, real-time data, and the IoT. Investments in cutting-edge technologies are necessary. UR cobot is not economical, it requires large amount of capital. The expense of training human workers for new jobs has increased. It has proven challenging for businesses to modernize their production lines for Industry 5.0. Because smart machines and highly skilled workers are needed to boost production and efficiency, adopting Industry 5.0 is expensive.

Confidentiality is a challenge for Industry 5.0 because trust in ecosystems is critical. The scale to interact with various devices is used in the industry to stand against future quantum computing applications to deploy IoT nodes. AI and automation in Industry 5.0 pose risks to the business, necessitating the use of trusted security. Because Industry 5.0 applications are focused on information and communication technology (ICT) systems, strict security requirements are required to avoid security challenges.

Technology acceptance and trust in technologies are critical. Technology adaptation to humans coincides with training people who use new technologies. Security, privacy, a lack of skilled workers, a time-consuming process, and a large budget are all current challenges. Adoption of Industry 5.0 is required to comply with industrial laws and regulations that can aid in the collaboration of smart machines and cobots (Angelopoulos et al., 2022; Pathak et al., 2022). Cognitive computing, human–machine interaction, and quantum computing are three future Industry 5.0 directions.

Industry 5.0 – Its Prospects for the Future

Using of cognitive computing which aims to convert human thoughts into a computerized model. Using self-learning algorithms, data mining, pattern recognition, natural language, and other techniques are used to simulate how the human brain works. Human–machine interaction refers to communication between humans and machines via a user interface. Gestures, for example, are used to attract attention because they allow humans to control machines through intuitive and natural behaviors. It is the Industry 5.0 future direction because it helps to keep humans at the center of the system and technologies to build in. Even the user interface aids in understanding people's actions and motivations.

Quantum computing is a type of computation that uses collective properties of quantum states to perform calculations, such as interference entanglement. Quantum computations are performed by the devices, which are referred to as quantum computers. It performs calculations based on the probability of the object's state before measuring it.

Conclusion

The mission of Industry 5.0 is to ensure that technologies and innovations benefit humanity. Following the recent COVID-19 pandemic, Industry 5.0 is required to concentrate on industry and technology resilience and sustainability. The global economic crisis has demonstrated that industry, innovation, and technology remain vulnerable. To address this weakness, Industry 5.0 solutions are expected to improve the resilience and robustness of industries and technologies. Workplaces and technologies must provide safety, security, and integrity. Identifying skill gaps and providing multiple training sessions is essential and necessary for businesses when implementing new technologies and the development of machine-human workplace integration. It has become common knowledge that change is a constant for businesses in all sectors, and companies must plan how to make sure their value chains can withstand disruptions and that there is a large enough, well trained workforce to meet demand for production, sales, and support.

The importance of talent management, and in particular the necessity to recruit and keep highly trained individuals, is highlighted by the "great resignation" wave, in which workers are quitting their employment at record rates and it is difficult to fill unfilled positions. The importance of resilience is highlighted by rising trade protectionism, overburdened shipping chains, and shortages of essential parts and supplies. Rising societal priorities increased legislative emphasis on clean energy, and increased attention to ESG considerations by the investment community are all appealing organizations to articulate sustainable strategies. In other words, a number of forces are pressuring forward-thinking businesses to include Industry 5.0 ideas in their strategy. Businesses must assess their resource footprint in light of the increasing regulatory and investor attention on decreasing carbon emissions and environmental effect. Analyzing the source of raw materials, the amount of waste produced, the environmental impact, the energy efficiency of operations, and the energy sources may all be part of this. Numerous businesses have made particular commitments to reduce their use of fossil fuels and switch to clean energy sources.

In addition, switching from petroleum-based materials to novel composites can lessen environmental effect, while promoting recycling and material repurposing activities can also aid in achieving goals. Although preparing for Industry 5.0 is important, there are several factors at work to push companies to adopt the fundamental values of human-centricity, resilience, and sustainability. Instead of reacting to an unexpected shock to the system, it is much preferable to seize the chance to get ready in advance. The technology-enhanced slogan Industry 5.0

promises to guide the next generation toward a balance of choices that promote smarter, greener, and more resilient industries. It goes beyond better, cheaper, and faster.

References

Angelopoulos, A., Michailidis, E. T., Nomikos, N., Trakadas, P., Hatziefremidis, A., Voliotis, S., & Zahariadis, T. (2022). Tackling faults in the Industry 4.0 era—A survey of machine-learning solutions and key aspects. *Sensors, 20*(1), 109.

Deepa, N., Pham, Q. V., Nguyen, D. C., Bhattacharya, S., Prabadevi, B., Gadekallu, T. R., & Pathirana, P. N. (2022). A survey on Blockchain for big data: Approaches, opportunities and future directions. *Future Generation of Computer Systems, 113*(10), 1–20.

Fraga Lamas, P., Lopes, S. I., & Fernández Caramés, T. M. (2021). Green IoT and edge AI as key technological enablers for a sustainable digital transition towards a smart circular economy: An Industry 5.0 use case. *Sensors, 21*(17), 5745.

Longo, F., Padovano, A., & Umbrella, S. (2022). Value-oriented and ethical technology engineering in Industry 5.0: A human-centric perspective for the design of the factory of the future. *Applied Sciences, 10*(12), 4182.

Majumdar, A., Garg, H., & Jain, R. (2021). Managing the barriers of Industry 4.0 adoption and implementation in textile and clothing industry: Interpretive structural model and triple helix framework. *Computers in Industry, 125*, 103372.

Pathak, A., Kothari, R., Vinoba, M., Habibi, N., & Tyagi, V. V. (2022). Fungal bioleaching of metals from refinery spent catalysts: A critical review of current research, challenges and future directions. *Journal of Environmental Management, 80*, 111789.

Chapter 8

Addressing the Complexity of the Digital Divide and the Role of Government in Addressing It: Role of Government in Bridging the Digital Divide

Khawaja Sazzad Ali and Anisur R. Faroque

Abstract

The digital divide refers to the gap among citizens of a country or across borders due to the lack of ease of access to digital means for some and the difficulty for others. The possession of electronic gadgets, smooth internet connectivity, and other forms of digital communication can have a wide gap in availability among countries. This gap is mostly influenced by factors that are of infrastructural, political, cultural, demographical, generational, and socioeconomic nature. On account of developed and developing countries, the gap is disseminated and thoroughly complex. Although the developed nations around the globe proved to have narrowed digital divide as a major source of development and advancement in respective countries, it is quite challenging for emerging economies to adhere to the same processes for development. For an emerging economy, the prudent cost-benefit analysis carried out by the government can have varying effects on undertaking projects related to minimizing the digital divide. Nevertheless, the importance of narrowing the gap of the digital divide is unparalleled, and governments of emerging economies are realizing the benefits of it and investing their resources accordingly. Furthermore, information technology can be a catalyst in facilitating processes that save a lot of costs, bring holistic quality improvements, and implement effective and efficient government policies that lead to digitalization and sustainable consumption of resources. Consequently, governments are getting actively involved in the digitalization of their respective countries to turn their smart cities into more intelligent ones. Even so, it is important to understand that taking one policy to address all citizens is not realistic. Hence, understanding the foundational knowledge

Fostering Sustainable Businesses in Emerging Economies, 127–145
Copyright © 2024 Khawaja Sazzad Ali and Anisur R. Faroque
Published under exclusive licence by Emerald Publishing Limited
doi:10.1108/978-1-80455-640-520231009

of the citizens, the demand of the population under various sectors, framing well-rounded policies with alternatives, and effectively and efficiently implementing them are extremely crucial.

Keywords: Digital divide; sustainable development; e-government; emerging economy

Digital Divide

In this ever-changing world, science and technology are shaping our foreseeable future. It is bringing innovation and exploring new options leading to ground-breaking discoveries. This has been mainly possible due to the digitalization that the world is currently going through. Sophisticated electronic devices that can solve months' problems in seconds with internet connectivity connecting and bringing all people together under the same roof to communicate is essentially making us more efficient, but is it always the case? The developing nations around the world would argue over their digital divide. The digital divide refers to the division of people having a different range of accessibility to information and communication technologies (Cullen, 2001). Emerging economies have to face multifaceted challenges on an ongoing basis. Their population mostly living under the poverty level puts downward pressure on comprehending the means to achieve such accessibility (Okunola, Rowley, & Johnson, 2017). As much as this gap can be visible across borders, it can even exist within a country. This gap is mostly influenced by factors that are of infrastructural, political, cultural, demographical, generational, and socioeconomic nature.

Infrastructural factors include the necessary means to set up information and communication technology in a country (Mills & Whitacre, 2003). Information and communication technology is important to a country as it lets a country ride the wave of technological innovation and eases the form of communication across people within and outside a country. Telecommunication is one aspect of it. It is the service provided by the telecom industry which includes call time, cellular data, and international roaming. For a country to succeed and bridge the gap of the digital divide, it is of utmost importance to have strong network services. The United States has Silicon Valley located in California, a hub of Information and Communication Technology (ICT) and start-ups, which solely works to innovate the landscape of the country based on the technological aspects of life. From providing a smooth and efficient lifestyle through numerous applications to bringing innovations that are strengthening connectivity across borders, the government of the United States is developing their citizens and other parts of the world to be better equipped with the same level of technical skills (Reggi & Gil-Garcia, 2021). When the mass population of the world receives the same products, it is easier to trade across borders and give both the producers and consumers better negotiation for the goods and services. On the contrary, third-world economies such as Sudan and Afghanistan have the worst possible telecommunication services in the world. Does the political situation affect the digital divide?

As aforementioned, political reasons too can play a notorious role in widening the gap. Both Sudan and Afghanistan have dreadful political systems. The government of the respective countries failed to provide their citizens the means to have smooth connectivity, as tested by Ookla, one of the pioneers in testing internet and mobile connectivity. However, how does a government benefit from it? All the answers may just lead to one straight fact: corruption. Corruption is extremely high in the said economies. It is also seen that the legislative body of the country provide one or two telecom companies to take charge of the entire country encouraging monopolistic behavior (Olken & Pande, 2012). Those companies, in turn, charge as they like making a hefty profit for themselves but deprive the population of the country of having the desired utility level. This also allows the governments to run and control the media as they prefer. One of the best examples can be North Korea in this case. The government of the country does not allow its citizens to communicate outside their borders, and in some cases, it is prohibited to communicate freely within their own country. This gives the ultimate power to the government to dictate as they like abandoning all senses of democracy (Byman & Lind, 2010).

Demographical factors such as age and gender can have a massive impact on the digital divide. The possession of electronic gadgets, smooth internet connectivity, and other forms of digital communication can have a wide gap in availability and may not be equally divided among the males and females of a country. However, the more important factor to worry about is the generational gap that exists in every country. The technological advancements we see today were not present in our forefather's generations. The elderly citizens of a country may not have an interest in technology as they have no prior knowledge. This creates a gap between the millennial and Generation Z age cohorts. Nevertheless, a lot of people may also argue that socioeconomic reasons can aggrandize the digital divide, but researches show no strong correlation between the two (Zhao, Collier, & Deng, 2014). A relevant example can be the sudden development of COVID-19 and its impact on countries around the world. Governments created websites for people to register for the vaccination program streamlining the process; however, in emerging economies such as Bangladesh, many people did not have the access to information and communication technology to register themselves to avail the services. They had to go to internet hubs to register them, and this discouraged thousands. This challenge was absent in countries that are technologically advanced and have minimal digital divide among their population.

E-Government

The sole responsibility of any government is to govern the well-being of its citizens. It can be by producing an adequate budget to meet all demands and supplies. It can also be enacting effective policies for the betterment of the citizens of the country. The improved business environment also falls under the umbrella of government's governance as businesses seek to expand outside the borders of a country. E-governance refers to connecting all three parties: government, the citizens of the country, and the businesses in a country together with the means of electronic support (Kumar, 2017). This does not mean only having websites will serve the purpose, but the way a government encourages everyone in the country for embracing information and communication technology is the predicament.

A good example that can be considered for this purpose is the vaccination project. With the sudden appearance and the destruction of the COVID-19 pandemic all over the globe, governments had to swiftly adhere to ways to vaccinate the people of their respective countries, which also meant the bigger the country in terms of population, the harder it ought to be. Nevertheless, first-world countries such as the United States, China, Canada, the United Kingdom, and India had successfully launched the registration program and got their citizens to be vaccinated (Ramsetty & Adams, 2020). Now, this was easy given the accessibility to the necessary means to register in the first place, which does not only include internet connectivity and electronic support but also the knowledge of the population itself. These governments were previously investing in their ICT sectors and encouraged people to take part in sustainable development. All these aforementioned countries comprise the majority of the population of the world, yet they succeeded in their tasks. However, governments from lower income countries were bombarded with challenges. First, they had to wait for the major countries to take action on the predicament and follow their steps in terms of minimizing the impact and loss but more importantly about the development of vaccines and other precautionary steps. Second, they needed to invest heavily in the accessibility of such a registration program. People from these third-world countries having a disseminated digital divide found it difficult to be a part of it. Third, the governments had to invest more in educating the population about the measures taken by the government and how common people could avail of them. This lack of knowledge seemed to be one of the biggest barriers to the said issue. Therefore, the importance of good governance through e-government is unparalleled and can shape the future of a country unimaginably.

Role of Government in Minimizing the Digital Divide

The number of people, both in developed and developing countries, using the mobile network and internet connectivity is increasing exponentially. More people are trying to communicate online with their families and friends. Even the traditional emailing system has recently taken a hit by the presence of social media in the workplace. The digital divide that we talked about earlier can be categorized into two broad categories or points of view: access point of view and skill point of view (Belanger & Carter, 2006). The access point of view mainly comprises sociodemographic factors such as ethnicity, age, income, and education. Alongside, the skill point of view includes general computer use and the purpose it is used, use of the internet, and other computer and smart devices experience. As seen earlier why digital divide can be extremely complex and overcoming the challenges is of utmost importance, the government has a major role to play.

Any policies taken by a government have to be well backed by proper research. The policies have to be cost-effective, efficient, technologically innovative, manageable, and socially acceptable. Therefore, one policy may not govern all the issues underlying the digital divide predicament due to its complexity, rather a portfolio of policies is needed with alternative options to reach out for inclusion of every individual in the country. The best way, perhaps, is to go for Cost-Benefit Analysis. Cost-Benefit Analysis refers to the analysis of a project that consists of various costs such as installation cost, maintenance cost, implementation cost, social cost, environmental cost, and many more. The benefits considered can be both tangible and intangible. These future costs and benefits are discounted to the present value subject to a fixed rate of return which is set by the analysts based on the market return. This is a comprehensive way to weigh all the policies available for the policymakers to choose the best policy or policies out of a menu of choices.

Nevertheless, all governments should encourage sustainable consumption and aim for sustainable development. This refers to the limited consumption of only the resources that are required for a process without putting pressure on it for the future generation. This induces sustainable development by encouraging everyone to adhere to processes that bring long-lasting benefits. A relevant example can be MicroMentor, an online platform to support female entrepreneurs to minimize the digital divide.

MicroMentor Shaping the Future

MicroMentor is a cost-free mentorship platform for women entrepreneurs all over the world. Being established in 2008, the organization has served over 13,000 women entrepreneurs in just over a decade (MicroMentor, 2022). The main idea of this innovative platform is to collaborate with mentors and mentees all over the globe despite having a form of geographical, cultural, financial, and language barriers. This idea helped all the people availing the service to take up projects that have an everlasting impact on the world contributing to sustainable development.

A program led by Mercy Corps and well supported by the US government (Programs-For-Corporations-and-Governments, 2022), MicroMentor has succeeded in minimizing the global digital divide. Many entrepreneurs all over the world face multifaceted challenges, which leads them to not pursue their dreams that could change the world. Many, even after pursuing, cannot keep up with the business demands or simply just fall out of the loop. MicroMentor's responsibility is to guide these entrepreneurs to efficiently use of their resources to reach a successful outcome. This in turn has created a wider range of job opportunities for people around the globe. The US government supported the initiative by providing them with resources as the program fosters a culture that thrives on a wider skillset. Additionally, the mentors, donated over 50 million pro-bono USD to the mentees to encourage them in their entrepreneurial journey (MicroMentor, 2022). Furthermore, renowned companies such as Apple, Chevron, MasterCard, and JP Morgan Chase & Co. are to name a few global partners of the program (Programs-For-Corporations-and-Governments, 2022).

From providing training programs on basic software skills needed to run and take decisions in small companies to teaching global market insights and providing a holistic industry view, MicroMentor has encouraged thousands of women from emerging economies to turn their dreams into reality. Anita Ramachandran, the Executive Director of the company, believes that women across the world face many more challenges than men in general (About MicroMentor, 2022). These challenges are multifold if emerging economies are considered. For example, in emerging economies, the wage rate is lower along with other social and cultural challenges adding more pressure on women to pursue any entrepreneurial activity. Subsequently, every start-up business or any form of business possesses a certain level of risk that cannot be mitigated. Many find this discouraging and that is where MicroMentor contributes. However, more importantly, MicroMentor aims for sustainable development that has a long-lasting impact by providing the means necessary to these women to have them on board to launch their businesses. This chapter will next look into a few distinct countries on how they have minimized their digital divide and what role their government plays in achieving it. These distinct cases will try to highlight the complexity of the digital divide among different countries and how E-government can implement policies to bridge the gap.

The Case of the United States

In 1996, the government of the United States realized the digital divide the country had was creating a bigger social divide. People who did not have internet access were not being able to avail of online government services and were going through lots of hassles. Their predicament was further elevated when people from both the Democratic and Republican parties could not take part in the "point and click" debate during the US national convention in 1996 (Sipior & Ward, 2022). They could not exercise their rights to vote only in person, which caused long queues of people to stand idle. The government realized the bottleneck and invested in providing more and more public internet access. This way more people could have access to free internet for their work or pass their leisure time in public.

An exploratory analysis was carried out to observe the effect of e-government inclusion and whether it bridges the gap of the digital divide. One hundred fifty-eight households from William Penn Housing Development that had less to no technological access were selected for the analysis (Sipior & Ward, 2022). The methodology of the research conducted both qualitative and quantitative data for observing a holistic view of people. The research followed the *Assets-Based Community Development Model* to see how the society of William Penn Housing Development could be empowered through e-government inclusion. The hypothesis was that the more people can be brought under the roof of the internet and technology, the more self-sufficient the members of the community can be. The results highlighted among the 158 households, 60% required a job and were not skilled due to not having proper means, i.e., a computer or internet. Twelve percent of the households did report necessary computing skills to work at corporates, but unfortunately none of them had any access to a computer to work remotely if needed (Sipior & Ward, 2022). This small housing development, located in Pennsylvania, with a population of 39,000, reported many disturbing issues. Drug abuse among the people, teenage pregnancy, poor performance in academia, vandalism, murders, and poor electrical and sewage system are to name a few. The author Sipior and Ward (2022) and team found that the lack of connection with the mainstream society and external factors pose threat to the society of William Penn Housing Development.

To subdue the issue laid out, the local government along with Villanova University's Institute for Teaching and Learning launched a training program. The law firms in the neighborhood provided 15 fresh personal computers followed by 14 refurbished ones donated by the local schools (Sipior & Ward, 2022). A Community Center was booked to train the individuals in the society. The training program was found to be effective among the members of the community which further spread positive word of mouth among the community influencing more people to sign up. A second location was soon booked to cater to the demand of the local community. People were also able to take their personal computers to their homes to practice. 15 more refurbished personal computers were donated. Upon successful completion of the training program, the participants were given certificates and free computers which boosted their morale and empowered them to be self-sufficient (Sipior & Ward, 2022). Although the lack of internet connectivity persisted, receiving free computers encouraged them to gain computational skills and expertise. They were given a range of tasks that tested a wide range of skills. As more and more people gained basic computer skills, the analysis of the data suggested that governmental websites incurred more traffic. People were also able to retain the information available on websites and name at least one government website when asked.

The biggest lesson the government acquired from this investigation is that they need to listen to the citizens more closely and streamline the technologies available to harness higher human capital. If their demands are well met, people are more likely to return multifold. Usage of computers was an important skill that many people found interesting which eventually increased the awareness and traffic for government websites. More people were interested in availing of online services rather than waiting in lines for hours which brought a paradigm shift. The members of the community were also found to be partnering with external parties for trade and commerce inducing sustainable development.

Digital Divide and Role of E-Government in European Economies

The European economies too did not fall behind in realizing the importance of minimizing the gap between the people in society in terms of their access to technology and the ability to use it. Eurostat's Community Statistics in Information Society collected micro-data over a decade from 2008 to 2017 (Botrić &

Božić, 2021). They wanted to find out the digital divide among all the European countries along with the impact of different age cohorts on the adoption of e-government services. The institute followed the *Heckman selection methodology* that tries to explain three types of effects; first, distinct effects on young and old due to gender, size of their respective household, and overall population density. The second effect this form of methodology tried to figure out the similar effects among the different age cohorts due to their economic activity. Thirdly, and lastly, the adverse effects on young and old due to their education level were found to be crucial.

Although prior research showed that approximately all citizens aged between 25 and 34 used the internet, it was quite the opposite for the elderlies in the communities (Botrić & Božić, 2021). Even though the senior citizens could benefit from the adoption of e-government services, there was a significant demotivation among them from using it. The European governments has been investing a lot of resources since the late 1990s; however, the adoption of e-government services is substantially low. The government thought it would be widely accepted due to its cost reducing policies, improving the overall quality of the services provided, and ultimately helping the government to take more effective policies. However, the older age cohort seemed to completely shun the project. In 2005, the government tried to enforce the e-government declaration which moved some part of the population toward their agenda of having all the citizens to inclusion and ease of accessibility of these online services with increased trust but all were spoiled due to the COVID-19 pandemic.

The findings of this research were quite interesting yet complex. The researchers used three dummy variables which included acquiring information from websites, downloading official forms, and submitting the completed forms. Even though different countries had similar population levels, their young and old age cohort behaved differently. The Irish senior citizens tend to use government websites for their services while the younger age cohort of Estonia seemed to use the websites more (Botrić & Božić, 2021). The researchers associated this change in behavior with socioeconomic reasons as Italy, another European country, showed a similar behavior as young people tend to live with their parents even after turning 18, implying their lesser usage of government websites because of it is usually navigated by their parents. Downloading online forms indicated active participation of users and required some level of computational skill and expertise. This variable showed lower participation and engagement among the people of the countries. However, the older population from the Netherlands, Ireland, and the United Kingdom showed a higher level of engagement, while younger people from Estonia and Finland showed higher engagement in going to government websites and navigating through them to acquire their desired information and download forms (Botrić & Božić, 2021).

The next step of the research showed the outcomes perhaps the governments across countries were trying to retrieve. Completing the forms required moderate to advanced computer skills that many did not possess. The older cohort reported that they did not have the necessary skills to complete the forms and submit them. This is the place where government needed to focus on for including more people to have necessary computer skills and overall inclusion in the digitalization of the country. To highlight the main findings from the paper:

- Older males had the necessary skills more than females to navigate through government websites. The younger cohort did not show such a correlation.
- Household income had a positive correlation with the usage of computers and the internet. The higher the level of income for a household suggested the higher the chance of possession of technological means.
- Elderlies from rural areas had a lesser chance of inclusion compared to their similar part in urban areas. People are more likely to adopt services in less dense areas.
- The higher the level of education, the more the attainment of necessary computer skills among the netizens. This, however, is arguable as the foundational level of education did not previously provide computer skills and expertise and requires implementation of specific policy toward it.

The ease of user interface particularly played an important role in adopting e-government services bridging the gap of the digital divide. Younger people generally showed more interest in availing of these services from websites regardless of their gender or education level.

All in all, the European countries showed a wide range of data. This demanded the governments to enact a portfolio of policies as previously discussed to find the best possible way to minimize the gap by streamlining the technologies and to foster culture of sustainability in their economies.

The Efforts of India

India is one of the most populous countries in the world. Along with the population explosion, the country also suffers from a lack of electricity, tele density, internet industry, and several other challenges. Having several states with people from numerous backgrounds, the digital divide is quite vivid in this country. To mitigate the issue, the government has taken some initiatives such as Akashganga, Akshaya e-centers, Bhoomi etcetera (Rao, 2005).

Over a billion citizens coming from various backgrounds add upward pressure to the digital divide. India has 18 different languages recognized so far, however, the literacy rate was 74.37% as of 2018 (India Literacy Rate | Macrotrends, 2023). The IT industry is also thriving but access to Information and Communication Technologies is the main issue the country is facing at the moment due to the infrastructural prerequisites not being met. These infrastructural prerequisites include electricity generation, tele density, the internet industry, and IT penetration. India had produced only 363 kW of electricity compared to the major technology powerhouses like Hong Kong which had generated 4959 kW of electricity (Rao, 2005). Tele density refers to the density of telecom companies or subscribers within a given population frame. India had one of the lowest tele density in the world with around only 16% presence of telecom subscribers in urban areas as of 2003. The IT sector too did not penetrate the population quite well. Due to the high price of computers, majority of the people cannot simply afford personal computers putting huge pressure on the digital divide. The internet industry in the early 2000 was not flourishing. Only 0.4% of the population were internet subscribers. Only 193 licensed internet service providers were available all over the country. As of 2003, India saw only 3.5 million internet subscribers (Rao, 2005). This low rate was caused by low IT penetration, high costs associated with internet connectivity but having a poor connection, and higher prices of personal computers. Nevertheless, the country has developed multifold in the past couple of decades proving to be a giant across industries.

With all these issues at hand, the Indian government announced "Internet for all" policy to shape society and in turn the whole country into a knowledge country. The digital divide does not only hamper the communication medium but it can slow down trade and commerce. Realizing the importance of bridging the gap, the government of India had undertaken a lot of policies which include every household having one telephone in urban areas whereas in rural areas with a population of 2000 people. In every 5 kilometers, there must be digital data facilities available for the rural people. This policy is expected to grow Voice Over Internet Protocol (VOIP) lowering the cost and making it affordable for the Indians. All these policies are strictly governed by the IT Task Force and the Ministry of Information Technology. The government also took initiatives to widen the technology options for better connectivity among people. Apart from traditional terrestrial wireless connectivity, the government also launched satellite connection which was much easier and did not require setting up issue. On the other hand, terrestrial wireless technology included Wi-Fi, cellular data, wireless pay phone, multi-access radio etcetera. Wireline technology included Integrated Services Digital Network (ISDN), Digital Subscriber Line (DSL), Power Line Communication (PLC), and cable-based broadband (Rao, 2005). Along with them, the government also launched IT-based programs:

- *Akashganga*: Milk is one of the nutritious drinks that are consumed by people of India from all layers of background. To facilitate the production and distribution of milk better, the government of India launched a program known as Akashganga. Located in 600 places and running for 8 hours every day around the year, the program has provided a multifold increment in milk production and supply.
- *Passenger Reservation System*: The Railway Ministry saw the gap in communication among the people from different states and heavily invested in building a better communication infrastructure. The railway system soon reduced the digital divide among the population.
- *Akshaya e-centers*: This program was launched all across Kerala. A training program for the locals was set up to provide them with basic IT training enhancing their computational literacy skills and expertise. The program was spatially distributed, so that people from all phases of life can participate and earn knowledge and necessary skills for e-commerce and trade.

- *Bhoomi*: Joining forces with National Informatics Center (NIC), the government of India launched this program to record all land ownerships. As this process was previously done manually, people had to wait in lines for hours to avail of the services which also involved bribery. However, upon implementation of Bhoomi, people could fill up the necessary forms online and document their land ownership.
- *Gyandoot*: 35 Internet Kiosks were placed in every five blocks of Madhya Pradesh State to elevate the knowledge of IT among the people (Rao, 2005). This program's main aim was to influence people to learn foundational to advanced computer skills which will later help them to be self-employed in their entrepreneurial journey.
- *Information Village Research*: This program aimed to empower villagers of the country with knowledge about different aspects of life; for example, the effective ways of farming, planned birth and family development, instant health care, fighting against social taboos, and many more. This volunteer-led program was found to be highly effective as the elders were observed to pass down the knowledge to the youth which is further likely to the generations henceforth.
- *TARAhaat*: This event led to the penetration of the internet into the daily lives of rural people around the country. This program aimed to engage people in e-trade and e-commerce via websites to retrieve information from the internet to tap into the markets that were previously left untouched. This brought a fortune for the country as more people engaged in freelancing bringing foreign currency into the country.
- *Warana Project*: This project was based on providing a marketing platform to people across the country. The wired communication services allowed people to sell agricultural products influencing numerous states to initiate a similar program.

South Africa and Its Efforts in Bridging the Digital Divide

South Africa, being one of the poorest countries in the world, faces multifaceted challenges. While the majority of the population lives in poverty, the government can barely invest in infrastructure to minimize the digital divide (Okunola et al., 2017). Most of the investments go to support other aspects of the livelihood of the population. The digital divide is orchestrated by humongous inequality across genders, races, and economic aspects followed by rural areas having weak information technology infrastructure, and an absence of governmental support (van Deursen & van Dijk, 2018). Although the presence of mobile phone usage is vivid, fixed line usage is quite absent from mainstream communication channels along with poor internet connectivity.

Table 1 adapted from Mphidi (2010) highlights the condition of the digital divide in South Africa. With only three mobile operators, the telecommunication companies charge a higher call rate than the ones in the neighboring countries

Table 1. Distribution of Information and Communication Technology.

Indicators	Numbers
Population	47,390,900
GDP	USD 200.5 billion
GDP per capita	USD 4,230
Gini coefficient	57.8
Main (fixed) telephone lines	4,729,000
Tele-density or Tele subscribers (fixed)	9.90%
Number of fixed line operators	2
Mobile telephone subscribers	39,066,000
Tele-density (mobile)	68.20%
Number of mobile operators	3
Internet subscribers (estimated)	5,100,000
Broadband internet subscribers	283,839
Number of personal computers	5,300,000
Number of internet service providers	355
Number of television sets	10,000,000
Number of television stations	6
Number of radio stations	130

Source: Mphidi (2010).

(Mphidi, 2010). The number of internet service providers and television stations are also minimal, enhancing the digital divide.

Nevertheless, observing other countries receiving benefits of e-governance, South Africa is also investing in developing its infrastructure. However, this poses several challenges:

- *Privacy*: A lot of personal details of individuals are stored in the government directory which induces a threat to the privacy of the citizens.
- *Security*: Any breach of data can result in a huge number of personal information being leaked which can deteriorate the security and safety of individuals.
- *Economic turbulence*: People from lower income groups naturally have lesser access to information and communication technology increasing the divide.
- *Education*: The level of education divides the population; the more a person is educated, the more they are likely to use the internet and have the necessary computer skills and literacy.
- *Accessibility*: Accessibility varies greatly among rural and urban areas mainly due to the government's lack of interest in sustainable development.

- *Awareness and confidence among citizens*: It has been found through research that citizens are concerned about their details being stolen by anonymous sources. This makes it even harder for the government to persuade the citizens of the country.
- *Lack of leadership*: The South African government failed to show leadership on bigger platforms. Any misconduct in the past is expected by the government to take accountability.
- *Legal framework*: The legal framework of the government is not too strong. Perpetrators can easily get away with their misconduct.
- *Bureaucratic government*: Bribing is extremely high as many government officials are found to be connected to different cases of misconduct.

Upon its birth in 1994, South Africa tried to rope in e-governance as it has over 30 websites for the citizens to avail services. Although the country is by far the best one in the entire continent of Africa, it is still struggling to minimize the gap of the digital divide due to its natural complexity embedded in the country. The State Information and Technology Agency (SITA) along with the government is relentlessly trying to have all the companies in the country have user-friendly websites (Mphidi, 2010). This will enhance the inclusion of the citizens and engage them in a manner that fosters sustainable development. They are doing this by a wide range of applications which includes government documents and forms being available to the citizens to avail a wide range of services, tenders and vacancies advertisements, search and feedback facilities, and useful links to different websites. These steps showed an overall growth in the numbers of people having access to their desired information bridging the digital divide.

Bangladesh and Its Take on Digital Divide

Bangladesh, being a developing country, has a bigger digital divide than the countries that fall in the same economic category. With a population of over 16 million, Bangladesh faces a multifaceted challenge due to its exponentially increasing birth rate. The country needs a holistic developmental approach to mitigate the issues such as traffic congestion, in the health care industry, education system, and other aspects of life. The current government has undertaken a wide range of projects to mitigate the issues aforementioned which include mega-projects that connect divisions across the country saving a lot of costs and time along with e-governance. The government has announced the slogan "Digital Bangladesh" which aimed to digitalize Bangladesh by 2021 (Rahman, 2016). This included delivering internet connection to every corner of the country, providing training programs in rural and urban places alike to enhance computer literacy skills and expertise, affordable computers and an internet connection, and a smooth mobile network (Hoque, Mahiuddin, & Alam, 2022). People can now avail online services with the luxury of sitting at home, making online payments anywhere in the world, serving clients across borders, and even receiving tele-medicine services. The projects undertaken have proved to bring fortune for

Bangladesh as importers are eyeing the country as a hub of technologically smart individuals.

Nevertheless, this was no easy feat and Bangladesh still has a lot of room for improvement. The major challenges the government had to endure along the way were:

- *Lack of sufficient electricity*: The country is facing one of the hardest challenges it ever faced that is a lack of sufficient electricity. Major development projects require a high amount of electricity along with industries, schools, hospitals, and households. However, the country does not have sufficient electricity to meet these ever-rising demands. Roughly 30% of the population (Hoque et al., 2022) has continuous access to electric connections which puts upward pressure on the digital divide.
- *Lower bandwidth of internet*: The speed of internet in Bangladesh is tested to be one of the lowest in the world. However, the price of obtaining and maintaining a connection is quite high which discourages the majority of the rural population to not buy a connection increasing the digital divide.
- *Lack of ICT infrastructure*: The government does not have a strong ICT infrastructure as many governmental offices are found to have computers providing poor performance. Many computers are also found to be sitting idle due to a lack of proper planning and research while setting up an office. The websites too are not well maintained and often contain incorrect information.
- *Accessibility among demotivated employees*: A lot of employees are found not to use personal computers. This is mostly because of the low-grade computers provided in the first place, but some are not interested in using them due to their lack of knowledge of computers. Some government employees still do their everyday tasks manually consuming a great deal of their time making the overall process slow.
- *Extreme bureaucracy and presence of middleman*: People are often found to be exploited while using government services. The presence of a middleman creates a bottleneck for the processes to be going smoothly. People often need to pay a high amount of money to these middlemen to get their work done. Bureaucracy is also present in the structure of a ministry. This hierarchy consumes a lot of time for the citizens that could have been spent elsewhere.

Nevertheless, the government seeing the success of its neighboring country India has implemented policies based on a few models explained below that focuses on minimizing the digital divide among the population through good e-governance and being registered as a digital country.

- *Broadcasting Model*: This model aims to spread the usage of e-governmental services to the mass population (Hoque et al., 2022). As aforementioned, many people find it enigmatic to use a computer because of not having the necessary skills and refrain from using the websites. The government created a bunch of websites to empower these individuals by making it easier for them to access their desired information. People can confirm the validity of the information provided by cross-checking with the local source if needed. This way people can assess their rights and responsibilities well and take well-rounded decisions.

- *Critical Flow Model*: The model allows the information with significant importance to flow to the target audience. In everyday life, we are bombarded with information, and not all this information carries the same weight. If people were fed the right and only the information they require, that would likely make us more efficient and productive. The model uses media to disseminate critical information to the targeted people intended to save time. This reduces the bottleneck and dependability on others to receive the needful information.
- *Comparative Analysis Model*: Comparative Analysis Model is the most effective model implemented by the government, however, it could not get the popularity it deserves (Hoque et al., 2022). The model aims to compare information that is available to public and private websites with the already known information circulating. This helps the government to better govern its population by understanding the perception of people regarding a certain topic. This also allows the government to revise its policies if required to better fit and serve the population of the country. The comparative analysis model uses information before and after a certain change is implemented to better understand the effectiveness of the project.
- *Mobilization and Lobbying Model*: This model is the most frequent model used by the government to strengthen the connection with the rest of the world. The model aims to build virtual partners globally who share similar values to take planned, directed and strategic decisions on a particular aspect. This does not only create a strong bond among the countries but also exchanges ideas to use strict e-governance for sustainable development of the countries involved. The diversity among the parties involved strengthens this model and is widely used around the world.
- *Interactive Service Model*: This model is an accumulation of all the previously explained models. This model aims to engage the citizens in a way where they can convey their problems or concerns about a certain issue to the governmental body who in turn can take a solid approach to cater to the needs of the citizens of the country. Engaging people in this way empowers them and enhances faith in the government.

As depicted in Table 2, e-governance in Bangladesh has brought several positive changes. The hierarchal bureaucracy has declined, coordination among departments along with the relationship between government and the citizens has improved, services are available online and can be availed by anyone from any corner of the world, and customization according to one's needs are to name a few of the benefits of e-governance had on the citizens of Bangladesh.

With all the successes in the past, Bangladesh has been ranked 148 out of 193 countries (Rahman, 2016) in the world in E-Government Development Index (EGDI) and has improved two steps from the last time the assessment was carried

Table 2. Paradigm Shifts in Public Service Delivery After E-Governance.

	Paradigm Shifts in Public Service Delivery	
	Bureaucratic Paradigm	**E-Government Paradigm**
Orientation	Production cost-efficiency	User satisfaction and control. Flexibility
Process organization	Functional rationality, departmentalization. Vertical hierarchy of control.	Horizontal hierarchy, network Organization, information sharing.
Management principle	Management by rule and mandate	Flexible management, interdepartmental team work with central coordination
Leadership style	Command and control	Facilitation and coordination, innovative entrepreneurship.
Internal communication	Top down. Hierarchical	Multidirectional network with central coordination, direct communication.
External communication	Centralized, formal, limited channels	Formal and informal direct and fast feedback, multiple channels
Mode of service delivery	Documentary mode and interpersonal interaction	Electronic exchange, non face to face Interaction
Principles of service Delivery	Standardization, impartiality, equity	User customization, personalization

Source: Hoque et al. (2022).

out. The country has a long way to go, but even small steps will add value. However, the country needs to strictly govern the people and eliminate any form of bureaucracy and crime.

Discussion

The presence of the digital divide can be found across the globe. From one of the strongest economies like the United States, to a developing economy like Bangladesh, the digital divide may not simply correlate with economic conditions. It is quite evident that economic conditions play a role, but other determinants are equally important and demand to be addressed to minimize the digital divide. The determinants according to various research included age, gender, household income, lack of ICT infrastructure, absence of good governance, and many more.

It is also evident that governments of emerging economies have to cater to other needs of the country inducing less investment in minimizing the digital divide. Emerging economies have to face multifaceted challenges on an ongoing basis. Their population mostly living under the poverty level puts downward pressure on comprehending the means to achieve such accessibility. As much as this gap can be visible across borders, it can even exist within a country. This gap is mostly influenced by factors that are infrastructural, political, cultural, demographical, generational, and socioeconomic reasons (Helbig, Ramón Gil-García, & Ferro, 2009). Nevertheless, decreasing the digital divide empowers people from all spheres of life. It can also bring an increased amount of trade and commerce inducing sustainable development. As seen earlier why digital divide can be extremely complex and overcoming the challenges is of utmost importance, the government has a major role to play.

Any policies taken by a government have to be well backed by proper research. The policies have to be cost-effective, efficient, technologically innovative, manageable, and socially acceptable. The main goal of the government is to streamline the processes in SDGs and technology to minimize the digital divide. Therefore, one policy may not govern all the issues underlying the digital divide predicament due to its complexity; rather a portfolio of policies is needed with alternative options to reach out for inclusion of every individual in the country. The best way, perhaps, is to go for cost-benefit analysis. Additionally, the models enacted by various governments were also found to be fruitful as they are providing promising results. However, as seen previously, a country implements a wide range of policies, and this is quite realistic based on the fact that people have a different range of knowledge or accessibility to digital processes. One policy would not be effective compared to portfolio of policies being implemented. Nevertheless, only making information and communication technology available to the public is not enough as people need to be trained properly to sustain the knowledge they acquire and use it in their lives. As seen in the case of the USA, the training programs at Penn Housing were very effective and it also influenced other people to take up the training as the people living in that society understood the importance of computer literacy skills and expertise. It is also important to note that people who could not afford personal computers were given refurbished computers to be taken to their respective homes to practice. This gesture is truly commendable and circulated positive word of mouth in the neighborhood influencing others.

Sustainable development is another aspect governments should be focusing on as the resources are depleting at an alarming rate. Both developed and developing countries are susceptible to change in climate, and using resources sustainably can help mitigate the issue. Furthermore, economies can receive benefits even in the long run from attaining a process that focuses on sustainable development. Minimizing the digital divide is one way countries try to reach sustainable development. It reduces inequality among people regarding knowledge, skills, and expertise.

To conclude, the importance of e-governance in minimizing the digital divide is unparalleled. Governments across the world need to focus on e-governance and strictly maintain them to streamline a smart society into an intelligent one, which in turn will lead to sustainable development. This will lead to global prosperity and lead newer and better innovations shaping the world.

References

About MicroMentor. Micromentor.org. (2022, September 26). Retrieved from https://www.micromentor.org/about/

Belanger, F., & Carter, L. (2006). The effects of the Digital Divide on e-government: An emperical evaluation. In *Proceedings of the 39th Annual Hawaii International Conference on System Sciences* (HICSS'06). doi:10.1109/hicss.2006.464

Botrić, V., & Božić, L. (2021). The digital divide and E-government in European economies. *Economic Research-Ekonomska Istraživanja, 34*(1), 2935–2955. doi:10.1080/1331677x.2020.1863828

Byman, D., & Lind, J. (2010). Pyongyang's survival strategy: Tools of authoritarian control in North Korea. *International Security, 35*(1), 44–74.

Cullen, R. (2001, September 23). *Addressing the digital divide.* Files.eric.ed.gov. Retrieved from https://files.eric.ed.gov/fulltext/ED459714.pdf

Helbig, N., Ramón Gil-García, J., & Ferro, E. (2009). Understanding the complexity of electronic government: Implications from the digital divide literature. *Government Information Quarterly, 26*(1), 89–97. doi:10.1016/j.giq.2008.05.004

Hoque, S., Mahiuddin, K., & Alam, S. (2022, September 25). *E-governance: A way forward to digital Bangladesh.* doi:10.2139/ssrn.2279312

India literacy rate 1981-2023. MacroTrends. (2023). Retrieved from https://www.macrotrends.net/countries/IND/india/literacy-rate

Kumar, A. (2017). E-governance to smart governance. *SSRN Electronic Journal.* doi:10.2139/ssrn.2970329

MicroMentor. Micromentor.org. (2022, September 26). Retrieved from https://www.micromentor.org/

Mills, B., & Whitacre, B. (2003). Understanding the non-metropolitan-metropolitan digital divide. *Growth and Change, 34*(2), 219–243. doi:10.1111/1468-2257.00215

Mphidi, H. (2010, September 25). *Digital divide and E-governance in South Africa.* Retrieved from https://citeseerx.ist.psu.edu/viewdoc/download?doi=10.1.1.544.2678&rep=rep1&type=pdf

Okunola, O., Rowley, J., & Johnson, F. (2017). The multi-dimensional digital divide: Perspectives from an e-government portal in Nigeria. *Government Information Quarterly, 34*(2), 329–339. doi:10.1016/j.giq.2017.02.002

Olken, B. A., & Pande, R. (2012). Corruption in developing countries. *Annual Review of Economics, 4*(1), 479–509.

Programs-For-Corporations-and-Governments. Micromentor.org. (2022, September 26). Retrieved from https://www.micromentor.org/programs-for-corporations-and-governments/

Rahman, M. (2016, September 25). *E-governance and Bangladesh.* Retrieved from https://www.google.com/amp/s/www.thedailystar.net/25th-anniversary-special-part-1/e-governance-and-bangladesh-210577%3famp

Ramsetty, A., & Adams, C. (2020). Impact of the digital divide in the age of COVID-19. *Journal of the American Medical Informatics Association, 27*(7), 1147–1148. doi: 10.1093/jamia/ocaa078

Rao, S. (2005, September 25). Bridging digital divide: Efforts in India. *Telematics and Informatics*, (22), 361–375. Retrieved from https://citeseerx.ist.psu.edu/viewdoc/download?doi=10.1.1.477.3812&rep=rep1&type=pdf

Reggi, L., & Gil-Garcia, J. (2021). Addressing territorial digital divides through ICT strategies: Are investment decisions consistent with local needs? *Government Information Quarterly, 38*(2), 101562. doi:10.1016/j.giq.2020.101562

Sipior, J., & Ward, B. (2022, September 25). *Bridging the digital divide for E-government inclusion: A United States case study*. Academic-publishing.Org. Retrieved from https://academicpublishing.org/index.php/ejeg/article/download/433/396

van Deursen, A., & van Dijk, J. (2018). The first-level digital divide shifts from inequalities in physical access to inequalities in material access. *New Media and Society, 21*(2), 354–375. doi:10.1177/1461444818797082

Zhao, F., Collier, A., & Deng, H. (2014). A multidimensional and integrative approach to study global digital divide and e-government development. *Information Technology and People, 27*(1), 38–62. doi:10.1108/itp-01-2013-0022

Chapter 9

Blockchain Technology for Secure and Intelligent Industry Applications

Vasim Ahmad, Lalit Goyal, Tilottama Singh and Jugander Kumar

Abstract

This chapter explores the significance of blockchain technology in protecting data for intelligent applications across various industries. Blockchain is a distributed ledger that ensures the immutability and security of transactions. Given the increasing need for security measures in industries, understanding blockchain technology is crucial for preparing for its future applications.

This chapter aims to examine the use of blockchain technology across industries and presents a compilation of existing and upcoming blockchain technologies for intelligent applications. The methodology involves reviewing research to understand the security needs of different industries and providing an overview of methods used to enhance multi-institutional and multidisciplinary research in areas like the financial system, smart grid, and transportation system.

The findings highlight the benefits of blockchain networks in providing transparency, trust, and security for industries. The Responsible Sourcing Blockchain Network (RSBN) is an example that utilizes blockchain's decentralized ledger to track sustainable sourcing from mine to final product. This information can be shared with auditors, corporate governance organizations, and customers.

The practical implications of this chapter are significant, serving as a valuable resource for industries concerned with identity privacy, traceability, immutability, transparency, auditability, and security. Understanding and implementing blockchain technology can address the growing need for secure and intelligent applications, ensuring data protection and enhancing trust in various sectors.

Keywords: Distributed ledger technology; security; intelligent applications; smart grid; privacy; business; and industry

Fostering Sustainable Businesses in Emerging Economies, 147–165

Copyright © 2024 Vasim Ahmad, Lalit Goyal, Tilottama Singh and Jugander Kumar

Published under exclusive licence by Emerald Publishing Limited

doi:10.1108/978-1-80455-640-520231010

Introduction

The blockchain is a chain of blocks that functions as a decentralized, peer-to-peer database of ever-growing records. The blockchain's initial block has no parent block; We looked at the research to see if public blockchains, consortium blockchains, and private blockchains all use the same parts of the technology (Dhanalakshmi & Babu, 2019). Fig. 1 depicts the blockchain's structure, which must be evaluated from multiple perspectives to achieve a deeper understanding of this technological marvel (Raj, 2022).

Each transaction block contains a Merkle root reference. In the block header, you can find the hash of the last block, the mining statistics that were used to make the block, and the root of the Merkle tree. The blockchain contains transactions as well. Each block has a header that contains a link to the block's transactions; if any transaction is modified, the block's header must be updated as well (Dhanalakshmi & Babu, 2019).

Blockchain technology could make many applications and services for big data much better because it is decentralized and secure. This article gives a thorough introduction to blockchain technology with a focus on big data. It pays special attention to existing methods, opportunities, and possible outcomes. First, we will give an introduction to blockchain technology and big data, along with an explanation of the motives behind combining the two. After that, we look at a variety of different blockchain services for big data, such as blockchain for the

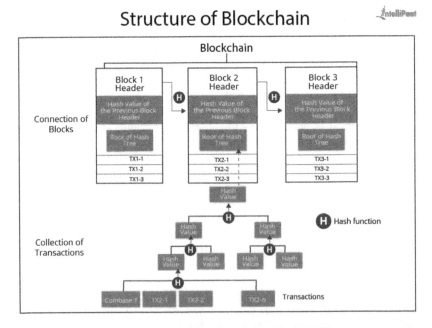

Fig. 1.   Blockchain Structure (Raj, 2022).

secure collecting of massive volumes of data, data storage, data analytics, and data protection. Lastly, we conclude by discussing some implications of these findings. The next step is for us to investigate the most recent research on how blockchain technology can be implemented to make use of big data in a variety of settings, including smart cities, smart health care, smart transportation, and the smart grid (Deepa et al., 2022).

A method based on blockchain technology has been developed in order to encourage mobile nodes to gather data in an effective manner and safeguard the data collection process in ad hoc networks. In addition, blockchain was utilized in conjunction with edge computing in order to enhance data quality, carry out compute-intensive operations required by Internet of Things (IoT) devices, and guarantee those devices' safety (Wu, Wang, Ma, & Leung, 2021). Computers, to enhance data quality, carry out compute-intensive processes necessary for IoT devices, and protect such devices (Wu et al., 2021). We looked into people's concerns regarding their privacy and the safety of using blockchain technology.

Numerous Industries Utilize Blockchain Technology

Using an immutable, shared database that members can only access with authorization, industry-specific blockchain technology employs an immutable, shared ledger. A network's organizations interact to determine what kind of information and actions each other organization and member can access. Blockchain is sometimes known as a trustless network. This isn't because business partners can't trust one another; rather, they don't have to in order for the network to perform correctly. This faith is founded on blockchain technology's enhanced security, increased transparency, and immediate traceability. In addition to overcoming trust difficulties, blockchain technology has further economic benefits, such as lower costs due to increased speed, efficiency, and automation. Blockchain eliminates or substantially reduces the need for third-party or inter-mediary transaction verification by reducing paperwork and human error (IBM Blockchain, n.d.). Blockchain enables all stakeholders to directly participate in the management of industrial processes by facilitating decentralized management of business-to-business activities. The Responsible Sourcing Blockchain Network (RSBN) enables blockchain by enabling verification of each process's compliance with the blockchain network's community-established industrial standards (Mendling et al., 2018). RSBN provides an immutable record of an asset's history that can be used to analyze its origin, components, updates, maintenance, and operations. Each modification to an ecosystem-relevant resource can be recorded on the blockchain, ensuring both the data's integrity and the time of modification.

A business model is the way a company does business and runs its operations to gain a competitive edge and improve its products in order to create value for all of its stakeholders. A business model is also known as a business strategy (Amit & Zott, 2012). Businesses digitalize their business models to increase their compet-itiveness due to the realities of a dynamic market, technological advancements, and fluctuating client demands (Li, 2020). The blockchain, which was initially used in the banking sector, is now used to transfer digital data across industries. By altering the way digital transactions are executed, a blockchain can provide businesses with new capabilities (Zhu, Peko, Sundaram, & Piramuthu, 2021). Specific blockchain applications for commercial operations, such as supply chain management, were prioritized during development (Wang, Chen, & Zghari-Sales, 2021). Blockchain technology can create a unique digital infrastructure in businesses, which could lead to the creation of new business models (Tiscini, Testarmata, Ciaburri, & Ferrari, 2020). Utilizing various sorts of blockchains is accompanied by its own set of perks and cons. There are three types of blockchains: consortium, public, and private. What differentiates one blockchain from another is the level of data accessibility, decentralized governance, and operational complexity that each type of blockchain delivers (Morkunas, Paschen, & Boon, 2019). A public blockchain is open to all parties, so data access is not restricted (Bauer, Zavolokina, Leisibach, & Schwabe, 2019).

Table 1 shows the pros and cons of public, consortium, and private blockchain networks based on their technological properties (access to data, operational complexity, and decentralized control) in terms of the value of stores, the value of networks, and the value of chains. These advantages and disadvantages are brought about as a result of the fact that public, consortium, and private blockchain networks all utilize blockchain technology. Table 1 shows a comparison of the value of the stores, networks, and chains in the public, consortium, and private blockchain networks. The ability to create value is particularly dependent on two different skills. The ability of the network to foster collaboration among its members is the first consideration. On the other hand, data validation raises one's level of confidence in the dependability of transaction security, which in turn encourages trustworthy cooperation (Chong, Lim, Hua, Zheng, & Tan, 2019). Data validation, on the other hand, makes transactions permanent, limiting experimentation and actor interaction flexibility (Chen & Bellavitis, 2020). The second quality is an expert level of competence in the handling of transactions. In many industries, the process of creating value for customers through the modification of products is rethought by tracing the quality of services and the customer's journey (Behnke & Janssen, 2020). Nonetheless, ā controller can jeopardize user privacy, which undermines the creation of value (Tiscini et al., 2020).

The way a blockchain delivers value shows how far technology has come in making service delivery more efficient. Two factors determine the extent to which technology enhances efficiency. To begin, the success of a process is dependent on the speed and security of the disintermediation mechanism's operations, which leads to an increase in the number of transactions. Despite this, disintermediation increases the operational complexity of permissionless networks. This, in turn, makes service delivery administration more complicated and increases the likelihood of a halt in operational activity. Second, the effectiveness with which value is supplied indicates the ability to communicate with a larger audience. Despite the potential for blockchain technology to generate network effects, there is a risk that the system's scalability will be jeopardized if too many people have access to the data (Kundu, 2019). The blockchain has an influence on value capture that is

Table 1. Business Model Roles and Value Setups to Blockchain Technical Qualities, Benefits, and Hazards.

Functions of Business Models	Blockchain Benefits and Risks	Value Shop	Value Network	Value Chain
Value Creation	Trustable Collaboration	Public Consortium	Public Consortium	Public Consortium
	Inflexible Transactions	Public Consortium	Public Consortium	Public Consortium
	Controlled Value		Private Consortium	Private Consortium
	Privacy Issues		Public	Public
Value Delivery	Service Delivery		Public Private Consortium	Public Private Consortium
	Service Disruption		Public	Public
	Network Effect	Public	Public	Public
	Scalability Challenge	Public	Public	Public
Value Capture	Cost Efficiency	Public Consortium	Public Private Consortium	Public Private Consortium
	Increased Investment	Public	Public	Public
Blockchain Type	Technical characteristics of the blockchain			
Public Blockchain	*"accessibility – permissionless, control over transactions – decentralized, complexity – high"*			
Consortium Blockchain	*"accessibility – permissioned, control over transaction – partially decentralized, complexity – medium"*			
Private Blockchain	*"accessibility – permissioned, control over transactions – centralized, complexity – low"*			

diametrically opposed to how it will affect an organization's cost-to-revenue structure. Even though there is evidence that using a blockchain could cut down on the costs of tracking, monitoring, and storing information (Ahluwalia, Mahto, & Guerrero, 2020), building and maintaining blockchain infrastructure requires significant resources (Notheisen, Shanmugam, & Cholewa, 2017). From a technical point of view, the information on this page gives a complete look at how public, consortium, and private blockchain systems work. A study of the pros and cons of different technologies in relation to the functions and value configurations of business models is also included.

Blockchain Technology for Security and Privacy in Industry

Using blockchain technology to track how goods and services are used to see how well quality standards are being met and to find out what customers want so that services can be tailored to their needs may make it possible to regulate prices (Behnke & Janssen, 2020). When companies use transactional data to improve products and services and offer solutions that add value, customers become part of the value-making process. The customers stop just watching and start taking part in the process of creating value (Sena, Bhaumik, & Sengupta, 2019). The personalization leads to "lock-in effects," or the desire to do business with the same company again, as well as more brand loyalty and higher switching costs (Hanninen, Smedboe, & Mitronen, 2018). Although the inclusion does not materially alter the offering, it does increase the products worth (Frank, Mendes, & Ayala, 2019).

Accessibility to data, authenticity of data, and centralized control are prerequisites for value management via customization and quality assurance. If a customer has confidence in a company and is certain that their information will not be misused, they may grant that company access to their personal information (Bauer et al., 2019). The "procedures validate and authorize the data provided by different system actors help build trust between a company and its customers" (Zheng, Xie, Dai, & Chen, 2017). Businesses access data in a dynamic manner in order to obtain information and expand the value of their services, while ensuring that the system-stored data is reliable (Bauer et al., 2019). Therefore, from a purely technical standpoint, value control authority is bestowed (Behnke & Janssen, 2020). Tracing data is an integral component of both public and consortium blockchain networks and anyone with network access can perform this operation. Business models that serve as value chains and value networks make it easier to manage value (Chong et al., 2019; Zhang, Yi, & Wang, 2021).

In value-shop firms, such as open innovation platforms, organizations (i.e., service providers) cede control over transactions and value creation to other platform-accessible parties (Chong et al., 2019). This suggests that customers modify value offerings via a cycle of problem identification, resolution, implementation, and evaluation (Stabell & Fjeldstad, 1998). According to (Chong et al., 2019; Xu, Lu, Liu, Zhu, & Yao, 2019) the data recorded using consortium blockchain in financial sector value-network organizations leads to the creation of risk-control and sophisticated credit models. These strategies make it possible to provide services more quickly and reduce the financial risks for both the company and its customers. Control between trading parties can be demonstrated through the validation and evaluation of sensitive business data in a blockchain-based consortium network, fostering cooperation among the network's members (Chang & Chen, 2020; Rahmanzadeh, Pishvaee, & Rasouli, 2020). At each step of a trade, embedded smart contracts check to make sure that procedures follow the rules (Dai & Vasarhelyi, 2017). This allows importers to identify and comprehend transactional and supply chain bottlenecks, allowing them to address the issue's root cause (Chang & Chen, 2020). Other businesses can employ private blockchain technologies like chain security to create value networks that mediate all stakeholder interactions. Through mediation, the lack of control improves how well a business works, lowers the risk of investments, and saves money for all stakeholders (Chong et al., 2019). Also, removing middlemen from the relationship between customers and businesses makes customers more likely to trust businesses, which is good for the customer journey (Kumar, Ramachandran, & Kumar, 2020).

Using private blockchain technology is radically changing how food is grown and delivered (Zhao et al., 2019). Because distributed ledgers make data easier to access, users can track a product's path through the supply chain and be sure that industries are following safety, quality, and regulatory standards (Tiscini et al., 2020). Tracing the food supply chain both upstream and downstream is made possible when all of the actors in the supply chain are brought together into a single system, known as a consortium (Behnke & Janssen, 2020). Behnke and Janssen (2020) give the example of chain draft as another example of a blockchain platform that was built through a partnership. It makes possible to build a trustworthy framework for the exchange of value that streamlines existing corporate activities like purchasing administration and gives customers more power (Chong et al., 2019). According to O'Leary (2017) IBM and Maersk worked together to make a system that turned all paperwork into digital files and gave full visibility into how products were delivered.

Data accessibility and decentralized control harm data privacy (Lu et al., 2019; Tiscini et al., 2020). Privacy is crucial to corporate operations because privacy concerns can reduce a company's social worth (Bocken, Short, & Rana, 2014; Dempsey, Bramley, & Power, 2011; Evans et al., 2017). Public blockchains increase the likelihood of privacy breaches (Feng, He, Zeadally, Khan, & Kumar, 2019). Within unrestricted network access makes it easier for unauthorized actions to occur (Notheisen et al., 2017). Even though they add a lot to the system's complexity and deployment costs (Anderson, Holz, Ponomarev, & Rimba, 2016; Ateniese, Bonacina, Faonio, & Galesi, 2014; Kiayias, Russell, David, & Ouroboros, 2017), privacy measures make it harder for bad people to break into public blockchain networks. These barriers include the implementation of "proof of cost," "proof of stake," and "proof." The identities of the other actors have been established due to the fact that the members of the group have been preverified. The decision as to whether or not new members are allowed to join is made either by the leaders of the group or by the existing members of the network. According to Morkunas et al. (2019), the increased secrecy is a direct result of the private nature of transactions. Second, permissioned blockchains, also known as private and consortium blockchains, allow data access only with network participants' consent. This restricts who can access the data. This is the case despite the fact that the network's central authority has control over the transactions that take place on the permissioned blockchain (Zheng et al., 2017). Therefore, subjects of consent-based personal data provision are users of both private blockchain systems and consortium blockchain technologies.

Utilization of Blockchain in Multiple Industries Using a Prudent and Secure Strategy

Using a blockchain helps industries improve their service delivery by enabling interactions between organizational stakeholders that are both efficient and secure. These interactions are made possible by the credibility and accessibility of the data (Chen & Bellavitis, 2020; Karamchandani & Srivastava, 2020; Morkunas et al., 2019). Because of how the decentralized trust system works, a third party is no longer needed to act as a middleman between a provider and a recipient. As a result, procedures are enhanced both inside and outside of companies, improving interoperability (Bauer et al., 2019; Chen & Bellavitis, 2020; Morkunas et al., 2019). Using a blockchain to decentralizedly connect multiple organizations makes it possible to capitalize on synergies between industries. Access to customer information by all parties involved in a transaction simplifies and improves the efficiency of business operations (Morkunas et al., 2019). Using data validation procedures guarantees that the blockchain network's records are secure and cannot be altered (Bauer et al., 2019).

Permissionless and permissioned blockchains can benefit from decentralization and improved data access and authenticity (Chen & Bellavitis, 2020; Chong et al., 2019; Morkunas et al., 2019; Zavolokina, Ziolkowski, Bauer, & Management, 2020). Therefore, the optimization of service delivery may be advantageous for business models enabled by blockchain in a variety of industries. For example, logistics solutions based on blockchain technology ensure the seamless integration of all supply chain participants, which is necessary to satisfy the requirements of interorganizational agreements. Using smart contracts, the process of transferring ownership of an item from one participant in a logistics system to another can be completely and automatically automated. These contracts can automatically respond to data submissions in order to finalize the agreements (Caro, Ali, & Vecchio, 2018). By validating transaction-related documents, smart contracts can expedite the closing of deals when a relationship exists between a buyer and a seller. Therefore, this expedites the purchasing process for all involved parties (Morkunas et al., 2019). The use of intermediaries in financial transactions may become obsolete with the advent of blockchain technology. It has the potential to strengthen ties amongst consumers as well. Users can make wire transfers and other financial activities across national borders (Morkunas et al., 2019).

The efficiency of transferring resources and information within an organization can be improved by using digital mediation or getting rid of middlemen by using private blockchain technology in value networks. In order to speed up the delivery of goods and services, traditional supply chains are being rethought. Blockchain technology is being used in this process (Chong et al., 2019). By putting together a group of companies that use private blockchain networks, service throughput time can be cut in two different but related ways (Kumar, Kandpal, & Ahmad, 2023; Gerth & Heim, 2020). Due to the elimination of intermediaries and the sharing of data between organizations, both parties engaged in international trade have the opportunity to benefit from increased export efficiency (Kumar et al., 2023). The distributed ledger technology has the potential to become a way to build on-demand internet services that don't give up users' privacy. This might be a significant step forward in the evolution of the internet (Gerth & Heim, 2020; Li, Barenji, & Huang, 2018). Likewise, public blockchains could facilitate online learning services, thereby accelerating the process of acquiring educational credentials such as diplomas and degrees (Sun, Wang, & Wang, 2018).

By using this technology in manufacturing industries to track component production and make quick prototypes, the time between having an idea and putting a product on the market can be cut down by a lot (Mandolla, Petruzzelli, & Percoco, 2019). Consortium blockchain applications enhance the effectiveness of consortium network members' business operations (Chong et al., 2019; Qiao, Zhu, & Wang, 2018). Smart contracts can be used to automate payment processing, which can speed up the approval of transactions and the shipping of goods in the context of how a business works (Chong et al., 2019). Regarding public blockchain networks, they are utilized in the implementation of food supply chain traceability systems. Customers now have access to previously unavailable services as a result of the newly constructed system (Chong et al., 2019). When businesses implement blockchain technology, service disruptions may occur (Behnke & Janssen, 2020; Chong et al., 2019; Janssen, Weerakkody, Ismagilova, & Sivarajah, 2020). A public blockchain network poses a greater threat than a private or consortium blockchain network due to the fact that its processes for certifying data and restricting data access are distinct. Three things make private blockchain networks and consortium blockchain networks more adaptable and able to work with each other than public blockchain networks (Chong et al., 2019; Zavolokina et al., 2020). First, the initial participation of new group members is limited in blockchain systems that are either private or consortium-based. The group may be accessed by its members, a regulatory agency, or a consortium. This limitation is applicable to both public and private blockchains (Morkunas et al., 2019). Transactions that take place on a public distributed ledger, on the other hand, have the potential to cause delays. The public blockchain experiences a high volume of traffic due to the participation of external users, resulting in a delay in data processing (Okon, Elgendi, Sholiyi, Elmirghani, & Jamalipour, 2020). Therefore, constraining users' access to data and participation in network activities helps maintain a manageable number of users, which increases throughput, decreases latency, and increases bandwidth (Morkunas et al., 2019; Wang et al., 2017). Second, the security mechanism of the public blockchain is one of its most vulnerable components (Zheng et al., 2017). Checking each digital record that is added to a block takes more time because of the way the process works. This is done to ensure that public networks are kept secure (Yli-Huumo, Ko, Choi, & Park, 2016).

The cryptographic protocols used to secure data may contain vulnerabilities that expose the data to the public, or they may demand excessive computational power (El Ioini, Pahl, & Helmer, 2018; Gennaro, Goldfeder, & Narayanan, 2016). This suggests that security breaches may hinder value delivery (Zheng et al., 2017). Third, the fact that there are many different kinds of people in public blockchain communities makes it more likely that the blockchain will split or split into many branches. Because of this, there is a chance that the rules that govern the system will need to be changed, and there is also a chance that value chains could be impacted (Islam, Mäntymäki, & Turunen, 2019). Due to the fact that blockchains can split into multiple branches, this is possible.

The blockchain's decentralized system, which has led to the integration of all participants into the platform and made network effects possible, is primarily responsible for enabling this development (Kundu, 2019).

Blockchain technology accelerates player interactions, which, in the long run, results in an expansion of the network's scope (Fu, Wang, & Zhao, 2017). In order to achieve a positive network effect, it is crucial to have both high data accessibility and decentralized control. The distributed ledger makes it possible to provide access to a large number of participants, thereby encouraging widespread adoption of the blockchain's services. The greater the number of individuals adopting a technology, the more widespread its adoption will become (Schmidt & Wagner, 2019). Due to network effects, it is easier for platforms with decentralized authorities and open access to deliver security solutions to their intended audience. This is because these platforms cater to a larger population (Abbatemarco, De Rossi, & Gaur, 2020). As the number of entities in the network grows, the decentralized trust structure makes sure that no one entity can control the network. This means that all entities in the network have the same chance of making a transaction. This is accomplished by preventing a single entity from gaining control of the network (Chen & Bellavitis, 2020). Due to the fact that there must be an adequate level of blockchain diffusion for value to be created and delivered, the deployment of a public blockchain is a technical prerequisite for the capability to do so. The network continues to expand while retaining its decentralized structure because participation does not require prior authorization (Schmidt & Wagner, 2019).

Implementing a private blockchain or consortium blockchain in industries that operate as value chains or value networks results in the introduction of new governance structures for existing activities. The controlled value advantage is enabled by the implementation of new governance. Companies can act as value controllers to customize and improve their products and services while monitoring data exchange. Such actions enable the development of complementary services with added value, which may result in a lock-in effect (Amit & Zott, 2001; Direction, 2017; Hanninen, Smedlund, & Mitronen, 2018). This effect is what motivates individuals to conduct multiple transactions. Car Dossier could, for instance, tailor its products and services to the preferences of its customers by utilizing the blockchain's potential. Possibilities include tailoring packages to the specifications of specific vehicles, determining *"pricing strategies, and offering discounts based on a customer's purchase history"* (Bauer et al., 2019).

The mapping of blockchain-enabled BMI design elements to value chains shown in Table 2 indicates that value chains will employ blockchain technology's distributed ledger rather than networks or value stores.

The blockchain will be used to store information regarding the safety level, which will be susceptible to modification. Each node consistently adds data to the blockchain. The generated information on the security quality of the link is then

Table 2. Overview of the Private, Consortium, and Public BMI Design Components, Value Drivers, and Value configurations.

BMI Design	Value Configuration	Blockchain Benefit	Blockchain Type	Value Drivers	Examples
New Activities	Value chain	Trustable collaborations	Public, consortium	Novelty, efficiency	Collaboration in the creation of digital assets and novel solutions utilizing blockchain technology.
		Service delivery	Public, consortium, private	Novelty, lock-in, complementarity, efficiency	Monitoring and tracing systems that make it possible to produce and distribute goods and services more quickly.
		Network effects	Public	Novelty, efficiency	A rise in the number of users participating in systems opens to the public.
		Cost efficiency	Public, consortium, private	Novelty, efficiency	Development of novel production processes and distribution strategies, which result in a price reduction for the end product.
	Value shop	Trustable collaborations	Public, consortium	Novelty, efficiency	Providing support for the collaborative development of applications.
		Network effects	Public	Novelty, efficiency	Extending the reach of the community of codevelopers working on open-access platforms.

Table 2. (*Continued*)

BMI Design	Value Configuration	Blockchain Benefit	Blockchain Type	Value Drivers	Examples
New Structure	Value network	Cost efficiency	Public, consortium	Novelty, efficiency	Improved efficiency in the creation and implementation of individualized solutions.
		Trustable collaborations	Public, consortium	Novelty, efficiency, complementarity	Innovative types of cooperation between various organizations and commercial systems.
		Service delivery	Public, consortium, private	Novelty, lock-in, efficiency	On-demand online services
		Network effects	Public	Novelty, efficiency	Increasing the influence of stakeholders as a result of decentralized governance.
		Cost efficiency	Public, consortium, private	Novelty, efficiency	Disintermediation without the need for trust, reduction of transaction costs, and reduction of both financial fraud and security risks.
New Governance	Value network	Controlled value	Private, consortium	Novelty, lock-in	Because of the validation and security of the transactions, stakeholders are confined within the network.
	Value chain	Controlled value	Private, consortium	Novelty, complementarity	Agricultural and food goods' ability to be tracked, along with other associated services.

packaged into individual blocks, at which point it becomes unalterable proof. On the safety blockchain, all information pertaining to an employee's safety is permanently stored. The precautions data is entered into the computer's processing area, where it is analyzed and evaluated. The level of the employee's commitment to safety is rated in accordance with the results of the evaluation. On this basis, employees will have a clear understanding of their own safety qualities and will be able to visualize safety-related information. This will allow for the most efficient personnel distribution. Every piece of construction-related safety data collected throughout an employee's career is added to a blockchain and stored there so that a comprehensive analysis of construction workers' protective abilities can be conducted. Human resources, technical training, psychological training, safety management, departments dealing with tangential issues, employee safety data, etc., are examples of departments that could become nodes in the safety blockchain. Construction workers stand out among them (Yi, Sun, & Guo, 2016). Therefore, employees are restricted to only querying the data on the safety blockchain. Distributed ledger accounting and consensus services do not involve employee engagement. Using mobile phone applications or other techniques, construction workers can access their own safety-related information. All departments besides the department of construction workers are fixed nodes that participate in the blockchain's accounting and transactions. Across the many nodes, the blockchain technology can be implemented in a variety of distinct ways.

Training in psychological quality focuses primarily on enhancing employees' mental health, and the record form may also include training in safety skills. On the distributed ledger, the records of the individuals responsible for managing the coal mine are updated in real time to reflect any violations. It is essential that the information you enter be accurate and that you include details such as the time, location, process, and outcomes of the violation.

The information that has been provided concerning the architecture staff's level of expertise and level of security is accurate. Assessment management represents both employee safety inputs and outputs, and safety quality assessment administration is the cornerstone for employee safety information management. The blockchain has the potential to be utilized to record any and all employment information relevant to occupational health and safety for those joining the construction business. Because of the properties of the blockchain, it is feasible to validate the information as genuine and establish that it has not been tampered with in any way. Because of this, the blockchain is able to maintain the reliability of the data. Big data, cloud computing, artificial intelligence (AI), and various other technologies are used to analyze the safety information resources that architectural workers have access to. These analyses are performed by professionals. The purpose of these assessments is to determine the level of security and quality that are maintained by architectural workers. Following this step, information concerning the level of security provided by the system is posted to the blockchain.

This is done by giving each link a weight, using the right methods to evaluate safety and quality, and putting the data on the blockchain. As a result, blockchain, a new distributed technology that first gained popularity in the financial sector (Crosby, Pattanayak, & Verma, 2016), has been implemented in fields including energy, logistics, education (Chen, Xu, Lu, & Chen, 2018), training, the application library scene, and the building materials supply chain.

Blockchain technology was incorporated into the maritime information management system to achieve this objective. The benefits and underlying ideas of blockchain technology were what motivated this decision. The total security of a blockchain requires a consensus process. This indicates that all of the nodes that are part of the decentralized peer-to-peer system need to reach consensus on the current state of the blockchain. If a node makes an attempt to falsely portray the state of the blockchain, its record of the blockchain will not match the records kept by the other nodes', and the node's record will be disregarded and not added to the blockchain (Edwards, 2019). This group of consensus processes, which includes the nodes talking to each other, is a big part of what makes the blockchain secure. The blockchain verifies the legitimacy of transactions prior to adding them to the ledger. Across the many nodes, the blockchain technology can be implemented in a variety of distinct ways.

The human resources department of the construction company is very important to the development of the safety blockchain. Before putting identifying information like their name, age, and level of education on the blockchain, employees in any industry first set up personal information files. The system keeps track of the security training node and automatically gives it permission to do a transaction whenever it gets a request from the security training node. In addition to this, the system is responsible for maintaining follow-up documentation and ensuring the safety of personal security information. The term "security skill training" can apply to a wide range of activities that are carried out by companies in order to improve the level of operation of their workforce. Each instance of training has its own duration, objective, procedure, and outcomes, as well as its own information added to the blockchain.

Training in psychological quality focuses primarily on enhancing employees' mental health, and the record form may also include training in safety skills. On the distributed ledger, the records of the individuals in charge of managing the coal mine document violations in real time. To ensure that the information regarding an employee's safety and quality in the architectural field is accurate, the information must be entered correctly, including the violation time, location, process, and repercussions, among other details (Skiba, 2020).

Conclusion

This study analyzed both the positive and negative effects that the implementation of blockchain technology would have on business processes. The void outlined two distinct research project objectives. To ascertain whether public blockchains, consortium blockchains, and private blockchains share any aspects of the technology, we conducted a literature search. With this knowledge, we were able to ensure the safety of a wide range of businesses. Data security solutions from

RSBN that work well can be used by the organization that got them. Before the company can use blockchain technology to change the way it does business, it needs to adjust and align the skills and resources it already has. This is a necessary requirement that needs to be satisfied.

References

Abbatemarco, N., De Rossi, L. M., Gaur, A., & Salviotti, G. (2020). Beyond a blockchain paradox: How intermediaries can leverage a disintermediation technology. In *Proceedings of the 53rd Hawaii international conference on system sciences.*

Ahluwalia, S., Mahto, R. V., & Guerrero, M. (2020). Blockchain technology and startup financing: A transaction cost economics perspective. *Technological Forecasting and Social Change, 151.*

Amit, R., & Zott, C. (2001). Value creation in e-business. *Strategic Management Journal, 22,* 493–520.

Amit, R., & Zott, C. (2012). Creating value through business model innovation. *Sloan Management Review, 53*(3), 41–49.

Anderson, L., Holz, R., Ponomarev, A., Rimba, P., & Weber, I. (2016). New kids on the block: An analysis of modern blockchains. *arXiv [cs.CR].* http://arxiv.org/abs/1606.06530

Ateniese, G., Bonacina, I., Faonio, A., & Galesi, N. (2014). Proofs of space: When space is of the essence. In *International conference on security and cryptography for networks* (pp. 538–557). Springer.

Bauer, I., Zavolokina, L., Leisibach, F., & Schwabe, G. (2019). Exploring blockchain value creation: The case of the car ecosystem. In *Proceedings of the 52nd Hawaii international conference on system sciences.*

Behnke, K., & Janssen, M. F. W. H. A. (2020). Boundary conditions for traceability in food supply chains using blockchain technology. *International Journal of Information Management, 52.*

Bocken, N. M., Short, S. W., Rana, P., & Evans, S. (2014). A literature and practice review to develop sustainable business model archetypes. *Journal of Cleaner Production, 65,* 42–56.

Caro, M. P., Ali, M. S., Vecchio, M., & Giaffreda, R. (2018). Blockchain-based traceability in agri-food supply chain management: A practical implementation. *IoT Vertical and Topical Summit on Agriculture, 1–4.*

Chang, S. E., & Chen, Y. (2020). When blockchain meets supply chain: A systematic literature review on current development and potential applications. *IEEE Access, 8,* 62478–62494.

Chen, Y., & Bellavitis, C. (2020). Blockchain disruption and decentralized finance: The rise of decentralized business models. *Journal of Business Venturing Insights, 13*(e00151), e00151. doi:10.1016/j.jbvi.2019.e00151

Chen, G., Xu, B., Lu, M., & Chen, N.-S. (2018). Exploring blockchain technology and its potential applications for education. *Smart Learning Environments, 5*(1). doi:10.1186/s40561-017-0050-x

Chong, A. Y. L., Lim, E. T. K., Hua, X., Zheng, S., & Tan, C.-W. (2019). Business on chain: A comparative case study of five blockchain-inspired business models.

Journal of the Association for Information Systems, 1308–1337. doi:10.17705/1jais. 00568

Crosby, M., Pattanayak, P., & Verma, S. (2016). Blockchain technology: Beyond bitcoin. *Applied Innovation*, *2*(6–10).

Dai, J., & Vasarhelyi, M. A. (2017). Toward blockchain-based accounting and assurance. *Journal of Information Systems*, 5–21.

Deepa, N., Pham, Q.-V., Nguyen, D. C., Bhattacharya, S., Prabadevi, B., Gadekallu, T. R., ... Pathirana, P. N. (2022). A survey on blockchain for big data: Approaches, opportunities, and future directions. *Future Generation Computer Systems: FGCS*, *131*, 209–226. doi:10.1016/j.future.2022.01.017

Dempsey, N., Bramley, G., Power, S., & Brown, C. (2011). The social dimension of sustainable development: Defining urban social sustainability. *Sustainable Development*, *19*, 289–300.

Dhanalakshmi, S., & Babu, G. C. (2019). An examination of big data and blockchain technology. *International Journal of Innovative Technology and Exploring Engineering*, *8*(11), 3118–3122. doi:10.35940/ijitee.k2497.0981119

Direction Getting "freemium" business model right: Key to remarkable success or a costly trap. (2017).

Edwards, J. (2019). *What is blockchain technology? How blockchain works, who's using it and why it's much more than just bitcoin.* Retrieved from https://www.finder.com. au/blockchain-guide

Evans, S., Vladimirova, D., Holgado, M., Van Fossen, K., Yang, M., Silva, E. A., & Barlow, C. Y. (2017). Business model innovation for sustainability: Towards a unified perspective for creation of sustainable business models. *Business Strategy and the Environment*, *26*, 597–608.

Feng, Q., He, D., Zeadally, S., Khan, M. K., & Kumar, N. (2019). A survey on privacy protection in blockchain system. *Journal of Network and Computer Applications*, *126*, 45–58. doi:10.1016/j.jnca.2018.10.020

Frank, A. G., Mendes, G. H., Ayala, N. F., & Ghezzi, A. (2019). Servitization and Industry 4.0 convergence in the digital transformation of product firms: A business model innovation perspective technological. *Technological Forecasting and Social Change*, *141*, 341–351.

Fu, W., Wang, Q., & Zhao, X. (2017). The influence of platform service innovation on value co-creation activities and the network effect. *Journal of Service Management*, *28*, 348–388.

Gennaro, R., Goldfeder, S., & Narayanan, A. (2016). Threshold-optimal DSA/ ECDSA signatures and an application to Bitcoin wallet security. In *International conference on applied cryptography and network security* (pp. 156–174). Springer.

Gerth, S., & Heim, L. (2020). Trust through digital technologies. In *Blockchain in online consultancy services proceedings of the 2020 the 2nd international conference on blockchain technology* (pp. 150–154).

Hänninen, M., Smedlund, A., & Mitronen, L. (2018). Digitalization in retailing: Multi-sided platforms as drivers of industry transformation. *Baltic Journal of Management*, *13*(2), 152–168.

IBM Blockchain. (n.d.). *Benefits of blockchain. Ibm.com.* Retrieved from https://www. ibm.com/in-en/topics/benefits-of-blockchain

Ioini, N. E., Pahl, C., & Helmer, S. (2018). *A decision framework for blockchain platforms for IoT and edge computing.* SCITEPRESS.

Islam, A. N., Mäntymäki, M., & Turunen, M. (2019). Why do blockchains split? An actor-network perspective on Bitcoin splits technological forecasting and social change. *Technological Forecasting and Social Change, 148*.

Janssen, M., Weerakkody, V., Ismagilova, E., Sivarajah, U., & Irani, Z. (2020). A framework for analysing blockchain technology adoption: Integrating institutional, market and technical factors. *International Journal of Information Management, 50*, 302–309.

Karamchandani, A., & Srivastava, S. K. (2020). Perception-based model for analyzing the impact of enterprise blockchain adoption on SCM in the Indian service industry. *International Journal of Information Management, 52*.

Kiayias, A., Russell, A., David, B., Ouroboros, R. O., & Oliynykov, R. (2017). Ouroboros: A provably secure proof-of-stake blockchain protocol. In *Annual international cryptology conference* (pp. 357–388). Springer.

Kumar, R., Kandpal, B., & Ahmad, V. (2023). Industrial IoT (IIOT): Security threats and countermeasures. In *2023 International Conference on Innovative Data Communication Technologies and Application (ICIDCA)*, Uttarakhand, India (pp. 829–833), doi:10.1109/ICIDCA56705.2023.10100145

Kumar, V., Ramachandran, D., & Kumar, B. (2020). Influence of new-age technologies on marketing: A research agenda. *Journal of Business Research, 125*, 864–877.

Kundu, D. (2019). Blockchain and trust in a smart city. *Environment & Urbanization Asia, 10*(1), 31–43. doi:10.1177/0975425319832392

Li, F. (2020). The digital transformation of business models in the creative industries: A holistic framework and emerging trends. *Technovation, 92–93*(102012), 102012. doi:10.1016/j.technovation.2017.12.004

Li, Z., Barenji, A. V., & Huang, G. Q. (2018). Toward a blockchain cloud manufacturing system as a peer to peer distributed network platform. *Robotics and Computer-Integrated Manufacturing, 54*, 133–144.

Lu, L., Chen, J., Tian, Z., He, Q., Huang, B., Xiang, Y., & Liu, Z. (2019). Educoin: A secure and efficient payment solution for MOOC environment. In *IEEE international conference on blockchain (blockchain) IEEE* (pp. 490–495).

Mandolla, C., Petruzzelli, A. M., Percoco, G., & Urbinati, A. (2019). Building a digital twin for additive manufacturing through the exploitation of blockchain: A case analysis of the aircraft industry. *Computers in Industry, 109*, 134–152.

Mendling, J., Weber, I., Aalst, W. V. D., Brocke, J. V., Cabanillas, C., Daniel, F., . . . Dustar, S. (2018). Blockchains for business process management-challenges and opportunities. *ACM Transactions on Management Information Systems, 9*, 1–16.

Morkunas, V. J., Paschen, J., & Boon, E. (2019). How blockchain technologies impact your business model. *Business Horizons, 62*, 295–306.

Notheisen, B., Shanmugam, A. P., & Cholewa, J. B. (2017). Trading real-world assets on blockchain. *Business & Information Systems Engineering, 59*, 425–440.

Okon, A. A., Elgendi, I., Sholiyi, O. S., Elmirghani, J. M., Jamalipour, A., & Munasinghe, K. (2020). Blockchain and SDN architecture for spectrum management in cellular networks. *IEEE Access, 8*, 94415–94428.

O'leary, D. E. (2017). Configuring blockchain architectures for transaction information in blockchain consortiums: The case of accounting and supply chain systems. *Intelligent Systems in Accounting, Finance and Management, 24*, 138–147.

Qiao, R., Zhu, S., Wang, Q., & Qin, J. (2018). Optimization of dynamic data traceability mechanism in Internet of Things based on consortium blockchain. *International Journal of Distributed Sensor Networks, 14.*

Rahmanzadeh, S., Pishvaee, M. S., & Rasouli, M. R. (2020). Integrated innovative product design and supply chain tactical planning within a blockchain platform. *International Journal of Production Research, 58,* 2242–2262.

Raj, R. (2022, December 29). *How does blockchain work? – Blockchain transaction – Intellipaat.* Intellipaat Blog; Intellipaat. Retrieved from https://intellipaat.com/blog/tutorial/blockchain-tutorial/how-does-blockchain-work/

Schmidt, C. G., & Wagner, S. M. (2019). Blockchain and supply chain relations: A transaction cost theory perspective. *Journal of Purchasing and Supply Management, 25.*

Sena, V., Bhaumik, S., Sengupta, A., & Demirbag, M. (2019). Big data and performance: What can management research tell us? *British Journal of Management, 30,* 219–228.

Skiba, R. (2020). Blockchain technology as a health and safety contributor in the transport and logistics industry – Human resource requirements. *International Journal of Innovative Science and Research Technology, 5*(4), 544–550. doi:10.38124/ijisrt20apr685

Stabell, C. B., & Fjeldstad, O. D. (1998). Configuring value for competitive advantage: On chains, shops and networks. *Strategic Management Journal, 19,* 413–437.

Sun, H., Wang, X., & Wang, X. (2018). Application of blockchain technology in online education. *International Journal of Emerging Technologies in Learning, 13.*

Tiscini, R., Testarmata, S., Ciaburri, M., & Ferrari, E. (2020). The blockchain as a sustainable business model innovation. *Management Decision, 58,* 1621–1642.

Wang, Y., Chen, C. H., & Zghari-Sales, A. (2021). Designing a blockchain enabled supply chain. *International Journal of Production Research, 59,* 1450–1475.

Wang, J., Wu, P., Wang, X., & Shou, W. (2017). The outlook of blockchain technology for construction engineering management. *Frontiers of Engineering Management.* 67–75.

Wu, Y., Wang, Z., Ma, Y., & Leung, V. C. M. (2021). Deep reinforcement learning for blockchain in industrial IoT: A survey. *Computer Networks, 191*(108004), 108004. doi:10.1016/j.comnet.2021.108004

Xu, X., Lu, Q., Liu, Y., Zhu, L., Yao, H., & Vasilakos, A. V. (2019). Designing blockchain-based applications a case study for imported product traceability. *Future Generation Computer Systems, 92,* 399–406.

Yi, X., Sun, H. B., & Guo, Q. L. (2016). Electricity transactions and congestion management based on blockchain in energy internet. *Journal of Power System Technology, 40*(12), 3630–3638.

Yli-Huumo, J., Ko, D., Choi, S., Park, S., & Smolander, K. (2016). Where is current research on blockchain technology?-A systematic review. *PLoS One, 11.*

Zavolokina, L., Ziolkowski, R., Bauer, I., Management, G. S., & Schwabe, G. (2020). Management, governance and value creation in a blockchain consortium. *MIS Quarterly Executive, 19,* 1–17.

Zhang, H., Yi, J.-B., & Wang, Q. (2021). Research on the collaborative evolution of blockchain industry ecosystems in terms of value co-creation. *Sustainability, 13.*

Zhao, G., Liu, S., Lopez, C., Lu, H., Elgueta, S., Chen, H., & Boshkoska, B. M. (2019). Blockchain technology in agri-food value chain management: A synthesis of applications. *Challenges and Future Research Directions Computers in Industry*, *109*, 83–99.

Zheng, Z., Xie, S., Dai, H., Chen, X., & Wang, H. (2017). An overview of blockchain technology: Architecture, consensus, and future trends. In *IEEE international congress on big data* (pp. 557–564). BigData Congress. IEEE.

Zhu, X. N., Peko, G., Sundaram, D., & Piramuthu, S. (2021). Blockchain-based agile supply chain framework with Io. *Information Systems Frontiers*, 1–16.

Chapter 10

Is New Wine in a New Bottle? Re-Engineering Poverty Architecture Through the Finnish Model of Education in India

Tushar Soubhari, Sudhansu Sekhar Nanda and Mohd Asif Shah

Abstract

Finland's globally accepted teaching practices are purely based on common sense, and holistically promote equity over excellence. "New Wine in a new bottle" literally means unlearning old thoughts and relearning new skills updated to changes in the world recouping to new trends and establishing ourselves full-fledged meeting the demand of the hour. The question of why India still doesn't get enough Noble Prizes in required disciplines is still unanswerable. Still in India, there exist the archaic forms of the classroom setting with little room for flexibility and no educational freedom; moreover, with a highly pressurised testing environment. With the increasing population of Indian set-up, most of the teachers are underpaid and are less satisfied with the amount of effort they put in and their pay scale. A paradigm shift could be expected in India's educational landscape post the introduction of the National Education Policy 2020; by reducing the academic workload for students and improving their holistic intelligence thereby. The NEP framework has been structured based on certain practical pedagogies from the Finnish context. The 5+3+3+4 model would encourage students to make their communication more effective, prioritising creativity, critical thinking, and personality development; say, various experts. There is a direct connection between education and poverty level in an economy. If the system lacks quality, then it would adversely affect the economic functioning of a nation. This study highlights the cases from both the Indian and Finnish contexts, clarifying the loopholes in our education system and what lessons could be incorporated from the Finnish model; so as to devise a policy at the national level for re-engineering the impoverished situations, keeping in

Fostering Sustainable Businesses in Emerging Economies, 167–186
Copyright © 2024 Tushar Soubhari, Sudhansu Sekhar Nanda and Mohd Asif Shah
Published under exclusive licence by Emerald Publishing Limited
doi:10.1108/978-1-80455-640-520231011

mind sustainable architecture. This chapter is the first of its kind not ever published elsewhere and is original in nature.

Keywords: Finnish model; educational freedom; NEP; creativity; personality development; sustainable architecture

Introduction

Rebottling an old wine into a new bottle doesn't sound good scientifically as excessive air oxidizes the wine perishing the bottle and therefore, the wine pours out. Cataloging the past teachings from the Holy Bible, it was quoted that reframing learning approaches through updated insight could help us to cross the turbulent waves of uncertainty even in times of crisis. The chaotic moments in students' life as an individual start, when they face the competitive world immediately waiting to hunt for a job. The dilemma here lies in the fact that would there be any guarantee for the students to get the right job based on the limited, impractical knowledge that he/she has possessed through their assigned curriculum throughout their studies. In fact, our Indian Educational system needed to be blamed for this negative change. Where does India lie in the global education system (Goyal, 2019). This is the question of the hour. After three decades time, obviously, there had been a rethink in the entire system for which a drastic change is expected to happen in the coming future. Who is responsible for that change? It's none other than ourselves since we have accepted a change to be the CHANGE amid lots of challenges in the global market.

The Indian educational system had been previously functioning based on the frames outlined by Lord Macaulay. After three decades of experimental observations with different innovative approaches to teaching and learning methods; there has been public acceptance to go for the adoption of the "New National Educational Policy- 2020"; the mission achieved under the chairmanship of the former ISRO Chairman Dr. K. Kasturirangan, in due course of achieving the Sustainable Development Goal (SDG) Goal-4 by the year 2030; ensuring inclusive and equitable quality education through the promotion of lifelong opportunities for everyone. The rich heritage of Indian value-based education could be traced back to the times of Takshashila, Vikramshila, Nalanda, and Vallabhi who were scholarly enough to contribute to multidisciplinary teachings across countries. The pursuit of knowledge, truth, and wisdom was considered superior in the Indian school of thought.

Loopholes in the Indian Educational System

It was possible to compare the Indian educational system before and during the British colonial era, and to see a dramatic change. Historically, the "Gurukul" method of education has placed its students in classrooms located beneath a canopy of trees, where they can benefit from increased oxygen levels and a conducive environment for learning. However, after hearing the recommendations of Lord Macaulay, the traditional educational system was changed and the contemporary educational system was implemented. In 2010, after India gained its independence, one of the six essential rights established by the constitution was the right to an education. With this new program, called "Sarva Shiksha Abhiyan," all children aged 6 to 14 were able to get a free public education. Preschool, kindergarten, grade school, middle school, and high school are the foundational levels of education, followed by postsecondary and tertiary programmes (Abhijeet, 2014). India's educational system has long been praised for its excellence. Nonetheless, the timing is not yet right to showcase the abilities. While many people lack access to basic services, those who do tend to leave for countries with higher wages and higher concentrations of skilled workers. Every effort is being made by the government to ensure that every child in India has access to a quality education. Thus, the literacy rate is on the rise, but there are still obstacles to overcome.

The UNESCO State of Education in India 2021 assessment found that there were 11.16 lakh unfilled teaching vacancies. It proved beyond a reasonable doubt that there was a deficiency in classroom educators. Moreover, educators were saddled with an abundance of extracurricular duties, which took their attention away from kids. National Institute of Education Planning and Administration (NIEPA) research indicates that instructors spend only around 19% of their time actually teaching, with the rest going toward administrative tasks that have nothing to do with student learning. In addition, little accountability has been exercised by the Government sector because Government instructors have a lifetime guarantee of job security regardless of their performance.

In our country, academic performance is a proxy for potential. Students who score above 90% are frequently viewed as "bright," while those who score below average are often viewed as "weaklings with no substantial future." Our colonial masters' model of curriculum is still in use today, unaltered and with an unhealthy focus on academic achievement at the expense of students' well-rounded growth. Generations of students have proven themselves to be "bookworms" by relying on their inherited knowledge of literature and history at the expense of actually contributing to society. There is very little opportunity for students to engage in hands-on exploration and investigation, and instead the curriculum focuses almost exclusively on theoretical concepts. Students are seldom allowed to deviate from the prescribed curriculum and are rarely encouraged to explore topics beyond the classroom. Our methods of instruction are quite boring, and they lack any semblance of flexibility or innovation. For the most part, students have to sit through lengthy lecture hours from which they may or may not take away anything of value. To combat this, an engaging approach to instruction not only benefits students but also piques their genuine curiosity about the topic, encouraging them to learn more. In the Indian educational system, the end-of-year results and board examinations are of the utmost importance, and pupils who do not perform well on these tests may be the targets of mental bullying, humiliation, and a loss of confidence. Extracurricular activities like sports, art, and music aren't valued by society, parents, or schools. Because of the high priority placed on academics, it is not uncommon to see professors exploiting the time provided for sports and other co-curricular activities to instead complete their own lesson plans. Not every young person has dreams of becoming an astronaut; some may instead pursue careers in the arts, athletics, or oratory, or public speaking. The problem with the Indian education system as it stands today is that all these students will be subjected to the same curriculum and pedagogy, even though much of what they are learning will be obsolete by the time they reach their twenties. While it's clear that students need to learn the basics, the requirement that they do so for a whole decade before they can choose their major seems antiquated. The criteria for what constitutes "excellent subjects" in our system must be revised. Despite our foresight in the mathematical and scientific communities, our talents are not limited to those fields. Other social and literary topics need to be given the same level of consideration. Instead of discovering one's true calling in middle age, students would benefit greatly from a curriculum shift that included creative topics alongside the traditional math and science.

It's not just the curriculum that's outdated; instructors and their practises also need a major facelift. The way we teach is out of date. Unfortunately, the only method of instruction we have is the traditional chalkboard and chalk. There has been a surge in the adoption of online education, but only a fraction of students have made the transition. Our educators are ineffective, and so is the way we teach. The institution needs to help them acquire more modern teaching skills and become accustomed to agile e-learning techniques. Having a good instructor on hand can turn e-learning into a highly imaginative learning experience. The benefits of having a competent instructor and an effective agile learning strategy combined are substantial. Two hands are usually needed to clap. Lack of business and economics education and practical literacy skills is a problem in the Indian school system. We always know the definition of a procedure in layman's words, but we never know how to really carry it through. Because of how seriously we take our grades, we've completely neglected teaching skills that are actually useful in the real world, such as functional literacy. Along with this, there is absolutely no foundational information about economics or market dynamics taught in our curriculum. In order to better grasp the global financial system, pupils should be exposed to basic market education beginning in secondary school.

To our children, the system is delivering the message that they are not in responsibility of their own lives, which is a really harmful message to transmit. They need just comply with whatever rules are established, rather than taking initiative and prioritizing their own happiness. Children, according to experts, can benefit much from it. No wonder our kids are bored and unmotivated by school. What would it be like to have your every waking moment planned out for you? True, we are turning them into "mechanical robots," and that must be stopped. Without this, their originality would be lost. Kiddies are putting in countless hours of study, staying up late to cram for meaningless tests that nobody will remember anyway. Questions like "What am I excellent at?" "What do I want to do with my life?" "How do I fit into this world?" and many others seem to be completely ignored in today's schools. The computer system doesn't seem to be concerned. Many people who are extraordinarily gifted have struggled to succeed in the traditional educational system. To their credit, they were ultimately successful despite these setbacks. However, not everyone is able to. How much skill and potential is lost because it isn't acknowledged by the current system is unknown.

Typical classroom time in an Indian school is spent listening to lectures and reading textbooks. Students are not encouraged to go for physical exercise. As a result, there is now a chasm separating sports and the student body. They seem to be sluggish and indolent practically of the time. Because kids spend five hours a day doing nothing but sitting in a classroom. Sports education should be given equal weight to academic subjects so that students' minds and bodies are constantly challenged.

Your ability to communicate effectively is the most important skill you can bring to any position. People skills and the ability to articulate one's ideas clearly in front of an audience are fundamental requirements for almost any profession. Learning from one's peers is a great way to improve in this area. The government school teachers don't even bother to show up to work on a consistent basis. The resulting atmosphere at government schools is toxic for the youngsters who attend there. Constant vigilance and the establishment of stringent restrictions are necessary to avoid this.

Students who aren't given adequate possibilities and positions within their home country often look abroad for work. Brain drain describes this phenomenon. Because of it, we lose talented people of our country who could have aided in the development of the education sector or must have contributed toward the progress of our country. It was stated throughout 1996–2015 that more than half of the toppers of class 10th and 12th had relocated and were studying or worked elsewhere, especially in the US. The National Skill Development Mission, launched by the Indian government, seeks to educate 400 million Indians by 2022, but this won't be enough to halt the uprising.

Before the advent of the internet and the rise of experiential learning, the Indian education system relied heavily on textbooks and lecture halls. The abacus and Vedic Maths have given mathematics a fresh perspective. There were now a plethora of fresh educational opportunities and exciting new ways to learn. In a similar vein, the traditional educational curriculum emphasizes memorization over understanding. Student learning has no real-world context. Both parents and educators place a premium on academic success at the expense of pupils' capacity to apply what they have learned in the real world. As a result, education has become a rat race. However, with the implementation of the National Policy on Education 2020, that's all changed. Three educational policies were implemented in India. One occurred in 1968, another in 1986, and the third is scheduled for 2020. The fundamental goal of the National Policy on Education 1986 was to incorporate underprivileged groups by providing them equal opportunity in the sphere of education. On the other hand, the National Policy on Education 2020 takes a more comprehensive approach. The program is designed to help students acquire marketable skills and find work. The New Educational Policy 2020 is designed to address all the shortcomings of the existing educational policies. What

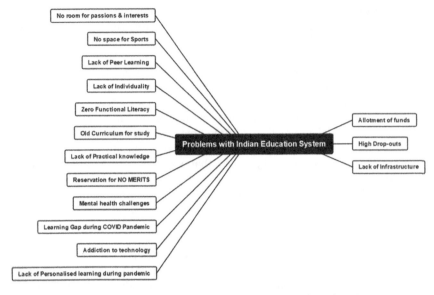

Fig. 1.   Showing the Problems With Indian Education System.
Source: Created by self with modifications from NEP report, 2020, MoE.

follows is a summary, in the form of Fig. 1, of the issues with our schooling system that have been mentioned above.

Features of NEP, 2020

Education "Quality," "Affordability," "Equity," "Access," and "Account-ability," all from the perspective of the system, are the primary concerns. By improving teacher preparation and reorganizing the educational system, NEP hopes to shift more resources into early childhood education and change the current examination system. Reforms for both K-12 and higher education are embedded in the policy.

A. Elementary Education: It proposes to replace the current 10+2 system with a 5+3+3+4 curriculum that is age-appropriate for students between the ages of 3 and 8, 8 and 11, and 11 and 18 years old. A child's developmental years between the ages of three and six are critical, and this program will introduce them into the formal education system.

B. Making the tenth and twelfth grade exams easier and teaching kids how to take tests effectively so they don't have to rely on memorization and retakes. Regulation of both public and private schools will be delegated to a new body called PARAKH (Performance Assessment, Review, and Analysis of Knowledge for Holistic Development).

C. Placing a premium on teaching students in their native tongue or a regional language until at least the fifth grade, teaching in both the student's native tongue and a second language, emphasizing extracurricular activities, beginning vocational education and 21st-century skills like coding in class 6 with internships, etc.

D. The National Council for Teacher Education (NCTE), in conjunction with NCERT, will evaluate student achievement and growth, and they will create a brand new, all-encompassing National Curriculum Framework for Teacher Education (NCFTE) 2021.

E. Post-secondary education: The goal is to double the GER (Gross Enrollment Ratio) from the current 26.3%–50% by 2035. A customizable, all-encompassing, and multidisciplinary undergraduate degree that can be completed in three to four years; students who complete the degree requirements and earn the necessary certifications can then forego the Master of Philosophy.

F. Establishing the Higher Education Commission of India (HECI), which will oversee all fields of higher education in India with the exception of the fields of medicine and law. College affiliation will be phased out over the course of 15 years, and a system will be put in place to gradually offer colleges greater independence.

G. Alterations Group: Establishing an Independent Organization, the National Educational Technology Framework (NETF), to Serve as a Forum for Discussion and Collaboration Regarding the Use of Technology to Improve Teaching, Assessment, and Administration.

H. For the purpose of evaluating students, a national assessment center PAR-AKH is being established. Its stated goals include the establishment of a Gender Inclusion Fund, the creation of Education Zones tailored to the needs of underserved communities, and the encouragement of the establishment of campuses of foreign universities in India. In comparison to the existing level of public investment in education (4.6% of GDP), the proposed increase would bring that number up to 6%.

The important Fundamental principles of NEP 2020 are discussed below in Fig. 2:
NEP 2020 suggested certain important recommendations which have been discussed below (Fig. 3):

Benefits of NEP 2020 Toward Student Community

Fig. 4 represents the summarised points on how NEP contributes to students' overall development in mere future:

The Way Forward Since 2020

It is crucial to have a clear vision and implement this at the grassroots level, where basic education is being inculcated, as the National Education Policy (NEP) seeks to enable inclusive, participatory, and holistic development and it has all which is needed in the twenty-first century. If carried out correctly, it has the potential to

Fig. 2.   Showing the Principles of NEP, 2020. *Source:* NEP 2020
Principles modified for the study from NEP Report, MoE.

provide India with its brightest and most capable workforce ever. It seems to reason
that if we continue to teach students using outdated methods and materials, fewer
and fewer young people in India will be able to find gainful employment. They are
leaving in droves toward the West in the name of "the learn and earn" in the hopes
of finding gainful employment. They have confidence in their ability to forge their
own paths professionally while abroad, and use this notion to guide their choices as
they shape their futures. The government of India recognized the value of the NEP
after small adjustments were made to account for predicted increases in school and
college dropout rates, college transfers, and so on.

Indian Model vs Finnish Model of Education

Students in Finnish schools are encouraged to evaluate their own performance
frequently (Aho, Pitkanen, & Sahlberg, 2006). Students are tasked with creating
their own educational experiences. Students are required to work together on
projects, and an emphasis is placed on those that span traditional topic areas. The

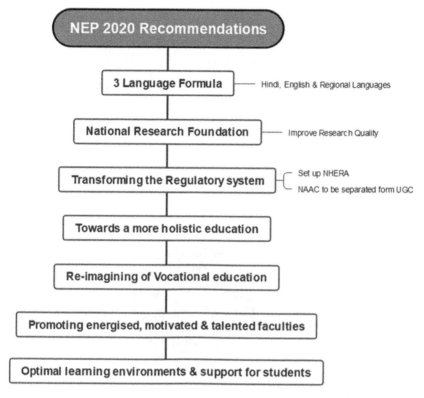

Fig. 3.   Showing NEP 2020 Recommendations. *Source:* Data
modified for the study from NEP 2020 Report, MoE.

primary goal of Finnish educational policy is to ensure that all Finnish citizens
have access to quality educational opportunities (Ministry of Education, Finland,
2009). These tenets are reflected in the design of the educational system. In other
words, there are few, if any, roadblocks in the way of students advancing through
the system (Gardner, 2010). Learning, not testing, is the main objective of schools
nowadays. In Finland, there are no standardized assessments given to students in
elementary school. Instead, subject-area educators are accountable for conducting
assessments based on the curricular goals for their courses. Almost all educational
and vocational programs receive funding from the government. Every level of
schooling is free of charge. The costs of a student's basic education, including
textbooks, lunches, and transportation, are covered entirely by the government
(Hargreaves, Halasz, & Pont, 2007). Students are expected to pay their own way
for textbooks and transportation costs in the secondary school level and beyond.
Also, there is a robust system of financial aid for higher education. Full-time
students in either higher education or secondary education can receive financial
aid (Finnish National Board of Education, 2008).

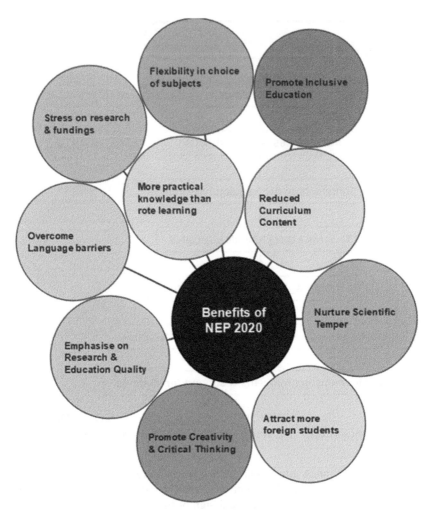

Fig. 4.   Showing the Benefits of NEP 2020. *Source:* Data modified
from the NEP 2020 Report, MoE.

Pedagogical Approach

Curriculum, instruction, and administration are all guided by a philosophy of
education that places a premium on students' agency and collaboration with
instructors and peers. The knowledge the student already possesses informs how
he or she processes and makes sense of the new material (constructive pedagogy
approach) (OECD, 2010). There is a political agreement that all children should
attend the same public schools and a belief that all children, regardless of

socioeconomic status or geographic location, are capable of excelling academically. An unwavering dedication to improving one's own teaching practices and a shared sense of accountability for students who are having difficulty is essential. Trust between the school and its surrounding neighborhood can flourish when limited funds are utilized to their fullest potential in the classroom (Burridge, 2010).

Modus Operandi of Finnish Education

- The curriculum has been recorded on a national basis to provide support for student learning and individual student well-being (Sahlberg, 2006).
- Schools, as well as students' learning results and evaluations, are inherently supportive.
- All teachers are required to have a Master's degree, and initial teacher training includes practical teaching training (Sahlberg, 2007).
- The teaching profession is highly regarded and popular in Finland, so students have their pick of the best teachers (Sahlberg, 2007).
- The goal is to provide information that will help schools and students improve.
- There are no national tests of learning outcomes and school ranking lists.
- In Finland, both elementary and secondary education majors focus heavily on content-based instruction (FNBE, 2010).

Privileges That Teachers Get in Finland

- Teachers who have a high degree of professional autonomy in the classroom are often regarded as subject-matter experts.
- Have a lot of responsibility in class and are given freedom to learn on their own.
- Be able to make important policy and management decisions for the school.
- Play a significant role in shaping local educational policies and development initiatives.
- Take charge of curriculum decisions and course materials.

Literature Review Excerpts Stating the Importance of the Finnish Model of Education

Juslin's research illustrates how the Finnish educational model has helped reduce poverty and how it might serve as a template for the development of similar models in other countries. Below, in Fig. 5, we can see how Hevner's 1936 seminal study on the subject of related works has been followed by subsequent investigations by various authors.

Juslin's work has been cited more frequently than that of any other author over a longer period of time, as seen in the above figure.

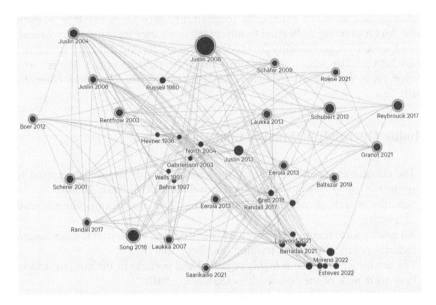

Fig. 5.   Showing the Literature Map From Research Works Compiled
Based on Importance of Finnish Education. *Source:* Data created using
LitMap research software © collected since 1980 till date.

Better the Education, Zero the Hunger, and End to Poverty

Getting rid of poverty is high on the United Nations' list of sustainable development goals since it is one of the most pressing issues affecting countries everywhere. Globally, over 783 million people are living on less than $1.90 a day, according to the United Nations, and if action is not taken soon, this number will rise. Education of the populace is the first step toward sustainable growth. The cycle of poverty can be broken through educational opportunities for those who want to break it. There is evidence that shows how education helps with things like health, nutrition, economic growth, and protecting the environment.

The United Nations Educational, Scientific, and Cultural Organization (UNESCO) estimates that 171 million people might be lifted out of extreme poverty if all pupils in low-income nations could read proficiently. The world's poverty rate might be reduced by more than half if all adults had completed secondary school. That's why ensuring that everyone has access to a high-quality education is one of the United Nations' 17 Sustainable Development Goals to accomplish by the year 2030.

Education Is Linked With Economic Growth

One reason why education is the key to escaping poverty is its correlation to a flourishing economy. Seventy-five percent of the global GDP growth between

1960 and 2000 was related to better math and science skills, according to a research published in 2021 by Stanford University and Munich's Ludwig Maximilian University.

Universal Quality Education for All Fights Inequality

According to the latest Oxfam report (2019), "good quality education may be liberating for individuals and it can operate as a leveller and equaliser within society" (Sekhri, 2011).

Inequality is one of the key reasons there is poverty in the world. People in extreme poverty are disproportionately affected by all forms of systemic discrimination (such as disability, religion, race, and caste). A quality education is a fundamental human right, and it may be a powerful tool in the fight against the structural inequalities that put some groups of people at the bottom of the social ladder (Chauhan, 2008).

Mathematical Model Depicting How Education Reduces Poverty

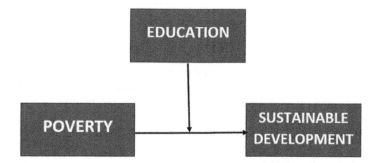

Fig. 6.   Showing a Model Representing How Poverty' Can Be
Trivialized Towards Sustainable Development via Education. *Source:*
Developed by Self Author.

The aforementioned model illustrates how education may be utilized to combat poverty and foster long-term economic growth.

Creating More Employment Opportunities

In times of economic uncertainty, it is not simple to get a work. Many times, we have to contend with a large number of other applicants for a small number of open positions. On top of that, there will be a larger pool of applicants vying for the same low-paying entry-level position if the applicant pool consists primarily of people with lower levels of education. However, if we take the time to get the training and education we need, we can improve our odds of finding a career that we enjoy.

Securing a Higher Income

Jobs that pay well and require expertise are more likely to go to those with advanced degrees and a wide range of work experience. If we put in the time and effort to learn as much as we can and improve our skills, we can guarantee that we will be able to live with relative ease.

Developing Problem-Solving Skills

An important advantage of formal education is that it equips students with the tools they need to think critically, rationally, and independently. There are many obstacles that young people must overcome when they enter adulthood, such as paying off college loans, finding gainful employment, saving for a down payment on a car and a house, etc. Humans are not only capable of thinking for themselves, but they are also adept at finding valid justifications and confirmations for their beliefs.

Introducing Empowerment

Changing a flaw into a strength requires an investment in one's education. It provides us with a range of resources and approaches to the challenges we face. But education's greatest benefit is that it gives us the mental nimbleness to respond quickly and effectively to any situation that arises. Educated women's increased confidence and ability to make sound decisions makes them less vulnerable to sexism and domestic violence, according to a wide range of studies (Sun, Sun, Geng, & Kong, 2018).

Creating Equal Opportunities

Those with higher levels of education are held to the same standards as their more poorly educated peers. Further, those who have completed their education tend to have broad minds that are receptive to new ideas and perspectives. The ability to provide for oneself through education is the key to personal liberty. To put it simply, it protects us from bad judgments and financial catastrophes.

Bridging the Borders

Online learning facilitates communication with groups and individuals all across the globe. Physical barriers have been eliminated. The ability to interact with people of other backgrounds and cultures expands perspectives and deepens our appreciation for one another (Meisalo, Lavonen, Sormunen, & Vesisenaho, 2010).

Giving Back to the Community

One of the benefits of an education is the realization of how important it is to reside in a safe and secure neighborhood. They are more likely to take part in initiatives that better their community and the world at large.

Improving the Economy

In most cases, employers look for candidates with strong academic credentials when offering high-paying positions. When a person improves their level of schooling and their resume, they increase their career opportunities. Those who come from disadvantaged backgrounds can help bring the poverty rate down by bettering themselves via education. Because education is about learning new things and using them wisely, it contributes to economic growth and helps individuals and communities (Matilainen, 2011).

Equating the Finnish Model to the Indian Model of Education Since the Introduction of NEP 2020

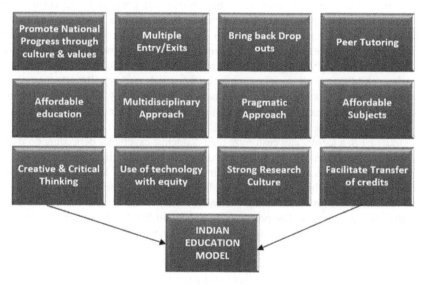

Fig. 7. Model Summarizing Features of Indian Education Post-Introduction of NEP 2020. *Source:* Modified based on data retrieved from NEP 2020 Report, MoE.

Findings of the Study

Due to its emphasis on grades, competition, and social status, India's school system prevents many kids from discovering and pursuing their true passions. There have been no modifications to NEP 2020 that would encourage students to relax and take pleasure in their study by adding global ideas that place a premium on creativity and critical thinking. The proposed reforms to Anganwadis raise serious questions about the feasibility of implementing NEP. A long-term answer is needed, and the NEP 2020s planned changes to the educational system won't provide that. Over time, it will need to be updated once again. An unrealistic goal of 6% of GDP for public spending has been set given the current situation of India's GDP. Challenges lie ahead in the areas of resource mobilization and application.

The Finnish Educational System has a lot to teach its Indian counterpart.

- The NEP was effective in that it led to the adoption of a new pedagogical framework of education that emphasizes the child's growth as a whole and attempts to eliminate the rote learning culture. However, the Finland Education System (FES) provides insights that we may adopt or draw inspiration from at every level of education, beginning with preschool and continuing through doctoral programs. A country like India places a premium on the fee structure more than any other factor. In Finland, the cost of preschool and kindergarten varies according to a family's annual income. Each person now has an opportunity to receive the finest education possible. And this is the age when children of all socioeconomic backgrounds are equally attentive, and their imaginations are at their most active. Transparency and a win-win situation for all parties are ensured when fees are structured in accordance with the amount of income tax a person pays.
- Under FES, a learner can customize their academic experience depending on their individual interests. They can also choose not to pursue a bachelor's degree at a university and instead pursue training in a specialized field. More talented people will emerge from India now than ever before because to the country's adaptable educational system and students' increased freedom and responsibility in making educational decisions. The people of India should live by the slogan "all are for education" (Kupiainen, Hautamaki, & Karjalainen, 2009).
- In Finland, local governments are in charge of educating and caring for children younger than school age. It's no secret that public schools in India are struggling. The fact that guardians and parents are so adamant about sending their kids to private schools speaks volumes about the quality of public education in that area. Regaining their former grandeur and student populations will require an emphasis on the holistic growth of children, as well as the employment of qualified educators, a coherent educational framework, and a functional physical plant.
- In Finland, compulsory schooling begins at age seven. Before entering formal school, a student has already developed a love of learning, a healthy curiosity and emotional range, and the mental agility to successfully navigate the

challenges it will inevitably present. Students are required to attend school for nine years, from Grade 1 through Grade 9. During this time, they are exposed to a variety of teaching methods and viewpoints on various topics, which allows them to draw their own judgments based on their own observations and experiences. That manner, the student's perspective is broadened and their views aren't limited to just one area of study. The end product is a cohesive lesson plan that organically weaves together concepts from throughout the curriculum.

- Educators' roles and expertise must be bolstered alongside that of their pupils, as they serve as the knowledge transfer medium. Educators need to learn not only what to teach but how to teach it. The ability to educate in a practical, rather than just theoretical, manner is a must for educators. Teachers who have a hand in deciding what students learn will have a deeper understanding of the material and will be better equipped to convey that understanding to their students. There should be support for raising the bar for becoming a teacher, as doing so benefits both students and schools in the long run (Centre for Civil Society, 2017).

- Without being overly harsh, it is fair to say that in Indian schools, the emphasis is on students completing their coursework, mastering the material presented in the classroom, and doing well on standardized tests. The problem with this system is that it conveys the message that all students must hustle or cram to be successful. As a result, students start viewing getting good grades on tests as the pinnacle of achievement. The purpose of education is not to cram facts into students' heads but rather to help them retain enough of their learning to use it in real-world contexts. There has been no revolutionary change brought about by the Finnish system. India needs to develop its own system soon.

Fig. 6 graphically depicts the aforementioned causes that may prompt India to embrace the Finnish model of education in an effort to alleviate poverty (Fig. 7).

Conclusion

While expanding access to education is important, it is not enough; the curriculum must also include opportunities for holistic growth. The current system of grading students requires urgent reform so that children are not made into public spectacles of their efforts. Embrace their natural inquisitiveness and encourage them to explore their interests early in their careers. The use of technology in education is becoming increasingly important. The introduction of technologies like smart boards, online materials, and interactive whiteboards has made it so that teachers have less work to do. Present-day students can access more online resources than ever before to aid them in their quest for knowledge. It's less of a struggle to grasp abstract ideas and memorize facts. India has to immediately begin funding and implementing more cutting-edge educational practices (and learning). To begin enforcing this at the ground level, the government, educators, and parents must collaborate. It is crucial to have a clear vision and implement this at the grassroots level, where elementary education is ingrained, as the NEP seeks to foster inclusive, participative, and comprehensive development, and it has all which is needed in the twenty-first century. If carried out correctly, it has the potential to provide India with its brightest and most capable workforce ever (Ministry of Education, Finland, 2008).

Suggestions

The current educational system is broken and has to be fixed immediately. One third of rural youngsters are completely unable to learn, as stated in the ASER 2020 assessment. The Indian government must prioritize the elementary and secondary education systems and ensure that all teachers receive adequate training. The focus should be on learning, not cramming. Education is crucial to any nation's development, so the focus should be on the students, not the grades (Weisskopf, 2004).

To help alleviate poverty, schools should provide individualized support services like counseling and ensure that all students have access to healthcare, nutritious meals at no cost, and a level playing field in the classroom.

Implications of the Study

Finland's educational policies are following a broad pattern. There should be less pressure, less unnecessary rules, and more compassion. Typically, a student's daily schedule will only include a handful of classes. They have ample opportunities to rest, rejuvenate, and eat. There are several 15- to 20-minute breaks throughout the day so that the kids may get up, move around, and relax. Teachers, too, benefit from this kind of setting (Gamerman, 2008). Rooms for teachers are provided in all Finnish schools so that educators have a place to unwind, get ready for the day, and mingle with one another. Teachers, like everyone else, have basic needs that must be met in order for them to perform at their highest potential in the classroom. Finnish pupils don't feel the need to strive for academic excellence because they have access to all the resources they require. Without the distractions of grades and filler assignments, students can concentrate on what really matters: developing as individuals. Finland is in the forefront because of its holistic approach to education and emphasis on equity rather than performance. For India to make progress toward a future with no hunger or poverty, the country must do the same kind of labor.

References

Abhijeet, S. (2014). Test score gaps between private and government sector students at school entry age in India. *Oxford Review of Education, 40*(1), 30–49. Retrieved from https://www.tandfonline.com/doi/abs/10.1080/03054985.2013.873529

Aho, E., Pitkanen, K., & Sahlberg, P. (2006). *Policy development and reform principles of basic and secondary education in Finland since 1968*. Prepared for the education working paper series, World Bank, Washington, DC. Retrieved from http://www. pasisahlberg.com/downloads/Education%20in%20Finland%202006.pdf

Burridge, T. (2010, April 7). Why do Finland's schools get the best results? *BBC News* [Online]. Retrieved from http://news.bbc.co.uk/2/hi/8601207.stm

Centre for Civil Society. (2017, December 2) *Direct benefit transfer in education: A policy blueprint.* Retrieved from https://ccs.in/sites/default/files/publications/dbt-in-education-policy-brief.pdf

Chauhan, C. P. S. (2008). Education and caste in India. *Asia Pacific Journal of Education, 28,* 217–234. doi:10.1080/02188790802267332

FNBE. (2010). *Structures of education and training systems in Europe.* Helsinki: FNBE. Retrieved from http://eacea.ec.europa.eu/education/eurydice/documents/ eurybase/structures/041_FI_EN.pdf

FNBE (Finnish National Board of Education). (2008). *Education in Finland.* Helsinki: FNBE. Retrieved from www.oph.fi/download/124278_education_in_finland.pdf

Gamerman, E. (2008, February 29). What makes Finnish kids so smart? *The Wall Street Journal,* Feature Article.

Gardner, W. (2010, February 26). Are quality and quantity possible in teacher recruitment? *Education Week* [Online]. Retrieved from http://blogs.edweek.org/ edweek/walt_gardners_reality_check/20/10/02/are_quality_and_quantity_possible_ in_teacher_recruitme nt.html

Goyal, S. (2019, December 2). Reservation in India advantages and disadvantages. *UPSC IAS PCS.* Retrieved from https://digitallylearn.com/reservation-in-india-advantages-and-disadvantages-upsc-ias-pcs/

Hargreaves, A., Halász, G., & Pont, B. (2007). *School leadership for systemic improvement in Finland.* Paris: OECD. Retrieved from www.oecd.org/dataoecd/43/ 17/39928629.pdf

Kupiainen, S., Hautamäki, J., & Karjalainen, T. (2009). *The Finnish education system and PISA.* Helsinki: Ministry of Education Publications, Helsinki University Print.

Matilainen, M. (2011). Finnish education model-pedagogical approach. Retrieved from. http://www.ims.mii.lt/ims/files/EducationmodelFinland_Marianne.pdf. Acce ssed on October 12, 2011.

Meisalo, V., Lavonen, J., Sormunen, K., & Vesisenaho, M. (2010). *ICT in initial teacher training, country report.* Paris: OECD Publishing. . Retrieved from http:// www.oecd.org/dataoecd/4/43/45214586.pdf

Ministry of Education, Finland. (2008). *Education and research 2007–2012: Development plan.* Helsinki: Helsinki University Print.

Ministry of Education, Finland. (2009). *Finnish education system in an international comparison.* Helsinki: Ministry of Education Policy Analyses.

OECD. (2010). *PISA 2009 results: What students know and can do: Student performance in reading,* Mathematics and Science (Volume I). Paris: OECD Publishing.

Sahlberg, P. (2006). Raising the bar: How Finland responds to the twin challenge of secondary education? *Revista de Curriculum y Formación del Profesorado, 10*(1).

Sahlberg, P. (2007). Education policies for raising student learning: The Finnish approach. *Journal of Education Policy, 22*(2), 147–171.

Sekhri, S. (2011, December 2). *Affirmative action and peer effects: Evidence from caste based reservation in general education colleges in India.* Charlottesville, VA: University of Virginia. Retrieved from https://pdfs.semanticscholar.org/81c2/ 848024da73d810693d2d56af2d77d0181603.pdf

Sun, H., Sun, W., Geng, Y., & Kong, Y. (2018). Natural resource dependence, public education investment, and human capital accumulation. *Petroleum Science, 15,* 657–665. doi:10.1007/s12182-018-0235-0

Weisskopf, T. E. (2004). Impact of reservation on admissions to higher education in India. *Economic and Political Weekly, 39,* 4339–4349. Retrieved from https://www.jstor.org/stable/4415591?seq=1

Websites

https://www.weforum.org/agenda/2018/09/10-reasons-why-finlands-education-system-is-the-best-in-the-world

https://www.smithsonianmag.com/innovation/why-are-finlands-schools-successful-49859555/

https://www.norad.no/en/front/about-norad/news/role-of-education-in-ending-extreme-poverty–taking-a-global-lead/

https://www.ccefinland.org/finedu

https://www.geeksforgeeks.org/national-education-policy-2020/

https://leadschool.in/blog/the-advantages-and-disadvantages-of-new-education-policy-2020/#:~:text=Reduced%20exam%20stress%3A%20The%20changed,broader%20options%20to%20learn%20now.

https://www.creatrixcampus.com/blog/The-National-Education-Policy-NEP-2020

https://ruralindiaonline.org/en/library/resource/national-education-policy-2020/?gclid=CjwKCAiAzp6eBhByEiwA_gGq5JaMknby-uEbd1Bnraz5izV03pYH3nUWA2SUS2eZripRwRw3NaLkeRoCycAQAvD_BwE

https://www.isrgrajan.com/10-loopholes-of-the-indian-education-system.html

https://senseselec.com/blogs/what-is-wrong-with-the-indian-education-system/

https://www.indiatoday.in/education-today/featurephilia/story/7-challenges-education-sector-faced-in-2022-2314975-2022-12-29

https://pib.gov.in/PressReleaseIframePage.aspx?PRID=1847066

https://byjus.com/free-ias-prep/indian-education-system-issues-and-challenges/

https://www.econtribune.com/post/loopholes-in-the-indian-education-framework

https://www.geeksforgeeks.org/challenges-in-indian-education-system/

https://www.financialexpress.com/education-2/lessons-india-can-learn-from-finlands-education-system/2434475/

Chapter 11

Leveraging Technology to Enhance Access to Healthcare and Manage Medical Waste: Practices from Emerging Countries

Zarjina Tarana Khalil and Samira Rahman

Abstract

Although healthcare and healthy living are integral to the Sustainable Development Goals (SDGs) for 2030, the coronavirus epidemic has dealt a devastating blow to these efforts. As governments and policymakers were compelled to shift their focus to lockdowns, sustenance, procurement, and distribution of vaccines, the momentum for health initiatives slowed, and the already fragile health systems of emerging markets were subjected to additional shocks. However, in many underserved regions of the globe, the introduction of technology has greatly facilitated the distribution and adoption of healthcare services.

This chapter highlights mini-cases from four emerging nations: Bangladesh, Nigeria, Vietnam, and the Philippines. Although the countries are emerging, each one of them are in a distinct stage of development and face a unique set of healthcare-related challenges. The chapter showcases how four different organizations based in these countries leveraged the use of technology to take healthcare services to underserved populations. In doing so, they addressed the key challenges of imparting healthcare: geographic accessibility, availability, financial accessibility, and acceptability.

This chapter concludes with a discussion of the implications of expanding healthcare industries leading to increased healthcare waste. To prevent mass population exposure to hazardous substances, the emergence of intelligent healthcare waste collection and disposal systems will be an absolute necessity. Hence, with the development of healthcare services, governments and policymakers need to mechanize smart waste management systems to safeguard humans, animals, and the environment.

Fostering Sustainable Businesses in Emerging Economies, 187–206
Copyright © 2024 Zarjina Tarana Khalil and Samira Rahman
Published under exclusive licence by Emerald Publishing Limited
doi:10.1108/978-1-80455-640-520231012

Keywords: Healthcare; emerging markets; waste management; technology; pandemic; health

Background

COVID-19 has been one of the most critical global health crises in recent years, affecting all nations to varying degrees. This magnitude of worldwide setback forced enterprises to reconsider their company strategy and operations (Heinonen & Strandvik, 2020). As a result of the pandemic, pharmaceutical companies are redesigning their marketing mix and partnership models to ensure affordable access to drugs. On the other hand, governments are investing in improving the quality and reach of public healthcare systems. Additionally, there are more social innovators who are cognizant of the health inequities across different markets. The combined efforts of these stakeholders help to push the agenda forward (Kyle, 2022). Overall, the progress is upward but there is still a long way to go with significant roadblocks.

As a result, it is crucial to devise strategies that will expand the reach of healthcare by leveraging technology and providing benefits to end users, including patients and policymakers. It needs to start with the very basics like efficient data collection and registration of patients with a unique ID. Previous research has shown that m-health and e-health have the potential to provide better access to healthcare facilities both for the patients and the service providers (Alam, 2019). Emerging markets with their diverse populations face significant obstacles in ensuring the equitable distribution of healthcare; technology may be used to bridge this disparity.

Technology as a Driver for Achieving the Sustainable Development Goals

In today's convergent and interconnected world, the effects of the digital revolution can be seen in every sector. The rapidity of technological progress has far-reaching implications for many sectors of our society and economy. Academic areas that are expanding fast include big data, the Internet of Things (IoT), machine learning, artificial intelligence (AI), robotics, 3D printing, biotechnology, nanotechnology, renewable energy, satellite, and drone technologies. Every industry benefits from technological advancements as it facilitates the process of boosting output, cutting down on waste, eliminating emissions, and improving resource management (Antoanela, 2021).

Today, sustainability in both lifestyle and infrastructure remains a formidable obstacle. The United Nation's recent report on the SDGs states that digitalization will be essential to accomplishing these goals for sustainability (UNCTAD, 2020). Since technology enables us to affect the lives of people on a global scale, it is time for technological innovation to create a sustainable future. Healthcare services are expected to benefit significantly from technological innovations, since all sub-sectors of biotechnology, health data management, and customized health solutions will contribute to the creation of innovative treatments in future (Hecht, 2018).

The pandemic has accelerated the global adoption of telemedicine and expanded its reach. Clinicians utilized technology-based systems to assist patients in a virtual environment for curative treatment and counseling services. With the aid of telemedicine, patients and physicians were able to communicate more readily, allowing those with symptoms to remain at home. This system has decreased expenses and saved lives. Even though Covid-19 infections have subsided with the advent of vaccines, people have realized the comfort and convenience of telemedicine, and the continued use of the service is highly prevalent.

While advances in technology and rising living standards have improved health indices worldwide, it is common knowledge that the healthcare industry is more skewed toward developed countries and affluent consumers. However, given that emerging markets/economies will be driven by the middle class, it has become imperative for both policymakers and the private sector to concentrate on the pre-middle class population, as ensuring their health will ensure productivity and sustainable economic growth (Deloitte UK, 2016).

Healthcare in Emerging Markets and Its Importance

Although there is unanimous agreement that good health is the basis of higher productivity, the reality is that not everyone can afford to "buy" health. Limited income and a lower level of awareness regarding health issues and facilities create a major gap in accessing and utilizing services. There is a vicious cycle between low income and lack of access to healthcare, as the former is a major contributor to the latter's negative effects on health, which in turn reduces the productivity of an individual, thereby further worsening the poverty situation. Many of the world's poor have less access to healthcare because developing nations have fewer physicians and hospital beds per capita than high-income nations. Also, in poorer countries, the majority of the health spending is borne by personal means as there is no provision or protection from the state/government (Peters et al., 2008). This in turn puts further pressure on people who are already deprived from the basic livelihood needs (Schanz, 2019).

Peters et al. (2008) suggested a conceptual framework that evaluates the ease of access to healthcare services on the basis of four dimensions:

(1) *Geographic accessibility* – physical distance from the point of service delivery and the user.
(2) *Availability* – Providing the appropriate care to those in need, including short waiting times, qualified personnel, and adequate supplies.
(3) *Financial accessibility* – The link between the pricing of services (which is somewhat influenced by their expenses) and the desire and ability of users to pay for those services. This dimension also covers the economic effects of healthcare expenditures.

(4) *Acceptability* – The awareness of health service professionals to the social and cultural needs of particular patients and communities.

Several socio-economic and demographic factors are expected to contribute to further pressurize the healthcare systems of emerging countries:

(1) *Aging population* – the number of people aged 65 and older is projected to double in 15 years.
(2) *Increasing middle-class population* – by 2030, the proportion of the middle-class income will be 59%.
(3) *Evolving disease patterns* – As incomes increase, non-communicable diseases, particularly chronic ailments, become more prevalent along with obesity.
(4) *Burden on public finances* – Financial strain on the government has led to a rise in the use of private payers to mediate healthcare transactions and increase the efficiency and efficacy of healthcare systems while reducing overall costs.

There are three goals that emerging countries should aim toward, with their digital health initiatives (Meloan & Iacopino, 2017):

(1) Increasing Access and Coverage
(2) The improvement of service quality
(3) Cost minimization and optimization

There is a wide gap between the affluent and the poor (underprivileged) in today's emerging markets. Each of these four factors contributes to the imbalance in emerging markets when it comes to the distribution of healthcare.

Geographic Accessibility: One of the major barriers to the accessibility of healthcare in developing countries is due to the absence of infrastructure. The majority of growth and development is concentrated in urban areas (Deloitte UK, 2016). Hence, the opportunity cost of travel time and travel cost often hinders accessing the service. The problem was aggravated even further during the pandemic with lockdowns and a lack of service personnel in the healthcare sector.

Availability: The measure of availability is the ability to access healthcare services as needed. In developing countries, this is a pertinent issue. Although seemingly there are modern hospitals and private healthcare facilities in many of the emerging megacities, the sheer volume of the population often becomes a challenge for capacity management. Along with that, there is a significant dearth of medical professionals, including doctors, nurses, and paramedics. Hence, even for people with financial resources, the availability cannot be guaranteed.

Financial Accessibility: The procedures of financing health services in under-developed nations have been one of the most contentious issues pertaining to health services. In some countries, introduction of user fees reduced the utilization of services, while in others it increased the utilization (Peters et al., 2008).

Unavailability of insurance policies for majority of the population is another common factor in these countries.

Acceptability: Since healthcare as a service is a high-involvement one, it must adhere to prevailing cultural norms. The inequities of health services in developing countries also implies that patients have preferences for different types of providers, ranging from formally trained medical doctors, traditional medicine practitioners, village doctors to uncertified doctors sitting in pharmacies. Studies on developing countries reveal that the acceptability of the health services vary based on the local contexts. Hence, it is imperative for services to build awareness and localize in order to gain acceptance.

The barriers in emerging markets include capacity and access, infrastructure and data, health workforce, patient education and awareness, and quality and safety (Stucke & Chen Lee, 2020). Poor roads, limited transportation options, and unpredictable supply of water and electricity complicate delivery of healthcare in many of the regions. Physicians in emerging markets are often seen to migrate to other countries for better prospects and lifestyle. For example, Chicago is said to have more Ethiopian-trained doctors practicing there than in all of Ethiopia itself. Although access to health information is extremely convenient today, emerging markets still see a lot of premature deaths from non-communicable diseases, due to lack of health literacy among patients. Through the use of technology, easier and more equitable dissemination of information to patients can help in preventing chronic diseases and deaths. As mentioned before, quality remains at the core of health service delivery. In order to serve these markets, healthcare providers need to come up with new business models which include reverse pricing, single serving, frugal innovations and localization strategies Through the use of technology, quality and safety can be boosted by empowering both the patients and the service providers (Stucke & Chen Lee, 2020).

Despite these challenges, there are several notable organizations operating in these markets that are leveraging the power of technology to bring healthcare to the deprived population. Each of these organizations face a unique set of challenges given they are based in different countries, targeting different segments of the population and utilizing different forms of technology. Four such operations are highlighted in the cases below.

Case 1

Friendship – Bringing Health to the Doors of the Marginalized Communities

Friendship is a nongovernment organization which was born out of the passion of its founder Runa Khan. Born in an aristocratic family, as a child, Khan was moved by the ordeals that were faced by the people in the low-lying areas of Bangladesh as she observed them while visiting her native town. Her empathy and passion drove her to find a way to serve them, and thus came Friendship into being. Friendship is currently serving approximately 4.2 million people over 22 of the 492 upazilas (i.e., counties) of Bangladesh, bringing health to their doors alongside other services like education, training, and lessons on institutional voids.

Friendship healthcare system follows a 3-tier structure giving it a holistic approach.:

Tier 1: Hospital Ships

Friendship has two hospital ships (floating hospitals) and one land hospital at Shyamnagar that provides comprehensive primary and secondary healthcare to patients. The care is offered through a medical team serving permanently on the hospital ships, complemented by an expert pool of local and visiting foreign doctors who run periodic specialized health camps. The two hospital ships are the Lifebuoy Friendship Hospital and the Emirates Friendship Hospital. Five more ships are being donated by the Islamic Development Bank (ISDB) out of which two are absolutely ready to start functioning in the beginning of 2023.

Tier 2: Satellite Clinics

Satellite clinics consist of mobile paramedical health teams that visit communities on a periodic basis (fortnightly or monthly) and provide basic primary care, including preventative services. The establishment of these clinics is announced beforehand, so that the communities are aware of the facilities being available. Friendship also works with the government to support the government initiatives in the implementation of its immunization programs and family planning programs. One of the major issues in developing countries is the lack of data, and this is where Friendship does the commendable job of maintaining health records of each individual of the community and make necessary referrals as required.

Tier 3: The Friendships Community Medic Aides (FCMs)

The FCMs can be considered the local brand ambassadors as they move about the community and take health door to door. One of the means in which Friendship localizes itself is by recruiting women living in the local communities, training them in basic medical services such as hygiene, nutrition, and diagnostics, care for women during pregnancy, labor and delivery, postnatal care, and family planning. In addition to providing primary care, these ladies also build health awareness in their communities and liaise with the satellite clinic team as and when required.

Leveraging Technology to Enhance Health Access

Geographic Accessibility: In 2014, Friendship started the process of digitization of its services with the introduction of the mHealth. The mHealth app was developed by Friendship but is now also being used in Uganda and Slovakia. Through the mHealth app, the FCMAs are able to provide basic treatment plans to the communities. The mHealth is an artificial intelligence (AI)-based algorithm driven app, which gives the FCMAs the ability to run 80 algorithms for primary care. A team of doctors and the technical team worked together to develop the algorithms, covering a wide range of diseases. The system has been made such that, with the advent of time, more algorithms can easily be added. The data collected from these algorithms are also helpful in categorizing diseases based on regions as they demonstrate common patterns.

Additionally, through location devices, each community is marked and monitored, and the nearest larger facilities are also made available to the FCMAs so they may refer patients as per the situation. Each community household is registered in the system that allows for GPS location. Additionally, all the health centers are also registered. Currently Friendship has also regionalized the nearest healthcare centers, so patients or beneficiaries from a particular village/ community are referred to the nearest healthcare facility. Hence, it is easier to identify the nearest facility and therefore facilitates in the entire process. This has also been made possible due to location devices and digitization.

The location devices also act as a remote monitoring system for the FCMAs. Each one of them have a daily schedule of visiting certain number of households and by pinpointing them it is possible to ensure whether they are making the required number of visits.

Availability: The primary objective behind the inception of Friendship was to make healthcare services available to the marginalized population of Bangladesh. These people live in the "chars" (low lying flood- and erosion-prone islets adjacent to major rivers) and for the longest time, were deprived of basic facilities for health. With their 3-tier healthcare system, the services are made available to the beneficiaries. The hospital ships provide comprehensive treatment facilities with advance technology. Medical teams from countries like France also hold specialized camps for specific treatment like cataract surgery. Technology helps in establishing communication and also locating the ships as sometimes medical teams arrive in seaplanes.

The satellite clinics consist of FCMAs, a paramedic, and a medical staff along with a program officer. The communities are informed well ahead regarding the schedule of the clinics as the planning and scheduling for the whole year is done by the organization. Communities come to the clinics and discuss their health issues. Through the mHealth app, they are given basic treatment. At times, the clinics also focus on particular issues like malnutrition in a courtyard session. For example, if a child is found to be stunted, the data are recorded in the mHealth app. Depending on the level of stunting, they are given a specific treatment plan as well as a demonstration of the kind of food the child should be having. Additionally, follow-up schedules are also recorded in the mHealth app, and the FCMAs will receive messages in their mobiles, reminding them to follow up with the patients. Some follow ups may be in one month, while others may be in 6 months. These reminders help the FCMAs to remember and visit the patients for the follow ups.

At present, Friendship employs 680 FCMAs who are serving 200 households each which are extremely difficult to reach. Therefore, the reach is approximately 136,000 households in total. The FCMA is provided with a smartphone with the mHealth app. They also have basic hygiene and sanitary items for sale to the households which enhances their entrepreneurship skills as well. They visit the households within the community regularly to check on people's health. If they find someone is ill, they open the app and start to enter the symptoms. Based on the symptoms, an algorithm-based treatment plan is generated. If the symptoms are beyond the FCMAs capacity, the algorithm refers it to the doctor center. As soon as the doctor gets to see the entry, they go the mHealth app and provide a prescription through SMS, which reaches the FCMA. The transaction is also recorded in the main system. Previously, the doctor center was centralized, but now, in order to better manage capacity, the center has also been decentralized. Depending on the location, the doctor available in the nearest ship or health center will be contacted for the consultation. If the doctors are too busy, doctors available in the central medical center are contacted. Therefore, through the use of technology, a connection is being established between a resident of an extremely remote area and an MBBS-qualified doctor.

Another very crucial service that Friendship is providing is the participation in the Prescrip-Tec Project. This project is dedicated toward cervical cancer and is functional in four countries, India, Slovakia, Uganda, and Bangladesh. Through the use of images and AI, cervical cancer is detected, and the data is also being used for research by the International Center for Diarrheal Disease Research, Bangladesh (ICDDR,B). By using the Gene Expert machine in two locations, the Emirates Friendship Hospital and Shyamnogor Medical Center and special cartridges designed for cervical cancer, they are facilitating the process of cervical cancer detection. Cervical cancer is the second highest cancer prevalent in women, and for women in marginalized communities, this is an absolute silent killer. Making the technology available to these women and training the FCMAs to properly guide them is paving the path for more tests and treatment.

Financial Accessibility: Friendship provides the services for free for these marginalized communities. Beneficiaries have to pay Tk. 5, a very nominal fee collected as a token money just so that the beneficiaries feel a sense of dignity. On the other hand, the fact that Friendship is taking the service to them saves them any other out-of-pocket costs including transportation. At the same time, it is also reducing the opportunity cost – if a poor farmer has to skip his work to travel and take his family member to a healthcare facility for a basic service, it also entails a significant opportunity cost, which is saved by the door-to-door service of Friendship.

Acceptability: The mHealth is designed in English and Bangla. The app is made as simple as possible, so that someone with very low literacy rate is able to operate the app. Localization is done through hiring local people, and that entails a feeling of trust. At the same time, as they can see the immediate results (the fact that the FCMA is able to give them basic treatment plan or is able to connect them to a doctor, establishes their faith in the system. Friendship is also respectful of local culture. Each household is segregated as a separate household based on the fact that if families are cooking separately. As soon as children are married and they cook separately, that is counted as a separate household or "*khana bhittik*" (based on food in Bangla). Each household is registered, and the number of people in each household is also registered. This entire registration process and data is digitized and available in the mHealth app, which was a huge ordeal previously, as it had to be done manually.

The mHealth has a dashboard, and data from various levels are visible on the dashboard. The *chars* do not always have a network. The mHealth system is functional without a network, but data transfer will require internet connection. Hence, the FCMA is able to carry on with their work offline, but as soon as they have access to network, the data will be automatically transferred to the central database. Friendship also has eHospitals, which is the digitization initiative of the entire service system. Through this automated integrated process they wish to upgrade and include the ships within the eHospital system. In order to link the various platforms, they are connected through a system called Beneficiary Information System (BIS), in order to avoid duplication of beneficiary. The hospital ships are powered by VSAT technology, whereby there is complete network coverage at all times, no matter how remotely the ships are docked.

Case 2

Zipline in Nigeria: Bringing Healthcare to Remote Communities Using Drones

Zipline is a US-based instant logistics provider and boasts of cutting-edge skills in inventory management, on-demand distribution, logistics, information technology, and performance management (agbetiloye, 2022). The organization has become well-known due to its revolutionary drone delivery method. Their use of technology has enabled them to expand access of healthcare making it more equitable, at the same time, enhancing affordability by decreasing costs through efficiency (Zipline – Instant Logistics, n.d.). Their contribution to the health sector has also earned them several awards and accolades, particularly for their proactive role in delivering Covid-19 vaccines.

The Kaduna State in Nigeria is home to a sizable population and makes a significant contribution to Nigeria's gross domestic product. However, the lack of safety in the state's current modes of transportation is a big barrier to trade in the area. Due to a partnership with the Kaduna State Government, Zipline is able to distribute medical supplies to hundreds of health facilities, making the healthcare system in this region more adaptable, responsive, and accessible to its citizens. Zipline operates three warehouses in Kaduna, encompassing an area of 46,000 square kilometers and supplying over 500 medical facilities that collectively care for 9.4 million people. There are over 200 different drugs and vaccines that are delivered by the company, and they have ambitions to grow to include more (Zipline, 2022). By integrating their capabilities into the existing healthcare infrastructure, Zipline has modernized the delivery of medical treatment.

In emerging markets, support from local governments is integral for proper functioning, and Zipline has a successful partnership with the State Government. According to the Health Commissioner of Kaduna State, Amina Mohammed Baloni, sound investment in the supply chain is required to make health systems more efficient, effective, and equitable. To guarantee this growth, such collaborations are necessary to provide improved health outcomes and healthier communities (Zipline, 2022).

Leveraging Technology for Meeting the Challenges

Geographic Accessibility: Nigeria has a population of 211.4 million, and nearly half of them live outside of cities. Vaccines and other services that have a limited shelf life and require a cold chain have a difficult time reaching this demography. Cold chain equipment is uncommon and dependent on an unreliable electricity grid that does not cover the entire country, while traditional land transit is impeded by weather or poor road quality (Zipline – Instant Logistics, n.d.).

Zipline creates and manages networks of cutting-edge medical-grade distribution centers known as hubs. Site of each hub is determined in collaboration with health system partners, considering population coverage, health burdens, geographic reach, and aircraft route optimization. Each hub maintains inventory for an infinite number of distant treatment clinics within a service area of 22,500 square kilometers. The use of delivery drones enables Zipline to reach locations inaccessible to conventional health care providers, hence expanding the availability of health care to people who were otherwise deprived. Kaduna state governor Nasir El Rufai highlighted Zipline's significance by stating that Zipline improves the state's ability to distribute medical commodities to health facilities across the state, even those in the most remote and inaccessible rural clinics, health centers, and hospitals (Ezze, 2022).

Availability: Zipline is ensuring availability in several ways. Every terminal is constantly open (24/7) and operating at full capacity, allowing daily cargo transit of 500 kg. They can also monitor their inventory levels in real time. The program generates unit IDs for each product, and stock is tracked in real time so that a comprehensive inventory picture is available at every point in the supply chain. In this manner, all inventory movements are controlled and safeguarded by fulfillment center-specific digital workflow protocols. Hence, there is no human error because self-reporting is not used. Thirdly, everyone in the supply chain has complete insight into current inventory levels and distribution history data. This drastically decreases the chances of theft and waste. Hub teams maintain regular connection with hundreds of health institutions, allowing them to collect unique data points on behalf of partners to measure KPIs and evaluate demand patterns. Using their monthly and seasonal reports, decision-makers may enhance forecasting and distribution, therefore decreasing stock-outs, overstocking, expiry dates, and waste. As a consequence, supply chain teams make more informed decisions based on the data.

Affordability: Although Zipline does not deal with end customers and thereby do not have much control over the pricing of services, their efficiency helps in cost reduction, which acts as a catalyst for the adoption of such services. With the drones, they are able to reach remote areas, saving the costs for additional infrastructure or investment. In addition, health care providers may issue directives using standard communication channels, such as WhatsApp or the phone, streamlining interactions and eliminating the need for specialized hardware, software, or double-entry of data (Zipline – Instant Logistics, n.d.).

Acceptability: Studies on drivers of success for affordable solutions in emerging markets reveal that, in order to understand the local context, it is imperative for companies to have an operational presence or strong partnership with local entities (Stucke & Chen Lee, 2020). Zipline has both – a strong partnership with the local state government and an operational presence catering to the local needs. This has led to better connectivity with the local community, which has shown a level of trust in the brand itself. A local resident stated that drone delivery of healthcare supplies was appreciated because most areas in the region required urgent healthcare services and were appreciative to the government for this unique health sector endeavor (Ezze, 2022).

Quality: Zipline ensures the accurate tracking and delivery of its products, thereby ensuring service quality. A significant challenge in developing nations is also the storage of medical products, especially those requiring specific temperatures. Zipline has state-of-the-art warehouses that use FEFO fulfillment standards to never let products go bad. All Zipline operation centers in Ghana and Rwanda have reduced losses to below 0.02%. Zipline's statewide hubs eliminate the need for expensive, high-maintenance cold chain equipment at service points. Every distribution facility has medical-grade refrigerators, freezers, and blood banks to store and deliver perishable commodities at exact temperatures (2–8°C, −20°C, and −70°C), so patients may get their drugs immediately regardless of their location. Drone flying requires strict governmental approval. Aircraft on regular routes follow national airspace flight plans monitored in real time by national air traffic controllers. Flights land at hubs and are managed by specialists, making boarding faster and safer. Zipline's punctuality and thoroughness ensure that patients receive their products even in bad weather (Zipline – Instant Logistics, n.d.).

Case 3

Jio Health − A Digital Health Ecosystem in Vietnam Fostering Preventive Care

Vietnam's Jio Health is a human-centered and technology-driven healthcare service. It started as a US-based venture before sensing the immense opportunities in the thriving emerging markets and relocating to Vietnam. In just 50 years, Vietnam has emerged as one of the Indo-Pacific region's fastest-growing economies. With a population of 95 million and a fast-growing youth, the country has enormous scope for a variety of sectors and healthcare is one of them (Abirami, 2020).

The digital health startup was launched in 2014, and it operates an online and offline healthcare ecosystem. At present it is based in Ho Chi Minh city but has plans to expand to other cities as well. On the digital side, it provides telemedicine and e-prescriptions via its mobile app on Android and iOS devices. It operates smart clinics, 300 Jio-branded community pharmacies, and home care on demand

(Adam, 2022). It offers a variety of healthcare services, including primary care, chronic illness management, pediatrics, and auxiliary care, through its platform of 150 multispecialty care providers.

COVID-19 has promoted the notion of self-care among patients, and technological advancement is assisting individuals in adopting a healthy lifestyle. The Vietnamese are also more concerned with "healthcare" than "sickcare," therefore enhancing their physical and emotional health equally (Jen, 2022). This trend toward emphasizing self-care is also one of the most practical means of disease prevention, hence reducing the load on the health system. Promoting self-care among the general populace is considered to be an effective strategy for alleviating the economic burden brought on by Vietnam's aging population. In response to shifting expectations, a growing number of health sector institutions in Vietnam are investing in the development of a self-care-centric ecosystem (Ng, 2020).

Jio Health caters to a wide range of customers as they have a whole range of services dedicated to the patients. The fundamental factors that make self-care possible are:

a. Applicability to all healthcare needs: For regular check-ups, monitoring, and screening.
b. Flexibility from staff: Consultations offered at home, office, online, or clinics.
c. Integrated digital solutions: Patients' data are stored and continuously updated in the mobile phones (Ng, 2020).

Leveraging Technology to Meet the Challenges of Accessibility

Geographic Accessibility: Through offerings including home visits, drug delivery, and online reservations, Jio Health hopes to eliminate boundaries between online and offline healthcare. They're serving as a road map to help people take care of themselves by making the healthcare system more open and accommodating. Their online and offline presence enhances their reach beyond cities, to a larger market base. Jio has ambitious goals to expand its clinical service offering to more customers and employers, to assist the establishment of additional Smart Clinics in existing and new locations, to expand its provider and clinical support teams, and to encourage technical platform innovation. Jio Health employs an omni-channel strategy that integrates preventative, multispecialty care management, and supplementary diagnostic and pharmaceutical services to improve healthcare outcomes (Bual, 2022).

Availability: Jio Health ensures availability in several ways. Jio's goal is to create an all-encompassing healthcare system by offering services including in-home consultations, an online pharmacy, round-the-clock virtual care, and annual plans for individuals, families, and businesses. Additionally, they have very recently launched a smart clinic which is one of the core elements of the comprehensive health ecosystem. It has all the necessary equipment and enough room for patients and physicians to meet face to face, making it the company's most tangible asset. The Smart Clinic, the "home of technology-based health-care," offers cutting-edge diagnosis and treatment by a team of highly qualified physicians. Appointments at the Smart Clinic are simple to schedule, electronic health data are readily available, and patients may use telemedicine to consult with a group of highly trained medical experts. Finally, they have a team of 150+ doctors covering 14+ specialties, to meet the diverse healthcare needs across all departments. Having access to these doctors virtually through the use of technology ensures their availability.

Affordability: Jio Health has partnered up with more than 40 reputed insurance providers in Vietnam in order for patients to have affordable access to healthcare. Patients are able to enjoy direct billing coverage. The company also helps the patients with paperwork and insurance claims, the majority of which is done online. Its full-stack ecosystem (integration) is addressing all critical pain points for patients which adds convenience and reduces transaction time, thereby making them the trusted brand for quality care at affordable costs for the masses.

Acceptance: Healthcare is a high involvement service and patients appreciate time and attention from the doctors. The Jio Health app is very user-friendly and the interface has been designed to make it very similar to the app of Uber or Grab, as Jio Health knew patients are familiar with that interface. Additionally, the process of registering oneself is very simple and can be completed in a matter of clicks. This familiarity and user friendliness led to a higher adoption of the app itself. The online and offline care services are tightly integrated with its lab information systems, e-pharmacy, and clinical operating system, thus enabling consumers to have a cohesive end-to-end healthcare journey that encompasses appointment booking, consultation, diagnostics, treatment, and home delivery of prescriptions, acting as a one stop solution.

Quality: Given the rate of technological disruptions, tech-based organizations are required to invest in the maintenance and upgradation of their equipment. Jio Health prioritizes the upgradation of its facilities and generously invests in new technology. On the other hand, constant training for all care providers and customer support teams is undertaken based on customer input to enhance the customer experience at all touchpoints. Building a solid healthcare model for the new era requires a real healthcare provider–public collaboration with customer participation (Ng, 2020).

Case 4

The National Telehealth System (NTS): Addressing Challenges of the Philippines Healthcare System

The Philippines comprises of 7,107 islands, of which only about 1,200 are inhabited. The geography makes rural health care difficult as there is an unfair distribution of doctors with the majority of doctors serving the metropolitan cities. The three cities with the most doctors are Metro Manila (4,029), Central Luzon (3,553), and South Luzon (3,251). These numbers are in stark contrast to the fact that only about 4.5% of all doctors work in poor, rural areas (World Health Organization. Regional Office for the Western Pacific, 2013).

To address this issue, the Philippines Department of Health (DOH) has a program called Doctors to the Barrios (DTTB) where the government deploys freshly graduated doctors to neglected rural communities or geographically isolated and disadvantaged areas (GIDAs). These GIDAs have daunting topography making them inaccessible. To overcome this challenge, the government introduced the National Telehealth System (NTS). The National Telehealth Center (NTHC), a research center affiliated with the University of the Philippines Manila, established and operates the NTS. The NTS addresses the demand for remote medical professional services and care for isolated, low-income individuals. Telehealth is a potential solution to the issues of a limited healthcare workforce and remote population. The NTS is a telemedicine platform that attempts to provide patients access to specialized treatment in underserved and physically remote places.

Geographic Accessibility and Availability

NTS is a telemedicine initiative that assists rural residents in receiving specialized care. This platform connects rural primary care practitioners with experts from major hospitals (Juban, Salisi, Mier, Mier-Alpano, & Ongkeko Jr, 2020). NTS users form a network of health providers who overcome geographical remoteness and mal-distributed resources. Philippines' extensive mobile phone use benefits the NTS. The shareholders including DTTB physicians, specialists, and patients facilitated the telemedicine platform's development. Since 2007, 2,710 NTS consultations were completed, 2,517 through SMS, and the remainder via email. Clinicians from 175 health facilities utilize NTS, covering over five million Filipinos (Juban et al., 2020). The NTS represents a significant advancement for the government's eHealth efforts and bridges the urban–rural divide by linking individuals who would otherwise be separated and underserved (Juban et al., 2020).

Success Story: A newly deployed DTTB referred to a 50-year-old man suffering from myocardial infarction in one of our most remarkable tele-cardiology cases.

> In this instance, the referring DTTB physician was uncertain about how to interpret the electrocardiogram (ECG), but his keen clinical eye (based on the patient's symptoms and physical examination) enabled him to call the specialist via the NTS platform. The specialist was immediately available and confirmed the referring physician's initial ECG interpretation. The NTS saved a patient's life by sending him to the closest hospital, where he was successfully treated.

> This example demonstrates how NTS assisted an inexperienced physician in managing a patient by involving a more seasoned

clinician, thereby enhancing patient care and lowering medical errors (Juban et al., 2020).

As a result of the NTS, people in locations with limited access to healthcare, such as those without reliable electricity or other infrastructure, are able to receive treatments. This platform assisted millions of people and saved lives, particularly during the Covid-19 pandemic (Balinbin, 2022). In these nations like the Philippines, the COVID-19 outbreak has severely hindered the provision of basic health treatment, inpatient admissions, and surgical procedures. As a response to the COVID-19 crisis, service providers, government regulators, and other civil society organizations in the Philippines have all advocated for the implementation of telemedicine (Villaraza et al., 2020). Several authorities and corporations have developed COVID-19 hotlines, websites, and mobile apps for teleconsultations in the Philippines. Despite its general acceptance as a viable method to extend the reach of scarce healthcare practitioners and resources during an epidemic, telemedicine is not widely employed due to its high costs, technological limitations, data privacy concerns, and patient safety risks.

Affordability and Acceptability: According to Enrique A. Tayag (Director of the DOH's), cultural barriers and poor infrastructure caused insufficient telemedicine services in the Philippines. One of the major cultural difficulties is the generation gap, with elders preferring face-to-face consultation and younger people possibly being more engaged on social platforms and making decisions outside of the telemedicine realm (Balinbin, 2022). Additionally, the difficulty of rural residents in acquiring cellphones and the quality of their internet connection are two of the biggest obstacles to the widespread use of telemedicine. Patients in rural areas usually schedule tele-counseling sessions for the evenings as then the internet connection is typically more stable. Although telemedicine has the potential to greatly improve patient care, the advent of 5G will be required to fully realize this promise (Balinbin, 2022). Some Filipinos are not tech-savvy and would rather have in-person meetings as they give the customers more freedom of expression. Tele counseling is challenging if the client has no private place and if they can't be left alone. Furthermore, mothers also expressed reluctance to use telemedicine for their children due to possibilities of a misdiagnosis and some find the service costly as well. Concerns relating to privacy issues are also another key problem which was also raised by some users of internet resources (Balinbin, 2022). Despite all the setbacks, there is gradual increase in the adoption.

The four cases illustrate that despite the challenges of operating in emerging countries, including lack of infrastructure, doctors and paramedics as well as prevalent divide of urban–rural population and digital adoption, with the use of technology, organizations are successful in meeting the pressing needs of health.

Healthcare Waste Management

Although the primary focus of this chapter is on the delivery of health services through the use of technology, healthcare services also generate a lot of waste which requires proper management for safeguarding the health of the communities. Developed countries utilize more smart-systems for the disposal of medical wastes which is very different from emerging countries. However, as technology trickles down to these markets, smart disposal of medical wastes should also be on the agenda.

Healthcare waste encompasses all medical waste produced within health facilities, research centers, and laboratories and also includes household health-care waste. Infectious organisms, genotoxic or cytotoxic chemical composition, toxic or hazardous compounds, biologically aggressive drugs, radiation, and used sharp objects like injection needles and vials all increase the risk posed by healthcare waste. A safe healthcare waste management system is required to prevent the release of chemical or biological hazards microbes that could endanger patients, healthcare staff, and the general public. Since healthcare waste and by-products come from a wide range of materials, segregation and sorting waste in a hospital prevents infections, and also helps cut down on greenhouse gas emissions, persistent organic pollutants (POPs), mercury, and other dangerous waste (World Health Organization, 2017).

According to WHO (2018) report, developed economies create up to 0.5 kg of hazardous waste per hospital bed per day, compared to 0.2 kg in low-income nations. However, in low-income nations, it's common for medical waste to not be segregated into hazardous and non-hazardous wastes, thus the actual amount of hazardous waste and its impact is much higher. As Asia is the fastest growing economic region with half the world population, a huge accumulation of waste is an inevitable byproduct of this growth. The governments of developing countries in Asia prioritize providing citizens with food, shelter, and clothing, but they often overlook the importance of properly disposing of the medical waste. Since health and the environment are inextricably interwoven, it is crucial to take a coordinated approach when helping developing countries deal with healthcare waste disposal challenges (Ananth, Prashanthini, & Visvanathan, 2010).

Medical wastes are most commonly disposed of through incineration, secure landfilling, encapsulation, and disposal in cement kilns (WHO, 2018). In general, the detoxification of infectious and sharp waste by steam (e.g., autoclaving) or other non-burn technologies should be favored for the treatment of infectious waste (World Health Organization, 2017). In the lower middle-income countries, more than 90% of medical waste is incinerated without a reduction device which results in releasing harmful dioxins and heavy metals after combustion (Liu, Qu, Lei, & Jia, 2017). Moreover, the medical waste incineration plants in these nations employ obsolete and potentially hazardous technology which leads to heavy emission of dioxin and other harmful chemicals in the environment. The second most common approach to treating medical waste is autoclaving, which uses heat to disinfect the waste in a safe and effective way, but is only used in few countries due to cost and esthetic concerns (HCWH, 2020).

Most countries have policies for the disposal of pharmaceutical waste, but none have a policy regarding the handling and management of hazardous and cytotoxic chemicals. It is suggested, in accordance with the Basel Convention, to prioritize waste treatment processes that reduce the creation and release of chemicals or harmful pollutants. The lower middle-income countries need pharmaceutical, chemical, and radioactive waste management strategies incorporated in their national plan, governed by international and local legislation. In lower- and middle-income countries where medical waste has not been well handled, the recent COVID-19 pandemic has worsened the scenario due to increased demand, usage, and disposal of medical waste, notably abandoned protection gears and single-use plastics (Singh, Ogunseitan, & Tang, 2022; Sinthiya, Chowdhury, & Haque, 2022). The absence of the holistic approach in waste management during the COVID-19 pandemic has already resulted in ecological and health consequences worldwide. According to the International Solid Waste Agency (ISWA), in poor and middle-income nations in particular, the collapse of the waste management system is possible if medical and municipal wastes are not methodically and efficiently segregated at the source (Singh et al., 2022). Therefore, an intelligent waste management system must be established to make trash collection more effective, economical, and environmentally friendly by leveraging the use of modern technologies (BigRentz, 2021; Sinthiya et al., 2022).

The term "smart waste management" refers to a method that employs the use of cutting-edge technology to dispose of waste in a way that's not only effective, but also environmentally friendly and inexpensive. This automated approach is significantly different from standard waste management systems since it provides the quickest and most efficient route, intelligent monitoring, reduces wasted fuel costs, and saves time. Most of these systems incorporate the Internet of Things (IoT) and AI models to better monitor and manage the collection of waste and archives data in real time, to improve garbage collection efficiency and foster future innovation (BigRentz, 2021; Sinthiya et al., 2022).

Conclusion

In low- and low-middle-income nations, a lack of integrative techniques and technological adaptation hinders the proper medical waste management. In these countries, health-care waste challenges include lack of awareness about health hazards, absence of training in proper waste management, the dearth of waste management and disposal systems, and considering waste management as a low priority. With coordinated and comprehensive approaches and the right technology adaptation, medical waste management can be incorporated into the economy more quickly and effectively, according to studies. It is particularly dependent on the acceptance and financing of innovative medical waste treatment technology, as well as the implementation of sustainable concepts utilized in many industrialized and industrial countries. The World Health Organization (WHO) recommends that the first step in medical waste management is source reduction (i.e., minimizing waste output) and effective segregation of the waste. If this is not practicable, then all wastes should be addressed as medical waste to avoid health hazards.

Success in hospital waste management will contribute toward the achievement of the UN Sustainable Development Goals, including:

(1) *SDG-3* – Good Health and Well-being.
(2) *SDG-6* – Clean Water and Sanitation.
(3) *SDG-8* – Decent Work and Economic Growth.
(4) *SDG-12* – Responsible Consumption and Production.
(5) *SDG-13* – Climate Actions (HCWH, 2020).

Low- and middle-income countries in particular need to recognize medical/healthcare waste management as a vital public service and invest in appropriate standards, training, immunizations, and living circumstances. Countries must implement a safe medical waste disposal strategy to prevent stockpiling and community contamination. Despite all obstacles, ecologically sound medical waste management can be achieved through the development and adoption of advanced innovative treatment technologies, products, and ideas that assist in driving the medical system toward an environmentally safe and healthy economy.

References

agbetiloye. (2022, June 7). Zipline is set to revolutionise the health supply chain in Nigeria. *Ventures Africa*. Retrieved from https://venturesafrica.com/how-zipline-will-revolutionise-the-health-supply-chain-in-nigeria/
Abirami. (2020, October 11). *How Jio health is changing MedTech landscape industry in Vietnam*. Investocracy News Technology.
Adam, A. (2022, March 11). Vietnamese digital health startup Jio health nets $20M in series B round. *Mobi Health News*. Retrieved from https://www.mobihealthnews.com/news/asia/vietnamese-digital-health-startup-jio-health-nets-20m-series-b-round
Alam, M. M. (2019). Foreign direct investment in Bangladesh: Analysis of government policy framework, sector wise impact and future of FDI growth. *International Journal of Management and Accounting, 3*(3), 60–82.
Ananth, A. P., Prashanthini, V., & Visvanathan, C. (2010). Healthcare waste management in Asia. *Waste Management, 30*(1), 154–161.
Antoanela, I. (2021, August 31). How tech helps advance the UN sustainable development goals. *The Recursive*. Retrieved from https://therecursive.com/how-tech-helps-advance-the-un-sustainable-development-goals/
Balinbin, A. L. (2022, March 2). Telehealth offers Filipinos a lifeline amid pandemic. *Business World Online*. Retrieved from https://www.bworldonline.com/top-stories/2022/03/03/433553/telehealth-offers-filipinos-a-lifeline-amid-pandemic/
BigRentz. (2021, October 15). *8 innovative smart waste management technologies*. BigRentz. Https://Www.Bigrentz.Com. Retrieved from https://www.bigrentz.com/blog/smart-waste-management
Bual, H. (2022, March 9). Vietnam-based health tech startup Jio health bags $20M in series B round. *Vietcetera, rprises*.
Deloitte UK (2016). *Healthcare for the pre-middle class in emerging economies* [White paper]. Retrieved from www2.deloitte.com/content/dam/Deloitte/sg/Documents/risk/sea-risk-healthcare-in-emerging-economies.pdf

Ezze, R. (2022, July 18). *Zipline drones bridge delivery gap, as more Nigerian states join in*. Retrieved from https://www.logupdateafrica.com/cargo-drones/zipline-drones-bridge-delivery-gap-as-more-nigerian-states-join-in-1345970

HCWH. (2020). *Health care waste management and the sustainable development goals*. Health Care Without Harm. Retrieved from https://noharm-global.org/issues/global/health-care-waste-management-and-sustainable-development-goals

Hecht, J. (2018, November 30). *How technology is driving change in almost every major industry*. Forbes. Retrieved from https://www.forbes.com/sites/jaredhecht/2018/11/30/how-technology-is-driving-change-in-almost-every-major-industry/

Heinonen, K., & Strandvik, T. (2020). Reframing service innovation: COVID-19 as a catalyst for imposed service innovation. *Journal of Service Management, 32*(1), 101–112.

Jen. (2022, July 8). Telehealth, integrated medical technology: Healthcare trends in the industry 4.0. *Vietcetera*. Retrieved from https://vietcetera.com/en/telehealth-integrated-medical-technology-healthcare-trends-in-the-industry-40

Juban, N., Salisi, J., Mier, A., Mier-Alpano, J., & Ongkeko Jr, A. (2020). *National Telehealth System, Philippines*. [Online]. World Health Organization & UNICEF/UNDP/World Bank/WHO Special Programme for Research and Training in Tropical Diseases. Geneva: Social Innovation in Health Initiative. Retrieved from www.socialinnovationinhealth.org

Kyle, G. (2022, May 12). *Closing the health care gap: Why innovation matters*. APCO Worlwide. Retrieved from https://apcoworldwide.com/blog/closing-the-health-care-gap-why-innovation-matters/

Liu, Y., Qu, Y., Lei, Z., & Jia, H. (2017). Understanding the evolution of sustainable consumption research. *Sustainable Development, 25*(5), 414–430.

Meloan, M., & Iacopino, P. (2017). *Scaling digital health in developing markets: Opportunities and recommendations for mobile operators and other stakeholders*. London: GSMA.

Ng, M. (2020, December 28). Jio health: A 3-year journey to a complete health ecosystem. *Vietcetera*. Retrieved from https://vietcetera.com/en/jio-health-a-4-year-journey-to-a-complete-health-ecosystem

Peters, D. H., Garg, A., Bloom, G., Walker, D. G., Brieger, W. R., & Rahman, M. H. (2008). Poverty and access to health care in developing countries. *Annals of the New York Academy of Sciences, 1136*, 161–171. doi:10.1196/annals.1425.011

Schanz, K.-U. (2019). Healthcare in emerging markets: Exploring the protection gaps. *The Geneva Association*, 1–39.

Singh, N., Ogunseitan, O. A., & Tang, Y. (2022). Medical waste: Current challenges and future opportunities for sustainable management. *Critical Reviews in Environmental Science and Technology, 52*(11), 2000–2022.

Sinthiya, N. J., Chowdhury, T. A., & Haque, A. K. M. (2022). Artificial intelligence based smart waste management—A systematic review. *Computational Intelligence Techniques for Green Smart Cities*, 67–92.

Stucke, A. & Chen Lee, S. (2020). *Enabling health technology in emerging markets* (pp. 1–8).

UNCTAD. (2020). *The impact of rapid technological change on sustainable development* (Science, Technology and Innovation – Current Issues). Retrieved from https://unctad.org/system/files/official-document/dtlstict2019d10_en.pdf

Villaraza, Acosta, A.-F. M., & Siao, K. C. C. (2020, April 15). *Addressing COVID-19 with healthcare in a digital economy*. Lexology. Retrieved from https://www. lexology.com/library/detail.aspx?g=b773868a-86f8-47e4-b6c6-e0b4704d9258

WHO. (2017). *Report on health-care waste management (HCWM) status in Countries of the South-East Asia Region*. World Health Organization. Regional Office for South-East Asia.

WHO. (2018). *Health-care waste [fact sheets]*. World Health Organization. Retrieved from https://www.who.int/news-room/fact-sheets/detail/health-care-waste

World Health Organization. (2017). *Safe management of wastes from health-care activities: A summary (WHO/FWC/WSH/17.05)*. World Health Organization. Retrieved from https://apps.who.int/iris/handle/10665/259491

World Health Organization. Regional Office for the Western Pacific. (2013). *Human resources for health country profiles*: Philippines: WHO Regional Office for the Western Pacific. Retrieved from https://apps.who.int/iris/handle/10665/207680

Zipline, T. (2022, June 13). Zipline gets ready to takeoff in Nigeria. *The Medium*. Retrieved from https://medium.com/@zipline/zipline-gets-ready-to-takeoff-in-nigeria-8a1d1c5ba1d7

Zipline—Instant Logistics. (n.d.). *Zipline*. Retrieved from https://www.flyzipline.com/

Chapter 12

A Study of Stimulating Sustainable Women Empowerment Through Fintech Applications

Ajay Sidana, Richa Goel and Mashiur Rehman

Abstract

The introduction highlights the historical gender gap in financial empowerment and how Fintech, particularly in the wake of COVID-19, has facilitated financial inclusion for women in India, offering digital solutions to overcome social restrictions. The objective of this chapter is to assess the impact of Fintech on sustainable women empowerment in India. The methodology involves surveying 230 women in Delhi NCR and analyzing factors such as financial literacy, decision-making, financial freedom, security, employability, career growth, and gender equality. The results indicate that Fintech has improved financial awareness and security for women, empowered them in financial decision-making, and fostered professional growth. The implications suggest that the Fintech industry plays a promising role in achieving gender equality by providing women with access to financial instruments, leading to increased economic contribution, personal confidence, and freedom. Fintech has the potential to reduce gender inequality and financial vulnerability at a macro level, empowering women to actively participate in the economy and contributing to sustained gender equality and economic growth.

Keywords: Sustainable; women empowerment; Fintech; technology; women; gender equality

Introduction

United Nations' 2030 Agenda for Sustainable Development placed a strong emphasis on women empowerment and achieving gender equality for a more equal society. It has been listed as the fifth among Sustainable Development

Fostering Sustainable Businesses in Emerging Economies, 207–221
Copyright © 2024 Ajay Sidana, Richa Goel and Mashiur Rehman
Published under exclusive licence by Emerald Publishing Limited
doi:10.1108/978-1-80455-640-520231013

Goals (SDGs) laid out in the Agenda 2030 and includes benchmarks for achieving a better future through gender empowerment. Over the past decade, continuous technological advancement has led to major strides in achieving gender equality through women empowerment in our society. Yet, the gender divide between men and women remains largely unabridged over one critical aspect of living, i.e., economic empowerment. Due to patriarchal setup in most societies, financial solutions and products have traditionally been the domain of men and out of reach for women. However, especially since COVID-19 pandemic, digital financial solutions via Fintech mobile Apps have paved the way for women to access financial resources unlike ever before. The availability of e-wallets and mobile banking facilities have opened up new avenues of financial resource management for women, even while following conventional social constraints of time and movement. As Fintech apps have grown in popularity due to their ease and convenience, the female gender stands to benefit in more ways than one. Hence, the shift in this dynamic brought on by Fintech Apps is interesting to be viewed from the lens of women empowerment. The present study takes a close look at the role of Fintech apps as a sustainable solution toward women empowerment in society.

Fintech as a term stands for financial technology. As Fintech apps, it refers to the latest leaps forward in mobile technology, which allows people to manage, monitor, save, and invest money. The monetary transactions that flow through these apps are secure and efficient. These apps are mobile and easy-to-adopt in their interface, making payments and transactions through these apps convenient and time-saving. To put it simply, Fintech apps are safe, effective, easy to use, and productive for all users irrespective of age or gender.

Today, the scope of the Fintech industry is incredibly vast, encompassing everything from mobile banking services to making investments, taking loans and even venturing in real estate. Some functions offered under the umbrella term of Fintech today include online payments and transactions, online banking, market trading, cryptocurrency trade, digital lending and credit, digital wallets, and collective financing, etc. Some globally popular Fintech apps include Paypal, Venmo, Stripe, and Alipay, while some popular Fintech apps used in India are PayTM, Cred, Razorpay, Finly, and more. As digitalization becomes prevalent in our modern society, the Fintech apps industry has also seen a rapidly accelerated growth. According to Deloitte report (2022),[1] it is predicted that the global Fintech market will be worth $213 billion in 2024, a huge rise from $140 billion in 2020. Additionally, the industry is expected to grow at over 12.6% per year. As per KPMG[2] Report (2021), investments in the Fintech industry has multiplied three times over since 2015. As Fintech continues to grow, there remains no doubt that it will have a powerful impact on all aspects of our society.

---

[1]https://www2.deloitte.com/content/dam/Deloitte/nl/Documents/financial-services/deloitte-nl-fsi-fintech-report-1.pdf.
[2]https://assets.kpmg/content/dam/kpmg/xx/pdf/2022/02/pulse-of-fintech-h2-21.pdf.

One of the core ways that Fintech has greatly influenced the society is by breaking barriers to financial inclusion for the discriminated sections of the society. Fintech apps have allowed unbarred access to crucial resources and facilities of financial planning, management, and execution. This has given newfound agency to the economically disadvantaged sections of society like women, who had been excluded from economic matters due to their social barriers. Traditionally, the social barriers to financial empowerment of women include lack of knowledge or awareness about financial matters and tools, or lack of experience and opportunities for savings and investment. Due to low awareness and exposure, women are also more likely to be scammed or be irresponsible with their finances (Agrawal, 2022). Women can find it tougher than men to avail credit or insurance, which hampers their entrepreneurial growth and restricts their choices. These factors lead to several challenges and difficulties in economic and social development of women. To make matters worse, women have also been sidelined in making important financial policy decisions which only exacerbates their plight. The lack of financial awareness also leads to low investment in their personal and professional growth, leading to long-term economic disadvantages in life. However, with the coming of Fintech apps, the unfettered access to digital financial solutions – irrespective of barriers like gender, age, or class-can serve as a great equalizer.

As Fintech continues to grow, it has the potential to impact women in many ways. For one, it could help women open up more money and better manage their finances. Fintech companies could provide a safety net to alleviate risks that women face on day-to-day basis. It has also been accelerated by the schemes and campaigns promoted by the government. The promotion of micro-entrepreneurship through Fintech can further integrate women in the economic cycle. For example, e-wallets and mobile banking have made it easier for women to get money and save money, which has removed social restrictions on time and movement.

As stated by the GSMA Mobile Report (2022),[3] more women than ever are using smart phones with mobile internet adoption in South Asia, with the largest change in gender gap coming from India. Despite these strides in digital empowerment, there has been a significant gender schism when it comes to financial empowerment for women in India. However, especially since COVID-19, digital financial solutions or Fintech has opened up many opportunities for women to access financial resources. As per the report above by GSMA (2022), shifting market dynamics over the past few years and the affordability of internet amid lockdown restrictions during COVID-19 were the major driving factors for Indian women to take interest in becoming more digital-savvy and claiming their decision-making. The same reasons were reflected in the report by Newsvoir (2022),[4] where it was found that the pandemic resulted in Indian women

---

[3]https://www.gsma.com/mobilefordevelopment/blog/the-mobile-gender-gap-report-2022/.
[4]https://inc42.com/buzz/india-has-more-fintech-adopters-at-87-compared-to-global-average-of-64-report/.

adopting financial technology services at a much higher rate than the global percentage. In 2022, India has the highest number of Fintech adopters in the world at 87% as compared to the global adoption of 64%. It is therefore imperative to look closely at the association between access to Fintech and improved status of women in society.

Presently, while relevant literature reviews exist in the field of impact of Fintech on women's lives, it may be seen that a majority of such reviews are focused solely on a particular facet of women development such as financial literacy, or rely solely on secondary data as obtained from existing journals. Additionally, the existing literature in this field has also been left suddenly outdated due to the vast changes brought in by the pandemic. This development has rendered the existing research lacking relevance to the present day scenario. Additionally, these studies have not explored the impact of access to Fintech from the perspective of professional growth and employability of women. To add to this gap, not much research has been accomplished in the field of Fintech and its sustained impact in pursuing gender equality as globally desired. Lastly, the studies available on this topic have largely been concentrated in western developed countries where Fintech adoption is not restricted by social norms like those prevalent in developing countries like India. The stark cultural and social differences in these backgrounds merit further research for establishing a nuanced conclusion.

And thus, considering the discussion above, the preexisting research in this field was extracted and analyzed in this study. By applying the literature methodology, this research paper has pondered over three major research questions, namely:

R1: How has access to Fintech apps impacted women empowerment?

R2: How can the impact of Fintech apps on women empowerment be measured?

R3: Can improved access to Fintech apps lead to gender equality via women empowerment in a sustainable fashion?

The findings of this study shall have potential benefits to several stakeholders in the area of study delegated to Fintech apps and their impact on society. The study will be a worthy addition to further research regarding the role of Fintech apps on the empowerment and equality of women, particularly considering their economic upliftment. It is evident that access to Fintech apps can result in improved quality of life for women through the development of financial awareness and informed confidence regarding their economic decisions. The findings will be of practical implication to women in general, but specifically to social leaders and policymakers, administrators, application developers, and other professionals in the field. This study will champion more evidence-based decisions regarding the development of women-friendly technologies that enable their development by bridging gender gaps and empowering them in their routine lives. At a wider scale, this study will have implications on the policy decisions regarding facilitating the access to Fintech apps for women so as to further the cause of gender quality by empowering women to take their financial decisions.

The research is organized as follows: Section 2 is "Review of Literature" which provides a comprehensive overview of research already existing in this field. In this section, detailed analysis on the role of Fintech apps and their merits toward women who have access to have been discussed from the les of women empowerment. Section 3 of this paper discusses the research methodology where a survey has been conducted which collected the data from some respondents which has been further analyzed for drawing an evaluation and conclusion. Using multiple factor analysis, the importance and impact of access to Fintech apps on women empowerment has been evaluated based on six independent key variables. In section 4 of the paper, the Analysis and Interpretation of the data has been presented. The relationship between the dependent and independent variables of access to Fintech apps has been analyzed. In section 5 of the paper, a discussion has been presented based on findings obtained from the analysis conducted in the study. Section 6 of the study presents a theoretical framework based on the findings of the study, to show the relationship between access to Fintech apps and sustainable gender equality as given in SDGs under Agenda 2030. Lastly, section 7 of the study provides the future scope and conclusion of the present study.

Review of Literature

Discussions around Fintech Apps and their applications for improving the status quo of women have been studied with various lenses over the last few years. In the current section, a comprehensive review of relevant literature in this field has been presented in a structure following the chronology of research questions as provided in the introduction to this paper. At the end of the review, some research gaps have been highlighted. These gaps in the existing literature have laid the foundation for the present paper.

Fintech Apps

To understand the impact of access of Fintech apps on women empowerment, it is important to first establish the meaning and scope of Fintech Apps as perceived in this study. The present sub-section seeks to establish the meaning and nature of Fintech apps and their role in the empowerment of their female users.

Fintech or financial technology refers to the digitalization of financial services. As per Arora (2020), these digital mediums deliver financial services using the Internet without being reliant on a physical branch of a bank or financial institution. Ozili (2018) further admits that Fintech is a broad term which does not have a rigid definition, but rather it includes all services, products, technologies and infrastructure which allows individuals or companies to make payments, transactions, savings, or access credit facilities via online means. As per Gomber, Koch, and Siering (2017), Fintech includes mobile and app services. Similarly, OECD (2018) expands the definition and ambit of Fintech to include "development of business products and models which rely on such technologies". In the effort to provide a stickler definition, Gomber et al. (2017) have stated that Fintech includes innovative technologies that are based upon the internet or automated information processing. Schueffel (2017) listed that modern Fintech companies employed various technologies in their operations including block-chain ledger technology, big data, internet of things, cloud computing, and artificial intelligence. Arora (2020) also pointed out those digital platforms such as marketplaces which act as mediators between online borrowers and lenders. Arner (2014) has broadly classified the evolution of Fintech into three stages, with the third and current stage beginning from the 2008 global financial crisis as a turning point.

In the present study, researchers have focused on the use of Fintech as limited to mobile applications available to the public for making routine financial transactions and investments.

Role of Fintech Apps

According to Arora (2020), digitalization of financial services has led to increased financial access and inclusion. Nguse et al. (2022) asserted in their study that financial inclusion of marginalized or discriminated sections was imperative to the collective growth of the economy. Siddik (2017) provides that useful and affordable financial products and services enable the financial inclusion for SMEs and individuals, which is the major engine of socioeconomic development. Hess and Klapper (2021) have also highlighted the need for mass-scale financial services which are accessible to poor people (Nasir, Lee, Pea, & McKinney de Royston, 2021). Fintech has the potential to empower people to manage their own finances and achieve self-reliance and freedom. Philippon (2016) stated that Fintech was a suitable and efficient financial system with reduced social costs. According to Fu and Mishra (2020, pp. 20–38), Fintech apps offer several benefits

Table 1. Brief List of Benefits Offered by Fintech as Per Previous Studies.

Impact of Fintech Apps	Citations
Increased access to financial resources	Arora (2020), Gomber et al. (2017)
Greater financial knowledge	Bunyamin and Wahab (2017), Riza and Wijayanti (2021)
Enhanced financial inclusion	Lwanga Mayanja and Adong (2017), Osabuohien and Karakara (2018)
Promote savings	Björkegren and Grissen (2018), Hess and Klapper (2021)
Increase economic growth	Bunyamin and Wahab (2017), Riza and Wijayanti (2021), Sioson and Kim (2019)
Improve well being	Gomber et al. (2017), Sioson and Kim (2019)
Match borrowers and lenders	Fu and Mishra (2020, pp. 20–38), Nasir et al. (2021), Schueffel (2017)

Source: Author.

such as accessibility, cost-savings, efficiency, and customer-friendliness. Additionally, the study found that mobile banking services made microcredit services more widely available and easily accessible, thus improving entrepreneurial capital investment (Table 1).

Women's Access to Fintech Apps

Several studies in the recent past have highlighted the need for financial inclusion of women in order to reduce gender divide in the society. A study on Ethiopian women by Nguse et al. (2022) also provided that financial inclusion of women was critical to the growth of the nation as a whole. According to Kim (2022), women have faced backwardness because poor financial awareness and literacy have crippled their development in relation to men. As pointed out in their study, Sioson and Kim (2019) found that women face a multitude of challenges in being financially equal to their male peers. A number of sociopolitical barriers can hinder women from financial access such as preexisting family or social responsibilities, and mindset or attitude barriers. Unlike men, women generally experience a lack of control over financial instruments and also suffer under unequal division of labor. Due to low awareness and exposure, women are also more likely to be scammed or be irresponsible with their finances (Agrawal, 2022). Women can also find it tougher than men to avail credit or insurance, which hampers their professional growth and restricts their choices. Additionally, for women who wish to invest in their own finances, social support is low (Fanta & Mutsonziwa, 2016, p. 1; Njagi & Onyango, 2019). Most women also face different risks when invested in the stock market: from losing money if the stock market crashes, to being left out of the biggest developments in the stock market. Thus, despite the many advances made in the twenty-first century, there still exists large-scale gender inequality which becomes especially evident for economic affairs. In this scenario, digital solutions via mobile apps have indeed been a key enabler in the inclusion of women to matters of economic growth. By providing them with access to affordable and accessible financial products and services, Fintech can help women become more financially secure. Thus as Fintech continues to grow, it has the potential to impact women in many ways, and help them get closer to an equal status in the society gradually and sustainably.

Over time, Fintech-enabled financial inclusion can thus help women in developing a better psychological state by enhancing their sense of self-worth, financial independence and the right to control their life.

How Fintech Apps Help in Empowering Women

As pointed out in a study of impact of mobile money on the financial inclusion of Nairobi women by Kim (2022), Fintech services enabled women with higher financial security and increased their inclusion in financial institutions. Fintech has the potential to revolutionize how women spend their money, by empowering them to manage their own finances and get what they need from life without reliance on men (Riza & Wijayanti, 2021). This has helped to remove gender barriers for attaining micro-credit, accumulating savings, delving into investment options, and developing confidence in financial participation (Sioson & Kim, 2019). Thus, the inclusion of women in financial institutions is one key facet of Fintech that can have a positive impact on their empowerment.

(1) Financial literacy – Fintech apps could help women open up more money and better manage their finances. Additionally, Fintech apps can provide a new way for women to communicate with each other and get advice on financial matters. As per Bunyamin and Wahab (2017), Fintech enhances the financial capability of an individual, and plays an active role in their financial well-being. Improved financial literacy through Fintech leads to higher participation of individuals in economic life (Robino et al., 2018).

(2) Financial decision-making – Several researchers state that women can contribute to growth not only by building businesses but also by better managing their financial resources (DiCaprio, Yao, & Simms, 2017; Kim, 2022). Having access to and use of a range of financial services enhances not only the contribution of women and women-led business to growth, but also contributes to women's autonomy, allows for better use of their personal and household resources, and reduces the vulnerability of their households and businesses. Gender gap in financial inclusion can act as an enabler of countries' development, economic growth, inequality reduction, business evolution, and social inclusion (Fu & Mishra, 2020; Riza & Wijayanti, 2021).

(3) Freedom – The past literature is unanimous in stating that women empowerment is a critical issue for the future of humanity. As women become more empowered and have control over their lives, they are able to better emancipate themselves from patriarchy and socioeconomic discrimination. However, much work remains to be done in order to empower women completely. By providing women with access to affordable, accessible financial products and services, Fintech has been able to play an important role in helping these women become more financially secure (Agrawal, 2022; DiCaprio et al., 2017). This will allow them to reduce their reliance on men for financial support, which would be beneficial not just for themselves but also for their families and social lives.

(4) Security – Fintech has the ability to help empower women by providing them with affordable and accessible financial products and services. By contributing to female empowerment, Fintech can play an important role in helping women become more financially secure (Riza & Wijayanti, 2021). This will allow them to reduce their reliance on men for financial support, which would be beneficial not just for themselves but also for their families and social lives. Having access to and use of a range of financial services enhances not only the contribution of women and women-led business to growth, but also contributes to women's autonomy, allows for better use of their personal and household resources, and reduces the vulnerability of their households and businesses. They can also enable women to accumulate savings and improve their productive capacity. Fintech can also empower women in their

strides toward reducing extreme poverty and boosting the economic and productive capacity, leading to a better life.

(5) Career Growth – Fintech companies could provide a safety net (such as credit, savings or insurance) to alleviate risks that women face on day-to-day basis. The promotion of micro-entrepreneurship through Fintech can further integrate women in the economic cycle. A few Indian Fintech platforms are already supporting MSMEs and SMEs that are working with rural women in industries such as handicrafts, food and healthcare in India. Several Fintech apps also facilitate the participation of women in government programs and welfare schemes. Fintech startups are using technology to promote entre-preneurship among rural women by extending differential financial solutions and enabling them to invest through low interest microcredit. In a study on women by Fu and Mishra (2020, pp. 20–38), it was concluded that micro-finance through Fintech solutions led to higher financial inclusion for small-scale women entrepreneurs and improved their business performance.

(6) Employability – Fu and Mishra (2020) stated that improved financial inclusion had the potentiality that reduces the fundamental barrier of edu-cation of the poor families. In case of income barrier, financial inclusion directly increases or tries to increase the income of the poor family. By availing themselves of education loans on these Fintech apps, women can re-educate themselves and invest in training for professional jobs and skills. These loans can directly empower women to seek out better professional avenues for themselves and improve their employability. Such benefits are sustainable and have a lasting and positive generational impact (Table 2).

Table 2. Brief Summary of Features Offered by Fintech Apps and Their Consequent Outcome for Women.

Outcome	Fintech App Features
Financial literacy	Knowledge of financial terms, saving measures, government schemes for marginalized sections
Financial decision making	Access to investment portals, mutual fund schemes, microfinancing, money transfer
Financial freedom	Access to 24 × 7 banking facilities, business loans
Security	Insurance plans, Savings, Instant Loans for women, application to welfare schemes, money transfer
Career growth	Higher education loans, salary-based loans, stock investment options
Employability	Higher Education Loans, Relocation loans, Financial awareness

Source: Author.

Despite the overwhelming positives of Fintech apps, some studies have also warned about the potential misuse and security issues brought by Fintech apps. Ozili (2018) warns that it should be noted that Fintech providers are profit-seeking corporations and thus can be biased in picking and choosing their user base. These biases can take the form of gender stereotypes, which can act to alienate women from digital financial services. Additionally, Sioson and Kim (2019) state that needs of the underserved sections of society should be encouraged to be addressed in the promotion of Fintech apps. The author argues that Fintech apps can be efficient in closing the gender gap only as long as the Fintech services remain easily affordable, accessible, and relevant for women. The rise in digital innovation has set in motion a metamorphosis that has the potential to further advance their financial inclusion. By providing women with access to affordable, accessible financial products and services, Fintech has taken several steps forward in helping these women become more financially empowered.

Fintech, Women Empowerment, and Sustainable Gender Equality

As per Kabeer (2005), gender equality and women empowerment are directly connected to each other. Higher participation in economic affairs along with access to financial education and safety empowers women to make bold choices for themselves, and raise themselves to occupy equal status as men. Guaranteeing equal rights to women and ensuring opportunities for them to reach their full potential is critical to attaining gender equality. According to the UNDP (2015) paper on "Trade, Gender and Poverty",[5] women constitute 50% of the world's population yet they own a dismal 1% of the world's wealth. Sundar (2017) highlights how women in many places still lack rights to own land or inherit property obtain credit, or earn equivalent incomes and escape job discrimination. As agreed upon by Ogato (2013) and Sen and Mukherjee (2014), empowerment of women is of major concern in ensuring gender equality and achieving sustainable development for our world. Sioson and Kim (2019) and Farahani, Esfahani, Moghaddam, and Ramezani (2022) have also linked the benefits of Fintech for women to achieving sustainable development through increased gender equality in our world. As per Farahani et al. (2022), Fintech can work toward mitigating the impact of social or economic upheavels in the society and ensure equality of economic access over time.

Research Gaps

As is evidently clear from the review conducted above, there exists a collection of literature on the topic of Fintech apps, and their role in the society, particularly toward development of women.

---

[5]http://www.undp.org/content/undp/en/home/librarypage/poverty-reduction/trade-gender-and-poverty.html.

However, some key research gaps cannot be left unaddressed since these gaps make the current research lacking in their scope.

Firstly, currently available research in this field is insufficient in exploring the relationship between Fintech Apps and empowerment of women from the viewpoint of multiple factors pertaining to financial confidence and development. The vast majority of existing studies are focused on the challenges and constraints in adoption of Fintech apps among women, and do not delve into the actual impact of Fintech apps on this section of the study. The current study fulfills that gap by diving into the consequent impact of Fintech apps post the access is granted to women.

Secondly, the available studies pertaining to role of Fintech on women empowerment have measured the factors of financial literacy and financial decision-making as a singular factor. However, these factors are separate and independent of each other and thus must be evaluated separately. The present study treats these factors as equal and independent variables in order to shed more light on the role of Fintech on these aspects of financial empowerment for women.

Thirdly, the available research in this field has not delved into the topic of sustainability of Fintech app solutions for women empowerment. This study has fulfilled that gap by assessing the impact of Fintech on improvement in the professional growth of women, thus evaluating whether Fintech apps can pose as a long-term solution for women empowerment. The study has also assessed the impact of Fintech on gender equality as a whole, in order to confirm the true positive influence of women empowerment against the male counterparts in the society.

Research Methodology

The methodology underlying the present research is based on primary quantitative data obtained from women with confirmed access to Fintech apps. In keeping heed with the restrictions imposed on public outing by national and state government in India, the researcher has chosen to conduct the research based on a short sample survey among 230 women in Delhi NCR, India. Survey data allows a researcher to collect quantitative information which is based upon the judgments of selected people. Moreover, primary data sources aid the researcher in obtaining raw and practical data that may be further analyzed to reach a conclusion. A total of six factors were extracted that will be used for explaining the dominating factors. These are namely, financial literacy, financial freedom, decision-making, security, career growth, and employability.

In addition to the collected empirical data, the researcher has also conducted a survey of recently available journal articles and authentic sources. The journal articles mentioned in this study have been curated from Google Scholar, PubMed and Scopus. A vast majority of the articles have been assessed from a period of past five years i.e. 2017–2022. Articles belonging to pre-2017 have outdated information about the current status and scope of existing technologies that form the modern Fintech apps. Thus, the articles prior to this period have been considered only for definitions or conventional theories and have not been taken in consideration otherwise.

Analysis and Interpretation

As per Table 3 total six factors are extracted that will be used for explaining the dominating factors by using factor analysis.

Findings

Finding of the study shows that by applying the factor analysis, there are six factors which have been extracted that show the effectiveness of Fintech app on sustainable women empowerment i.e., financial literacy, financial freedom, decision-making, security, career growth, and employability.

Theoretical Framework

Based on findings from this study and the supporting literature reviewed, a theoretical framework can be constructed as produced here in Fig. 1. The independent variable in this study is Fintech Usage, whereas the effects of FU on factors related to finance and women are the dependent variables. Additionally, at the next level, the variable of Sustainable Gender Equality (SGE) is also dependent on the effects of Women Empowerment (WE).

Future Scope and Conclusion

The present study was undertaken to evaluate the impact of Fintech on sustainable women empowerment in developing economies like India. By using empirical data, the study has identified that access to Fintech has indeed resulted in improving the quality of life for women and played a role in uplifting their status in society across different spheres. Thus, it can be stated that Fintech has played a positive role in facilitating women's financial empowerment. This conclusion was

Table 3. Author's Own Calculation.

Factor Name	Reliability
Financial literacy	0.751
Financial freedom	0.917
Decision making	0.650
Security	0.867
Career growth	0.969
Employability	0.870

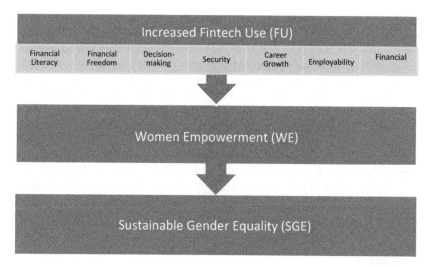

Fig. 1. Theoretical Framework Showing the Factors Influencing Sustainable Gender Equality Through the Use of Fintech Among Women.

reached through a study of Fintech's influence cross six independent variables. It may be interesting to witness how future researchers can expand upon this study's findings. Going forward, more studies can be undertaken to replicate this model and probe deeper within the nuances of the six variables discussed in the present study. There remain several under-researched facets of Fintech which can provide grounds for future studies in this field. For instance, interested researchers may find it worthwhile to study the role of Fintech in closing socioeconomic demographic dividends like intercaste income gaps. Additionally, the present study is limited to evaluating the impact of Fintech on the lives of women living in an urban area, i.e., NCR Delhi. However, this limitation may be overcome with future studies that focus on widening the area of study to include women from semi-urban and rural areas as well. The present study will also gain from such inclusions and showcase a more effective snapshot of the reality.

In conclusion, the study has found that access and use of Fintech has benefited women in multiple ways and paved the way for their economic and social empowerment. Based on the empirical data, it stands proven that women have gained much from their access to Fintech. Fintech has resulted in improved financial awareness and literacy among its women users. Emboldened with the newfound financial knowledge, women have also been able to make informed financial decisions for them, thus leading to greater freedom in economic matters. Their ability to make their own independent financial decisions has also enabled a greater sense of financial security in a society where women are often bereft of resources. As a consequence of these changes in the status quo, the access to Fintech apps has led to an increase in the confidence levels of women. The study also found that there was a direct and positive linkage to the impact of this financial confidence on the career trajectory of women. Women with access to Fintech apps saw a career growth for themselves. Fintech apps helped women to gain equality to their male counterparts in terms of financial know-how and thus raising their employability in higher income roles in the modern workplaces. Thus, the present study conclusively shows that improved access to Fintech apps plays a major role in empowering women. Finally, as the number of internet users grows over time with greater access to digital devices and modern technologies, the role of Fintech apps is expected to only increase and grow more significant in the coming years. It is expected that Fintech will continue to play a pivotal role in shaping the financial awareness among women from poorer or backward territories in the future. Thus, the positive impact of Fintech on achieving greater gender equality through women empowerment is a sustainable strategy for years to come.

References

Agrawal, R. (2022). Role of Fintech companies in increasing financial inclusion. *Journal of Applied Management-Jidnyasa, 14*(1), 24–36.

Arner, D. W. (2014). *FinTech and RegTech: Opportunities and challenges.* Asian Institute of International Financial Law University of Hong Kong.

Arora, R. U. (2020). Digital financial services to women: Access and constraints. In *Gender bias and digital financial services in South Asia.* Bingley: Emerald Publishing Limited.

Björkegren, D., & Grissen, D. (2018, May). The potential of digital credit to bank the poor. In *AEA papers and proceedings* (Vol. 108, pp. 68–71).

Bunyamin, M., & Wahab, N. B. A. (2017). The impact of financial literacy on finance and economy: A literature review. *International Journal of Research, 4*(07).

DiCaprio, A., Yao, Y., & Simms, R. (2017). *Women and trade: Gender's impact on trade finance and fintech.* Asian Development Bank Institute. Working Paper 797.

Fanta, A. B., & Mutsonziwa, K. (2016). *Gender and financial inclusion.* Policy research paper, (01).

Farahani, M. S., Esfahani, A., Moghaddam, M. N. F., & Ramezani, A. (2022). The impact of Fintech and artificial intelligence on COVID 19 and sustainable development goals. *International Journal of Innovation in Management, Economics and Social Sciences, 2*(3), 14–31.

Fu, J., & Mishra, M. (2020). The global impact of COVID-19 on FinTech adoption. *Swiss Finance Institute Research Paper.*

Gomber, P., Koch, J. A., & Siering, M. (2017). Digital finance and FinTech: Current research and future research directions. *Journal of Business Economics, 87*(5), 537–580.

Hess, J., & Klapper, L. (2021). *Financial inclusion, women, and building back better (No. 35870).* The World Bank Group.

Kabeer, N. (2005). Gender equality and women's empowerment: A critical analysis of the third millennium development goal 1. *Gender and Development, 13*(1), 13–24.

Kim, K. (2022). Assessing the impact of mobile money on improving the financial inclusion of Nairobi women. *Journal of Gender Studies, 31*(3), 306–322.

Lwanga Mayanja, M., & Adong, A. (2017). *A pathway to financial inclusion: Mobile money and individual savings in Uganda* (No. 676-2016-46605).

Nasir, N. S., Lee, C. D., Pea, R., & McKinney de Royston, M. (2021). Rethinking learning: What the interdisciplinary science tells us. *Educational Researcher, 50*(8), 557–565.

Nguse, T., Desalegn, G., Oshora, B., Tangl, A., Nathan, R. J., & Fekete-Farkasne, M. (2022). Enhancing women economic empowerment through financial inclusion: Evidence from SMEs in Ethiopia. *Polish Journal of Management Studies, 25*(1).

Njagi, N. W., & Onyango, D. O. (2019). Challenges faced by women entrepreneurs in their efforts towards poverty reduction in Mukuru Kwa Njenga; Embakasi east constituency, Nairobi, Kenya. *Developing Country Studies, 9*(60), 68–83.

OECD. (2018). *Education at a glance 2018: OECD indicators.* Paris: OECD Publishing.

Ogato, G. S. (2013). The quest for gender equality and women's empowerment in least developed countries: Policy and strategy implications for achieving millennium development goals in Ethiopia. *International Journal of Sociology and Anthropology, 5*(9), 358.

Osabuohien, E. S., & Karakara, A. A. (2018). ICT usage, mobile money and financial access of women in Ghana. *Africagrowth Agenda, Africagrowth Institute, 15*(1), 14–18.

Ozili, P. K. (2018). Impact of digital finance on financial inclusion and stability. *Borsa Istanbul Review, 18*(4), 329–340.

Philippon, T. (2016). *The fintech opportunity (No. w22476).* National Bureau of Economic Research.

Riza, A. F., & Wijayanti, D. M. (2021). Kartini in the pandemic: Women's economic empowerment through synergy of digital banking, Fintech, and E-commerce. *Journal of Islamic Economy and Community Engagement, 2*(1), 114–129.

Robino, C., Trivelli, C., Villanueva, C., Sachetti, F. C., Walbey, H., Martinez, L., & Marincioni, M. (2018). Financial inclusion for women: A way forward. *G20 Insights: Social Cohesion and the Future of Welfare Systems*, 1–9.

Schueffel, P. (2017). *The concise fintech compendium.* Fribourg: Switzerland.

Sen, G., & Mukherjee, A. (2014). No empowerment without rights, no rights without politics: Gender-equality, MDGs and the post-2015 development agenda. *Journal of Human Development and Capabilities, 15*(2–3), 188–202.

Siddik, M. N. A. (2017). The does financial inclusion promote women empowerment? Evidence from Bangladesh. *Applied Economics and Finance, 4*(4), 169–177.

Sioson, E. P., & Kim, C. J. (2019, April). *Closing the gender gap in financial inclusion through Fintech.* Asian Development Bank Policy Brief (2019–2023). ISSN: 2411-6734.

Sundar, I. (2017). Gender equality and women empowerment. *International Journal of Humanities and Social Sciences, 7*(1), 7–21.

Chapter 13

Role of Sustainable Development Goal and Digitalization in Hospitality Industry: A Systematic Literature Review

Pratim Chatterjee and Rita Karmakar

Abstract

Purpose: This chapter aims to list the literature that document the role of hospitality industry achieving Sustainable Development Goals (SDGs), and to summarize those contributions, related to the literature. Extensive literature review was also conducted to explore a critical analysis of sustainable digitalization of the hospitality industry.

Design/Methodology/Approach: The article has undertaken a systematic literature review of all the significant research area of almost last two decades. Keyword searches were performed in Google Scholar search engine, where timeframe of "2001–2023" was used to filter the desired article. Total 141 research articles were primarily identified after the initial search. After screening the articles for relevance or duplicates, finally 107 articles were considered for this study.

Findings: This study figures out those environment-related SDGs which is considered essential for the hospitality industry. This study found the importance of adopting digitalization in hospitality sector to build inclusive environment and providing seamless experience to customers while focusing on both positive and negative aspects associated with digital transformation.

Originality/Value: Hospitality industry of numerous countries around the world are now exploring by implementing SDGs and Digitalization in their business practices. This study will provide insight to policymakers as development and usage of digital technologies and implementing SDGs in their practices are crucial for the sustainable transformation of hospitality industry. Sustainable transformation of hospitality sector not only improves

Fostering Sustainable Businesses in Emerging Economies, 223–245
Copyright © 2024 Pratim Chatterjee and Rita Karmakar
Published under exclusive licence by Emerald Publishing Limited
doi:10.1108/978-1-80455-640-520231014

services and helps us to make wiser choices when planning for a trip but also positively impact both physical and psychological well-being.

Keywords: Hospitality industry; Sustainable Development Goals (SDGs); digital technology; sustainability; sustainable digitalization; critical analysis

Introduction

Sustainability is defined as satisfying the need of present generation without compromising the resources of the future ones (Morris, 2004). Hotels and resorts, irrespective of its size and location, need to take responsibility safeguarding the planet's natural resources. To gain a competitive edge over their competitors, organizations must now develop their marketing strategy adhering to the social, regulatory, and environmental rules and approve future opportunities targeting to be known as environmental leaders (Fraj, Matute, & Melero, 2015; Hall, Daneke, & Lenox, 2010). Green marketing orientation can assure the combination of the society, consumer, companies, and the environment to achieve a green marketing model (Chung, 2020; Ou, Wong, & Huang, 2021). To make sustainability strategies beneficial and to get competitive edge, organizations need to maintain cordial relationship with their stakeholders (Iraldo, Testa, Lanzini, & Battaglia, 2017). To improve the environmental, social as well as economic performance level of the organization, management need to consider adopting green building practices (Ahn & Pearce, 2013).

The Green Hotels Association (2014) defined green hotels as "environmentally friendly properties whose managers are eager to institute programs that save water, save energy, and reduce solid waste – while saving money – to help protect our one and only earth" (para. 8). An eco-hotel or environmentally sensitive hotels are those that have altered all its policies, practices, and equipment to minimize the environmental impact (Noor, Nor, & Kumar, 2014). Sustainable hotels are inclined with positive reputation and more value among customers compared to their nongreen counterpart. Mainstream accommodation establishment like hotel and supplementary accommodation establishment like homestays are advised to engage in green practices for revamping their brand image and decreasing environmental degradation (Batabyal, Chatterjee, Pandit, Goswami, & Kumar, 2021; Chandran & Bhattacharya, 2019; Lim, 2016; Pasanchay & Schott, 2021). To improve the environmental, social, and economic performance level of the hotel, developers of a hotel need to consider adopting green building practices (Ahn & Pearce, 2013).

On September 25, 2015, the 2030 Agenda for Sustainable Development and 17 SDGs with 169 targets as a universal and transformative development strategy were acquired by the United Nations General Assembly that include all features of sustainability, namely, to eradicate poverty, promote prosperity and well-being for everyone, and to safeguard the planet (Abdou, Hassan, & El Dief, 2020; Baicu, Oehler-Sincai, & Popescu, 2019). As a global effort, the Millennium Development Goals (MDGs) were introduced in 2000 to mark the indignity of poverty, hunger, prevent diseases, and include all children under primary education, among other development priorities (UNGA, 2014). The SDGs are the successor development tool to the MDGs (Nanda, 2016; Yiu & Saner, 2014). The SDGs are a key element of the United Nations 2030 agenda (UN, 2015). The agenda encourages sustainable development by way of observing and managing the use of natural resources and boosting conservation efforts, generating employment opportunities for local communities while fostering local culture and products to expand the economic welfare for developing and underdeveloped countries (UNWTO & UNDP, 2017; Rasoolimanesh, Ramakrishna, Hall, Esfandiar, & Seyfi, 2020). The 17 SDGs, as illustrated in Fig. 1, convey the global challenges experienced, that includes poverty, inequality, climate change, environmental degradation, peace, and justice. Based on the reports (UN, 2020), the SDGs and associated targets are consolidated and inseparable and globally pertinent, considering realities of different nation, magnitudes, and levels of improvement besides keeping in mind national policies and priorities.

The United Nations Development Program Strategic Plan (UNDP, 2017) 2018–2021 established various guidelines about the contribution of the hospitality industry in SDG. Jones, Hiller, and Comfort (2017) argued that the tourism and hospitality industry can offer to the implementation of the SDGs, at the same time developing numerous market opportunities. Hospitality industry will impart into SDGs for two reasons. Firstly, it is particularly related to the threat of climate change, which influences seasonality. Second, being a part of the global industry, hospitality industry has become a major economic sector for many developed and developing countries. For this reason, major hospitality companies have incorporated the SDGs into their corporate social responsibility (CSR) programs (Jones & Comfort, 2019). Rhama and Setiawan (2022) stated that hospitality and tourism industry is no different from consumptive behavior, and it is only in the early stages of boosting SDGs, especially SDG 6, 7, 13, and 15.

Fig. 1.   Sustainable Development Goals. *Source:* UN (2015).

Hospitality sector has not reached the full potential, the deadline of which is 2030, because of the delay in exploring SDGs and the effects of the COVID-19 pandemic. The SDGs framework contributes the hospitality industry with an opportunity to explore the sustainability initiatives as most of the tourists demand hospitality products considering social, economic, and environmental factors (Fleming, Wise, Hansen, & Sams, 2017). Hospitality industry is now more than ever engrossed on the contribution of SDGs in its mission, vision, core values, business objectives, societal objectives, and building a sustainable or eco-friendly hotel offer (Alvarez-Risco et al., 2020; Robert, Parris, & Leiserowitz, 2005).

Education is the backbone of a society. Quality education helps in nation building. Quality education (SDG 4) aims at creating an inclusive environment, and equitable education that promotes holistic development of learners as well as society at large. Technology can be a powerful tool for achieving education for sustainable development (ESD). Technological advancement has revolutionized the education system by introducing the concept of green education which creates environmental awareness and inculcates philanthropic values among learners. Green education enables students to be problem solver and being reflective and thereby presenting advanced solutions to problems. Technological advancement in education also played a crucial role in making education accessible for all even in the most difficult time created by the sudden outbreak of COVID-19. Learning from Home (LFH) models were introduced and were broadcasted through local channels to provide easy access to education at different levels of society, especially to those who are unable to access internet and get quality education. Mohanty and Dash (2018) suggested that technological advancement in education facilitates skill development in addition to acquiring academic knowledge and consequently making learners more adaptive and effective in day-to-day life. The market value of educational technology from elementary level of education to higher education will be increased by 10.4 billion by 2025 (The economist, 2022). Ministry of human resource, Government of India (GoI) introduced DIKSHA (Digital Infrastructure for Knowledge Sharing) to make education accessible via e-content-based curriculums like QR coded Energized Textbooks (ETBs) and training courses for teachers. Direct to Home (DTH) channel was introduced with study material developed in sign language and is also available on YouTube to educate visual and hearing-impaired students. Not only GoI but also corporates extended their CSR programs for providing laptops with academic software, digitally enriched contents, and proper infrastructural facilities. Digitalization in the education system automatized administrative aspects of education such as sharing content, automated grading, and attendance, and consequently teachers can invest more time in the core activities (Bongiorno, Rizzo, & Vaia, 2018). In a nutshell, advanced technology offers endless opportunities for learners by providing seamless experiences. The smart technology and virtual reality such as Microsoft Teams/Zoom meetings/Google Meet/Tencent (VooV), virtual education platforms (Blackboard, Moodle, Canvas, etc.) played crucial role during COVID-19 lockdown and kept the entire teaching–learning system running even in complete lockdown (Senbekov et al., 2020). Despite unending opportunities, some obvious limitations are overdependence on smartphones, addiction to harmful online content, and excessive screen time causing health and psychological issues with the passage of time (Sharma, 2020).

Technological advancement in health care has led to significant innovation in healthcare sector. Technology has redefined different aspects of health care system such as patient care, hospital management, course of treatment and innovative drugs, etc. Primarily the technology has improved the working style of physicians by making their work easy, faster, and less time consuming and thereby reducing the number of errors to a large extent. The obvious consequence is patient satisfaction and increased trust. Artificial intelligence (AI), cloud computing, big-data analytics, Internet of Things (IoT), deep learning, and blockchain technology facilitate the identification and treatment of major medical and clinical problems (Tian et al., 2019; Wang & Tang, 2020). Khan et al. (2021) studied the role of smart technology such as the drones, robots, AI, and sensor technology in alleviating the spread of COVID-19 pandemic and thereby ensuring the survival of mankind. During COVID-19, autonomous robots were used to tackle the quick spread of infection through interhuman contagion by sanitizing and disinfecting large areas with minimal effort and time. Robots were also utilized for delivering food and medicines to COVID-19 patients in hospitals without direct human contacts (Chen, Marvin, & While, 2020; Ozkil et al., 2009; Yang et al., 2020).

Of late, tourism sector has been expanded globally and has become one of the fastest financially growing industries. This sector has been emerged as a key engine of the socioeconomic development of developed and developing countries. It generates employment opportunities, financial securities and promotes gender equality and, consequently, reinforces altogether an environment of overall growth. Tourism is also one of the vital sources of three main pillars (social, economic, environmental) of sustainable development. Sustainability in general is a major concern for industries including hospitality industries where sustainability is one biggest issue. The rapid growth of hotel industries may have some negative impact on the environment as by and large hotels consume relatively large amount of energy and resources to survive; the study related to promoting environmental preservations by hotel industries is utmost important in order to promote healthier quality of life and thereby promote sustainable development in the long run. Many hotels have already started taking initiatives of implementing eco-friendly initiative. Bender (2020) analyzed the findings of a survey conducted by TripAdvisor and revealed that around 62% of travelers think of environmental issues before finalizing their stay at a hotel and other hotel-related services. This study also suggested that around 69% travelers tend to choose eco-friendly hotel in next 12 months. An intriguing finding is that around 84% of travelers believe that environmentally friendly practices do not have any impact on the comfort and luxury of travelers as they have already used some of the green practices such as 88% saved electricity by switching off lights while not at hotel room, 78% reused towels, and 58% supported recycling.

Hotel industries had invented many eco-friendly strategies to support eco-friendly movement and thereby supporting conservation principle which ensures the development of industries in future. Implementing sustainable practices also helps to keep environment free from pollution hence ensuring the faster development of industries.

Sustainability in the hospitality industry is a multifaceted approach. Han, Lee, Trang, and Kim (2018) suggested that hedonic and utilitarian values of customers may be increased by adopting certain green practices such as water conservation and waste reduction management. Customer loyalty was also influenced by green practices to a great extent. Jauhari (2014) emphasized on number of factors involved in green practices such as designing of green hotels, energy consumption, modern technology, and human resource management practices. Green hotel practices reduce operation and consequently increases hotel's profits, customer satisfaction, and loyalty and hence gaining competitive advantage in the long run, but very little studies have been conducted to determine the role of green hotel practices in achieving SDGs, especially in developing countries. With the advent of technology, there is a need to convert the resources of hospitality sectors into intelligent resources to achieve sustainability. There are several benefits of using technology in hotel rooms such as reducing electricity and water consumption, creating environmental awareness, facilitating the quality of experience at destination and overall satisfaction of travelers (Hák, Janoušková, & Moldan, 2016). This also guarantees the sustainable development by integrating travelers' satisfaction and quality service provided during stay at hotels.

Kim, Ritchie, and McCormick (2012) mentioned that use of technology in hotel rooms helped in solving customer's problem in much faster and efficient manner, and consequently customers tended to revisit the hotels and expressed satisfaction. The use of AI in hospitality has revolutionized the concept of tourism and revolutionized the hospitality services by adding new dimensions and strategies in increasing customer satisfaction. Henn na Hotel in Japan is the first hotel fully operated by "robots." Papathanassis (2017) incorporated the idea of AI in different hospitality services beginning with front desk to the delivery of customers' services such as hotel room cleaning, room assistance, etc. Using robots in hotels have both pros and cons. Robots can perform duties more consistently and flawlessly compared to human being. Robots can do duties 24×7 throughout the year without requiring any work break and motivation. They are also more accurate and faster than human being. Using robots, hotels can run with a smaller number of employees and consequently gaining more and more profit. Alpin Hotel in Poiana, Brasov, is another example for using technology in facilitating sustainability. The hotel utilized many sustainable strategies. With the help of new technology, the stored rainwater can be controlled for purity and temperature. Solar panels were installed to collect raindrops to produce energy not only for the usage of hotels but also for public usage. Technology was also used effectively in managing waste and transforming into energy. To avoid long que and waiting time at the time of check-in and check-out, the hotel automatized check-ins and check-outs system. The other obvious consequences of automatic check-ins and check-outs system are reducing cost, eliminating errors, and thereby gaining customer satisfaction and loyalty. Guests also can choose available rooms based on their preferences through the Hotel App. The app also eases the interaction between customers and hotel reception and offers e-invoice facilities. To provide unique experience, digitalized keys (signature RFID locks) are used not only in hotel rooms but also accessing other areas of hotel such as the gym, swimming pool, etc. Chatbots are the easiest and professional way to relate to guests all the time, and closer interaction between customers and the hotel management can be done by using NFC (Near Field Communication) technology, by linking the tags to Google+, Facebook, Twitter, and so on. Technology not only smoothens the customer verification process but also enhances customer security by transmitting the hotel keys directly over phone. Customers are provided tablets that will always keep them connected to the hotel staff and authorities and thereby fostering a sense of being protected all the time during their stay. Automatic controlling of room temperature, room ambiance and starting a flow of water in the bathtub and smart sockets added great value to customers' experiences. Digitalized applications not only increase the level of satisfaction of guests but also inculcate a sense of environmental awareness during their stay at hotels and even beyond that. Customers start liking these sustainable practices and try to apply some of them at home as well and thereby becoming more and more responsible toward the society. Printed images on hotel room walls depicting the culture of a society and country facilitates the guests' satisfaction by adding esthetic value and presence of robots for room service and other hotel-related activities not only make the travel experience enjoyable but also ensure the future visit to a large extent and thereby become much more profitable to hotels. Moreover, it is high time to rethink their services and products by amalgamating the advanced technology and human touch to attract guests by increasing their satisfaction and loyalty. Japan's Henn na hotel, first hotel, used robotics in front desk and in service assistance such as cleaning rooms, luggage storage, etc., to achieve level of excellence in service (Rajesh, 2015). Markoff (2014) reported that Aloft Hotels used robots which can use elevator and call the guests for delivering desired products at the doorstep. Hilton hotels launched a robotic caretaker Connie which can interact with guests and was able to provide information related to hotel services and amenities, information on sightseeing, local travels and was also able to improve future answers. Adopting technology in hotels increases operational efficiency with minimization of errors and labor cost. Introduction of advanced technology also allows customer to browse online menu with images and descriptions of menu items, order online (Curtis, 2016), and enable customer for contactless payment and thereby facilitating guests' seamless experience. Not only that but also advent of technology allows guests to engage themselves in recreational activities while waiting for the order to be cooked. The adoption of technology was done by Pizza Hut by recruiting humanoid robot Pepper which converses with customers to take order and accept payments from them as well. Conveyor restaurants (Ngai, Suk, & Lo, 2008) and roller-coaster restaurants (Blinder, 2014) used automated process of food ordering via touch screen and delivering the order via a conveyor belt and tracks look like roller coaster tracks. Eatsa, 100% automated restaurant, provides customers with tablets to place orders and payment by eliminating human waiters and cashiers. They have stated using technology not only in delivering food but also in cooking process by introducing 3D printing of food (Prisco, 2014). The major value addition of food prepared with the help of technology is the improved quality as well as providing meals having different nutritional value. Hotels also appoint robot chefs who can prepare sushi (Sushirobo, 2016), noodles (Elkins, 2015), sausage (Filloon, 2016), burgers (Momentum Machines, 2016), mixed drinks (Sloan, 2014), and coffee (Fowler, 2017).

Abdou et al. (2020) considered only SDG 6, SDG 12, SDG 7, and SDG 13 where hotels can contribute positively. Whereas Alvarez-Risco et al. (2020) focused on the SDGs on hotels starting from SDG 1 to SDG 9. Anna de Visser-Amundson (2022) adopted a multi-stakeholder partnership to fight food waste in the hospitality industry by emphasizing on SDG 12 and SDG 13. Fleetwood (2020) explored the role of hospitality on SDG 2, SDG 3, and SDG 8. Matteucci (2020) analyzed opportunities for Hilton Worldwide Holdings, Inc. (Hilton), Melia Hotels International (Melia), and Sun Limited (Sun) hotels focusing SDG 8, SDG 12, and SDG 17. Whereas Rhama and Setiawan (2022) observed direct connection between SDG 6, SDG 7, SDG 13, and the global hotel industry. Though, out of 17 SDG's, 12 are directly related to the hospitality industry, with the best possible efforts of the authors any single literature combining all these 12 SDG'S could not be found. So, this chapter aims to fill this gap by synthesizing all 12 SDGs which are related to hospitality industry in one single literature. In addition to this, this chapter also tries to put together the positive and negative impact of sustainable digitalization on hospitality industries and community at large. The "icing on the cake" would be the discussion on the negative psychological impact of sustainable digitalization on different stakeholders.

Thus, the main objectives of this study can be considered as follows:

- To conduct a systematic literature review on the role of the hospitality industry in achieving SDGs.
- To explore a critical analysis of sustainable digitalization of the hospitality industry.

Methodology

The research was done via a systematic review process, through the analysis of 107 research articles in various formats (journals, research books, and online websites) with objective of obtaining information on role of hospitality industry in achieving SDGs and critical analysis of sustainable digitalization of hospitality industry (Terjesen, Hessels, & Li, 2013). Systematic review process presumes designing the plan of research, searching the literature through a systematic process, screening out relevant articles, and synthesizing the selected literature (Pickering, Grignon, Steven, Guitart, & Byrne, 2015). The authors started the research project by designing a plan of the research, which established because of the relevance of the current topic. The initial step was to formulate the questions that the authors desired to answer in the research, which developed in searching existing literature on sustainability in hotels and related topics included in the existing literature. Step 2 was determining the criteria that were used to ascertain the usefulness of the articles that would be reviewed, to gain a wide array of opinions, and viewpoint on the topic. References of only post 2000 were considered as the timeframe of the article. The third step was to search on Google Scholar for all articles relating to "sustainability in hotels", which resulted in 12,60,00,000 articles. The authors then applied filters such as timeline of "2001–2023", which then led to 2,10,00,000 results. At this point, the authors decided to consider articles that included "sustainability in hotels" within the title, to achieve a narrower scope of information, which yielded 141 results. In Step 4, after screening the article for relevance or duplicate and validity as per the objective of this study, 107 research articles were finally selected for this chapter. In step 5, the authors began the content analysis, and started the first drafting of this chapter.

Findings and Discussion

As per the first objectives, rigorous literature review was conducted on the role of hospitality industry achieving SDGs. Role of hospitality industry to achieve the 17 SDGs with 169 targets as a universal development strategy as per 2030 Agenda for Sustainable Development is observed in the the section "Role of Hospitality Industry Achieving SDG". Similarly in next section critical analysis of the SDG for the hospitality industry has been explored. As per the second objective, critical analysis of sustainable digitalization of hospitality industry is observed in the section "Critical analysis of sustainable digitalization of hospitality industry".

Role of Hospitality Industry Achieving SDG

The hospitality industry is considered as a threat to the environment because of its enormous consumption of primary natural resources like water, energy along with discharge of huge amount of raw and solid waste material. It will have a negative impact on the environment had these measures are not managed properly in a hotel (Kasim, 2009; Mensah, 2006). As the year 2030 draws closer, when the agenda 2030 on SDGs will lapse, there is a need to take some serious measure to achieve those goals. Among the 17 SDGs, we tried to figure out those environment-related SDGs which are related to hospitality industry. Though Mabibibi, Dube, and Thwala (2021) stated that hospitality and tourism have the potential to contribute directly and indirectly to all the 17 SDGs and related 169 targets, others argued and confined the role of hospitality industry in some of the SDGs among the total 17. So based on the review of literature, we focused our study about the role of hospitality industry with the below mentioned SDG's.

Role of the Hospitality Industry to SDG 1

No Poverty: There are various ways hospitality industry can contribute to the eradication of poverty and boost the economic condition for the local community directly or indirectly. All the accommodation sector, both primary and alternate establishment, takes care of the economic part of different types of people staring from hotel owner, employee, supplier or vendor, local government, local shop owner, transport authority, tourist guide, and other people associated to hospitality and tourism (Lee & Jan, 2019; Scheyvens & Hughes, 2019).

Role of the Hospitality Industry to SDG 2

Zero Hunger: Food waste is a big problem in the hospitality industry. In this scenario, Boulden (2017) estimates 20% of food waste, which could have been avoided. Wirtz and Zeithaml (2018) pointed out that establishment can carry out their activities maintaining proper quality and standards to become more profitable. Implementation for effective hospitality business practices in food logistics, storage, and preparation will reduce costs of waste collection and disposal (Papargyropoulou, Lozano, Steinberger, Wright, & Ujang, 2014).

Role of the Hospitality Industry to SDG 3

Good Health and Well-Being: Sonmez, Apostolopoulos, Lemke, Hsieh, and Karwowski (2017) explained the contribution of hospitality industry to achieve SDG 3, in the form of occupational health. It is the duty of hospitality industry to take care of its employees and customers. Restriction in smoking in the hotel and responsible alcohol consumption for the health and well-being of in room guest and guest in different food and beverage outlet is one of the biggest challenge and responsibility of hospitality industry which initiates a tradeoff between profitability and social responsibility (Borchgrevink, 2017).

Role of the Hospitality Industry to SDG 4

Quality Education: Education can be a routine activity of the hotel which can be beneficial for the employees and their children. Hotel can offer different training program for their employees and bear the educational expenses of their ward as a part toward SDGs (Khoo-Lattimore & Jihyun Yang, 2018). These types of sustainable activities will have a huge impact on customer satisfaction that finally leads to revisit intention of the customer and increase the positive word of mouth publicity (Boo & Busser, 2018).

Role of the Hospitality Industry to SDG 5

Gender Equality: In the hospitality industry, there are several corners for the gender equality contribution. Empowering rural women, better pay, and more professional training could improve female workers in hospitality industry. Dashper (2019) explained the advantages of a mentoring program in hotels in the United Kingdom for assisting women overcome gendered barriers in their workplace. With the establishment of AI in the hotel industry, gender equality issues can also be observed, as mentioned by Pritchard (2018) who intimates that the robots being made available for attention and taking care of the guest are "feminine", while the "male" robots are intended for different types of hard work like assembly and repair of equipment's.

Role of the Hospitality Industry to SDG 6
Clean Water and Sanitization: Water-related problem has been always a major environmental concern since long times, for establishment in hospitality and tourism (Gossling et al., 2011). Also, Han and Hyun (2018) pointed out that hospitality industry can sustainably differentiate themselves by water conservation measure, reusing and recycling of guest room and bathroom linen and thus promoting the hotel to the environment concerned guest as a benchmark. Kasim, Dzakiria, and Ahmad (2017) mentioned size of the hotel as an influencing factor for being responsible to the environment. As per their observation, large hotels can easily take efficient water management measurers as compared to small- and medium-sized hotels or budgeted establishment.

Role of the Hospitality Industry to SDG 7
Affordable and Clean Energy: Hospitality industry is greatly responsible for clean and renewable energy resources. Bianco, Righi, Scarpa, and Tagliafico (2017) explored energy-saving means in the Italian hotel sector, by evaluating the consumption level, estimating the maximum energy savings possibility, and examining the implementation of an energy efficiency model. They opined that primary energy savings of 1.6 TWh (13%) can be achieved in 2030 through the execution of sustainable energy efficiency measures.

Role of the Hospitality Industry to SDG 8
Decent Work and Economic Growth: Decent work in the hospitality field is a necessity, and for this it is essential to measure the baseline in the workers and to develop a measuring instrument for that (Alvarez-Risco, Estrada-Merino, & Perez-Luyo, 2020). Schneider and Treisch (2019) found that like other industry flexible working hours and the suitable environment to balance professional and private life are the most important job attributes for hospitality industry employees. Zhang, Torres, and Jahromi (2019) evaluated working conditions and health risks/hazards for hospitality management workers. Management of hospitality industries have responsibilities in offering healthy eating and weight control programs, smoking cessation, and other sessions to the employees.

Role of the Hospitality Industry to SDG 9
Industry, Innovation, and Infrastructure: Innovation processes are essential for the survival and growth of the hospitality industry in this competitive era. As per Oslo Manual (OECD, 2018), four types of innovation are observed in the hospitality industry, namely a. product innovation, b. process innovation, c. marketing innovation, and d. organizational innovation. As hospitality industry is

continuously changing along with the changes of consumer taste and preference, hotels need to innovate their infrastructure and services on a continuous basis.

Role of the Hospitality Industry to SDG 12

Responsible Consumption and Protection: The significance of this SDG lies in the globally accepted sustainable consumption and production (World Tourism Organization and United Nations Development Programme, 2017, p. 30). Sustainable consumption is need of the hour in hospitality industry and creates immense opportunities for a long-term approach. It begins with achieving sustainable resource practices to implementing the unsustainable use of natural ones through responsible suppliers, to using clean energy. Moreover, maintaining ecological footprint has a direct impact on economic growth and sustainable development (Haar & Kostense-Smit, 2018, p. 28). Additionally, the tourism and hospitality industry could contribute to attaining goal 12 by embracing sustainable consumption and production (SCP) methods, like efficient technologies for air, water, and energy, recycling and reusing waste treatment, pollution reduction, local purchase, and community involvement.

Role of the Hospitality Industry to SDG 13

Climate Action: With regards to SDG 13, hotels need to use renewable energy sources like solar and wind power to reduce the consumption of energy in the hotel for the benefit of the climate. The hotel must replace fossil fuel to a great extent with renewable energy sources as a part of sustainable development practices.

Role of the Hospitality Industry to SDG 17

Partnerships for the Goals: Goal 17 of SDG is an opportunity requiring constant monitoring and actualization in the hospitality industry. With a total of 19 targets identified within this goal, hospitality industry can be benefited by possible exploration of inter-sectoral collaboration and partnership in an ever-changing and competitive environment. Successful hospitality and tourism companies stand by establishing value and long-lasting relationships with customers (Hannon, Kuhlmann, & Thaidigsmann, 2016). Through fruitful collaborations with other sectors, the hospitality industry can enjoy leverage by implementing circular economy concepts for value creation.

Critical Analysis of the SDG for the Hospitality Industry

The basic concept of sustainable development reflects the natural conflict between the human and environmental systems (Dasgupta, 2013; Redclift, 2005). Although the major players of the hospitality and tourism industry show their commitment to corporate sustainability, the strategic objective within the industry is mainly focused on business efficacy and cost savings rather than by any fundamental concern for sustainability (Gabriela, 2016; Jones et al., 2017).

Though tourism and hospitality industry are observed to have an essential role to play toward a more sustainable future, the leading hotel brands of the industry need to address a few challenges as a meaningful contribution for the achievement of the SDGs.

The UN-adopted SDGs as adopted in 2015 have been criticized for being inconsistent, difficult to quantify, execute, and monitor (Spaiser, Ranganathan, Bali Swain, & Sumpter, 2016; Swain, 2018; Swain & Wallentin, 2020). The leading hospitality and tourism companies are now facing with the dilemma whether to map their existing strategies onto the SDGs or to develop new sustainability strategies to meet sustainability development goals (Jones et al., 2017). In addressing the mapping of sustainable development activities to operational activity, Price Waterhouse Coopers (2015) denied the existence of proper tools and techniques which map SDGs to a business presently. They also opined that though some organizations are developing their own goals and methodology for the implementation of the SDGs, consistency of those approaches are missing. The SDGs furnish a list of targets, yet hardly any clear priorities and explanation on how these goals can be achieved are being provided (BaliSwain, 2018). Jones and Comfort (2019) advised to fulfill the sustainability development goals, the leading hotel groups of the world must focus on the SDGs themselves, acquire a more extensive approach to fulfill their priorities for the SDGs, and convey the measurement issues.

Critical Analysis of Sustainable Digitalization of Hospitality Industry

Advanced technology revolutionized many industries and hospitality is no exception. The use of technology has transformed the overall service quality, and consequently revenue, cost effectiveness, and competitive advantage has been maximized to a large extent (Camilleri, 2018; Cohen & Olsen, 2013; Lam & Law, 2019; Law, Leung, & Buhalis, 2009; Xiang, 2018). Technological upgradation in hospitality sector ensures the outstanding travel experience for guests and thereby improving sustainability. Technology has been integrated impeccably into all three phases of the guest cycle: presale, point of sale, and postsale phases to provide a holistic digital service experience for the guests. Guests-facing systems such as automatic check-in and check-out services, keyless entry services, control of in-room functions, etc., improve guest satisfaction by inculcating a sense of empowerment (Wang, So, & Sparks, 2017). Many hotels such as Hilton and Starwood hotels, Mondarian SoHo, The Plaza, and The Marlin offer seamless experiences to their guests by providing automatic check-in and keyless entry service using their mobile apps, controlling in-room functions as well as checking weather and flight information through a TV remote interface and placing tablet in the hotel rooms (DePinto, 2016). Guest-facing systems offer guests with location-based services such as digitally guided tours, recommendations of local events and attractions, as well as suggestions for dining and entertainment options which add one more layer to guest satisfaction. These services enable guests not only to explore the surroundings during their stay at hotels but also maximizing the profit of hospitality service providers (HSPs) by engaging guests to local sites and establishments. Advancement of technology also significantly influences the back-of-house (BoH) management systems, for example, in rooms, IoT units such as thermostats, motion sensors, and ambient light sensors help in controlling temperature and lighting when the rooms are not occupied which leads to decrease in energy cost by 20%–45% (DePinto, 2016). Technological innovation not only facilitates guest satisfaction but also enables HSPs to generate customer profile which can be used in future to design personalized treatment in order to repeat business and thereby maximizing profit and loyalty. BoH management systems help in building online brand value by maintaining cordial customer relationship and involving guests in providing review through online portals (Lee & Jeong, 2014). BoH management systems also monitor online reviews and take necessary actions for negative reviews as a single negative review may hamper the image of organization.

Despite having immense contribution of technology in hospitality sector, they may have some potential threats. Some researchers (Buhalis et al., 2019; Ivanov, 2019; Rebecca & Yeoman, 2012; Webster & Ivanov, 2020) stated that over-dependence on digital technology result in jobs shifting from human to nonhuman employees that is replacing human attendants by robot attendants. Over-dependence of AI led to the increment of employees' turnover intention in the hotel industry (Li, Bonn, & Ye, 2019). Styvén and Wallström (2019) reported that some hotels may be resistant to adopt digitalization due to paucity of highly skilled employees who can use technology in their day-to-day life. Adoption of technology has brought about certain changes in the organizational culture and creating an environment of uncertainty among employees with respect to the importance and appropriateness of their existing skill sets to adjust with the new culture and thereby hampering the well-being of employees to a large extent. In order to restore the well-being of employees, management needs to identify major digital competencies and skill sets required for effective adjustment with the changed scenario and train employees (who are ready to upgrade themselves) accordingly (Arkhipova & Bozzoli, 2018; Svahn, Mathiassen, & Lindgren, 2017; Warner & Wäger, 2019). In case of hiring, organizations also need to hire only those people who have required competencies and skill sets. Management also needs to keep it in mind that to adapt to the technological advancement, acquiring new skill sets and competencies are not only required but also the flexible mind set is crucial in order to constantly adjusting with the technological upgradation. For successful implementation of technological adoption is only possible under the guidance of transformational leaders who can guide sub-ordinates to develop vision and values to accept the effective usage of technologies, organizations also need to set up goals and trainings which will empower employees to bring about certain changes which will help them to adapt to technological advancement and thereby increasing the sustainability (Hemerling, Kilmann, Danoesastro, Stutts, & Ahern, 2018, pp. 1–11; Sousa, Santos, Sacavém, Reis, & Sampaio, 2019). In addition to all these, the potential threats of cyber-attacks and security breaches have been increased to a large extent with the excessive use of advanced technology in day-to-day life.

Technological progress has resulted in irreparable damage to the environment. Technological misuse has led to environmental pollution (social, water, air, etc.)

and global warming. Excessive use of electronic gadgets (smart phone, tablets, laptop, etc.) resulted in high radiation which caused many health issues. Scarcity of natural resources and ecological imbalance are the significant negative outcome of excessive use of advanced technology (Adil, 2022). Negative impacts of technology also include damaging ozone layer, nonrecyclable waste produced by technology and deforestation (Adil, 2022).

Conclusion

The objectives of this study are twofold: firstly, determining the role of technology in achieving sustainable goals in hospitality sector; secondly, to analyze critically the role of sustainable digitalization of hospitality industry. It has been clearly observed in this study that hospitality industry has a prominent role toward the society by properly implementing the SDGs. This study reveals that digital transformation is the key driving force of sustainability. This study explains the importance of adopting digitalization in hospitality sector to build inclusive environment and providing seamless experience to customers. This study also focuses on both positive and negative aspects associated with digital transformation. The critical analyses reveal that technology revolutionizes the hospitality sector by increasing customer gratification, profit of hotels, and making services faster and almost flawless. It also contributes to business model innovations and impact societies' sustainable development. This study also highlights that technology has some negative impacts on hospitality sectors. The negative consequences include damaging environment such as depletion of natural resources, pollution, and ecological imbalance. The negative impact is not only restricted to environmental damage but also adversely influence mental health and well-being. Introducing robots and AI in hospitality may lead to employee turnover, resistance to accept, and deal with sudden technological changes. This study also suggests that in order to implement effective technological adoption, proper training may be organized so that employee get opportunity to learn desired work behavior. Transformational leadership training for manager is also need of the hour as transformational leaders can only supervise people to be most effective with rapidly changing environment.

Implications

This study has several implications. Digital technology encourages innumerable opportunities for industries to improve their performances by reducing errors and making work faster and consequently providing quality service to customers. Quality customer service also ensures customer loyalty, long-term relationship, and thus become more competitive and increasing visibility in the market. This chapter outlines many critical enhancements that need to be taken into consideration while implementing technology. This may have valuable managerial implications as it acts as a framework for effective implementation of technological advancement keeping in mind the probable cons associated with technology. Being aware of probable cons of technological advancements industries will be able to save their resources and thereby being more responsible to employees as well as society at large. Hospitality industry also can explore about its contribution for the implementation of SDGs in its all department. There is no doubt that this study will add value to the innovative business model which will deal effectively with the probable cons and improve hospitality services by capturing real-time data. This study will also provide insight to policymakers as development and usage of digital technologies and implementing SDGs in their practices are crucial for the sustainable transformation of hospitality sector. Sustainable transformation of hospitality sector not only improves services and helps us to make wiser choices when planning for a trip but also positively impacting both physical and psychological well-being.

Limitation and Scope for Future Research

Though a modest number of articles are reviewed in this study, still it has few limitations. Firstly, only articles that are written in English are considered in the study. Secondly, only those SDGs are cultured here which are related to hospitality industry, so SDG 10, SDG 11, SDG 14, SDG 15, and SDG 16 were not considered. Relation between hospitality industry and these five SDGs, i.e., SDG 10 that mentions reduced inequalities, SDG 11 that mentions sustainable cities and communities, SDG 14 that mentions that mentions life below water, SDG 15 that mentions life on land, and SDG 16 that mentions peace, justice, and strong institution will be an area to be explored in future hospitality research. There is enormous scope of future research to explore the contribution of SDGs for attracting the attention of the guests in a hotel for the purpose of survival and growth in this ever-competitive era. Though sustainable digitalization is essential for hospitality industry, acceptance level of the employees especially at the senior levels is a matter of concern. So further study needs to focus on how to effectively build the mentality of employees of a hospitality establishment at all levels to adapt the digitalization for overall development and growth.

References

Abdou, A. H., Hassan, T. H., & El Dief, M. M. (2020). A description of green hotel practices and their role in achieving sustainable development. *Sustainability*, *12*(22), 9624. doi:10.3390/su12229624

Adil, M. (2022). *Positive and negative effects of technology on the environment*. Retrieved from https://techstonz.com/positive-negative-effects-technology-environment/

Ahn, Y. H., & Pearce, A. R. (2013). Green luxury: A case study of two green hotels. *Journal of Green Building*, *8*(1), 90–119. doi:10.3992/jgb.8.1.90

Alvarez-Risco, A., Estrada-Merino, A., & Perez-Luyo, R. (2020). Sustainable development goals in hospitality management. *International Sustainable hospitality management*, *24*, 159–178.

Arkhipova, D., & Bozzoli, C. (2018). Digital capabilities. In *CIOs and the digital transformation: A new leadership role* (pp. 121–146). Cham: Springer.

Baicu, C. G., Oehler-Sincai, I. M., & Popescu, D. (2019). Bioeconomy and social responsibility in the sustainable hotel industry. *Amfiteatru Economic, 21*(52), 639–653.

Bali Swain, R. (2018). A critical analysis of the sustainable development goals. In W. Leal Filho (Ed.), *Handbook of sustainability science and research* (pp. 341–355). *World Sustainability Series*. Cham: Springer. doi:10.1007/978-3-319-63007-6_20

Batabyal, D., Chatterjee, P., Pandit, A., Goswami, S., & Kumar, D. (2021). Assessing the choice of supplementary accommodation for the new normal urban areas in West Bengal, India. *Journal of Contemporary Issues in Business and Government, 27*(2), 1413–1420. doi:10.47750/cibg.2021.27.02.153

Bender, A. (2020). *Survey: Two-thirds of travelers want green hotels.* Retrieved from https://www.forbes.com/sites/andrewbender/2013/04/22/survey-two-thirds-of-travelers-want-green-hotels-heres-how-to-book-them/?sh=120cf5eb2e2f

Bianco, V., Righi, D., Scarpa, F., & Tagliafico, L. A. (2017). Modeling energy consumption and efficiency measures in the Italian hotel sector. *Energy and Buildings, 149*, 329–338.

Blinder, R. (2014). World's largest roller-coaster themed restaurant opens in Abu Dhabi. *Daily News. Erişim Tarihi Haziran, 15*, 20. Retrieved from http://www.nydailynews.com/life-style/world-largestroller-coaster-restaurant-opens-article-1.2029683

Bongiorno, G., Rizzo, D., & Vaia, G. (2018). *CIOs and the digital transformation: A new leadership role* (pp. 1–9). Springer International Publishing. doi:10.1007/978-3-319-31026-8_1

Boo, S., & Busser, J. A. (2018). Tourists hotel event experience and satisfaction: An integrative approach. *Journal of Travel & Tourism Marketing. 35*(7), 895–908. doi:10.1080/10548408.2018.1445066

Borchgrevink, C. P. (2017). Predicting alcohol consumption in hospitality populations using sense of coherence. *Journal of Tourism and Hospitality Management, 5*(1), 38–46.

Boulden, J. (2017). Ikea is slashing its food waste thanks to Winnow startup. *CNN Money*. Retrieved from http://money.cnn.com/2017/09/08/smallbusiness/ikea-foodwaste-winnow/index.html

Buhalis, D., Harwood, T., Bogicevic, V., Viglia, G., Beldona, S., & Hofacker, C. (2019). Technological disruptions in services: Lessons from tourism and hospitality. *Journal of Service Management, 30*(4), 484–506. doi:10.1108/JOSM-12-2018-0398

Camilleri, M. A. (2018). The promotion of responsible tourism management through digital media. *Tourism Planning & Development, 15*(6), 653–671. doi:10.1080/21568316.2017.1393772

Chandran, C., & Bhattacharya, P. (2019). Hotel's best practices as a strategic driver for environmental sustainability and green marketing. *Journal of Global Scholars of Marketing Science, 29*(2), 218–233. doi:10.1080/21639159.2019.1577156

Chen, B., Marvin, S., & While, A. (2020). Containing COVID-19 in China: AI and the robotic restructuring of future cities. *Dialogues in Human Geography, 10*(2), 238–241. doi:10.1177/2043820620934267

Chung, K. C. (2020). Green marketing orientation: Achieving sustainable development in green hotel management. *Journal of Hospitality Marketing & Management*, *29*(6), 722–738. doi:10.1080/19368623.2020.1693471

Cohen, J. F., & Olsen, K. (2013). The impacts of complementary information technology resources on the service-profit chain and competitive performance of South African hospitality firms. *International Journal of Hospitality Management*, *34*, 245–254. doi:10.1016/j.ijhm.2013.04.005

Curtis, S. (2016). Pizza Hut hires ROBOT waiters to take orders and process payments at its fast-food restaurants. *Mirror*. Retrieved from http://www.mirror.co.uk/tech/pizza-huthires-

Dasgupta, P. (2013). *The nature of economic development and the economic development of nature*. Cambridge Working Papers in Economics. CWPE 1349. Cambridge: University of Cambridge.

Dashper, K. (2019). Mentoring for gender equality: Supporting female leaders in the hospitality industry. *International Journal of Hospitality Management*, *88*, 102397. doi:10.1016/j.ijhm.2019.102397

De Visser-Amundson, A. (2022). A multi-stakeholder partnership to fight food waste in the hospitality industry: A contribution to the United Nations sustainable development goals 12 and 17. *Journal of Sustainable Tourism*, *30*(10), 2448–2475. doi:10.1080/09669582.2020.1849232

DePinto, J. (2016). Trends for the Internet of Things in hospitality. *Hotel Online*. Retrieved from https://goo.gl/2He5iU

Elkins, K. (2015). *This restaurant has a new secret weapon: A robot that slices the perfect noodle faster than any human*. Retrieved from http://www.businessinsider.com/noodle-slicing-robot-could-revolutionize-the-restaurant-industry-2015-5

Filloon, W. (2016). *Bratwurst-cooking robot is a feat of German engineering*. Retrieved from http://www.eater.com/2016/7/19/12227128/bratwurst-robot-sausage-cooking-germany

Fleetwood, J. (2020). Social justice, food loss, and the sustainable development goals in the era of COVID-19. *Sustainability*, *12*(12), 5027. doi:10.3390/su12125027

Fleming, A., Wise, R. M., Hansen, H., & Sams, L. (2017). The sustainable development goals: A case study. *Marine Policy*, *86*, 94–103. doi:10.1016/j.marpol.2017.09.019

Fowler, G. A. (2017). Robot baristas serve up the future of coffee at Cafe X. *The Wall Street Journal*. Accessed on February 4, 2017.

Fraj, E., Matute, J., & Melero, I. (2015). Environmental strategies and organizational competitiveness in the hotel industry: The role of learning and innovation as determinants of environmental success. *Tourism Management*, *46*, 30–42. doi:10.1016/j.tourman.2014.05.009

Gabriela, B. C. (2016). Some economic dimensions of sustainable development. *Journal of Economic Development, Environment and People*, *5*(3), 1–4.

Gossling, S., Peeters, P., Hall, M., Ceron, J. P., Dubois, G., Lehmann, L. V., . . . Scott, D. (2011). Tourism and water use: Supply, demand and security an international review. *Tourism Management*, *33*(1), 1–15. doi:10.1016/j.tourman.2011.03.015

Green Hotels Association. (2014). *What are green hotels?* Retrieved from http://www.green.hotels.com

Haar, R., & Kostense-Smit, E. (2018). Sustainable development goals – A business perspective. *Deloitte*. Retrieved from www2.deloitte.com/content/dam/Deloitte/nl/Documents/risk/deloitte-nlrisk-sdgs-from-a-business-perspective.pdf

Hák, T., Janoušková, S., & Moldan, B. (2016). Sustainable development goals: A need for relevant indicators. *Ecological Indicators, 60*, 565–573. doi:10.1016/j.ecolind.2015.08.003

Hall, J. K., Daneke, G. A., & Lenox, M. J. (2010). Sustainable development and entrepreneurship: Past contributions and future directions. *Journal of Business Venturing, 25*(5), 439–448. doi:10.1016/j.jbusvent.2010.01.002

Han, H., & Hyun, S. S. (2018). What influences water conservation and towel reuse practices of hotel guests? *Tourism Management, 64*, 87–97. doi:10.1016/j.tourman.2017.08.005

Han, H., Lee, J., Trang, H. L. T., & Kim, W. (2018). Water conservation and waste reduction management for increasing guest loyalty and green hotel practices. *International Journal of Hospitality Management, 75*, 58–66. doi:10.1016/j.ijhm.2018.03.012

Hannon, E., Kuhlmann, M., & Thaidigsmann, B. (2016). Developing products for a circular economy. In C. Murphy & J. Rosenfield (Eds.), *The circular economy: Moving from theory to practise* (pp. 22–25). McKinsey & Company. Retrieved from www.mckinsey.com/business-functions/Sustainable development goals sustainability/our-insights/the-circular-economy-moving-from-theory-to-practise?cid=eml-web

Hemerling, J., Kilmann, J., Danoesastro, M., Stutts, L., & Ahern, C. (2018). *It's not a digital transformation without a digital culture*. Boston Consulting Group.

Iraldo, F., Testa, F., Lanzini, P., & Battaglia, M. (2017). Greening competitiveness for hotels and restaurants. *Journal of Small Business and Enterprise Development, 24*(3), 607–628. doi:10.1108/JSBED-12-2016-0211

Ivanov, S. (2019). Ultimate transformation: How will automation technologies disrupt the travel, tourism and hospitality industries? *Zeitschrift für Tourismuswissenschaft, 11*(1), 25–43. doi:10.1515/tw-2019-0003

Jauhari, V. (2014). *Managing sustainability in the hospitality and tourism industry: Paradigm and directions for the future*. Toronto, ON: Apple Academic Press.

Jones, P., & Comfort, D. (2019). Sustainable development goals and the world's leading hotel groups. *Athens Journal of Tourism, 6*(1), 1–14. doi:10.30958/ajt.6-1-1

Jones, P., Hillier, D., & Comfort, D. (2017). The sustainable development goals and the tourism and hospitality industry. *Athens Journal of Tourism, 4*(1), 7–18. doi:10.30958/ajt.4.1.1

Kasim, A. (2009). Managerial attitudes towards environmental management among small and medium hotels in Kualalumpur. *Journal of Sustainable Tourism, 17*, 709–725. doi:10.1080/09669580902928468

Kasim, A., Dzakiria, H., & Ahmad, R. (2017). Does the size of the company influence the innovative responses of water management in the hotel sector? *Advanced Science Letters, 23*(1), 369–372.

Khan, H., Kushwah, K. K., Singh, S., Urkude, H., Maurya, M. R., & Sadasivuni, K. K. (2021). Smart technologies driven approaches to tackle COVID-19 pandemic: A review. *3 Biotech, 11*(2), 1–22. doi:10.1007/s13205-020-02581-y

Khoo-Lattimore, C., & Jihyun Yang, M. (2018). The constructions of family holidays in young middle-class Malaysian Chinese children. *Journal of China Tourism Research*, 62–77. doi:10.1080/19388160.2018.1513884

Kim, J.-H., Ritchie, J., & McCormick, B. (2012). Development of a scale to measure memorable tourism experiences. *Journal of Travel Research, 51*(1), 12–25.

Lam, C., & Law, R. (2019). Readiness of upscale and luxury-branded hotels for digital transformation. *International Journal of Hospitality Management, 79*, 60–69. doi: 10.1016/j.ijhm.2018.12.015

Law, R., Leung, R., & Buhalis, D. (2009). Information technology applications in hospitality and tourism: A review of publications from 2005 to 2007. *Journal of Travel & Tourism Marketing, 26*(5–6), 599–623. doi:10.1080/10548400903163160

Lee, T. H., & Jan, F. H. (2019). Can community-based tourism contribute to sustainable development? Evidence from residents' perceptions of the sustainability. *Tourism Management, 70*, 368–380. doi:10.1016/j.tourman.2018.09.003

Lee, S. A., & Jeong, M. (2014). Enhancing online brand experiences: An application of congruity theory. *International Journal of Hospitality Management, 40*, 49–58. doi:10.1016/j.ijhm.2014.03.008

Li, J. J., Bonn, M. A., & Ye, B. H. (2019). Hotel employee's artificial intelligence and robotics awareness and its impact on turnover intention: The moderating roles of perceived organizational support and competitive psychological climate. *Tourism Management, 73*, 172–181. doi:10.1016/j.tourman.2019.02.006

Lim, W. M. (2016). Creativity and sustainability in hospitality and tourism. *Tourism Management Perspectives, 18*, 161–167. doi:10.1016/j.tmp.2016.02.001

Mabibibi, M. A., Dube, K., & Thwala, K. (2021). Successes and challenges in sustainable development goals localization for host communities around Kruger National Park. *Sustainability, 13*(10), 5341. doi:10.3390/su13105341

Markoff, J. (2014). Beep. Says the Bellhop. *The New York Times*. Retrieved from https://www.nytimes.com/2014/08/12/technology/hotel-to-begin-testing-botlr-a-robotic-bellhop.html?_r=0

Matteucci, V. (2020). How can the hospitality industry increase corporate value aligned with sustainable development goals? Case examples from Hilton, Meliá and Sun. *Worldwide Hospitality and Tourism Themes, 12*(5), 509–523.

Mensah, I. (2006). Environmental management practices among hotels in the Greater Accra Region. *International Journal of Hospitality Management, 25*, 414–431. doi: 10.1016/j.ijhm.2005.02.003

Mohanty, A., & Dash, D. (2018). Education for sustainable development: A conceptual model of sustainable education for India. *International Journal of Development and Sustainability, 7*(9), 2242–2255.

Morris, N. (2004). What is sustainability? *Power Engineer-IEE-, 18*, 11–11.

Nanda, V. P. (2016). The journey from the millennium development goals to the sustainable development goal. *Denver Journal of International Law and policy, 44*, 389–412.

Ngai, E. W. T., Suk, F. F. C., & Lo, S. Y. Y. (2008). Development of an RFID-based sushi management system: The case of a conveyor-belt sushi restaurant. *International Journal of Production Economics, 112*(2), 630–645. doi:10.1016/j.ijpe.2007.05.011

Noor, M., Nor, A., & Kumar, D. (2014). Eco friendly 'activities' vs eco friendly 'attitude': Travelers intention to choose green hotels in Malaysia. *World Applied Sciences Journal, 30*(4), 506–513.

OECD. (2018). *Oslo manual.* Retrieved from https://www.oecd.org/science/oslo-man-20-20-9789264304604-en.htm

Ou, J., Wong, I. A., & Huang, G. I. (2021). The coevolutionary process of restaurant CSR in the time of mega disruption. *International Journal of Hospitality Management, 92,* 102684. doi:10.1016/j.ijhm.2020.102684

Ozkil, A. G., Fan, Z., Dawids, S., Aanes, H., Kristensen, J. K., & Christensen, K. H. (2009). Service robots for hospitals: A case study of transportation tasks in a hospital. *IEEE International Conference on Automation and Logistics,* 289–294. doi:10.1109/ICAL.2009.5262912

Papargyropoulou, E., Lozano, R., Steinberger, J. K., Wright, N., & Ujang, Z. B. (2014). The food waste hierarchy as a framework for the management of food surplus and food waste. *Journal of Cleaner Production, 76,* 106–115. doi:10.1016/j.jclepro.2014.04.020

Papathanassis, A. (2017). R-tourism: Introducing the potential impact of robotics and service automation in tourism. *Ovidius University Annals, Series Economic Sciences, 17*(1), 211–216.

Pasanchay, K., & Schott, C. (2021). Community-based tourism homestays' capacity to advance the sustainable development goals: A holistic sustainable livelihood perspective. *Tourism Management Perspectives, 37,* 100784. doi:10.1016/j.tmp.2020.100784

Pickering, C., Grignon, J., Steven, R., Guitart, D., & Byrne, J. (2015). Publishing not perishing: How research students transition from novice to knowledgeable using systematic quantitative literature reviews. *Studies in Higher Education, 40*(10), 1756–1769. doi:10.1080/03075079.2014.914907

Prisco, J. (2014). Foodini machine lets you print edible burgers, pizza, chocolate. *CNN.* Retrieved from http://www.cnn.com/2014/11/06/tech/innovation/foodini-machine-print-food/

Pritchard, A. (2018). Predicting the future of tourism gender research. *Tourism Perspectives, 23,* 144–146. doi:10.1016/j.tmp.2017.11.014

Rajesh, M. (2015). Inside Japan's first robot-staffed hotel. *The Guardian, 14.* Retrieved from https://www.theguardian.com/travel/2015/aug/14/japan-henn-na-hotel-staffedby-robots

Rasoolimanesh, S. M., Ramakrishna, S., Hall, C. M., Esfandiar, K., & Seyfi, S. (2020). A systematic scoping review of sustainable tourism indicators in relation to the sustainable development goals. *Journal of Sustainable Tourism,* 1–21. doi:10.1080/09669582.2020.1775621

Rebecca, T. L. Y., & Yeoman, I. (2012). Imagine staying in a Shanghai hotel bedroom in 2050? *Research in Hospitality Management, 1*(2), 85–95. doi:10.1080/22243534.2012.11828280

Redclift, M. (2005). Sustainable development (1987–2005): An oxymoron comes of age. *Sustainable Development, 13*(4), 212–227. doi:10.1002/sd.281

Rhama, B., & Setiawan, F. (2022). Sustainable development goals in the tourism industry (case study of the hospitality industry in central Kalimantan, Indonesia). *Journal of Environmental Science and Sustainable Development, 5*(1), 165–175. doi:10.7454/jessd.v5i1.1148

Robert, K. W., Parris, T. M., & Leiserowitz, A. A. (2005). What is sustainable development? Goals, indicators, values, and practice. *Environment: Science and*

Policy for Sustainable Development, 47(3), 8–21. doi:10.1080/00139157.2005. 10524444

Scheyvens, R., & Hughes, E. (2019). Can tourism help to "end poverty in all its forms everywhere"? The challenge of tourism addressing SDG1. *Journal of Sustainable Tourism, 27*(17), 1061–1079.

Schneider, A., & Treisch, C. (2019). Employees' evaluative repertoires of tourism and hospitality jobs. *International Journal of Contemporary Hospitality Management, 31*(8), 3173–3191. doi:10.1108/IJCHM-08-2018-0675

Senbekov, M., Saliev, T., Bukeyeva, Z., Almabayeva, A., Zhanaliyeva, M., Aitenova, N., ... Fakhradiyev, I. (2020). The recent progress and applications of digital technologies in healthcare: A review. *International Journal of Telemedicine and Applications*, 92–103. doi:10.1155/2020/8830200

Sharma, S. (2020). Educational technology – A pathway to a sustainable world. *The CSR Journal: Integral Part of the Solution.* Retrieved from https://thecsrjournal.in/educational-technology-a-pathway-to-a-sustainable-world

Sloan, G. (2014). Robot bartenders? This new cruise ship has them. *USA Today.* Accessed on February 4, 2023.

Sonmez, S., Apostolopoulos, Y., Lemke, M. K., Hsieh, Y. C. J., & Karwowski, W. (2017). Complexity of occupational health in the hospitality industry: Dynamic simulation modeling to advance immigrant worker health. *International Journal of Hospitality Management, 67*, 95–105. doi:10.1016/j.ijhm.2017.08.006

Sousa, M., Santos, V., Sacavém, A., Reis, I., & Sampaio, M. (2019). 4.0 leadership skills in hospitality sector. *Journal of Reviews on Global Economics, 8*, 105–117. doi:10.6000/1929-7092.2019.08.11

Spaiser, V., Ranganathan, S., Bali Swain, R., & Sumpter, D. (2016). The sustainable development oxymoron: Quantifying and modelling the incompatibility of sustainable development goals. *The International Journal of Sustainable Development and World Ecology*, 457–470. doi:10.1080/13504509.2016.1235624

Styvén, M. E., & Wallström, Å. (2019). Benefits and barriers for the use of digital channels among small tourism companies. *Scandinavian Journal of Hospitality and Tourism, 19*(1), 27–46. doi:10.1080/15022250.2017.1379434

Sushirobo. (2016). *Sushi machines.* Retrieved from http://www.sushirobo.com/#machines

Svahn, F., Mathiassen, L., & Lindgren, R. (2017). Embracing digital innovation in incumbent firms. *MIS Quarterly, 41*(1), 239–254. Retrieved from https://www.jstor.org/stable/26629645

Swain, R. B. (2018). A critical analysis of the sustainable development goals. *Handbook of sustainability science and research*, 341–355. doi:10.1007/978-3-319-63007-620

Swain, R. B., & Yang-Wallentin, F. (2020). Achieving sustainable development goals: predicaments and strategies. *The International Journal of Sustainable Development and World Ecology, 27*(2), 96–106. doi:10.1080/13504509.2019.1692316

Terjesen, S., Hessels, J., & Li, D. (2013). Comparative international entrepreneurship a review and research agenda. *Journal of Management, 20*(10), 1–46. doi:10.1177/0149206313486259

The economist. (2022, April 1). Educational technology market size in India in 2020, with projection for 2025 by segment. *The economist.* Retrieved from https://www.statista.com/statistics/1235210/india-edtech-market-size-bysegment/

Tian, S., Yang, W., Le Grange, J. M., Wang, P., Huang, W., & Ye, Z. (2019). Smart healthcare: Making medical care more intelligent. *Global Health Journal, 3*(3), 62–65. doi:10.1016/j.glohj.2019.07.001

United Nations. (2015). *Transforming our world: The 2030 agenda for sustainable development. Resolution adopted by the general assembly on 25 September 2015.* United Nations A/RES/70/1. Retrieved from https://sustainabledevelopment.un. org/content/documents/21252030Agenda for Sustainable Development web.pdf

United Nations. (2020). *Sustainable development goals.* Retrieved from https://sdgs.un. org/

United Nations General Assembly. (2014). *Report of the open working group of the general assembly on sustainable development goals.* U.N. Doe. A/68/970. United Nations.

United Nations World Tourism Organization and United Nations Development Programme. (2017). *Tourism and the sustainable development goals – Journey to 2030.* UNWTO.

Wang, Y., So, K. K. F., & Sparks, B. A. (2017). Technology readiness and customer satisfaction with travel technologies: A cross-country investigation. *Journal of Travel Research, 56*(5), 563–577. doi:10.1177/0047287516657891

Wang, Z., & Tang, K. (2020). Combating COVID-19: Health equity matters. *Nature Medicine, 26*(4), 458–458. doi:10.1038/s41591-020-0823-6

Warner, K. S., & Wäger, M. (2019). Building dynamic capabilities for digital trans-formation: An ongoing process of strategic renewal. *Long Range Planning, 52*(3), 326–349. doi:10.1016/j.lrp.2018.12.001

Webster, C., & Ivanov, S. (2020). Robotics, artificial intelligence, and the evolving nature of work. In B. George & J. Paul (Eds.), *Digital transformation in business and society* (pp. 127–143). London: Palgrave Macmillan. doi:10.1007/978-3-030-08277-2_8

Wirtz, J., & Zeithaml, V. (2018). Cost-effective service excellence. *Journal of the Academy of Marketing Science, 46*(1), 59–80. doi:10.1007/s11747-017-0560-7

World Tourism Organization and United Nations Development Programme. (2017). *Tourism and the sustainable development goals – Journey to 2030.* Retrieved from www.undp.org/content/dam/undp/library/Sustainable%20Development/UNWTO_UNDP_Tourism%20and%20the%20SDGs. pdf. Accessed on May 27, 2020.

Xiang, Z. (2018). From digitization to the age of acceleration: On information tech-nology and tourism. *Tourism Management Perspectives, 25,* 147–150. doi:10.1016/j. tmp.2017.11.023

Yang, G. Z., Nelson, B. J., Murphy, R. R., Choset, H., Christensen, H., Collins, S. H., … Kragic, D. (2020). Combating COVID-19—The role of robotics in managing public health and infectious diseases. *Science Robotics, 5*(40), 55–89. doi:10.1126/scirobotics.abb5589

Yiu, L. S., & Saner, R. (2014). Sustainable development goals and millennium development goals: An analysis of the shaping and negotiation process. *Asia Pacific Journal of Public Administration, 36*(2), 89–107. doi:10.1080/23276665. 2014.911487

Zhang, T. C., Torres, E., & Jahromi, M. F. (2019). Well on the way: An exploratory study on occupational health in hospitality. *International Journal of Hospitality Management, 87,* 102382. doi:10.1016/j.ijhm.2019.102382

Chapter 14

Digital Payments Transformation in India: Trends, Issues, and Opportunities

Anupkumar Dhore, Vijay D. Joshi, Amir Hafizullah Khan and Sukanta Kumar Baral

Abstract

The purpose of this chapter is to examine the integration of technology-based solutions in the Indian banking industry, driven by the need for contactless services and addressing operational issues and customer complaints post-Covid-19. The study utilizes archival and observational research, drawing data from the internet to understand the changes in the acceptance and use of digital payments in India. The findings suggest that digital payments are poised for growth due to the increasing acceptance and popularity of personal device-based banking services. However, the limitations of the study restrict its applicability to the Indian context. The practical implications highlight the importance of technology in improving banking operations and efficiency, while the social implications emphasize the shift in people's mindset toward accepting and utilizing technology for everyday banking activities. This chapter also discusses government initiatives aimed at resolving issues and customer complaints arising from the increased use of technology in the banking industry. This chapter contributes to the understanding of the evolving digital payment scenario, technology-based banking services, and the payment infrastructure in India.

Keywords: Digital payment scenario in India; technology-based banking services; Indian government initiatives to encourage digital payment; payment infrastructure in India

Introduction

What is Digital Payment (RBI, 2022)?

Fostering Sustainable Businesses in Emerging Economies, 247–257
doi:10.1108/978-1-80455-640-520231015

Digital payment is an arrangement in which transactions are noncash-based. It uses payment system infrastructure to accomplish transactions.

Typically, a payment system infrastructure has the following components:

- Cards: Debit Cards and Credit Cards,
- Prepaid Payment Instruments (PPIs): Wallets and Cards,
- ATM Network,
- Micro ATMs, and
- Point of Sale (PoS) Terminals.

Exhibit 1 shows the present status of the payment system infrastructure in India.

Government Initiatives to Promote Digital Payment

The Indian digital payment system has seen significant development, improvement, and administrative support over the past few years. According to PricewaterhouseCoopers (PwC) and Reserve Bank of India (RBI) (2019), the

Exhibit 1. Payment Infrastructure in India (RBI, 2023).

| System | Volume (In Lakh) | | | |
	As on March 2022	January 2022	December 2022	January 2023
Number of Cards	9,912	10,110	10,206	10,280
Credit Cards	735	702	812	824
Debit Cards	9,177	9,408	9,394	9,456
Number of PPIs @	15,553	15,389	16,234	16,030
Wallets @	12,788	12,722	13,346	2,784
Cards @	2,765	2,667	2,888	13,246
Number of ATMs	2.52	2.46	2.57	2.58
Bank Owned	2.20	2.16	2.20	2.21
Others	0.31	0.30	0.37	0.37
Number of Micro ATMs @	9.16	7.78	14.19	14.75
Number of PoS Terminals	60.70	56.20	75.50	76.57
Bharat QR @	49.72	46.71	49.59	50.57
UPI QR*	1727.34	1,521.05	2,361.82	2,442.34

@: New inclusion w.e.f. November 2019.
*: New inclusion w.e.f. September 2020. Includes only static UPI QR code.

development of this sector in India and its connected subsystems has been particularly noteworthy.

PoS transactions are now more secure, thanks to RBI guidelines for the issue of chip-based cards with PIN. The risk of card skimming and cloning incidents at ATMs will be reduced if banks rebuild ATMs to accept and validate chip-based cards rather than cards using magnetic strips. The rationalization of merchant discounting rates has been done throughout time to lower transaction costs for the merchants. Customers no longer have to pay extra fees to use National Electronic Funds Transfer (NEFT) and Real Time Gross Settlement (RTGS). This is assisting in the advancement of huge noncash exchanges through electronic modes. The government/public authority has additionally expanded its emphasis on building up a "less money (noncash-based) society".

Different metropolitan authorities are embracing Bharat Bill Payment Services (BBPS) for bill payments. Government bearing on National Common Mobility Card (NCMC) and National Electronic Toll Collection (NETC) has helped start digitizing low-worth, high-volume money exchanges in the transport area.

Different partners like banks, public vehicle administrators, OEMs, installment framework administrators including card organizations, PPI backers, and monetary market foundation suppliers have assumed a significant part in building up the advanced payment mechanism in India.

In October 2018, the RBI passed operational interoperability regulations for PPIs. Users of mobile wallets can now transfer money between their wallets. With India's Unified Payment Interface (UPI) platform, users can transfer money from their wallets to bank accounts. It is anticipated that giving PPIs the ability to issue cards for withdrawals will level the playing field between payment banks and mobile wallet providers (PwC and RBI, 2019).

Global Digital Payment Scenario (WPR, 2022)

Covid-19 promoted the use of noncash payment systems and encouraged consumers and companies to integrate digital technology into their daily life. Instant payments and e-money transactions as a percentage of all noncash transactions are expected to grow in the next 5 years (from 2021 to 2026). Exhibit 2 shows global noncash transaction volume (in billion) by region for the period 2021–2022.

A large portion of the record rise in worldwide noncash transactions was contributed by the Asia-Pacific region (APAC), which had a Compound Annual Growth Rate (CAGR) of 25% (during 2021–2022). Some of the key factors driving growth in the APAC area include the widespread use of digital wallets, the rising popularity and acceptability of e-commerce platforms, and innovation in mobile payments.

The region leading the rise in noncash transactions will continue to be APAC. The phenomenal growth of mobile wallets in China over the past few years (based on platforms from Alibaba and Tencent) is still going strong. Although digital payment is still in its infancy in India, it will develop over the next few years,

Exhibit 2. Global Noncash Transaction Volume (in Billion) by Region for the Period 2020–2021 (WPR, 2022).

Region	Noncash Transactions (In Billion)		
	2021	2022	CAGR (2021–2022)
APAC	441	553	25.4%
The Middle East, Africa (MEA)	24	27	12.5%
Europe	255	287	12.55%
Latin America	66	72	9.1%
North America	204	218	6.86%
Global	**990**	**1,157**	**16.87%**

owing to a supportive legislative framework, upgraded infrastructure, and rising smartphone use and penetration.

Shifting user payment preferences, growth of the e-commerce industry, and governmental support are expected to drive 16.5% noncash transaction growth in the global areas from 2021 to 2026 (F). The payment behavior of the APAC region will drive the region's phenomenal 22.8% CAGR between 2021 and 2026 (F) (WPR, 2022).

Exhibit 3 shows the forecasting of global noncash transactions (in billion) by region for the period 2021–2026 (F).

As said in the report, the growth in volumes is also due to the increasing use of next-gen payment methods. These may include buy now pay later (BNPL) scheme, invisible, biometric, and cryptocurrency. If introduced in the market, the central digital currency (CDC) issued by the national regulatory bank of the respective country could also be there. All of these payment methods will have a significant contribution to achieving this volume growth.

Exhibit 3. Global Noncash Transactions (in Billion) by Region Forecast (F) (WPR, 2022).

Region	Noncash Transactions (In Billion)		
	2021	2026 (F)	CAGR (2021–2026)
APAC	441	1,232	22.8%
The Middle East, Africa (MEA)	24	42	12.1%
Latin America	66	100	8.6%
Europe	255	467	12.9%
North America	204	281	6.6%
Global	**990**	**2,122**	**16.5%**

Indian Digital Payment Scenario (RBI, 2023)

According to the data provided in Payment System Indicators and Payment & Settlement System Statistics by RBI, there is growth across volumes of all system components in India (See Exhibit 4).

According to the data provided in Payment System Indicators and Payment & Settlement System Statistics by RBI, there is the use of different types of payment modes and channels used while making transactions (See Exhibit 5).

It is seen that UPI transactions are growing steadily. These are governed and driven by apps (i.e., mobile applications) such as PhonePe, Google Pay, Paytm, Amazon Pay, etc. (Worldline, 2022). According to the data provided by the National Payments Corporation of India (NPCI), there were 782 crores of UPI transactions recorded in December 2022 (NPCI, 2023). This app-based payment method is now well-established and is likely to grow in the near future. Recently, NPCI has approved an additional six crore users on UPI for WhatsApp. With this, this messaging app can expand the service to 10 crore customers in the country (Appl, 2022).

Exhibit 4. Volume of Payments Across All System Components in India (In Lakh).

	Volume (In Lakh)			
System	Financial Year 2021–22	January 2022	December 2022	January 2023
Retail – Credit Transfers	577,934	57,367	90,675	92,396
UPI@	459,561	46,171	78,290	80,385
NEFT	40,407	3,630	4,855	4,800
Immediate Payment Service (IMPS)	46,625	4,400	4,860	4,745
Others	31,341	3,166	2,670	2,466
Direct – Debit Transfers	12,190	1,060	1,357	1,360
NACH	10,754	934	1,200	1,202
Others	1,436	126	157	158
Card Payments	61,782	5,151	5,223	5,103
Credit Cards	22,398	1958	2,556	2,593
Debit Cards	39,384	3,193	2,667	2,510
PPI-based	65,782	5,807	6,354	6,129
Wallets	53,013	4,613	5,012	4,874
Cards	12,769	1,194	1,342	1,255
Paper-based Instruments	7,000	597	608	573
Total Payments	726,767	70,163	104,435	105,766
Total Digital Payments	719,768	69,566	103,826	105,193

@: New inclusion w.e.f. November 2019.

Exhibit 5. Volume of Payments Across Different Types of Payment Modes in India (In Lakh).

Payment Mode/Channel	Volume (In Lakh)			
	Financial Year 2021–22	January 2022	December 2022	January 2023
Mobile Payments (Mobile app-based)	506,842	49,905	84,929	86,637
Internet Payments (Net Banking/Internet Browser-based)	40,825	3,564	3,664	3,538
Cash Withdrawal at ATM	65,240	5,555	5,890	5,752
Cash Withdrawal at Micro ATM	11,126	1,125	934	963
Cash Withdrawal at PoS Terminals	91.17	2.13	2.38	2.44

In the last 2 years, UPI's popularity has multiplied to the point where, in volume terms, the platform currently processes more peer-to-merchant (P2M) transactions than peer-to-peer (P2P) transactions. UPI was previously mostly utilized for P2P transactions (NPCI, 2023).

Challenges to Digital Payments

The market for digital payments is very heterogeneous, with customers of widely varying profiles and needs. Therefore, they have to use different ways for product promotion and distribution. In this context, social media can play a vital role in spreading the word.

Some of the factors listed below are expected to challenge the digital payment situation shortly (WPR, 2022).

- Technological uncertainty,
- Regulatory complexity, and
- Intensifying competition.

Technological Uncertainty

- New technology established banks.
- It could be challenging for banks to comprehend, put into practice, monitor, and control new technologies because they might call for significant operational and systemic changes.

- Technology-based solutions raise customer expectations.
- Emerging technologies have the potential to modify how things work and perhaps make things dangerously technical.

Regulatory Complexity

- The difficulties with regulatory compliance that banks are currently confronting add a (new) layer of complexity to the already complex payment environment.
- Complex situations arise as a result of compliance issues including nonintrusive security in the context of PSD2RTS (Open Banking Mandate).
- Given that there are numerous real-time payment systems in use worldwide, a lack of interoperability has an impact on the operational and financial health of banks.
- Open Banking Projects (OBP) are not supported or encouraged by Global Accreditation. Some nations (uniquely) have domestic card payment systems that may cause fragmentation (e.g., Rupay, MEPS, ALTO, NAPAS, FPOS, etc.).

Intensifying Competition

- Market share is in danger due to the advent of huge technology-based enterprises. The size of the internet behemoth, which is looking for more business opportunities in the developing financial services industry, poses a real threat. It includes everything from capable suppliers to demand aggregators and, in the end, service platform providers.

Recent Trends in Digital Payments

Some of the highlights of the World Payment Report 2022 are (WPR, 2022):

- The growth of noncash transactions has been fueled by a digital payments infrastructure that is becoming more established.
- Initiatives related to regulations and the industry have been numerous and extensive recently.
- Expectations of banks and other payment service providers from Small and Medium Businesses (SMBs) are increasing.
- Executives from payment service providers acknowledge that SMBs have unresolved technology and process problems.
- Payment companies can configure services, capabilities, and features on-the-fly, thanks to the composable architecture.
- Together with other financial service providers, central banks are investigating use cases for distributed ledger technology (DLT).

Another interesting aspect in this context is the central bank digital currency (CBDC). If introduced in the market, theCBDC could have an impact on digital payments as it is provided as an alternative (to people) in the form of a digital currency. A CBDC is the digital form of the country's flat currency. Instead of printing money, the central bank issues electronic coins or accounts backed by the full faith and credit of the government (CBDC1, 2022).

Ten countries have launched a CBDC and others may follow the same in near future. These include Nigeria, Jamaica, The Bahamas, and seven Eastern Caribbean countries having a common central bank. India has also joined this group now (CBDC2, 2022). According to the RBI statement, the CBDC test drive started on November 1, 2022, in the wholesale market for secondary trade in government bonds. The RBI has announced its first pilot project to use CBDC in the wholesale market for secondary trade in government securities.

The RBI has said that the retail digital rupee (e-R) pilot will launch on December 1 with four banks participating initially in it. The project will be run in Mumbai, New Delhi, Bengaluru, and Bhubaneshwar (CBDC3, 2022). A second pilot project on retail use of the digital rupee also started (on December 1, 2022) in the closed user groups.

Way forward for digital Payments in India (Razorpay, 2021)

Future developments in the fintech sector will make it more dynamic and offer safe trading platforms for the advancement of domestic digital payment systems. In terms of blockchain technology, cloud-based payments, cryptocurrencies, and other payment methods based on artificial intelligence (AI), machine learning (ML), and the Internet of Things (IoT), the nation has already made headway. According to Razorpay, digital payments have grown to 76% in the last 12 months, with a few first-time digital payment users. According to reports, India's digital payments industry has grown to $700 billion by 2022.

India's digital payments market has seen extraordinary growth in recent years since it was monetized in 2016, but the Covid-19 outbreak has also spurred the growth and adoption of online transactions. Users have switched to online banking and other digital payment options to access products such as essentials, groceries, retail, medical, and education. Meanwhile, the emergence of improved technology is one of the key drivers of the growth of the country's digital payments industry.

Government Initiatives (Initiative, 2021)

In August 2021, Prime Minister Narendra Modi inaugurated a scheme e-RUPI. This was a technology-based initiative that supports the personal and purpose-specific digital payment mechanism. This e-RUPI is a cashless and contactless payment method for digital payments. A quick-response (QR) code or SMS string-based e-voucher is delivered to the recipient's mobile phone. Users of this seamless one-time payment mechanism can redeem vouchers with service providers without access to a card, digital payment app, or internet banking.

It should be mentioned that technologically driven and technology-based things like digital payments are not always beneficial. The fact that more customers are complaining about using digital payments is evidence of this. From 1.6 lakh complaints in FY 2018 to 3.3 lakh in FY 2020, these have increased (Complaint, 2021). With the use of technology, the government and RBI are also tackling this problem. The "Integrated Ombudsman System" was developed by the government to address customer complaints about businesses under RBI regulation. This is an advancement in inclusivity (Ombudsman, 2021).

The Indian banking and financial services industry will be driven by technology in the post Covid-19 era (Jaya, 2021). The Indian banking industry, which was already experiencing rapid change, has been altered by the events of 2020. In the post Covid-19 era, the growth of public and hybrid cloud spaces, blockchain, microservices-based architectures, and AI will support this transformation.

In conclusion, the author believes that the pandemic has posed significant challenges to all industries, including banking in India. However, because it has the potential to alter the direction of development for the Indian banking industry, this may be viewed as an opportunity. Shri Shaktikanta Das, Governor of the RBI, asserts that increased technology adoption drives revenue, growth, and productivity. The banking industry will concentrate primarily on supporting the expansion of the rural economy, putting into action government programs, making use of technology to provide better services that are focused on the needs of customers, and supporting training and development programs. Digitalization and innovation can usher in a new era of prosperity for many, and a journey beyond Covid-19 will be driven by revenue growth and job creation (Das, 2021).

To explore the opportunities in the post Covid-19 era, the Indian government is encouraging the establishment of a digital economy by framing relevant policies. Increased use and acceptance of UPI and the introduction of CBDC are examples of the same.

An interesting aspect of this fintech revolution in India is that the other countries have started showing interest in the same.

Locally, UPI is becoming more well-liked and accepted. Other nations are also looking into the possibility of using the same (to improve their financial payment infrastructure). Singapore is a recent illustration (Singapore, 2023). Due to the platform's integration with PayNow, Indian citizens can now send money to and from Singaporeans using UPI. PayNow users in Singapore can send money from India in a similar way. Such alliances may also cover other nations.

Following Singapore, the RBI is in discussions with several nations, including Indonesia, the United Arab Emirates, and Mauritius, to establish a direct payment link of the UPI with networks in these nations (Others, 2023). This will make using mobile phones for fund transfers faster and less expensive. Even some Latin American nations have reportedly expressed interest, according to RBI sources.

Conclusion

To sum up the things, it may be summarized as below: (PwC and RBI, 2019; RBI, 2023; WPR, 2022)

The RBI claims that the digital payment mechanism aims to enhance the payment ecosystem by focusing on the following customer-focused aspects:

- Giving service providers and operators of payment systems more control.
- Making infrastructure a priority and enabling the ecosystem.
- Reducing the risks posed by cybersecurity to a minimum.
- Enhancing the customer experience.
- Implementing a regulation that looks to the future.
- Support for supervision that focuses on risk.

The use of technology to make it easy and convenient for customers to make payments has been emphasized in Digital Payment. With the development of new technologies, it was also evident that the landscape of payments is changing. It is becoming more complicated as new players enter the market, new technologies emerge, and shifting customer expectations cause more disruption.

It is concluded that (Indian) banks are responding to this shift in the market by innovating and working together to create synergies.

The technological assistance banks receive in providing their customers with a secure and efficient payment experience is crucial to the success of Digital Payment.

References

Appl. (2022). NPCI allows WhatsApp to extend UPI services to more users. Article published in the Times of India, Pune edition dated April 14, 2022.

CBDC1. (2022). Global central banks starts issuing digital currencies. Article published in the Times of India, Pune edition dated July 26, 2022.

CBDC2. (2022). RBI launches first pilot project for the digital rupee. Article published in the Times of India, Pune edition dated November 1, 2022.

CBDC3. (2022). RBI to pilot digital rupee for retail use from Dec. 1. Article published in the Times of India, Pune edition dated November 30, 2022.

Complaint. (2021). Digital doubled banking plaints two years: RBI Data. Article published in the Times of India, Pune edition dated Nov. 12, 2021.

Das S. (2021). Beyond COVID: Towards a Stronger, Inclusive, and Sustainable Economy. Keynote Address by Shri Shaktikanta Das, Governor, Reserve Bank of India - September 22, 2021 - Delivered at the 48th National Management Convention of the All India Management Association (AIMA).

Initiative. (2021). Government encouraging digital payment initiatives. Article posted on the Razorpay blog, published on August 10, 2021.

Jaya V. (2021). Technology will drive the Indian Banking industry post-Covid. Article published in Business Today, dated January 27, 2021.

NPCI. (2023). UPI Transactions Rise Over 7.82 Billion in December 2022. Outlook Money. January 2. Retrieved from https://www.outlookindia.com/business/upi-transactions-rise-over-7-82-billion-in-december-2022-here-s-how-upi-has-grown-over-the-years-news-250301. Accessed on February 20, 2023.

Ombudsman. (2021). Advertisement by RBI that promotes the launching of the Integrated Ombudsman Scheme. Published in the Times of India, Pune edition dated November 12, 2021.

Others. (2023). UPI may extend to UAE, Mauritius, and Indonesia. Article published in the Times of India, Pune edition dated February 24, 2023.

PwC and RBI. (2019). RBI Vision 2019-2021: The way forward. Prepared by PwC India - PricewaterhouseCoopers Private Limited [GM/August 2019/M&C-203].

Razorpay. (2021). Nation heads towards a cashless economy. Article by Vidyashree S. supported by Razorpay, published on August 10, 2021.

RBI. (2022). Payment System Indicators- July 2022. Reserve Bank of India (RBI) Bulletin. Retrieved from https://www.rbi.org.in/Scripts/PSIUserView.aspx?Id=14. Accessed on December 20, 2022.

RBI. (2023). Payment System Indicators- January 2023. Reserve Bank of India (RBI) Bulletin. Retrieved from https://www.rbi.org.in/Scripts/PSIUserView.aspx. Accessed on February 23, 2023.

Singapore. (2023). How Singapore-India UPI works? Article published in the Times of India, Pune edition dated February 22, 2023.

Worldline. (2022). *Nearly two out of every three payments are done via UPI, says Worldline India Digital Payment Report.* Article published in the Times of India, Pune edition dated July 1, 2022.

WPR. (2022). World Payments Report WPR 2022. Prepared by Capgemini. Retrieved from https://worldpaymentsreport.com/key-highlights.html/. Accessed on February 20, 2023.

Chapter 15

Integration of New-Age Technologies in Education System to Achieve Sustainable Development Goals (SDGs) in Emerging Economies

Vijay Prakash Gupta

Abstract

The use of cutting-edge technology in education has the potential to transform the learning experience and greatly contribute to the achievement of the Sustainable Development Goals (SDGs) in emerging economies. With the increased accessibility of technology and online resources, digital literacy has become an essential skill in today's world. Smart e-learning platforms have emerged as a new tool for offering education and training in emerging economies, while also boosting digital literacy.

This chapter will attempt to investigate the impact of new-age technologies on the educational system and how they can help emerging economies achieve the SDGs. This study looks at case studies from various emerging economies, analyzing how innovative technologies like digital learning, smart teaching and learning, mobile learning, online learning, artificial intelligence (AI), virtual reality, and gamification are used to improve education quality and promote SDGs. This chapter emphasizes the impact of technological integration on access to education, reducing inequality, and improving educational quality and relevance. This study also looks into how education may help promote environmental sustainability and economic growth. According to the findings, integrating new-age technologies into the education system can be a game changer in achieving SDGs in emerging nations.

Keywords: Digital literacy; smart E-learning; Smart Classrooms; skills and scientific attitude; ICT tools; SDGs

Fostering Sustainable Businesses in Emerging Economies, 259–280
Copyright © 2024 Vijay Prakash Gupta
Published under exclusive licence by Emerald Publishing Limited
doi:10.1108/978-1-80455-640-520231016

Introduction

History and Emergence of Education System

Education has a long history, going back to ancient times when information was passed down verbally and through practical apprenticeships. Several societies reserved education for the privileged few, such as priests and aristocracy. Yet, the modern formal education system began to evolve in the sixteenth century.

During Europe's Renaissance period, there was a renewed emphasis on the study of classical literature, mathematics, and the sciences. This resulted in the establishment of universities, which were originally established to train priests but were eventually expanded to include other professions such as law, medicine, and engineering. The first universities were founded in Italy, France, and Germany, and they swiftly spread throughout Europe and, eventually, around the world.

The first public school in the United States was created in Massachusetts in 1635, and it was quickly followed by the formation of other schools around the country. Many countries made public education mandatory in the nineteenth century, and governments began to construct public school systems. Meanwhile, the industrial revolution produced a demand for skilled labor, resulting in the establishment of vocational and technical schools.

Education became a key emphasis for governments around the world in the twentieth century, with many countries establishing laws requiring children to attend school until a particular age. The evolution of new technologies, such as computers, has also resulted in the incorporation of technology into education.

Education is now seen as a fundamental human right, and the majority of countries have developed public education systems that ensure equal access to education for all residents. Education's emphasis has switched to educating students for the workforce and supporting lifelong learning, as well as cultivating critical thinking, problem-solving, and other abilities required for success in the modern world.

Emergence of Modern Education System

The contemporary education system may be traced back to the Industrial Revolution, when a competent workforce was required to satisfy the needs of the new economy.

The following characteristics define the current educational system:

- *Compulsory Education:* In most nations, children between the ages of 6 and 16 are required to attend school. Governments mandate children to attend school, and parents who do not comply may be punished or suffer legal consequences.
- *Universal Education:* The modern educational system strives to educate all pupils, regardless of social class, gender, color, or religion.
- *Standardized Curriculum:* The modern education system is based on a standardized curriculum that includes language, mathematics, science, history, and social studies.

- *Teacher Education:* Teachers are taught in universities and other institutions to present a standardized curriculum and to promote their students' intellectual, emotional, and social growth.
- *Assessment and Evaluation:* Pupils' progress and achievement are examined and evaluated through a variety of tests, examinations, and other methods.
- *Technology Integration:* To increase learning and educational outcomes, technology has been integrated into the current educational system. Computers, the internet, and other digital technologies are used to distribute content, allow collaboration, and promote learning.

The modern educational system has been chastised for being overly focused on standardized testing and failing to address the requirements of all children. Attempts are being undertaken to improve the system so that it is more student-centered, customized, and inclusive, and so that students are better prepared for the challenges of the twenty-first century.

Importance of Education in Achieving Sustainable Development Goals

Education is a vital component in accomplishing long-term development objectives. Education is not only a fundamental human right, but it also plays a critical role in developing the required skills, information, and attitudes for long-term development. Education may help individuals and communities comprehend the environmental consequences of their actions and enable them to make educated decisions that lead to sustainable development.

Education can help reach long-term development goals in a variety of ways. For starters, education may raise awareness and comprehension of the SDGs, their targets, and the significance of achieving them. Education can also assist in the development of skills and knowledge required to solve long-term development concerns such as climate change, environmental degradation, and social inequality.

Furthermore, education may empower individuals and communities to actively participate in efforts to achieve sustainable development. Education may help to cultivate critical thinking, foster creativity, and foster innovation, all of which are necessary for promoting sustainable development.

Overall, education is a powerful weapon that can aid in the achievement of SDGs by providing individuals and communities with the knowledge, skills, and attitudes required to make informed decisions and conduct actions that promote sustainable development.

Sustainable Development Goals (SDGS) and Education

The United Nations approved the SDGs in 2015 to address global concerns and promote sustainable development. Education is an essential component of the SDGs, and the education system is vital to accomplishing many of them. Here are some examples of how the education system can help to achieve the SDGs:

SDG 4 – Education Quality: SDG 4 strives to provide inclusive and equitable quality education and to encourage opportunities for lifelong learning for everyone. The school system can help to achieve this goal by delivering high-quality education to all pupils, regardless of background or socioeconomic level.

SDG 5 – Gender Equality: SDG 5 seeks gender equality and the empowerment of all women and girls. The education system can help achieve this aim by ensuring equitable access to education for girls and encouraging gender-sensitive teaching and learning materials.

SDG 10 – Inequality Reduction: SDG 10 seeks to address disparities both within and between countries. The education system can help to achieve this goal by ensuring equal access to school and promoting education as a tool of social and economic mobility.

SDG 13 – Climate Action: SDG 13 strives to take immediate action to combat climate change and its consequences. This goal can be helped by improving environmental awareness and sustainability education in the educational system.

SDG 16 – Justice, Peace, and Strong Institutions: SDG 16 seeks to foster peaceful and inclusive societies for long-term development, to ensure equal access to justice for all, and to establish effective, responsible, and inclusive institutions. Peace education, human rights education, and civic education can all help to achieve this goal.

SDG 17 – Partnerships for the Goals: SDG 17 seeks to strengthen implementation mechanisms and revitalize the global partnership for sustainable development. The education system can help to achieve this goal by encouraging collaboration among governments, civil society, and the private sector to promote education and sustainable development.

Ultimately, the education system is crucial to accomplishing the SDGs and supporting long-term development. The education system may contribute to a more fair, peaceful, and sustainable world by delivering quality education that is inclusive, equitable, and accessible to everyone.

Overview of SDGs

The United Nations General Assembly established the SDGs in 2015 as a worldwide call to action to eradicate poverty, safeguard the environment, and ensure that all people experience peace and prosperity by 2030. Poverty, hunger, health, education, gender equality, clean water and sanitation, affordable and clean energy, decent work and economic growth, industry, innovation, and infrastructure, reduced inequalities, sustainable cities and communities, responsible consumption and production, climate action, life below water, life on land, peace, justice, and strong institutions, and partnerships for the goals are among the issues addressed.

The SDGs build on the Millenium Development Goals (MDGs), which were set in 2000 and aimed to reduce poverty, hunger, and sickness while also promoting gender equality, education, and environmental sustainability. While the MDGs were designed with developing countries in mind, the SDGs apply to all countries and need action from all stakeholders, including governments, the commercial sector, civil society, and individuals.

The SDGs seek to establish a framework for sustainable development that takes into account the economic, social, and environmental components of development. They realize the need for transformative change and advocate for a more inclusive, equitable, and long-term approach to development. The SDGs reflect a shared future vision and a road map for global action to achieve a more just and sustainable world for all.

Role of Education in Achieving SDGs

Education is a critical engine of economic growth, social development, and environmental sustainability, and hence plays a critical role in reaching the SDGs. Under the SDG framework, education is specifically acknowledged as a separate target (SDG 4), which asks for "inclusive and equitable quality education and lifelong learning opportunities for all." Here are some statistics and data that demonstrate the critical significance of education in accomplishing the SDGs:

Excellent education is a driver of economic growth and poverty reduction: UNESCO estimates that each additional year of schooling boosts an individual's earning capacity by 10%. Education also plays a crucial role in poverty reduction: it is estimated that if all pupils in low-income nations had access to basic reading abilities, 171 million people would be lifted out of poverty.

Gender equality cannot be achieved without education: Education for girls is one of the most powerful strategies to promote gender equality and empower women and girls. Educating girls has been demonstrated in studies to reduce child marriage, enhance health outcomes, and increase economic engagement.

Environmental sustainability requires education: education can assist raise knowledge about environmental challenges and promote sustainable habits. Environmental education initiatives, for example, have been found to improve people's knowledge and awareness of ecological systems and conservation challenges.

Education is required to achieve all SDGs: Education is a crucial enabler of the other SDGs. It can aid in the promotion of health and well-being (SDG 3), the reduction of disparities (SDG 10), and the promotion of peaceful and inclusive societies (SDG 16).

Notwithstanding the importance of education in achieving the SDGs, there are still major gaps in global access to education. According to UNESCO, an estimated 262 million children and adolescents are not attending school, with approximately 60% of them being girls. To attain the SDG 4 goal of inclusive and equitable quality education for all, it will be required to close these disparities and guarantee that all children have access to education that fulfills their requirements and promotes their development.

How Technology Can Support Education in Achieving SDGs

Technology, particularly in the field of education, has the potential to play a revolutionary role in reaching the SDGs. Here are some instances how technology might help education achieve the SDGs:

Access to education: Technology can help overcome hurdles to education access, particularly in low-income nations or locations with insufficient infrastructure. Those who may not have access to traditional classrooms, for example, can benefit from online courses and digital learning platforms. According to the United Nations, boosting access to technology and the internet could open doors for an additional 2.5 million students in sub-Saharan Africa alone.

Education of high quality: Technology can help to deliver high-quality education by providing new and innovative teaching techniques and materials. Virtual and augmented reality technology, for example, may offer immersive and engaging learning experiences, while artificial intelligence (AI) can tailor instruction and provide students with real-time feedback. According to EdTechXGlobal, the global edtech business will be worth $252 billion by 2020.

Skills development: Technology can help with the development of skills needed to achieve the SDGs, such as digital literacy and problem-solving abilities. Coding programs and other digital skills training, for example, can assist prepare young people for future careers. According to the World Economic Forum, the most in-demand abilities by 2022 will be analytical thinking, creativity, and complex problem-solving.

Data collection and analysis: Technology can help with the collection and analysis of data needed to track progress toward the SDGs. Digital tools, for example, can be used to assess student development and identify places where further assistance is required. According to a Brookings Institution analysis, the use of educational technology can assist bridge the knowledge gap between what is currently accessible on education systems and what is required to fulfill the SDGs.

While technology has the potential to help education achieve the SDGs, it is critical that it is used in an inclusive and fair manner. If technology is not available to all pupils or if it supports existing prejudices or inequalities, there is a risk that it will increase existing inequities. To ensure that technology positively supports the SDGs, it is critical to consider concerns of access, equity, and inclusion in its design and implementation.

New-Age Technologies in Education System to Achieve SGDs

In recent years, the incorporation of new-age technology has altered the education system, opening up new avenues for teaching and learning. Here are some examples of how new technologies are being integrated into the educational system:

E-Learning

The use of digital technology to distribute educational information and courses via the internet is referred to as e-learning. E-learning has grown in popularity because of its flexibility, accessibility, and low cost, allowing students to learn at their own speed and from any location.

E-learning, often known as online learning, is a method of learning that takes place via digital media over the internet. It has grown in popularity in recent years, particularly after the COVID-19 pandemic, which has compelled many schools and institutions to adopt online learning.

Here are some of the characteristics, types, benefits, and drawbacks of e-learning, as well as its application in the present educational system:

E-Learning Advantages

Self-paced learning allows students to learn at their own pace and on their own time.

Accessibility: E-learning is available at any time and from any location as long as there is an internet connection.

Multimedia: To enhance the learning experience, e-learning employs a variety of multimedia resources such as movies, photos, and interactive exercises.

Customized learning: E-learning can be customized to the needs and interests of individual students.

E-Learning Formats

- *Synchronous e-learning:* Synchronous e-learning occurs when students and teachers are both online at the same time and communicate in real time. Live video conferencing and online chat sessions are examples of synchronous e-learning.
- *Asynchronous e-learning:* Asynchronous e-learning allows students to access learning materials at their own leisure, eliminating the requirement for real-time contact. Prerecorded video lectures and online discussion boards are examples of asynchronous e-learning.

Benefits of E-Learning

Flexibility: E-learning allows students to learn at their own pace and on their own time, making it suitable for working professionals and busy people.

Cost-effective: Because there are no expenditures associated with travel, lodging, or physical classroom space, e-learning can be less expensive than traditional classroom learning.

Accessible: E-learning is accessible from anywhere with an internet connection, making it perfect for students who reside in remote places or who are unable to attend traditional classroom settings owing to impairments or other factors.

Personalized learning: E-learning may be adapted to specific student needs and interests, resulting in a more personalized learning experience.

Disadvantages of E-Learning

Lack of interaction: Because students may not have the same opportunities to connect with instructors and other students as they would in a typical classroom setting, e-learning can be isolating.

Technological difficulties: Issues such as sluggish internet speeds or software glitches can impair the learning experience.

Self-discipline: Because there is no actual classroom environment to keep pupils on track, e-learning necessitates self-discipline and drive.

The Importance of E-Learning in the Contemporary Educational System

Because of its flexibility, accessibility, and cost-effectiveness, e-learning has become a crucial instrument in the current educational system. It enables students to learn from wherever they are, at any time, and at their own speed. It also allows for personalized learning and the use of multimedia resources to improve the learning experience.

To summarize, e-learning is a valuable addition to today's educational system, offering an alternative to traditional classroom learning. While e-learning has advantages and problems, its flexibility, accessibility, and cost-effectiveness make it a significant tool for both students and instructors.

Learning Management Systems (LMSs)

LMSs are software systems that provide a platform for managing, distributing, and tracking educational content and courses. Teachers can use LMSs to create and distribute course materials, connect with students, and evaluate their progress.

It is a software application used to administer, document, track, report on, and provide educational courses, training programs, or learning and development programs.

Characteristics of LMS

- LMS provides for the creation, organizing, distribution, and tracking of courses.
- It provides for the development and management of learning content such as videos, quizzes, documents, and assessments.
- It allows users to be added, altered, and deleted, as well as their roles and permissions.

- *Reporting and analytics:* The LMS tracks and reports on student progress, performance, and other pertinent data.
- *Communication tools:* LMSs feature communication tools such as email, forums, and chat to allow learners and instructors to communicate.

Types of LMS

- *Cloud-based LMS:* It is one that is housed in the cloud and can be accessed through a web browser.
- *Self-hosted LMS:* A self-hosted LMS is hosted on the server of an organization, which necessitates IT support and infrastructure.
- *Open source LMS:* An open-source LMS allows users to edit, extend, and adapt the software by providing open access to its source code.
- *Commercial LMS:* A commercial LMS is a proprietary software tool that customers pay a fee to use.

Advantages of LMS

- *Flexibility:* An LMS allows students to access content and finish courses at their own pace and on their own time.
- *Cost-effectiveness:* An LMS decreases the costs associated with traditional classroom-based training, such as travel, lodging, and classroom space.
- *Scalability:* An LMS permits courses to be given to a large number of learners at once, with no restriction on the number of learners who can engage in a course.
- *Personalization:* An LMS enables personalized learning experiences by allowing learners to choose their own learning paths and access tailored content depending on their needs.

Disadvantages of LMS

- Technical concerns, such as sluggish internet speeds, software compatibility issues, and hardware issues, can all impair the learning process.
- Lack of face-to-face interaction: LMSs can be isolating because learners may not have the same opportunities to connect with instructors and other learners as they would in a traditional classroom setting.
- LMS is reliant on technology, which is susceptible to technical breakdowns and security risks.

Utility of LMS in the Modern Education System for SDGs

LMS is a crucial instrument in the modern educational system, particularly in the context of the SDGs. LMS can be utilized to support the SDGs in a variety of ways, including:

- Providing education to rural and disadvantaged communities: LMSs can assist in the delivery of education and training to people in remote or disadvantaged communities, thereby bridging the digital divide.
- Access to education can be increased by lowering the costs associated with traditional classroom-based training and allowing learners to learn at their own speed and on their own schedule.
- Encouraging lifetime learning: LMSs can help achieve the SDG of fostering lifelong learning by giving learners opportunities to build new skills and knowledge throughout their lives.
- Improving learning outcomes: An LMS can be used to create personalized learning experiences that are suited to individual learner needs, hence improving learning outcomes.

Virtual Reality (VR) and Augmented Reality (AR)

Virtual reality (VR) and augmented reality (AR) are two cutting-edge technologies that have gained traction in recent years. They provide a unique and immersive way to interact with digital content in the physical environment. VR and AR are immersive technologies that allow students to explore virtual settings and simulations, resulting in more engaging and interactive learning experiences.

Characteristics of VR and AR

- *VR* is a computer-generated environment that simulates an artificial world. It is accessed by a headset or other device that gives a fully immersive experience that includes sound, sight, and touch. Users can interact with and manipulate virtual things in a natural and realistic manner.
- *AR* is a technology that superimposes digital data on the actual environment. It is accessed via a mobile device or smart glasses and frequently requires the usage of location-based services. Users can see and interact with the environment's physical and digital features.

Classifications of VR and AR

- VR environments come in three varieties: fully immersive, semi-immersive, and nonimmersive. Fully immersive VR provides a full sensory experience that can be extremely realistic. Semi-immersive VR uses a headgear or a projection screen and is less immersive. Nonimmersive VR is often experienced on a computer screen with limited interaction with the surroundings.

• AR experiences are classified as marker-based, markerless, or projection-based. A physical marker is used to activate the digital overlay in marker-based AR. Markerless AR overlays digital information onto the environment using location-based services or object recognition. A projector is used in projection-based AR to generate a digital overlay on a physical surface.

The Benefits and Drawbacks of VR and AR

• *Advantages:* VR and AR have the potential to improve numerous industries, including education, health care, entertainment, and manufacturing. They offer immersive and engaging experiences that improve learning and training, aid in the visualization of complicated concepts, and enable distant collaboration.
• *Disadvantages:* The main disadvantages of VR and AR include the technology's high cost and complexity, the possibility of motion sickness or other undesirable physical impacts, and the necessity for specialist hardware and software.

VR and AR's Significance in Contemporary Education

By enabling immersive and engaging learning experiences, VR and AR have the potential to significantly revolutionize the education sector. They let students to interact and explore virtual settings, imitate real-world circumstances, and visualize complex topics. These are some concrete examples of how VR and AR might be used in education:

Virtual field trips: VR can take students to areas that are difficult or impossible to see in person, such as historical sites or natural wonders.

Science simulations: AR can help students visualize and engage with complicated scientific subjects like the human body or molecular structures.

VR can provide realistic training simulations for a variety of vocations, including health care, the military, and emergency services.

Overall, VR and AR have the potential to improve education by providing new approaches to engage students and promote learning. Its effectiveness, however, will be determined by how they are implemented and integrated into the curriculum.

Gamification

Gamification is the application of game design principles in educational environments to make learning more enjoyable and engaging. Gamification uses components like prizes, points, and leader boards to encourage students to learn and achieve academic goals.

Gamification is the use of game design and game principles to engage and encourage users in nongame environments. It has been used in a variety of industries, including education, to improve the learning process.

Characteristics of Gamification

Gamification is the use of game design features and mechanics in nongame contexts such as education, marketing, or business settings to engage and drive people to accomplish specific activities or behaviors. The key aspects of gamification are as follows:

- It is fundamentally goal-oriented, and it often entails identifying explicit objectives or results that users are expected to attain. These goals might range from finishing a task to acquiring a new skill to reaching a specific level of performance.
- Gamification is frequently centered on the usage of rewards and incentives to motivate users to participate with the experience and achieve their goals. Points, medals, levels, and other virtual or real-world prizes are all examples of rewards.
- It is feedback-driven. Feedback is an important component of gamification since it informs users about their progress and performance. Visual progress bars, leaderboards, and other types of feedback that offer users with a sense of success and promote continuing involvement are examples of feedback.
- It is fundamentally interactive, and it often entails user input and engagement. Completing tasks, competing against other users, or partnering with others to achieve common goals are all examples of this.
- It is supposed to be enjoyable and engaging for users, which is maybe its most distinguishing feature. This may be accomplished in a variety of ways, including the use of game-like visuals and animations, the creation of a sense of competition or challenge, and the use of storytelling and narrative to create a more immersive experience.
- Gamification captures consumers' attention and encourages continuing engagement by making the experience enjoyable and engaging.
- It uses the natural human need for competitiveness, achievement, and social engagement to improve the learning experience.
- It frequently makes use of digital technology like mobile devices and web-based platforms.

Types of Gamification

Points-based gamification entails rewarding users with points for performing specified tasks or reaching certain milestones.

- *Badges and prizes:* In this sort of gamification, users are awarded badges or rewards for accomplishing specified activities or reaching certain milestones.

- *Leaderboards:* With this style of gamification, a leaderboard is displayed that shows the ranking of users depending on their performance.

Benefits and Drawbacks of Gamification

Advantages: Gamification has the potential to increase motivation and engagement, promote self-directed learning, and improve learning outcomes. It can also provide immediate feedback and improve learning enjoyment.

Disadvantages: Gamification might be shallow and ineffective for all types of learners. It can also be distracting, with extrinsic rewards taking precedence over intrinsic motivation.

Significance of Gamifications in Contemporary Education

- Gamification can be an excellent method for improving learning in today's educational system.
- It can improve motivation and engagement: Using game elements that foster a sense of accomplishment and progress, gamification can make learning more engaging and exciting.
- Gamification can provide students with rapid feedback, allowing them to measure their progress and change their learning tactics accordingly.
- Gamification can improve learning outcomes by encouraging self-directed learning, teamwork, and problem-solving abilities.

Here are some concrete instances of how gamification might be applied in education:

- Language learning apps employ gamification to make learning more fun and interesting.
- Gamification is used in educational games to teach topics in science, mathematics, and other subjects.
- Gamification is used in online learning platforms to inspire students and track their progress.

Ultimately, gamification can be a valuable technique in modern education because it improves the learning experience while also encouraging student involvement and motivation. Its usefulness, however, will be determined by how it is implemented and integrated into the curriculum.

Artificial Intelligence (AI)

Artificial intelligence (AI) is being utilized in education to enhance personalized learning, provide student feedback, and automate administrative work. AI-enabled chatbots and voice assistants are also being used to provide students with immediate support and guidance.

AI is an area of computer science concerned with the development of intelligent machines capable of doing activities that normally require human intelligence, such as speech recognition, decision-making, and problem-solving.

Characteristics of AI

- *Learning:* AI systems can enhance their performance over time by learning from their experiences.
- *Adaptability:* AI systems have the ability to adjust to new conditions and contexts.
- *Autonomy:* AI systems can make judgments and behave without the need for human intervention. AI systems can reason and make decisions based on data and information.

Classifications of AI

- *Reactive machines*: These AI systems can only react to inputs and have no memory or ability to draw on previous experiences.
- *Limited memory:* Some AI systems can make decisions based on previous experiences.
- *Theory of mind:* These AI systems can understand other people's emotions and mental processes.
- *Self-awareness:* These AI systems are self-aware and understand their own existence.

Benefits and Disadvantages of AI

Benefits of AI include the ability to accomplish complicated jobs quickly and effectively, eliminate human error, and make smarter judgments based on data and knowledge.

Disadvantages include the fact that AI can be expensive to develop and implement, that it may displace human occupations, and that it is vulnerable to bias and inaccuracy.

Significance of AI in Modern Education

AI can be a beneficial tool for modern education in a variety of ways, including:

- *Personalization:* AI can assist personalize the learning experience by delivering personalized feedback and adjusting to each student's requirements and preferences.
- *Data analysis:* AI can assist educators in analyzing data and identifying patterns and trends to influence instructional decisions.
- *Accessibility:* By providing helpful technology and tools, AI can help make education more accessible to students with disabilities.

AI's Role in Sustainable Development Goals

AI has the potential to play a key role in the achievement of the United Nations SDGs. Among the ways in which AI can help to the SDGs are:

- *Improving health care outcomes:* By analyzing massive databases to discover illness patterns and advise treatment options, AI can assist improve health care outcomes.
- *Encouraging sustainable agriculture:* By employing sensors and data analysis to optimize planting and harvesting, AI can help farmers boost agricultural yields and reduce waste.
- *Lowering energy consumption:* AI can help reduce energy consumption by optimizing energy use and minimizing waste in buildings and transportation.

Ultimately, AI has the potential to generate sustainable development and improve people's lives in a variety of ways. Yet, it is critical to guarantee that AI is developed and deployed in an ethical and responsible manner in order to avoid unforeseen effects and harm.

Online Collaboration Tools

Online collaboration tools are digital platforms and applications that enable individuals and teams to collaborate remotely, regardless of where they are physically located. Because of the rise of remote work and the demand for more flexible working arrangements, these technologies have grown in popularity in recent years.

Features of Online Collaboration Tools

Real-time communication and messaging: Many online collaboration platforms include real-time chat and messaging features that allow team members to instantaneously engage with one another.

File sharing and storage: These solutions enable teams to share and store files in a centralized area, allowing them to collaborate on documents, presentations, and other projects more easily.

Several collaboration platforms incorporate project management features like task assignment and tracking, project timeframes, and progress reporting.

Several online collaboration platforms also provide video conferencing and screen sharing capabilities, which can be handy for remote meetings and presentations.

Merits of Online Collaboration Tools

Improved productivity: By offering a central site for communication, document sharing, and project management, online collaboration solutions can help teams operate more efficiently.

Flexible working arrangements: These solutions enable team members to work remotely and collaborate across time zones and regions.

Cost-effective: Several online collaboration tools are inexpensive or even free, making them a viable alternative for small enterprises and teams.

Demerits of Online Collaboration Tools

Security hazards: If some online collaboration technologies are not properly secured, they may represent security issues, potentially resulting in data breaches and information leaks.

Technical issues: Poor internet connectivity and software faults can occasionally impede the usage of online collaboration solutions, resulting in lost productivity.

Internet collaboration tools may limit personal interaction between team members, perhaps leading to social and emotional concerns.

SDG Contribution of Online Collaboration Tools

Online collaboration technologies can help to achieve the United Nations SDGs in the following ways:

- *SDG 4:* Quality education: Online collaboration tools can be utilized to support remote education and enable students in remote places or with low resources with access to educational resources.
- *SDG 8:* Decent work and economic growth: Internet collaboration technologies can help with remote work, allowing people to work from anywhere and opening new prospects for freelancing and self-employment.
- *SDG 9:* Industry, innovation, and infrastructure: Internet collaboration tools may help teams and organizations innovate and collaborate, boosting economic growth and fostering the creation of new technologies.
- *SDG 17:* Partnerships for the goals: Internet collaboration technologies can facilitate partnerships and collaboration across various organizations and stakeholders, allowing them to work more effectively together to achieve the SDGs.

Open Educational Resources (OERs)

Open educational resources (OERs) are educational materials that are openly licensed and freely available to anyone for use and/or repurposing. OERs include a wide range of resources, such as textbooks, lesson plans, videos, images, and interactive tools.

The use of OER has the potential to support education in achieving the SDGs in several ways:

- *Increased access to education*: OER can help overcome barriers to education access by providing high-quality educational materials to people who may not have access to traditional classroom resources. According to the United Nations Educational, Scientific and Cultural Organization (UNESCO), OER can help to bridge the education gap and reduce inequalities by providing education to people who might not otherwise have access to it.

- *Cost savings:* OER can be a cost-effective alternative to traditional textbooks and other educational resources. According to a study by the Babson Survey Group, the use of OER can save students an average of $128 per course. This cost savings can help to reduce financial barriers to education and make education more accessible to all.
- *Customization and personalization:* OER can be customized and repurposed to meet the needs of diverse learners. Teachers can modify OER to fit the specific needs of their students, and students can adapt OER to their own learning styles and preferences.
- *Collaboration and innovation:* The use of OER can foster collaboration and innovation in education. Teachers and students can collaborate on the creation and improvement of OER, and OER can be used as a starting point for new and innovative educational approaches.

To support the use of OER in achieving the SDGs, many organizations and initiatives have emerged to promote the creation, sharing, and use of OER. For example, the open education consortium (OEC) is a global network of educational institutions that promotes the use of OER, and the UNESCO OER recommendation provides guidelines for member states to support the creation and use of OER. Overall, the use of OER has the potential to support education in achieving the SDGs by increasing access to education, reducing costs, promoting customization and personalization, and fostering collaboration and innovation in education.

The incorporation of cutting-edge technologies in education has the potential to improve educational outcomes, enhance learning experiences, and better prepare students for the challenges of the modern world. Yet, it is critical that these technologies be used in ways that promote learning and suit the needs of all students.

Challenges and Limitations of Technology in Education

Technology has transformed the way we learn, yet there are significant problems and limitations to its usage in education. Some of the major issues and limits are as follows:

- *Equity and access:* Not all students have equal access to technology and the internet, which can worsen existing educational imbalances. Kids from low-income households or living in rural regions, for example, may not have the same resources as their counterparts from more affluent or metropolitan backgrounds.

- *Reliability and technical issues:* Technology may be unstable and prone to technical problems, which can disrupt the learning process and generate irritation for both students and teachers.
- *Distraction:* Students who are tempted to use their gadgets for noneducational purposes during class may be distracted by technology.
- *Personal involvement:* Technology-based learning does not always provide the human contact and engagement that face-to-face training does. This is particularly difficult for kids who thrive on interpersonal interactions and collaborative learning.
- *Overdependence on technology:* There is a risk of overdependence on technology, which can lead to a lack of critical thinking and problem-solving abilities, as well as an overemphasis on rote memorization and standardized testing.
- *Concerns about privacy and security:* Because personal information and data might be subject to cyberattacks or data breaches, technology-based learning can create privacy and security issues.
- *Cost:* The expense of integrating and maintaining technology in education, particularly for impoverished schools and districts, can be a substantial obstacle.

Despite these difficulties and restrictions, technology may be an effective tool for upgrading and improving education. It is critical to address these issues and discover methods to use technology in ways that maximize its promise while limiting its limits. This might entail guaranteeing stability and technical assistance, as well as balancing technology use with traditional face-to-face education and cooperation.

Best Practices for Integrating Technology in Education

- *Establish clear goals and objectives:* Incorporating technology into education may have several benefits for both instructors and students, but it is critical to approach this process with caution and purpose. Following are some examples of best practices for using technology into education:
- *Provide adequate training and support:* When adopting any technology into your classroom, it is critical to create specific goals and objectives for what you expect to achieve with the technology. This will assist you in selecting the best tools and tactics for your needs, as well as ensuring that technology is used successfully to support your teaching and boost student learning.
- *Give enough training and support:* In order to properly use technology, teachers and students must get adequate training and assistance. These might include professional development opportunities, online training, and troubleshooting help.
- *Select suitable tools and platforms:* There are several educational tools and platforms accessible, and it is critical to select the ones that best match your needs and align with your goals. Consider things like simplicity of use, compatibility with current systems, and the precise features and capabilities that will help you teach and students learn.

- *Encourage cooperation and communication:* Technology can help students and instructors collaborate and communicate more effectively. Encourage students to use online tools to collaborate on projects and tasks, and use technology to contact with students outside of class, such as email or messaging platforms.
- *Use technology to enhance, not replace, traditional teaching methods:* Utilize technology to supplement, not replace, existing teaching techniques: Technology should be used to supplement, not replace, traditional teaching methods. This includes incorporating technology into established teaching procedures, such as employing multimedia presentations to support lectures or giving online resources to assist readings and assignments.
- *Monitor and assess progress:* It is critical to monitor and assess the influence of technology on student learning, and to change your strategy as necessary. Gather input from students and track their progress to discover areas where technology is most helpful, and make improvements to ensure that it is used as effectively as possible.

Teachers may successfully integrate technology into their classrooms to boost student learning and meet their teaching goals by following these best practices.

The Future of Technology in Education

The future of technology in education is promising for achieving the SDGs, as evidenced by the following facts and data:

Access to education: The use of technology in education has already improved access to education in many parts of the world. According to a report by UNESCO, the number of out-of-school children in sub-Saharan Africa has fallen by 15 million since 2000, in large part due to the use of technology in education.

Personalized learning: A study by the Clayton Christensen Institute found that schools that implemented personalized learning saw significant improvements in student achievement, with 72% of students showing improved proficiency in mathematics and 50% showing improved proficiency in reading.

Collaboration and communication: The use of technology has already facilitated global collaboration and communication in education. For example, the Global Learning XPRIZE challenged teams to develop tablet-based software for teaching children to read and write in Swahili, resulting in a winning solution that is now being implemented in Tanzania.

Online education: Online education has already proven to be an effective tool for improving access to education. In 2020, the number of students enrolled in online courses worldwide surpassed 100 million for the first time, according to a report by Class Central.

Data-driven education: The use of data and analytics in education can help educators identify areas where students may be struggling, and provide targeted support and feedback. A report by McKinsey & Company found that data-driven education initiatives have the potential to improve student achievement by 10–20%.

Overall, the use of technology in education has already shown great promise in helping to achieve the SDGs, and is likely to continue to do so in the future.

Recommendations for Policymakers, Educators, and Stakeholders

The incorporation of cutting-edge technologies into the educational system has the potential to significantly improve emerging economies' ability to meet the SDGs. Here are some suggestions for policymakers, educators, and stakeholders on how to effectively integrate new-age technologies into the educational system:

Create a Comprehensive Plan: Policymakers should collaborate with education stakeholders to create a comprehensive plan for incorporating new-age technologies into the educational system. The plan should take into account the region's specific needs as well as the SDGs' goals. The plan should also identify the resources needed as well as the strategies for effectively implementing and monitoring the integration of cutting-edge technologies into the educational system.

Invest in Infrastructure: It is critical to invest in the necessary infrastructure in order to effectively integrate new-age technologies into the education system. This includes high-speed internet connectivity, computer labs, and other digital resources required for the implementation of cutting-edge technologies. Policymakers should prioritize the creation of the infrastructure required to support the integration of new-age technologies into the educational system.

Invest in Teacher Education: Educators are an essential component of integrating new-age technologies into the educational system. As a result, it is critical to invest in teacher education to ensure that they have the skills needed to effectively integrate new-age technologies into their teaching methods. Policymakers should create training programs that are open to all teachers, regardless of location or level of education.

Encourage Collaboration: Integrating new-age technologies into the education system necessitates collaboration among various stakeholders, including policymakers, educators, and the private sector. As a result, it is critical to encourage collaboration among all stakeholders. Policymakers should encourage private-sector participation and provide opportunities for educators and private-sector stakeholders to collaborate and develop innovative solutions for integrating new-age technologies into the education system.

Monitor and Evaluate Progress: Policymakers and educators should routinely monitor and evaluate the progress of new-age technology integration in the education system. This will aid in identifying areas for improvement and determining if the incorporation of cutting-edge technology is effectively helping to the accomplishment of the SDGs. Policymakers should utilize the information gathered to make educated judgments and adapt their tactics as necessary.

Conclusion

In order for emerging countries to make progress toward reaching sustainable development goals, the incorporation of cutting-edge technology into the educational system has emerged as an essential component. Because of the quick rate at which technological improvements are being made, it is increasingly essential to provide students with the information and abilities they need to be able to adjust to the shifting environment. The school system has to become more open to contemporary technology, which has the potential to improve education's overall quality while also making it more readily available and cost-effective. Students will be able to develop new skill sets, access relevant resources, and gain new knowledge in a variety of fields if the education system is updated to incorporate modern technology. This will make it possible for the United Nations to more effectively achieve the SDGs. This will result in the production of a skilled labor force, which will drive sustainable development, economic growth, and social development in countries that are still in the developing stage. In order to accomplish the SDGs and build a more sustainable future, it is essential for decision-makers, educators, and other stakeholders to collaborate on the implementation of modern technology into the educational system.

Bibliography

Bakhshi, H., Hogan, R., & Sengupta, I. (2016). *The promise and challenge of the age of data: Insights from the innovation landscape.* McKinsey & Company. Retrieved from https://www.mckinsey.com/industries/social-sector/our-insights/the-promise-and-challenge-of-the-age-of-data

EdTech Review. (n.d.). Integrating technology in developing countries. Retrieved from https://edtechreview.in/trends-insights/trends/359-integrating-technology-in-developing-countries

eLearning Africa. (2019). *ICT for education in developing countries: A systematic review.* Retrieved from https://ela-newsportal.com/wp-content/uploads/2020/02/ICT-for-Education-in-Developing-Countries-A-Systematic-Review-by-eLearning-Africa.pdf

Global Learning XPRIZE. (n.d.). Retrieved from https://learningxprize.org/

Global Partnership for Education. (2019). *The role of education in achieving the Sustainable Development Goals.* Retrieved from https://www.globalpartnership.org/blog/role-education-achieving-sustainable-development-goals

Horn, M. B., & Staker, H. (2015). *When personalized learning meets education technology.* Clayton Christensen Institute. Retrieved from https://www.christenseninstitute.org/publications/when-personalized-learning-meets-education-technology/

International Telecommunication Union. (2017). *Measuring the information society report.* Retrieved from https://www.itu.int/en/ITU-D/Statistics/Pages/publications/mis2017.aspx

Koutropoulos, A., Abajian, S., Waard, I. D., Hogue, R. J., & Keskin, N. Ö. (2018). Emerging technologies for education and development. *International Journal of Emerging Technologies in Learning, 13*(10), 4–16. https://www.online-journals.org/index.php/i-jet/article/view/6453/5561

Sarwar, M., Soomro, T. R., & Yasin, M. A. (2020). New technologies and the Sustainable Development Goals: A systematic review. *Sustainability, 12*(21), 9083. https://www.mdpi.com/2071-1050/12/21/9083

Shah, D. (2021). 2020: The year in online education. Class Central. Retrieved from https://www.classcentral.com/report/2020-online-learners-record/

Sisay, A. M. (2014). Technology integration in developing countries: An assessment of progress and challenges. *Journal of Education and Practice, 5*(18), 123–132. https://www.iiste.org/Journals/index.php/JEP/article/view/20479/21100

UNESCO. (2017a). The role of technology in achieving the Sustainable Development Goals. Global Education Monitoring Report. Retrieved from https://unesdoc.unesco.org/ark:/48223/pf0000365886

UNESCO. (2017b). Accountability in education: Meeting our commitments. Global Education Monitoring Report. Retrieved from https://en.unesco.org/gem-report/report/2017/accountability-education-progress

UNESCO. (2017c). *Education for Sustainable Development Goals: Learning objectives.* Retrieved from https://en.unesco.org/sdgs/education-database/learning-objectives

United Nations Department of Economic and Social Affairs. (2021). *Harnessing technology for sustainable development.* Retrieved from https://sdgs.un.org/sites/default/files/publications/2021_sustec_policybrief.pdf

United Nations Development Programme. (2017). *Technology and the SDGs: An action agenda for governments and partners.* Retrieved from https://www.undp.org/content/dam/undp/library/SDGs/SDG%20Integration/Technology%20and%20the%20SDGs.pdf

United Nations Development Programme. (2018). *Digital Transformation in Education: SDG good practices.* Retrieved from https://www.undp.org/content/undp/en/home/librarypage/poverty-reduction/digital-transformation-in-education.html

World Bank. (2016). *World development report 2016: Digital dividends.* Retrieved from https://openknowledge.worldbank.org/handle/10986/23347

World Economic Forum. (2016). *Transforming education with new technologies.* Retrieved from https://www.weforum.org/agenda/2016/05/transforming-education-with-new-technologies/

Index

Printed and bound by CPI Group (UK) Ltd, Croydon, CR0 4YY

25/02/2024